The Civil Rights Movement

MAGILL'S CHOICE

The Civil Rights Movement

Volume 2

Literacy tests – Zoning

385 - 766

edited by

The Editors of Salem Press

Salem Press, Inc.
Pasadena, California   Hackensack, New Jersey

Most of these essays originally appeared in *Racial and Ethnic Relations in America*, 1999. The rest first appeared in *Survey of Social Science: Government and Politics*, 1995; *American Justice*, 1996; and *Great Lives from History: American Series*, 1987. New material has been added.

∞ The paper used in these volumes conforms to the American National Standard for Permanence of Paper for Printed Library Materials, Z39.48-1992 (R1997).

Library of Congress Cataloging-in-Publication Data

The Civil Rights movement / edited by the editors of Salem Press.
p. cm. — (Magill's choice)
Includes bibliographical references and index.
ISBN 0-89356-170-3 (v. 1 : alk. paper) — ISBN 0-89356-171-1 (v. 2 : alk. paper) — ISBN 0-89356-169-X (set : alk. paper)
1. Afro-Americans—Civil rights—History—20th century—Dictionaries. 2. Civil rights movements—United States—History—20th century—Dictionaries. 3. United States—Race relations—Dictionaries. I. Salem Press. II. Series.
E185.61 .C6124 2000
305.896'073—dc21

99-046715
CIP

First Printing

PRINTED IN THE UNITED STATES OF AMERICA

Contents

The Civil Rights Movement

Literacy tests

In an election, a citizen is expected to be literate enough to read a printed ballot in order to cast a vote. It is unnecessary to exclude illiterates from voting, as their marks are likely to be random and therefore will not influence the outcome of an election.

After the Civil War ended in 1865, tests for literacy were adopted as voting requirements in many states. The aim was to exclude marginally literate persons from voting, in particular African Americans and recent immigrants. The way to exclude marginally literate persons was either to reject those applying to register to vote who had errors on their application forms or to ask such persons to explain esoteric provisions in the Constitution of the United States or other text to a voter registrar, who would turn down their application.

The Voting Rights Act of 1965 suspended all literacy tests in states in which less than 50 percent of the voting-age population had been registered or had voted in the 1964 election. The law had an immediate impact. By the end of 1965, a quarter of a million new black voters had been registered, one-third by federal examiners. In the Voting Rights Act of 1970, Congress prohibited the use of all literacy tests and similar tests as preconditions for voter registration.

Michael Haas

See also: Grandfather clauses; Poll tax; Voting Rights Act of 1965.

Little Rock school desegregation

In the *Brown v. Board of Education* decision of 1954, the Supreme Court declared segregation unconstitutional, but its 1955 implementation order allowed the lower courts to develop plans to desegregate. It was the first time that the Court had not ordered immediate establishment of a constitutional right. In a state such as Arkansas, moderate and reluctantly willing to accept political and legal (though not social) equality, this approach seemed to suggest that a gradual process would be possible. Trouble seemed unlikely.

Little Rock school superintendent Virgil Blossom planned to start by enrolling a few black students at Central High School in 1957 and working down the grades year by year. The children, eventually pared down to nine, were chosen for strong scholarship and character; they were from middle-class families. When school opened on September 3, however, these children met serious resistance.

Angry whites gather to protest against the integration of Little Rock's Central High School. *(Library of Congress)*

Governor Orval Faubus had decided that his best bet for future political success—most immediately a third term—lay in making himself the leader of the lower-class white segregationist element in the state. Despite the fact that he had not previously been particularly (or at least overtly) racist, Faubus announced that he could not keep the peace and called out the National Guard to keep order.

Daisy Bates, head of the local chapter of the National Association for the Advancement of Colored People (NAACP), realized that families served by Central High School were predominantly lower class and were likely to be stirred to resistance by the governor's statements. She organized the students to arrive in a group. They were turned away at bayonet point. One student, Elizabeth Eckford, did not get the message and arrived alone to face a mob of angry whites. Blocked from the school by armed Guardsmen and cursed and reviled by the mob, she was rescued by a reporter from *The New York Times* and an older white woman. Such scenes as these were reported by the press and broadcast on television. The nation was forced for the first time to face the true ugliness of its prejudice.

President Dwight D. Eisenhower met with Faubus on September 14 and got what he thought was a promise to abide by the Supreme Court decision. When Faubus reneged, the president, on September 25, ordered elements of the 101st Airborne to Little Rock. The soldiers escorted the black children to school and protected them for several weeks. Then the state National Guard, placed under federal authority, took over. Despite continuing harassment by white students, all but one of the nine was graduated from Central High.

In Little Rock, the *Brown* decision had been enforced, but resistance to school integration continued in many areas of the South. Faubus, who continued to fight, won a total of six terms as governor. The Little Rock crisis was a vital first step in desegregation, but it was no more than that.

Fred R. van Hartesveldt

See also: *Brown v. Board of Education*; Busing and integration; Civil rights; Civil Rights movement; Desegregation: public schools; National Association for the Advancement of Colored People; *Sweatt v. Painter.*

Los Angeles riots of 1992

The acquittal of four police officers charged with police brutality sparked the worst violence in the city's history from April 29 to May 1, 1992.

Before the Rodney King beating on March 3, 1991, many in the Los Angeles community believed that the Los Angeles Police Department (LAPD) had demonstrated a pattern of excessive force, particularly against minority groups. One significant example was Operation Hammer, begun in 1989, during which the LAPD allegedly rounded up African Americans and Hispanics without probable cause that they had had committed a crime, simply because of the way the suspects looked and because the police wanted to avert the threat of gang violence. As a result, the chief of the LAPD, Daryl Gates, was despised by many in the African American community. The videotape of Rodney King's beating by members of the LAPD, therefore, came as no surprise to the African American community of Los Angeles. It merely confirmed what they already thought: that police brutality and use of excessive force against minorities was a common practice.

The Beating of Rodney King The videotape, recorded by private citizen George Holliday in the morning hours of March 3, 1991, contained eighty-one seconds of footage. The footage that was seen throughout the United States was of King, a six-foot, three-inch African American weighing 225 pounds, prone on the ground, sustaining blows to his head, neck, kidney area, and legs from four policemen, who were kicking and smashing at him with their truncheons. Not in full view on the videotape were nineteen other police officers surrounding the four who were administering the beating. Also not in view were the onlookers who were pleading that the beating stop. The police paid no attention to them. As a result of the beating, King sustained eleven fractures to his skull, a crushed cheekbone, a broken ankle, internal injuries, a burn on his chest, and some brain damage.

Television viewers also did not see what preceded the beating. During the evening, King had consumed the equivalent of a case of beer. His blood alcohol level was twice the legal limit. He was on parole at the time and ran the risk of landing back in jail if he were caught speeding. Police, led by Stacey Koon, started chasing King as he sped through the streets of Los Angeles. The chase escalated to one hundred miles per hour at one point, before the police were able to stop King and force him out of his car. Nor did television viewers see King fighting with the police, even standing up after being stunned twice with a Taser gun. People saw only the prone body of an African American man being assaulted repeatedly by white police officers.

The Trial Four of the officers, including Koon, were charged with the beating at the end of March, 1991, in Los Angeles. Their attorneys moved for a change of venue for the trial, which was granted. The trial was held in the spring of 1992 in Simi Valley, a suburban town an hour's drive north of Los Angeles. The town was the home for a large proportion of LAPD officers and retirees and was dominated by law-and-order conservatives. Six men and six women, none of whom was African American, made up the jury. According to those who were present, the prosecution presented a weak and diffuse case. The defense, however, was strong. It played the videotape in slow motion over and over until its effect became trivialized. The defense also emphasized how King presented a threat to the police. Koon testified about King's "hulk-like strength and how he groaned like a wounded animal," conjuring up for the jury the image of police representing the "thin blue line" that protects the forces of civilization from the savagery represented by King. To those who had likely settled in Simi Valley to get away from the alleged evils and crime of the inner city, the message resounded. After thirty-two hours of deliberation, on April 29, 1992, the jury acquitted the four officers. The verdict was announced on television at 2:50 P.M.

The Riots At 4:00 P.M., in the South Central Los Angeles district near Florence and Normandie Boulevards, five African American gang members went to get some malt liquor at the Payless Liquor Store. They started to take it without paying, and the owner's son tried to stop them. One of the gang members smashed the son on the head with a bottle and allegedly said, "This is for Rodney King." Other gang members hurled the bottles they held through the store windows, while the owner pressed the alarm for the police. When two officers came, the suspects were not there.

At 5:30, at the corner of Florence and Normandie, eight black men wielding baseball bats started breaking the car windows of passing motorists. Eighteen police cars and thirty-five officers from the LAPD sped to the area. They arrested three suspects but left at 5:45. In the next hour, the crowd attacking cars grew to two hundred people. One of the victims was Reginald Denny, a white truck driver, who was pulled from his truck and beaten by African Americans, including Damien Williams, with a fire extinguisher. The police from the 77th district of the LAPD still stayed away. Chief Gates had left police headquarters at 6:30 to attend a fund-raising event in the affluent suburb of Brentwood.

By 7:30, the crowd at Florence and Normandie had started lighting fires. An hour later, the LAPD finally returned to the area and began to disperse the crowd. By that time, the fires, rioting, and looting had spread to other parts of the city. The riots continued for two more days; local news coverage flooded the airwaves with helicopter views of hundreds of fires throughout the city and normally law-abiding citizens looting goods from stores. On Friday, May 1, 1992, Rodney King appeared on television with the plea, "Can't we all get along?" When the riots ended that day in Los Angeles, more than fifty people had died, more than twelve thousand people had been arrested, and the property damage was estimated to be $1 billion. Throughout the nation, uprisings had started in Atlanta, Las Vegas, Minneapolis, New York, Omaha, and Seattle.

The riots in Los Angeles following the King trial caused more damage and spread across a wider area than those of the 1960's. Gates subsequently was replaced by an African American chief of police, Koon and a fellow officer were convicted of violating King's civil rights in federal court, Williams was acquitted of most of the charges in the beating of Denny, and King won a civil suit against the city of Los Angeles. These actions reinforced the perception of many that the criminal justice system treats whites and African Americans differently, whereas others argued that the riots were less the result of racial tensions than of a widening gap between "haves" and "have-nots" in U.S. society.

Jennifer Eastman

Core Resources

"Can't We All Get Along?" "The Fire This Time," and "Anatomy of an Acquittal" (*Time* 139, May 11, 1992), give a good overview of the events on April 29, 1992, and following. "Los Angeles, April 29, 1992, and Beyond: The Law, Issues, and Perspectives" (*Southern California Law Review* 66, May, 1993) contains a panoply of views on the trial and the riots. "Symposium—The Urban Crisis: The Kerner Commission Report Revisited" (*North Carolina Law Review* 71, June, 1993) discusses how the riots of 1992 differed from those of the 1960's.

See also: King, Rodney, case; Miami riots of 1980; Newark race riots; Race riots of the twentieth century; Watts riot.

Lynchings

Lynchings were a primary means of intimidation and control of blacks in the American South.

Lynching, the deadliest form of vigilantism, has a long history in America. At the time of the American Revolution, lynchings were used to punish Tories or British sympathizers. Until the 1850's, lynchings were associated with nonlethal forms of punishment such as beatings and tarring and feathering. In the years immediately before the Civil War, lynching took on its fatal connotation as it was used to suppress slave insurrections. Although lynching is often associated with hanging someone, lynching includes all sorts of violent acts, including flogging, dismemberment, torture, burning, and shooting.

History of Lynching After the Civil War, lynching became more widespread as former slaves came to be viewed as a threat by their former slavemasters. Accurate numbers on lynching are hard to come by, and it was not until 1872 that there was a systematic effort to obtain reliable data. Records kept by the Tuskegee Institute indicate that there were 4,743 lynchings in the United States between 1882 and 1968. Of those lynched, 3,446 (73 percent) were blacks and 1,297 (27 percent) were whites. Even these numbers underestimate what most scholars believe to be the actual number of lynchings. A more accurate estimate would be close to 6,000 lynchings.

Lynchings were most prevalent from the 1880's to the 1920's. During the last two decades of the nineteenth century, there was an average of 150 lynchings per year, with a high of 230 in 1892. Between 1901 and 1910 there was an average of 85 lynchings per year, and from 1911 to 1920 there was an average of 61 per year. Lynchings declined to an average of 28 per year during the 1920's, to 11 per year during the 1930's, and to 3 per year during the 1940's. From 1951 to 1985 a total of 10 lynchings were reported in the United

Hundreds of festively dressed whites gather near Waco, Texas, to watch a black man brutally killed. *(Library of Congress)*

States. Although almost every state experienced lynchings, 82 percent occurred in the South. Mississippi ranks first with 581, followed by Georgia with 530 and Texas with 493.

Grounds for Lynching Although lynching was often justified as a method of protecting white women from black rapists, only 25 percent of lynching victims were suspected of rape or attempted rape. In most cases, lynching victims were summarily executed before receiving any trial. Their guilt was never established at all, let alone beyond a reasonable doubt. The justification for lynching in the cases of rape was to protect the white woman from the agony of testifying in court.

Approximately 40 percent of lynchings involved murder or attempted murder allegations. Nine percent involved assault or robbery charges, certainly not capital offenses, and 2 percent involved blacks insulting whites, particularly white women. The most famous example of a black who was lynched for insulting a white woman was Emmett Till. Till, a fourteen-year-old Chicago native, was visiting relatives in Mississippi in 1955. Prodded by some friends, Till asked a white woman for a date. The woman immediately rejected Till and went to get a pistol. Till walked out of the store saying, "Bye, baby," and "wolf whistled" at her. Till's actions violated one of the major cultural taboos in the South, and he would pay with his life. That same day, the woman's husband and her half-brother abducted Till from the home he was visiting. Three days later, Till's decomposing body was found floating in the Tallahatchie River. Till had been beaten and shot before his weighted-down body was thrown into the river. The two white men who abducted Till were charged with his murder, but it took an all-white jury less than one hour to acquit them.

The Campaign Against Lynching Few individuals who participated in lynchings were ever prosecuted. Coroners' juries repeatedly concluded that the death had come "at the hands of parties unknown." Seldom was anything further from the truth. Often lynchings took on a festive air, and local newspapers provided complete coverage, sometimes including photographs. In the event someone was arrested for the crime, such as the two white men accused of murdering Emmett Till, they would be found not guilty by all-white juries.

Leading the effort to abolish lynchings were the Commission on Interracial Cooperation, headed by Will Alexander, and Southern Women for the Prevention of Lynching, led by Jessie Daniel Ames. Ames, one of the leading social reformers in the South, had forty thousand members in her organization within nine years of its establishment in 1930. When alerted about a possible lynching, Ames contacted women in the area who were members of her organization or sympathetic to its objectives.

One of the earliest objectives of the National Association for the Advancement of Colored People (NAACP), a civil rights organization established in

1909, was to pressure the U.S. Congress to pass a federal antilynching bill. On several occasions, the House of Representatives passed such legislation, but it was always filibustered by southern senators when it reached the Senate. In the late 1940's President Harry Truman appointed a President's Committee on Civil Rights (PCCR). The PCCR urged Congress to pass a federal antilynching law, but without success.

The NAACP met with greater success in attempting to mobilize public opinion against lynching. The NAACP investigated lynchings and often sent special investigators into areas where a lynching had occurred. The NAACP prepared written narratives of the lynchings, including photographs if available, and distributed them to any media outlet that would publicize the lynching. The effort was to try to shame the South into stopping this despicable practice.

Darryl Paulson

Core Resources

Among the best studies on lynching are Ray Stannard Baker's *Following the Color Line: An Account of Negro Citizenship in the American Democracy* (New York: Doubleday, Page, 1908); Richard M. Brown's *Strain of Violence: Historical Studies of American Violence and Vigilantism* (New York: Oxford University Press, 1977); James Chadbourn's *Lynching and the Law* (Chapel Hill, N.C.: University of North Carolina Press, 1933); Arthur Raper's *The Tragedy of Lynching* (Chapel Hill, N.C.: University of North Carolina Press, 1933); Walter White's *Rope and Faggot* (New York: Alfred A. Knopf, 1929); Stephen Whitfield's *A Death in the Delta: The Story of Emmett Till* (Baltimore: Johns Hopkins University Press, 1988); and Robert Zangrando's *The NAACP Crusade Against Lynching, 1909-1950* (Philadelphia: Temple University Press, 1980).

See also: Dyer antilynching bill; Ku Klux Klan; National Association for the Advancement of Colored People.

McCleskey v. Kemp

In *McCleskey v. Kemp,* the Supreme Court on April 22, 1987, rejected a death row inmate's claim that Georgia's system of sentencing people to death was unconstitutional because it discriminated on the basis of race.

In 1978, Warren McCleskey, a black man, was convicted of killing a white police officer during an armed robbery of a store in Atlanta, Georgia. McCleskey's jury—which consisted of eleven whites and one black—sentenced him to die in Georgia's electric chair. McCleskey sought a writ of *habeas corpus,* arguing, among other things, that the Georgia capital sentencing process was administered in a racially discriminatory manner and violated the

United States Constitution. According to McCleskey, the jury's decision to execute him violated the Eighth Amendment because racial bias rendered the decision arbitrary and capricious. Also, the equal protection clause of the Fourteenth Amendment was violated because McCleskey, a black man, was treated differently from white defendants in the same position.

To support his claim of racial discrimination, McCleskey offered as evidence a sophisticated statistical study performed by Professor David B. Baldus and his colleagues at the University of Iowa (the Baldus study). The Baldus study showed that race played a dual role in deciding whether convicted murderers in Georgia would be sentenced to death. First, the race of the murder victim played a large role in whether a defendant would be sentenced to die. According to the study, defendants charged with killing whites received the death penalty in 11 percent of the cases. Defendants charged with killing blacks received the death penalty in only 1 percent of the cases. After taking account of thirty-nine variables that could have explained the disparities on nonracial grounds, the Baldus study concluded that, in Georgia, defendants charged with killing white victims were 4.3 times as likely to receive a death sentence as defendants charged with killing blacks.

Second, the race of the defendant played an important role during capital sentencing. According to the Baldus study, black defendants were 1.1 times as likely to receive a death sentence as other defendants. Thus, the study showed that black defendants such as McCleskey who had killed white victims had the greatest likelihood of receiving the death penalty.

By a 5 to 4 vote, the Supreme Court ruled against McCleskey. The Supreme Court accepted the validity of the Baldus study but held that McCleskey failed to prove "that decisionmakers in his case acted with discriminatory purpose." In other words, McCleskey failed to show that his constitutional rights were violated because he did not prove that anyone involved in his particular case intentionally discriminated against him based on his race. Justice Lewis Powell's opinion for the majority expressed special concern that if the Court accepted McCleskey's argument—that racial bias impermissibly tainted capital sentencing proceedings—all criminal sentences would be subject to attack based on allegations of racial discrimination. The *McCleskey* decision is a landmark ruling in the modern era of capital punishment.

Warren McCleskey died in Georgia's electric chair on September 25, 1991. That same year Justice Powell, whose 5 to 4 majority opinion had sealed Warren McCleskey's fate, told a biographer that he would change his vote in that case (thus sparing McCleskey's life) if he could. Also, although executions had resumed in the United States in 1977, 1991 marked the first time in the modern era of American capital punishment that a white defendant (Donald "Pee Wee" Gaskins) was executed for killing a black person.

Randall Coyne

See also: Crime and race/ethnicity; Discrimination: racial and ethnic.

Malcolm X assassination

The February 21, 1965, murder of Malcolm X silenced an inspiring militant spokesman for African American rights.

Perhaps no twentieth century African American leader better expressed the anger and frustrations of urban African Americans than Malcolm X. During the 1960's Civil Rights movement, Malcolm X, the national spokesman of a black separatist Muslim sect known as the Nation of Islam, articulated in militant language the effects of the nation's historical pattern of racism against African Americans and the social consequences the country faced if significant change did not occur. Before his assassination in 1965, Malcolm X had come to symbolize the disenchantment of African American ghetto residents, a group who were disillusioned about the benefits of racial integration and becoming increasingly impatient with the dominant nonviolent philosophy of the Civil Rights movement.

Malcolm's Early Life Malcolm X was born Malcolm Little on May 19, 1925, in Omaha, Nebraska, to Louise Norton Little and J. Early Little. His father, a Baptist preacher, worked as an organizer for the Universal Negro Improvement Association, the black nationalist organization led by Marcus Garvey. In his later life, Malcolm too would consider himself a black nationalist. In 1931, Malcolm's father died mysteriously in East Lansing, Michigan, where the family had relocated. Thereafter, Malcolm's life was marked by a series of crises.

The impoverished family, now comprising Malcolm, his mother, and six siblings, was soon separated: Malcolm's mother was committed to a mental hospital and no longer influenced his development. Malcolm was placed in a foster home and began to get into trouble as he grew older. Hoping to change the direction of the troubled teen's life, Ella, an older half sister, brought him to live with her in Boston, Massachusetts. Although he possessed a good mind, he did not find school rewarding and dropped out to work at odd jobs. An attraction to street life overcame his interest in legitimate employment, however, and he gradually gravitated toward hustling, drugs, and petty crime.

For a time, Malcolm loved the culture of urban street life and seemed to flourish in it. In the 1940's, he wore the zoot suit and wide hat popular among young African American and Hispanic hipsters and patronized the night spots in Boston's Roxbury and New York's Harlem ghettoes. The seedy side of this life proved to be his downfall. His graduation to the more serious crime of burglary eventually landed him in prison, and at twenty years of age, he began serving six years of a ten-year sentence in Massachusetts' Charlestown and Norfolk penitentiaries.

Initially, Malcolm was hardly a model prisoner. In many ways, however, prison proved to be his redemption, for it was in prison that Malcolm converted to a version of Islam that changed his life. Largely through the efforts of his sisters and brothers, who visited him regularly, Malcolm was introduced to the ideas and philosophy of a little-known Muslim sect, the Nation of Islam, headed by Elijah Muhammad. Gradually, Malcolm abandoned his aggressive behavior, adopted Muslim prayer and life practices, and enmeshed himself in the teachings of Muhammad.

Malcolm as a Muslim Malcolm absorbed the Muslim interpretation of the history of races, an interpretation that explained how and why white people came to be regarded as "devils" and the oppressors of black people throughout the world. Based on Muhammad's teaching, Malcolm's own life experiences, and wide reading in history, politics, and economics, Malcolm came to understand how central the role of white people had been in causing the lowly conditions of African Americans. Muhammad could not have found another adherent with a wider breadth of knowledge about black and white race relations than Malcolm. Their attraction to each other and Malcolm's commitment to spreading Muhammad's message placed Malcolm in an ideal position for elevation to a more visible role in the Islamic organization.

Shortly after his parole in 1952, Malcolm was appointed minister of Temple No. 7 in Harlem by the Muslim leader. Articulate and intellectually gifted, Malcolm undertook his duties with a passion and energy unmatched by his peers. He increased the membership in his own temple and traveled throughout the country organizing new mosques. By 1959, the sect could boast of forty-nine temples nationwide and more than forty thousand members. In six years, temple establishment increased nearly tenfold, and Malcolm almost single-handedly accounted for this.

Malcolm X *(Library of Congress)*

By 1960, Malcolm clearly had emerged as the second most influential man in the Nation of Islam, and was the national spokesman for Elijah Muhammad. Malcolm was heard on the radio and seen on national television. Converts and sympathizers read about his views through the columns of the newspaper that he established, *Muhammad Speaks,* and in other African American urban newspapers for which he regularly wrote. In his Harlem street meetings, he railed against police brutality, and he quelled potentially explosive confrontations between African Americans and law enforcement officials. He continued to "fish" on the ghetto streets for new converts, appealing to them with a mastery of oratory that condemned white racism and the failure of liberal black and white leaders to address the real needs of the African American community. In no uncertain terms, he told listeners that African American men sought to present and defend themselves as men, violently if necessary. Change would occur in the United States, he said, either by the ballot or by the bullet.

Speaking Out In the span of a few short years, Malcolm's name was as familiar as that of Martin Luther King, Jr. Malcolm's national notoriety and influence sparked rivalry and jealousy within the ranks of the Nation of Islam, however. Even Elijah Muhammad, who had warned Malcolm of potential internal dangers from becoming too powerful, grew envious of his national prominence. Rival factions looked for ways to bring him down.

The opportunity occurred in December, 1963, following President John F. Kennedy's assassination, when Malcolm violated Muhammad's order for Muslims to remain silent about the murder. In an interview, Malcolm equated the president's death to "chickens coming home to roost," an impolitic remark that provided the excuse for Muhammad to punish him. Discredited and officially silenced for ninety days, Malcolm's influence within the Nation of Islam waned precipitously.

Unable to forge an effective reconciliation with Muhammad and increasingly determined to speak more broadly for African Americans independent of Nation of Islam constraints, Malcolm left the organization in early 1964 to form his own group, Muslim Mosque, Inc. A pilgrimage to Mecca, the Hajj, and subsequent travel to Africa expanded his understanding about the true nature of Islam, validated his status as an international personality, and helped him to define new agendas in his fight for black people worldwide. A new Malcolm with a new Islamic name, El-Hajj Malik El-Shabazz, hoped to accomplish his agenda through a more politically oriented organization of his making, the Organization of Afro-American Unity.

The Assassination Malcolm remained a marked man, however, and was unable to escape the vilification of enemies in the Nation of Islam. Privately and publicly, they denounced him as a traitor to Elijah Muhammad and placed him under surveillance. From many quarters, those threatened by Malcolm's mass appeal and influence called for violent retribution. In February, 1964, he and his family escaped death from a bomb that destroyed their home.

Malcolm's pleas for peace with the Nation of Islam could not stave off another attempt on his life. On February 21, 1965, while speaking before a crowd of several hundred followers in Harlem's Audubon Ballroom, Malcolm was felled by a fusillade of bullets. In March, 1966, a racially mixed jury found three men—Talmadge Hayer, Norman 3X Butler, and Thomas 15X Johnson—guilty of first-degree murder in Malcolm's death. Despite their conviction, conspiracy theories about Malcolm's death have remained, including theories implicating non-Muslims and even the U.S. government.

Robert L. Jenkins

Core Resources

George Breitman, Herman Porter, and Baxter Smith's *The Assassination of Malcolm X* (New York: Pathfinder Press, 1976) investigates the authors' claim of a cover-up regarding Malcolm's death. Karl Evanzz's *The Judas Factor: The Plot to Kill Malcolm X* (New York: Thunder's Mouth Press, 1992) is a detailed, documented account revealing the author's theory that the intelligence community was involved in Malcolm's death. Michael Friedly's *Malcolm X, the Assassination* (New York: Carroll & Graf, 1992) explores the various conspiracy theories advanced about Malcolm's murder and gives extensive coverage of his relationship with Elijah Muhammad. Bruce Perry's *Malcolm: The Life of a Man Who Changed Black America* (Barrytown, N.Y.: Station Hill, 1991) revises earlier images of Malcolm's life and public career, presenting a man whose childhood was burdened with hardship and violence and who was driven by the need for acceptance by the society he condemned as racist.

See also: Black Power movement; Civil Rights movement; King, Martin Luther, Jr., assassination; Nation of Islam.

March on Washington

Martin Luther King, Jr.'s Poor People's Campaign, carried out after King's death, was a major mass-participation event designed to dramatize to the nation and the government the plight of the poor. By 1967, King had come to see the Vietnam War and the War on Poverty as inseparable issues: The war overseas was taking needed money and government attention away from the more important goal of ending poverty in the United States. The Poor People's Campaign was designed to demonstrate the problem of poverty vividly and graphically by bringing thousands of poor Americans to Washington, D.C., to camp and lobby.

Organizing for this massive march on Washington was interrupted while King went to Memphis in support of a sanitation workers' strike. While there, he was assassinated, the event stunning the movement and the nation. The Southern Christian Leadership Conference (SCLC), now led by Ralph Abernathy, decided to carry out King's Poor People's March in his honor

Tents erected in "Resurrection City" in May, 1968. *(Library of Congress)*

and memory. From all parts of the nation, thousands of poor people of all races set out for Washington, arriving five weeks after King's death. They built Resurrection City, a campground-city, on the Washington Mall.

In the few weeks of its existence, Resurrection City provided "freedom schools" and free food and medical care for its poor residents. Demands were made on the government through such actions as marching to the Department of Agriculture and demanding an end to American hunger in a land of such plenty. Jesse Jackson, a longtime member of the SCLC and King associate, came into prominence, leading marches and giving speeches. Running a city sapped all the energy from the SCLC, however; the group had no time to plan other actions and no clear agenda. Then it began to rain. The rain and mud made life in Resurrection City miserable, and the protesters soon had to abandon the project.

A few government actions can be attributed to the Poor People's Campaign—provision of food to some of the country's neediest counties, some funding for low-income housing, and additional funds for the Office of Economic Opportunity—but, in general, the campaign had only very limited success.

Lisa Langenbach

See also: Civil Rights movement; King, Martin Luther, Jr., assassination; Southern Christian Leadership Conference; Student Nonviolent Coordinating Committee.

Marshall, Thurgood

As an advocate for civil rights and associate justice on the U.S. Supreme Court, Marshall (1908-1993) made a sustained commitment to equal justice under the law.

Thurgood Marshall was born July 2, 1908, in Baltimore, Maryland. His father, William Canfield Marshall, was employed as a waiter and came to be head steward at the affluent Gibson Island Club on the Chesapeake Bay by the time Marshall reached school age. Marshall's mother, Norma Arica Williams, taught in the Baltimore schools for more than thirty years. Both of their families had resided in Maryland for some time. The Marshall family enjoyed a comfortable, stable, middle-class existence. The achievement of this status by a black family less than forty years after the abolition of slavery in the United States is remarkable. Although Maryland, in general, and Baltimore, in particular, were quite well-known for their relatively large free black populations, even modest financial legacies were the exception rather than the rule for most blacks in those decades following the Civil War.

One of Marshall's great grandfathers had been a slave, but little is known about him. Marshall's paternal grandfather, Thoroughgood Marshall, served in the United States merchant marine for many years, and his maternal grandfather, Isaiah Olive Branch Williams, also spent a number of years traveling abroad. Both gave up a life at sea to settle in the Baltimore area; also, both owned and operated grocery stores.

Marshall grew up in a world of books, opera, and tales of adventure. He came into contact with black men who were important and influential in their own communities, and, consequently, he lived in a world of conversation, debate, curiosity, and political and racial awareness. He enjoyed a supportive, extended family network which protected and encouraged in him the growth and development of an independent, well-adjusted, and assertive personality.

Two ambitious, disciplined, and playful young men grew up in the Marshall household. Both sons earned undergraduate degrees at Lincoln University in Oxford, Pennsylvania. Opened in 1856, the historically black university offered the two Marshall youths unique educational and social opportunities. In addition to employing an all-white, essentially Princeton-trained faculty, the college attracted a variety of individuals from throughout the black community. Marshall's classmates included, for example, Kwame Nkrumah, who later led West Africa's Ghana to independence, and Nnamdi Azikiwe, who served as president of Nigeria between 1963 and 1966. Marshall's older brother, William Aubrey, chose medicine as his profession and became a surgeon. Only a quarter of a century before Marshall's graduation there were only 1,734 black doctors in the United States and even fewer black lawyers—only 728.

Before Marshall graduated from Lincoln, he married Vivian Burey and became more focused in his academic interests. He graduated at the top of his class and chose to attend Howard University Law School in Washington, D.C.

Marshall's school years do not, at first glance, seem to have anticipated his participation in a more equal, more fully integrated society. He grew up in an essentially segregated community, attended segregated public schools, a black university, and a predominantly black professional school. Clearly, this environment reflected the legacy of racism, yet Marshall's experiences during this period helped him to secure his racial identity, his long-standing principles, and his tendency to work and to fight for those things in which he believed. During this period, too, he came into contact with faculty members of vision who recognized his talent, challenging and directing the lanky, brash, and assertive young man in his preparations for a highly competitive profession. Particularly important was Marshall's association with Charles H. Houston, a Phi Beta Kappa at Amherst and a Harvard Law School graduate. Under Houston's tutelage, Marshall excelled as a law student; later, when Houston became counsel to the National Association for the Advancement of Colored People (NAACP), he hired Marshall as assistant counsel.

Legal Career Marshall began his law career when he was graduated from the Howard University Law School at the head of his class in 1933. His career began inauspiciously in Baltimore, Maryland, as the Great Depression hung over the nation. Marshall was not immune to the hardships most Americans were experiencing and found it necessary to supplement the meager income he earned in his law practice with money he earned by acting as counsel to the local NAACP branch. The young lawyer unknowingly took the first step in an association through which he would reach the top of his profession.

Thurgood Marshall, the first African American justice on the U.S. Supreme Court. *(Library of Congress)*

In 1936, Marshall's former law professor and mentor, Charles Houston, invited him to accept the position of assistant special counsel to the NAACP in New York. The regularity of the small salary attached to the position was attractive to Marshall, and he was happy to renew his association with Houston, one of the top black attorneys in the United States.

Significantly, Marshall moved from being a practicing attorney to being a politician-lawyer, from counselor to advocate. In 1940, he became director-counsel of the NAACP Legal Defense Fund. In this capacity, he came to be known as a "pioneer civil rights lawyer" and the "legal champion of black Americans." He was, from his earliest involvement with the NAACP, an important figure in what was emerging as a remarkable alteration of the legal position of blacks in the United States.

Although the NAACP's legal team enjoyed a number of successes and victories under Marshall's leadership, his greatest legal triumph was in 1954, when he successfully argued before the Supreme Court in *Brown v. Board of Education of Topeka,* and the Court decided unanimously that school segregation violated the equal protection provision of the Fourteenth Amendment to the Constitution. Thereafter, in addition to enjoying greater prominence in his profession, Marshall, as President Lyndon B. Johnson would remark at a later date, had "already earned his place in history."

Judicial Career Marshall's nomination, in 1961, to a federal judgeship on the United States Court of Appeals by President John F. Kennedy was almost anticlimactic given Marshall's earlier victory. He agreed to serve, however, and after lengthy debate by the United States Senate, he won confirmation.

Citing competence, wisdom, and courage, President Johnson selected Marshall to become solicitor general of the United States. He was speedily confirmed by the Senate and became the government's chief legal spokesperson. At the same time, Marshall became the first black person to hold that position. Marshall, thanks to the interest of Presidents Kennedy and Johnson, was becoming more broadly engaged in the legal profession and less narrowly identified with the Civil Rights movement. In 1967, only two years after Marshall was appointed solicitor general, President Johnson, in perhaps the most dramatic appointment of his administration, named Marshall as his candidate to fill the vacancy created on the United States Supreme Court by the retirement of Justice Tom Clark.

Johnson's political instincts were never better or his moral leadership more pronounced. As the nation anguished over urban unrest and the Civil Rights movement began to crest, Johnson chose Marshall and others—Robert Weaver, the first black to hold a cabinet post; Andrew Brimmer, federal reserve board governor; Patricia Harris, ambassador to Luxembourg; Walter Washington, mayor of Washington, D.C.—to assume significant public offices. In his autobiography, *The Vantage Point* (1971), Johnson said that he had not chosen these leaders for the color of their skin:

> But I also deeply believed that with these appointments Negro mothers could look at their children and hope with good reason that someday their sons and daughters might reach the highest offices their government could offer.

Johnson personally announced the appointment of Marshall on June 14, 1967. The American Bar Association (ABA) found Marshall's nomination "highly acceptable," and the Senate voted sixty-nine to eleven for his confirmation on August 30, 1967.

Marshall's credentials were extraordinary, but when an old friend of the new justice was asked to account for his success, he observed that Marshall was a tolerant person who could relax in his interpersonal relationships, had an unusual ability to put people at ease, and was earnest about finding solutions to human problems.

On the Supreme Court, Marshall proved to be a skilled and practical jurist who had special concern for the plight of the poor and disadvantaged. Ramsey Clark, former attorney general of the United States and son of Justice Tom Clark, has argued that Marshall's full power as a jurist and his concern for humanity were most clearly demonstrated in his application of the principles of the Constitution to the death penalty.

Assessment of His Career Marshall had a far-reaching, direct, and dramatic impact on American life. He was a pioneer in the Civil Rights movement, successfully argued the case of *Brown v. Board of Education* and numerous other cases before the Supreme Court, served on the United States Court of Appeals for the Second Circuit, served as solicitor general of the United States, and was appointed to the Supreme Court.

As an African American born early in the twentieth century, he overcame the restrictions of a segregated society and worked to advance the cause of blacks in the United States. Marshall has become both a symbol of equal opportunity under the law and of the commitment to the rule of law. Marshall urged blacks to use the courts to secure their legal rights, successfully arguing their cases before the Supreme Court. These cases established milestones in the areas of voting rights, fair housing, and integration. As an attorney, he worked tirelessly to obtain factual data to improve the existence of racism and its negative impact upon the lives of the powerless. Marshall brought to the Supreme Court an understanding of the consequences of unequal justice under the law, and he extended this understanding to the elderly, the poor, women, and those on death row.

In poor health, Marshall retired from the bench in 1991. He died on January 24, 1993, in Bethesda, Maryland.

Michael J. Clark

Core Resources

Randall W. Bland, *Private Pressure on Public Law: The Legal Career of Justice Thurgood Marshall* (Port Washington, N.Y.: Kennikat Press, 1973) examines Marshall's judicial behavior before his appointment to the Supreme Court, emphasizing Marshall's legal conservatism. Richard Kluger's *Simple Justice: The History of Brown v. Board of Education and Black America's Struggle for Equality* (New York: Vintage Books, 1975) is an excellent history of *Brown v. Board of*

Education that includes an invaluable account of Marshall's role in the decision. Bob Woodward and Scott Armstrong, *The Brethren: Inside the Supreme Court* (New York: Simon and Schuster, 1979), is a resourceful account of the Court with insights into Marshall's relationship with other justices.

See also: *Brown v. Board of Education*; Civil rights; National Association for the Advancement of Colored People Legal Defense and Educational Fund; Supreme Court and ethnic representation.

Miami riots of 1980

The Miami riots of 1980 constituted one of the most violent urban disorders in the United States since the 1960's. The random killing of whites, not merely the looting of stores, was the goal of the rioters. Yet if the excesses of the rioters were terrible, the provocation that moved them to these acts was also severe.

On December 17, 1979, Arthur McDuffie, a thirty-three-year-old African American insurance agent with no criminal record, was riding along the highway on his motorcycle when several officers of the Public Safety Department of Dade County ordered him to stop. When he refused to do so, he was pursued; when captured, he was beaten severely with nightsticks and heavy flashlights. McDuffie died a few days later from the injuries he had sustained at the hands of the police. This was the last of several incidents of alleged police brutality in the county in 1979: These included the shooting death of a teenager in Hialeah; the alleged sexual abuse of a prepubescent African American girl by a white police officer; and the severe beating administered by police to a black schoolteacher, after the police had raided his house in search of illegal drugs.

The Trial and Aftermath The state attorney for Dade County, Janet Reno, prepared a case against four Dade County police officers who had beaten McDuffie. The case was brought to trial on March 31, 1980, in the town of Tampa, on the state's gulf coast; it was believed that the officers could not get a fair trial in Miami. Because of peremptory challenges by the defense attorney, the jury before which the case was tried was all white. The jury's decision, handed down on Saturday afternoon, May 17, 1980, shocked Miami's African American community: The police officers were acquitted of all charges.

In the early evening hours of May 17, the anger of the black Miamians boiled over into violence; rocks began to fly, and mobs began to attack individuals. Later that evening, after a mob attempt to set fire to the Metro Justice Building was barely repulsed, the governor of Florida, Bob Graham, ordered the National Guard to Miami; it did not arrive in full force, however, until Tuesday. It was not until May 23 that the situation was returned to normal. As a result of the riots, 18 people died and hundreds were injured. There was eighty million dollars' worth of property damage and 1,100 people were arrested. Many Miami businesses were burned: African American, Cuban, and native-born white business owners all suffered.

Major arteries of traffic, used by motorists of all races and ethnic backgrounds, ran through Liberty City, a black area near Miami. In the evening hours of May 17, several white motorists, presumably unaware of the verdict, drove through that neighborhood, where they encountered maddened crowds, composed mostly of young people, bent on revenge. About 250 whites were injured that night in attacks by rioters; 7 whites died as a result of the injuries sustained. Of those who died, one middle-aged woman perished from severe burns when her car was set afire; a young sales clerk, a teenager, and a sixty-three-year-old Cuban refugee butcher died as the result of severe beatings. The reign of terror that night was mitigated only by the willingness of some courageous African Americans to rescue persons threatened by the mobs. The deliberate attacks on whites distinguished the Miami riot from the urban riots of the late 1960's, in which most deaths had occurred by accident.

In the days following that bloody Saturday, blacks were riot victims as well. Some of those killed were rioters; others were law-abiding individuals mistaken for rioters by the police; still others appear to have been random shooting victims of unknown white assailants. Most Miami-area African Americans were neither rioters nor heroes nor victims; they simply waited for the disturbances to end.

For the United States, the Miami riot of 1980 ended twelve years of freedom from major urban riots. Riots broke out again in Miami's African American ghetto in December, 1982; in January, 1989 (when a Hispanic police officer, William Lozano, shot and killed an African American motorcyclist); and in July, 1995. The later riots, however, were not as costly in lives or property as the 1980 outburst. In May, 1993, Lozano's acquittal by a jury in Orlando was not followed by violence.

The Miami riot of 1980 was an alarm bell, warning the United States of the sharp tensions between the races that still persisted a decade and a half after the legislative victories of the Civil Rights movement, and of the combustible possibilities that existed wherever blacks, native-born whites, and Hispanic immigrants lived side by side. The triggering of the Miami riot by an unpopular jury verdict rather than by immediate actions by the police foreshadowed the trajectory of the disastrous riot of April 29-May 1, 1992, in Los Angeles, California.

Paul D. Mageli

Core Resources

Paul Anderson's *Janet Reno: Doing the Right Thing* (New York: John Wiley and Sons, 1994) offers insights into the character and personality of a key player in the 1980 events. Raymond A. Mohl's "On the Edge: Blacks and Hispanics in Metropolitan Miami Since 1959" (*Florida Historical Quarterly* 69, July, 1990) traces the riots of 1980, 1982, and 1989 back to African American anger at Cuban success. Bruce Porter and Marvin Dunn's *The Miami Riot of 1980: Crossing the Bounds* (Lexington, Mass.: D. C. Heath, 1984) is a detailed book-length account of the 1980 riot. Alejandro Portes and Alex Stepick's *City on the Edge: The Transformation of Miami* (Berkeley: University of California Press, 1993) presents the May, 1980, riot as part of a long process by which Miami-area blacks came to see Cuban refugees, as well as native-born whites, as their oppressors. Jerome H. Skolnick and James J. Fyfe's *Above the Law: Police and the Excessive Use of Force* (New York: Free Press, 1993) compares the McDuffie incident with cases of police brutality in other U.S. cities and provides a good account of efforts within the Dade County police department, after 1980, to control the use of force by police.

See also: King, Rodney, case; Los Angeles riots of 1992; Race riots of the twentieth century; Watts riot.

Military and racial/ethnic relations

Racial and ethnic relations in the U.S. military became the center of attention with the integration of the armed forces in 1948 and the shift to an all-volunteer service in 1973. Sociological, ethical, and political concerns revolve around recruitment, promotion, and official military policy regarding race.

The regular service of minorities, especially African Americans, in the U.S. military is a relatively recent phenomenon. Before the Civil War (1861-1865), the U.S. military tradition was one of erratic militia-based service and sanctioned prejudice. Therefore, minorities played very little role in U.S. military life. The Civil War saw the first real attempt to incorporate blacks into the service, strangely enough, on both sides of that conflict. However, they were largely used in noncombat roles, especially in the South, and their use, though playing a marginally important part in the Union's victory, was hotly debated and carefully segregated. This segregation continued well into the twentieth century through two world wars.

The years immediately after World War II saw the first impetus for change. Various segregated black units and a few individual black servicemen (such as Dorrie Miller, a Navy hero at Pearl Harbor) had distinguished themselves in battle, and this opened the debate on the desegregation of the armed forces. President Harry S Truman initiated new policies on race relations in the military, and the services were mostly integrated by the start of the Korean War in 1950. The U.S. Navy, previously the most conservative branch, actually took the early lead in promoting equality within the ranks. Gradually, African Americans began gaining some ground, a few even rising to officer status. During the Vietnam War (1957-1975), a multitude of problems arose, many of which concerned black troops.

From Conscription to the All-Volunteer Force The United States' modern wars, from the Civil War to the Vietnam War, were largely fought by conscripts or draftees. In the two world wars, conscription and segregation went hand in hand. The wars in Korea and Vietnam, especially the latter, were the United States' first experience with draftees fighting in an integrated service. Although conscription was designed to promote equitable social and ethnic representation in the services, it was often alleged that blacks were overly represented and burdened with the risks of combat during the Vietnam War. Indeed, the poor and minorities appear to have suffered from the inequities of the draft, in large part because middle-class and more affluent people could more easily be excused from service or obtain deferments. This discrepancy was also caused by the war's increasing unpopularity. As the combat effectiveness of conscripts declined in the later years of the Vietnam War, the debate ensued as to the desirability of having an all-volunteer force (AVF).

Initially, opposition to ending the draft arose from many quarters. This opposition was based on notions that a large, all-volunteer force would be mercenary, ineffective, socially unrepresentative, and costly. Nevertheless, in 1970, a presidential task force known as the Gates Commission forwarded recommendations that an AVF was possible if military pay and benefits were raised to meet civilian standards. By 1973, the AVF was in place as the last U.S. troops left Vietnam. This AVF seemed to function well at first, but problems arose that led to a decline in quality of personnel for the next decade. The 1980's, however, saw two important changes occur: the onset of serious effort and spending to upgrade the AVF and the implementation of solid racial policies in the U.S. military.

The AVF and Race Relations The 1980's saw a marked improvement in the overall effectiveness of the AVF. Higher pay, better benefits, and more effective advertising have been cited as the cause. Enlistment eligibility requirements were raised considerably during this time. The number of blacks enlisting in the service continued to rise, reaching 22 percent in 1989. The greatest increase in black recruits occurred in the U.S. Navy, where enlistment doubled. Because of the higher eligibility standards, the educational and aptitude levels of all recruits, including minorities, continued to rise into the 1990's. With this higher-quality recruit came a concerted effort at improving race relations and the advancement prospects of minorities in the services. In some respects, an outward attempt was made to make the AVF not only combat effective but also an ideal model in the areas of cost-efficiency, team effort, and race relations. Efforts to improve recruits' sensitivity to race began as early as 1973, but the U.S. military consistently added policies throughout the years that have achieved a remarkable level of color-blind professionalism. Racial incidents underwent a steady decline and have been dealt with sternly. The military maintains a complex system of grievance procedures and racial protocol. Indeed, the U.S. military's record on race is, by most accounts, far better than its record on gender and other issues.

The issue of race and social representation is also a factor in both vocational placement and promotion through the ranks. For active-duty personnel, there appears to be equal representation in combat roles, while blacks occupy larger numbers of clerical, administrative, and logistical positions. A few experts have even suggested capping minority recruitment in some areas, although this would revive the issue of discrimination. The U.S. military boasts the largest percentage of minorities in command roles in its entire history, and an African American officer, General Colin Powell, served as chairman of the Joint Chiefs of Staff during the critical period of the Persian Gulf War. When that conflict erupted in early 1991, it was seen as a major test of the effectiveness of the AVF. Smart bombs and other high-tech weaponry may have garnered the attention of most viewers, but professional military men were quick to point out the readiness and steady professionalism of the men and women of the all-volunteer force that handily won the Gulf War.

Gene Redding Wynne, Jr.

Core Resources

S. A. Stouffer's *The American Soldier* (Princeton, N.J.: Princeton University Press, 1949) offers an account of the motives behind integration of the services. Bowman, Little, and Sicilia's *The All-Volunteer Force After a Decade* (Washington, D.C.: Pergamon-Brassey's, 1986) sheds some positive light on the emerging professional army of the period. D. Bandow's "An Involuntary Military: Paying More for Less," in *The Anthropo Factor in Warfare: Conscripts, Volunteers, and Reserves* (Washington, D.C.: National Defense University, 1988), edited by Lee Austin, clearly expresses some doubts. David R. Segal, in *Recruiting for Uncle Sam* (Lawrence: University Press of Kansas, 1989) deals with the attraction of new recruits to the service. For a firsthand look at the role of black troops in the new military, see Ronald Walters's *African-American Participation in the All-Volunteer Force*, testimony before the Committee on Armed Services, U.S. House of Representatives, March 4, 1991.

See also: Civil War and African Americans; Desegregation: defense; Military desegregation; Tuskegee Airmen.

Military desegregation

On July 26, 1948, President Harry S Truman established a major precedent in the history of equal opportunity for all races when he issued two executive orders. The first, 9980, allowed governmental employees to appeal discriminatory employment procedures to the Fair Employment Board, a subdivision of the Civil Service Commission. The second, 9981, potentially revolutionized race relations in the United States by integrating the armed forces of the United States.

The president's military desegregation order exhibited a characteristic bluntness that came to symbolize his presidency. "It is hereby declared," he commanded, "to be the policy of the president that there shall be equality of treatment and opportunity for all persons in the armed services without regard to race, color, religion, or national origin."

African Americans marching at the Democratic National Convention in 1948 to demand an end to segregation in the military. *(Library of Congress)*

Critics immediately lambasted the order. The *Baltimore Sun* accused Truman of trying to win African American votes. There may have been some merit to this charge: African American leader A. Philip Randolph quickly announced the cancellation of a civil disobedience campaign planned for August 18, 1948. However, when General Omar Bradley insisted that the U.S. Army would not participate until "the nation as a whole" joined the effort, Truman struck back. He would not equivocate on this issue; he would not retreat a single inch. The military was to obey. Unlike other presidents who tried but failed to protect civil rights in the military, Truman personally ensured the end of racial discrimination and segregation in the armed forces.

By January, 1950, Executive Order 9981 effectively integrated most of the military. For example, blacks and whites were working together in the U.S. Air Force, and some black officers now commanded white enlisted airmen. Changes in the Air Force did not attract much attention, however, since only 351 African American officers served in the corps, constituting less than 1 percent of the entire branch.

Similar advances, despite stubborn resistance by some officers, occurred in the U.S. Navy. By December 22, 1949, all black U.S. Marines experienced integrated basic training. The Navy also increased its promotional campaign to recruit more African Americans into its Reserve Officer Training Corps. African Americans previously relegated to the lowly rank of steward now found themselves being promoted to petty officer.

In the Army, however, integration proceeded at a slower pace. On June 7, 1949, Secretary of the Army Louis Johnson ordered the tempo increased. When that failed, African American newspapers called upon the president to intervene. Truman, however, allowed the process to develop at a natural rate, and the Army adhered to a 10 percent quota of African American troops until the beginning of the Korean War. As part of the war effort, the quota was removed, and African American enlistments dramatically increased, prompting Army commanders to desegregate basic training camps. African Americans increased to 11.4 percent of the Army within sixty days after North Korean troops invaded South Korea in June, 1950.

By the time Truman left office in January, 1953, he had reached his goal of nearly total integration of the U.S. military. Although his personal popularity with the U.S. public reached new lows in presidential polls, African American voters remained loyal to the Democratic Party. Executive Order 9981 no doubt played a major role in this significant development.

J. Christopher Schnell

See also: Civil War and African Americans; Military and racial/ethnic relations.

Milliken v. Bradley

In *Milliken v. Bradley* (1974), the U.S. Supreme Court decided that courts did not have the authority to order school desegregation plans that required moving schoolchildren across school district lines unless it could be shown that school district lines had been constructed in a manner designed to preserve segregation.

By the early 1970's, many urban school districts continued to operate schools with a majority black population because of the dearth of white students in those school districts. In 1971, the U.S. Supreme Court in *Swann v. Charlotte-Mecklenburg Board of Education* had held that urban school boards could be required to engage in extensive school busing to integrate their schools. The *Swann* decision, however, did not address the issue of how to integrate urban school districts that had few white students.

In the early 1970's, a group of black parents, with the assistance of the National Association for the Advancement of Colored People Legal Defense and Educational Fund, brought suit seeking to desegregate the Detroit school system. In 1972, federal district court judge Stephen Roth ruled that the Detroit schools were in fact illegally segregated and ordered a multidistrict desegregation plan involving the Detroit city school district along with fifty-three surrounding suburban school districts. One year later, the U.S. Court of Appeals for the Sixth Circuit affirmed, holding that the Detroit schools could not be adequately desegregated without such a multidistrict plan. Shortly thereafter, the U.S. Supreme Court agreed to hear the case.

In 1973, the Supreme Court had considered a similar multidistrict desegregation plan involving the Richmond, Virginia, schools. In that case, the Court had divided 4 to 4, with Justice Lewis Powell recusing himself because of his prior membership on the Richmond School Board. The Court took the Detroit case to decide the question of whether multidistrict desegregation plans were required when inner-city school districts could not otherwise be desegregated. In the meantime, the specter of multidistrict desegregation prompted a firestorm of activity in Congress, as many members of Congress backed both legislation and amendments to the Constitution restricting the ability of federal courts to order extensive desegregation plans.

The Supreme Court held in the *Milliken v. Bradley* decision, with a 5-4 vote, that a district court should not order an interdistrict remedy unless it could be shown that the school district lines had been constructed in a manner to preserve segregation or unless state government officials had taken other action that contributed to the interdistrict segregation. This was a burden of proof that would prove difficult to meet. The *Milliken* decision marked the first time that the Supreme Court had declined to refine existing school desegregation jurisprudence to further integrationist goals.

In the wake of the *Milliken* decision a few metropolitan areas did adopt interdistrict desegregation remedies, but, for the most part, the decision undermined desegregation efforts in America's cities. Unable to utilize an assignment plan that included children from surrounding suburban school districts, inner-city school boards were greatly restricted in their efforts to desegregate their schools.

Davison M. Douglas

See also: *Brown v. Board of Education*; Busing and integration; Discrimination: racial and ethnic; Segregation: de facto and de jure; *Swann v. Charlotte-Mecklenburg Board of Education.*

Million Man March

In October, 1995, an event known as the Million Man March took place in Washington, D.C. The march was significant in that it was successful in assembling nearly one million African American men in the nation's capital for a day of reckoning. Although the march's controversial sponsors, Louis Farrakhan and Benjamin Chavis, caused many Americans, particularly certain black leadership, to question the legitimacy of the event, the march did require the nation to focus on the various predicaments that confronted black men in the United States.

On October 16, 1995, men of African descent converged on Washington, D.C. They came from all over the United States. The majority were poor and working class, a sizable number were middle class, and some were affluent. They all came with the intention of becoming better men once they returned to their homes. The event was known as the Million Man March, and it was one of the major media stories of 1995.

Led by the controversial Nation of Islam leader, Louis Farrakhan, and a former National Association for the Advancement of Colored People (NAACP) leader, Benjamin Chavis, the march generated an ample amount of positive and negative publicity. Farrakhan is well known for his virulent anti-Semitic remarks, and Chavis was voted out of his position as NAACP president after it was disclosed that he had paid $332,400 in organizational funds to his former mistress. Farrakhan, by addressing the deepest concerns of many African Americans at a time when many other black politicians were alarmingly silent, managed to insert himself into the center of what was (and still is) an ongoing racial debate in the United States. Because of the march's success, many mainstream media pundits conceded that Farrakhan was a force to be acknowledged. Ted Koppel, on ABC's *Nightline*, stated that Farrakhan could be called "one of the most influential leaders in black America." During the march, Farrakhan advocated pride, love, and black self-reliance.

Several hundred thousand participants in the Million Man March gather on the Washington Mall, where large television screens were erected to relay proceedings from the Capitol steps. *(Reuters/Gregg Newton/Archive Photos)*

Dissenters From the outset, the event was mired in controversy. Many leaders, black and white, questioned the ability and/or sagacity of Farrakhan and Chavis to cosponsor a march that called for equality and brotherhood. Critics of Farrakhan pointed to his virulent anti-Semitic attacks on Jews and other minorities; critics of Chavis noted his larceny and infidelity. Both men were chided by many women and women's rights organizations for their deeply ingrained sexism.

Mary Francis Berry, chairperson of the U.S. Commission on Civil Rights, wrote a letter in the October, 1995, issue of *The Washington Post* in which she stated, "I do not trust Louis Farrakhan or Benjamin Chavis to lead us to the Promised Land." More than a few African Americans endorsed Berry's sentiments. A *U.S. News & World Report* poll taken in 1995 found that 31 percent (almost a third) of African Americans harbored an unfavorable impression of Farrakhan. Such disdain was echoed by many Jewish leaders as well. On September 19, 1995, the Anti-Defamation League of B'nai B'rith (a Jewish civil rights organization) took out a full-page advertisement in *The New York Times* aggressively denouncing Farrakhan. The advertisement stated, "This march will be led by the most mainstream anti-Semite in recent American history." Alvin Poussaint, a leading black psychiatrist at Harvard University Medical School, said that Farrakhan had to confront his controversial racist past. Poussaint argued that Farrakhan could not continue to speak out of both sides of his mouth and fail to take into account how his own remarks were interpreted.

The Million Man March also exposed the tension that existed between men and women in the African American community. Syndicated columnist Julianne Malveaux; Gloria Watkins, distinguished professor of English at City College in New York; and other prominent African American women denounced the event because of what they saw as the endemic paternalism and sexist message that the march promoted. Other African American women raised similar arguments. With the exception of poet Maya Angelou and the late Betty Shabazz (widow of Malcolm X), virtually no African American women were present at the march.

Supporters of the "no women allowed" policy argued that by prohibiting African American women from attending the march, African American men would be able to concentrate on themselves as individuals and their responsibilities as men, and would not be distracted. Opponents of excluding women from the march argued that such a decision demonstrated the lack of sensitivity that has always been a part of the Nation of Islam regarding women. By engaging in such an act, Farrakhan and his supporters had ignored the crucial role that African American women have played in the struggle for freedom. By relegating African American women to a secondary role, Farrakhan demonstrated either his historical ignorance or gross insensitivity toward his female brethren.

Economic Class Other supporters of the march participated out of a spirit of defiance. Although a sizable number of middle-class men attended the march, the majority of the men came from working-class backgrounds. These were men who had seen their economic prospects falter and had become increasingly distrustful of many successful people, white or black. This was also the group within the African American community that has most recently responded to the message of manhood, greater family responsibility, and black pride.

Farrakhan provided hope for many working-class blacks, who used the march to demonstrate their rage against and resentment of many mainstream Americans, black and white, who argued that African Americans should stay away from the march and that Farrakhan and Chavis were nothing more than two racist and sexist hatemongers who epitomized everything that was negative about black nationalism. On the contrary, for many blacks in this socioeconomic class, these two men embodied all that was absent in their lives. Farrakhan and Chavis were able to tap into the hopelessness, despair, and uncertainty that many of these men felt. Despite opposition, even the Million Man March's detractors conceded that the event was a success. The march put the spotlight on African American men and gave Farrakhan a renewed sense of visibility and importance.

Elwood David Watson

Core Resources

Scott Minerbrook's article in *U.S. News & World Report*, "The Right Man for the Job?" (October 16, 1995), debated whether Farrakhan had the moral and political resources to be a spokesperson for a march of one million men. Sylvester Monroe, in his *Time* magazine article "The Mirage of Farrakhan" (October 30, 1995), discussed the ambivalence that many Americans, both black and white, harbored toward Farrakhan. In the October 23, 1995, article "A Million Men, Minus One," *Time* magazine journalist Jack White criticized and dismissed Farrakhan and discussed his boycotting of the event. In the October 16, 1995, article "Marching to Farrakhan," *Time* magazine journalist David Van Biema talked about the events surrounding the Million Man March. Eric Pooley in his *Time* magazine article, "To the Beat of His Drum" (October 23, 1995), argued that Farrakhan had forced the nation to acknowledge the force he has in black America. The *Time* magazine piece "I, Too, Sing America" (October 30, 1995) examined the sociological impact that the march had on African American men. The October 9, 1995, *Newsweek* magazine article "Farrakhan on the March," written by Vern E. Smith and Steven Waldman, discussed how Farrakhan attempted to give exposure to the voice of a silent majority, the black underclass.

See also: African American women; Black nationalism; Million Woman March; Nation of Islam.

Million Woman March

The Million Woman March took place in Philadelphia, Pennsylvania, on October 25, 1997, and provided African American women the opportunity to discuss some key racial issues. The streets were filled with women pushing baby strollers, beating drums, and walking with the determination to be counted among the several hundred thousand women who attended the historic gathering. Participants carried the red, black, and green flag of the national African American movement and banners that showed the many areas from which they had traveled. The event was organized by activist and bookstore owner Phile Chionesu and was attended by many African American celebrities, including actors Blair Underwood, Margaret Avery, and Jada Pinkett, as well as Winnie Mandela, former wife of South African president Nelson Mandela.

The women marched to draw strength from one another and to focus on their common problems. The event provided a forum to address many issues that are not typically dealt with by women's groups. Some of the main issues discussed were human rights abuses against African Americans, the start of independent African American schools, and a demand for an investigation into allegations of Central Intelligence Agency involvement in the crack cocaine trade in African American neighborhoods. Most of the women left inspired to make changes in their communities, and Chionesu planned to hold a second Million Woman March.

Alvin K. Benson

See also: African American women; Million Man March; National Black Women's Political Leadership Caucus.

Minority and majority groups

Minority groups are defined by their powerlessness relative to other groups in a society, and majority groups are the reverse: They dominate other groups. This concept helps explain why and how conflict occurs in ethnically stratified societies.

"Minority group" and "majority group" are complementary concepts (one implies the other) that denote a hierarchical relationship of dominance and subjugation between groups. The terms carry much emotional and political baggage because of their association with two related concepts, "race" and "ethnicity." To understand minority and majority groups, one needs to distinguish between the sociological viewpoint just outlined and the meanings attributed to the terms by the ordinary person in the street. Sociologists tend to define the concepts strictly, whereas nonacademics define them loosely. This lack of precision lends itself to misconceptions, but it is also true that the sociological viewpoint has inherent problems.

Scholarly vs. Popular Definitions Anthropologists Charles Wagley and Marvin Harris have put forward a widely accepted definition of the term "minority group." In *Minorities in the New World: Six Case Studies* (1958), they argued that five characteristics identify these groups. First, they are relatively powerless compared with members of the dominant group. Second, they share distinctive cultural and/or physical characteristics that distinguish them from the dominant group. This fact, along with their powerlessness, exposes them to unequal treatment. Third, their distinctive traits cause minority groups to become self-conscious social units. Fourth, an established rule of descent exists for transmitting membership in minority groups across generations. Fifth, members of minority groups tend to marry within their groups.

Most social scientists agree that these criteria are not equally important. They view minority groups' relative powerlessness as the most important criterion distinguishing them from majority groups. For example, in *Majority and Minority: The Dynamics of Race and Ethnicity in American Life* (1991), sociologist Norman Yetman argues that "minority group" is synonymous with the term "subordinate," and "majority group" is synonymous with "dominant." The main implication of this viewpoint is that, contrary to what one might assume, members of minority groups can constitute a numerical majority in their society, and majority group members might be a numerical minority. The classic example of this is South Africa, where blacks, although they constitute approximately 75 percent of the population, were powerless under apartheid, while whites, constituting approximately 14 percent of the population, were dominant.

Sociologists distinguish between racial, ethnic, religious, and gender groups, on one hand, and minority and majority groups on the other. They view the latter twin concepts as subsuming the others. That is, majority groups and minority groups may consist of distinct races, ethnic groups, religious groups, and gender groups. These various types of majority/minority groups differ from each other symbolically. Thus, racial majority/minority groups are set apart by physical features, ethnic majority/minority groups by their unique cultural attributes, religious majority/minority groups by unique spiritual beliefs, and gender majority/minority groups by societal expectations of sex-linked characteristics. A minority and majority group might display a number of these characteristics simultaneously. An example of an overdetermined minority group would be black, Haitian, female Catholics.

Nonacademics often adopt a loose definition of minority and majority groups. They tend to ignore the latter concept and focus on the former. In this focus, "minority group" becomes synonymous with specific racial and/or ethnic groups, and the term "minority" is often used to refer to individuals belonging to these groups. Thus, in the United States, the term "minorities" is often understood to mean blacks and/or Hispanics. This is controversial, because such usage often occurs in a pejorative context and may be viewed as a way of attacking those two groups. Used in this way, the term "minority" can become a weapon in intergroup conflict.

Problems with Definitions Adopting the sociological viewpoint on majority/minority groups leaves less room for confusion. Nevertheless, this viewpoint also has problems. To begin with, it seems counterintuitive to suggest that numerical majorities can be, in fact, "minorities." This is not a problem when a group—for example, African Americans—is both numerically smaller and less powerful than the dominant group. As sociologist Pierre L. van den Berghe (*Dictionary of Race and Ethnic Relations*, 1988) has suggested, however, that colonial subjects who vastly outnumber their colonial rulers might take umbrage at the notion that they constitute a "minority." The problem is that the commonsense understanding of "minority" conflicts with sociological usage; therefore, the potential for confusion exists.

Van den Berghe even argues that this confusion is deliberate, since it serves useful political purposes. In pluralistic societies—such as the United States—that have instituted affirmative action programs to aid historically disadvantaged groups, being identified as a "minority group" can prove beneficial in some instances. The problem lies in deciding which groups are minority groups. Blacks and Hispanics are uncontroversial choices, but whether Jews, Japanese Americans, and Chinese Americans should be considered minority groups is more problematic and controversial. These groups, though numerical minorities, enjoy a level of socioeconomic success which far outstrips that of blacks and Hispanics. Thus, the term "minority group," with its connotation of powerlessness and relative deprivation, seems somewhat inappropriate. A fuzzy definition of "minority group," however, would give these economically successful groups a firmer claim to minority status and, with it, even greater access to societal resources. Van den Berghe suggests that similar confusion over the term "majority group" allows the tiny elite who exercise hegemony over the United States to cloud their identity and escape criticism by being lumped into a larger category—white Anglo-Saxon Protestants—who are perceived, mistakenly, as the dominant group.

Use of the Concept The concept of minority groups has long been used in Europe to describe national groups who, for whatever reason (for example, through conquest by another group), have come to form small enclaves in societies dominated by other groups. Early in the twentieth century, the concept was adopted by American sociologists seeking a comprehensive term to describe the multifaceted intergroup conflict that has been a recurring theme in American history. With respect to blacks, American Indians, the Chinese, and the Japanese, the conflict seemed to be racial; with respect to groups such as Eastern European Jews, the Irish, and Italians, the conflict seemed to revolve around religious and cultural differences. As noted above, the unifying thread was domination by one group (native whites) of these various other groups. This suggested to sociologists such as Donald Young the need for a word to encapsulate all these various conflicts. In *American Minority Peoples* (1932), he suggested that the term "minority groups" be used to describe the distinctive groups who found themselves in conflict with the white majority.

Since the time of Young's proposal, the minority group/majority group concept has gained widespread acceptance because of the universality of intergroup conflict following European decolonialization. This process created new states such as India and Pakistan, but it also led to widespread racial, ethnic, religious, and nationalistic conflicts. Not all of these can be described as minority group/majority group situations, but many are. Examples include the Rodiya and Sinhalese in Sri Lanka, the Hutu and Tutsi in Burundi, and the Osu and Ibo in Nigeria. In *Ethnic Groups in Conflict* (1985), Donald Horowitz gives numerous examples of such conflict occurring in formerly colonized areas.

The more industrially developed areas of the world are also the scene of numerous minority group/majority group conflicts. The conflict between blacks and whites in the United States is perhaps the best known, but to this could be added French Canadians and English-speaking Canadians, aboriginal Canadians and white Canadians, Australian aboriginals and white Australians, white New Zealanders and Maoris, and nonwhite immigrants and whites in the United Kingdom. Even more pressing examples are to be found in Eastern Europe, where the breakup of the former Soviet Union has allowed long-standing racial, ethnic, religious, and nationalistic hatreds to flare into open warfare. This breakup has combined with economic recession in Western Europe to reawaken antiminority fervor. Thus, in West Germany, Eastern European, Turkish, Vietnamese, and African immigrants have been repeatedly attacked by neo-Nazi groups. In France, agitation against Arab and African immigrants led the government to pass laws making it easier to track the movement of these immigrants. Even traditionally tolerant countries such as Denmark have experienced anti-immigrant sentiment. The prevalence of this type of conflict illustrates why the twin minority/majority group concept is likely to retain its utility.

Milton D. Vickerman

Core Resources

Donald Horowitz's *Ethnic Groups in Conflict* (Berkeley: University of California Press, 1985) contains numerous examples of intergroup conflict involving majority/minority situations. Peter I. Rose's *They and We* (4th ed., New York: McGraw-Hill, 1990) is a well-written and accessible book on racial and ethnic relations in the United States. George Simpson and J. Milton Yinger's *Racial and Cultural Minorities* (5th ed., New York: Plenum Press, 1985) presents an encyclopedic discussion of issues related to race and ethnicity. *Majority and Minority: The Dynamics of Race and Ethnicity in American Life* (5th ed., Boston: Allyn & Bacon, 1991), edited by Norman Yetman, is a collection of twenty-nine articles that gives a comprehensive overview of the field of race and ethnicity. Donald Young's *American Minority Peoples* (New York: Harper & Brothers, 1932) is an early book devoted to the subject of minority/majority relations; Young is said to have introduced the concept of minority groups into the sociological literature.

See also: Discrimination: racial and ethnic; Ideological racism; Minority voting districts; Psychology of racism; Racism: history of the concept.

Minority voting districts

The 1965 Voting Rights Act prohibited limiting the rights of all people to vote and called on the federal government to examine suspect elections. Specifically, it addressed efforts by whites in the American South to keep African Americans from voting. The act was successful in eradicating exclusionary practices and resulted in substantial increases in the numbers of African Americans who voted, but minority political disfranchisement still existed. Minorities remained proportionally underrepresented in elected offices nationwide.

The 1982 amendment mandated the creation of "majority-minority" voting districts in states with a history of racial disfranchisement. Such districts contain populations of minorities large enough to constitute a majority or elect a candidate of their preference. This is achieved through reapportionment, a process whereby districts are periodically redrawn by state legislatures, typically following the decennial U.S. census. Reapportionment ideally reflects the changes in population occurring since the last census count. However, districts were "gerrymandered" during reapportionment to preclude the election of minorities by dividing minority populations across districts. Such gerrymandering for political self-interest is commonplace and was named after Massachusetts governor Elbridge Gerry, who, in 1812, advocated a salamander-shaped voting district.

Redistricting to create minority voting districts has been successful if measured by the numbers of minorities elected to office in such districts. However, minority districts face constitutional challenges.

Robert P. Watson and Claudia A. Pavone Watson

See also: Disfranchisement laws in Mississippi; Redistricting; Representation: gerrymandering, malapportionment, and reapportionment; Voting Rights Act of 1965.

Miscegenation laws

State miscegenation laws were examples of explicit racial discrimination in U.S. statutory law; they criminalized and penalized the unions of persons of differing racial heritages and denied legal legitimacy to mixed-race children born to such interracial couples.

Thirty-eight U.S. states at one time had miscegenation laws in force; seven of those thirty-eight repealed their laws before 1900. All southern states (not including the District of Columbia) had miscegenation statutes. Many western states (including Arizona, California, Montana, Nevada, Oregon, Utah, and Wyoming), in addition to forbidding intermarriage between blacks and whites, also specifically prohibited unions between whites and Native Americans or whites and Asian Americans. Penalties upon conviction varied from a maximum imprisonment of more than two years in most of the South and some other states (ten years in Florida, Indiana, Maryland, Mississippi, and North Carolina) to sentences ranging between a few months and two years in other states. Enforcement of the laws was random and irregular.

The key case in ending miscegenation laws was *Loving v. Virginia* (1967). At the time that the U.S. Supreme Court heard the *Loving* case, sixteen states

Antimiscegenation tract published in the North during the 1860's. *(Library of Congress)*

still had miscegenation laws in force. Virginia's laws dealing with racial intermarriage were among the nation's oldest. They stemmed from statutes formulated in the colonial period (1691) and had been strengthened by more stringent miscegenation legislation passed in the mid-1920's in which whiteness was very narrowly defined. The codes that became law in 1924 were aimed primarily at discriminating against people of mixed African American and white heritage and/or of American Indian background.

In the *Loving* case, Richard Perry Loving, who was white, had married Mildred Delores Jester, who was African American, in Washington, D.C., in June, 1958. The Lovings made their home between Fredericksburg and Richmond in Caroline County, Virginia. They were issued warrants of arrest in July, 1958, and in January, 1959, they were convicted before the Caroline County court of violating Virginia's antimiscegenation statute. Their minimum sentences (of one year imprisonment each) were suspended on agreement that they would leave the state. They moved to Washington, D.C., until 1963, when they returned to their farm in Virginia and worked with attorneys Bernard Cohen and Philip Hirschkop of the American Civil Liberties Union (ACLU), who placed their case under appeal. The miscegenation law and the Lovings' convictions were upheld by the Virginia Supreme Court of Appeals in March, 1966, but in June, 1967, the U.S. Supreme Court overruled the appellate finding. The Supreme Court ruled that use of race as a basis for prohibiting marriage rights was unconstitutional under the Fourteenth Amendment's equal protection and due process provisions. The ruling nullified all remaining laws forbidding interracial marriage. Previous to the unanimous 1967 ruling, the U.S. Supreme Court had taken a conservative approach to this civil rights issue. It had repeatedly avoided reviewing lower court convictions based on state antimiscegenation laws (*Jackson v. Alabama*, 1954; *Naim v. Naim*, 1955; *McLaughlin v. Florida*, 1964).

Barbara Bair

See also: Biracialism; Blackness and whiteness: legal definitions; Interracial and interethnic marriage; One-drop rule; Race as a concept.

Mississippi Freedom Democratic Party

The Mississippi Freedom Democratic Party (MFDP) was founded to bring attention to the lack of political freedom in Mississippi. The Freedom Summer project had registered only sixteen hundred voters in Mississippi in 1964, and the ruling Democratic Party barred civil rights activists from attending party conventions. The Council of Federated Organizations (COFO) therefore created a new party and selected sixty-eight delegates and alternates to attend the Democratic Party's national convention in Atlantic City, New Jersey. Their mission was to contest the seats held by Mississippi's all-white delegation, arguing that the MFDP was the only truly democratic party in the state.

Efforts to promote African American suffrage in Mississippi go back to the 1950's, when voter education classes were conducted in churches to prepare people for the state's voter registration test. *(Library of Congress)*

Civil rights workers testified before the national Democratic Party's Credentials Committee about conditions in Mississippi. Fannie Lou Hamer, a sharecropper's daughter, delivered a riveting account of being threatened and beaten for attempting to register to vote. President Lyndon B. Johnson feared losing the support of white Democrats and tried to arrange a compromise that would allow the MFDP token representation. Even though white liberals and moderate civil rights leaders such as Martin Luther King, Jr., were willing to accept this compromise, a majority of the MFPD's members were not. This disagreement solidified the split in the Civil Rights movement between integrationist moderates and separationist radicals.

Robert E. McFarland

See also: Civil Rights movement; Council of Federated Organizations; Disfranchisement laws in Mississippi; Freedom Summer.

Missouri Compromise

The Missouri Compromise of 1820 was an attempt to pacify both northern and southern sectional interests by allowing slavery to exist in the southern part of the Louisiana Purchase territory.

Between 1818 and 1819 both the territories of Missouri and Maine petitioned the U.S. Congress to be admitted as new states. The Missouri Territory had been created from the Louisiana Purchase (1803) and was promised constitutional protection. However, Congress could not decide if the right of property applied to the institution of slavery. Should it be allowed in Missouri and the rest of the Louisiana Purchase, or did Congress have the moral responsibility to rectify the issue of slavery that had been avoided since the Constitutional Convention of 1787? It would take three sessions of Congress between 1818 and 1821 before Missouri was fully admitted as a state. The issue of slavery sparked by the ensuing debate spread throughout the country and threatened to cause disunion between the northern and southern regions.

The Issue of Slavery At the time that Missouri and Maine applied for statehood, the United States consisted of eleven free states and eleven slave states. This political balance had been achieved since 1789 by admitting a slave state and then a free state determined by geographical location and each region's past history with regard to slavery. This arrangement supplied each section with an equal number of senators (two per state) and attempted to equalize representation in the House of Representatives through the three-fifths clause.

The three-fifths compromise, added to the final draft of the Constitution, allowed slave states to count each slave as three-fifths of a person to balance their representative power against that of the more densely populated North. Nevertheless, the North had a majority of representatives in Congress (105 to 81). Missouri's admission as a free or slave state therefore became an important issue in the very body that would resolve it. Missouri threatened to extend the influence of the industrial free North in the Senate or provide the majority to the agrarian slaveholding South.

In 1818, Missouri's boundaries were approximately the same as those of today, and the territory was estimated to have 2,000 to 3,000 slaves. Slavery was a historical by-product of prior French and Spanish colonial policies. Missouri reasoned that slavery should be allowed to continue as it had in other territories that had been granted statehood since 1789.

In February, 1819, the House of Representatives responded to this debate by adopting the Tallmadge amendment. Representative James Tallmadge of New York proposed an amendment to the bill allowing Missouri to frame a state constitution. The two clauses in the amendment would restrict the further introduction of slavery into Missouri and provide that all children born to slaves would be free at age twenty-five. Both clauses passed the House. Southern senators were shocked by the bitterness of the debate in the House and the ability of the North to muster votes. They saw the Tallmadge amendment as the first step in eliminating the expansion of slavery. Voting along sectional lines, the Senate rejected both clauses.

Congress adjourned session until December 6, 1819. During this interim, Maine formed a constitution and applied for admission as a free state. Maine had been incorporated into the Massachusetts Bay Colony in 1691 but had started to agitate for separate statehood during and after the War of 1812. Its application for statehood as a free state seemed to provide a possible solution to the Missouri debate that threatened the stability of the young nation. On February 18, 1820, the Senate Judiciary Committee joined the two measures and the Senate passed Maine's and Missouri's applications for statehood but without mentioning slavery. This infuriated Maine, which had, as part of Massachusetts, outlawed slavery in 1780. What should have been a routine confirmation of new states became part of the most explosive issue to face the country. Maine would be allowed to separate from Massachusetts and gain statehood as long as Congress approved it by March 4, 1820, or the nine counties would revert back to Massachusetts. Even so, many of Maine's constituency urged that Maine's application fail so that slavery would not spread into Missouri.

Sectional Polarization Senator J. B. Thomas of Illinois offered a compromise amendment to the Senate bill that would admit Missouri as a slave state with the proviso that the remaining territories in the Louisiana Purchase above 36°30′, Missouri's southern border, would be free of slavery. The Northern-controlled House responded by rejecting this Thomas amendment and passed a proviso prohibiting the further introduction of slavery anywhere. The result was polarization along sectional lines. In turn, the Senate struck out the antislavery provision and added the Thomas amendment. Thus began the final debate over whether slavery would be allowed to expand.

Senator Rufus King of New York continued the debate by stating that Congress, under Article IV, section 3 of the Constitution, was empowered to exclude slavery from the territory and to make slavery an issue for statehood. "New states *may be* admitted by the Congress into this Union." A precedent had been established under Article IV, section 3 of the Constitution which forbade slavery in lands above the Ohio River in the Northwest Ordinance of 1787. Therefore, in the minds of many of the northern congressmen, they should take this opportunity to eliminate slavery from any point west of the Mississippi. In response, Senator William Pickering of Maryland stated that the United States was composed of an equal number of slave states and free states; Missouri should be allowed to determine its own fate.

Missouri responded with anger and frustration, asserting that the issue was not about slavery but rather the issue of state sovereignty. Congress had delayed its admission for years. Missouri, like other states, had the right to choose its property laws. In Missouri as well as the rest of the South, the issue swung from one dealing with slavery to one dealing with property rights and the equality of states within the United States. These issues captured the attention of citizens throughout the country and led to heated debates on all levels. For the first time, slavery was being justified and defended as a good way of life by not only southern politicians but also the southern clergy. Would the country be influenced by restrictionists who sought to control this institution, or would states' rights be preserved?

The Compromise A compromise between the two houses was eventually reached in a conference formed to break the deadlock. Speaker of the House Henry Clay of Kentucky stated that he would not support Maine's admission unless Missouri was admitted with no restrictions. The Senate took the House bill and inserted the Thomas amendment. The House under Henry Clay's leadership voted to admit Maine as a free state and Missouri as a slave state and restricted slavery north of 36°30′. It is interesting to note that seven of Maine's nine representatives in the Massachusetts delegation voted against Maine's admission so that their state would not be used to provide a solution to the slavery issue.

Missouri continued to be an issue when it presented a state constitution in November, 1820. As if to get the final word, the Missouri Constitutional Convention had incorporated into its constitution a provision excluding free blacks and mulattoes from the state. This provision incited the antislavery factions in the Senate and House and threatened to destroy the fragile compromise. A "Second Missouri Compromise" was needed which stated that Missouri would not gain admission as a state unless its legislature assured Congress that it would not seek to abridge the rights of citizens. The Missouri legislature agreed to this in June, 1821. On August 10, 1821, President James Monroe admitted Missouri as the twenty-fourth state. After waiting a short time, Missouri's state congress sought to have the last say when it approved statutes forbidding free blacks from entering the state.

The Missouri Compromise would stand for the next three decades. During that time it served to mark a clear delineation between the growing regional and sectional problems of the North and South and made states' rights the rallying cry for the South until the Civil War.

Vincent Michael Thur

Core Resources

Richard H. Brown's *The Missouri Compromise: Political Statesmanship or Unwise Evasion?* (Boston: D.C. Heath, 1964) contains primary source material showing views of contemporary leaders and varying perspectives of historians. R. Douglas Hurt's *Agriculture and Slavery in Missouri's Little Dixie* (Columbia: University of Missouri Press, 1992) is a study of the political and legal impact of the Missouri Compromise in a seven-county area along the Missouri River. Glover Moore's *The Missouri Controversy, 1819-1821* (Gloucester, Mass.: Peter Smith, 1967) is a significant monograph on the political compromise that signaled nineteenth century sectional controversies during the antebellum era.

See also: Bleeding Kansas; Compromise of 1850; Lincoln-Douglas debates; Proslavery argument; Slavery: history; Three-fifths compromise.

Montgomery bus boycott

The Montgomery bus boycott of 1955 and 1956, the first major effort by African Americans to fight entrenched discrimination through economic sanctions, sparked the early Civil Rights movement.

When the Supreme Court issued its decision in *Brown v. Board of Education* in May, 1954, ruling that racial segregation in public schools was unconstitutional, it marked the beginning of a period of dramatic change in the relationships between African Americans and whites. Until the mid-1960's, that change was hastened by the organized nonviolent resistance by many African Americans to laws and conditions that they regarded as discriminatory. The first occasion in which such tactics proved successful was a boycott of public buses in Montgomery, Alabama.

Although African Americans had achieved some hard-fought successes before 1954—most notably the desegregation of the armed forces—in many respects they remained a separate community, enjoying fewer rights and

Rosa Parks, whose refusal to give up her bus seat to a white man helped trigger the modern Civil Rights movement. *(Library of Congress)*

opportunities and less legal protection than whites. This was especially true in the Deep South, where the doctrine of "separate but equal" was held to apply to most areas of daily life and was used to justify a decidedly unequal segregation. Hundreds of laws, many of them passed in the late nineteenth century, restricted the rights of black southerners to eat, travel, study, or worship with whites.

The school desegregation ruling brought no immediate change to race relations in Montgomery. Once the capital of the Confederacy, this city of about 130,000 people—50,000 of whom were African American—continued resolutely in the old pattern of racial separation. The African American community of Montgomery had undertaken initial steps to challenge certain local segregation practices that were particularly offensive. E. D. Nixon of Montgomery headed the National Association for the Advancement of Colored People (NAACP) in Alabama. Because he worked as a sleeping-car porter, a unionized profession, he was less susceptible to attempts by the white establishment to control his behavior by threatening his job. Jo Ann Robinson helped lead the African American clubwomen in Montgomery, who provided a powerful organizational backbone among the small African American middle class in Montgomery. This nascent movement still lacked both a unified structure and a single issue to mobilize the African American community to push for civil rights.

Rosa Parks's Arrest The issue came to a head on December 1, 1955, when Rosa Parks, a seamstress at a Montgomery department store and formerly the secretary of the local NAACP chapter, refused to give up her seat to maintain a row of vacant seats between white and black riders on the public bus system in Montgomery, as required by law. She was arrested and charged with violating the segregation ordinance. Parks's action was in part spontaneous—she had not boarded the bus with the intent to violate any segregation ordinance. Yet she had attended the Highlander Folk School in Tennessee, where members of the community learned to become more effective, and a lifetime of enduring racial indignities had made her acutely aware of the evil nature of segregation.

Immediately, Montgomery's African American community sprang into action. Fred Gray, one of but four black lawyers in Alabama, contacted Clifford Durr, a liberal white attorney, to post bail for Parks. Nixon brought together two ministers, Ralph David Abernathy and Martin Luther King, Jr., with Jo Ann Robinson to plan for a massive boycott of Montgomery public buses, a majority of whose riders were African American. It would be necessary to arrange for transportation for scores of African Americans who did not own cars. To coordinate the massive undertaking, Montgomery's African American leaders created the Montgomery Improvement Association (MIA), presided over by King, the twenty-six-year-old pastor of Dexter Avenue Baptist Church. The boycott began on December 5, 1955.

The Response to the Boycott At first, whites reacted with indifference or amusement, until the bus company's revenues dropped by 75 percent. A series of meetings between the city commissioners, representatives of the bus company, and the MIA failed to produce any agreement on the African Americans' demands—courteous treatment by bus drivers; a first-come, first-served seating arrangement, with blacks filling the rear and whites the front of the bus; and the employment of African American drivers on routes that served predominantly African American neighborhoods of Montgomery. Instead, the city police department began to harass the carpools that had been set up by the MIA to provide alternative transportation, and they arrested some of the drivers. Police officers arrested King himself for speeding, and on January 30, persons unknown blasted King's house with dynamite. The houses of two other boycott leaders met a similar fate.

These acts of violence and intimidation affected the course of events in several ways. First, they united the African Americans in Montgomery, inspiring them to continue the boycott for more than a year. The violence also attracted national attention to Montgomery and led to substantial outside support for the boycott, assistance vital to its success. Finally, the violence served as a foil for the rhetoric of nonviolent resistance that King so eloquently articulated. In one mass meeting after another, he urged his followers to ignore hostile provocations, to confront their persecutors passively, and to refuse to fight back, relying on the moral authority of their actions to sway the hearts and minds of their antagonists.

While the boycott continued, the legal issues it raised were argued in federal courts. On February 1, 1956, five Montgomery women filed suit to have the Court strike down the city bus seating ordinance. The case was heard on May 11, by which time eighty-nine MIA members faced local charges for conspiracy to interfere with normal business. In November, city officials obtained an injunction against the MIA officials for running a carpool, which nearly brought the boycott to a halt. Nevertheless, the federal suit received a favorable hearing and was affirmed by the Supreme Court in *Browder v. Gayle* in November, and the Court ordered the seating on Montgomery buses desegregated on December 17, 1956. Four days later, King, Abernathy, and Nixon rode the bus downtown and were able to sit wherever they wanted.

Results of the Boycott The boycott succeeded for a number of reasons, not the least of which was the timely court ruling. It also benefited from fissures in the white community across gender, age, and economic lines. White, middle-class women often transported their black maids to and from work, unwittingly aiding the boycott. Within the Chamber of Commerce, a coalition of young businessmen called the Men of Montgomery demanded that the city fathers end the boycott because the city's tarnished image made it difficult to attract outside businesses.

Successful in its immediate objective, the boycott established a precedent for other economic protests over the next decade. Because of his role in the boycott, Martin Luther King, Jr., emerged as the most important spokesperson for African Americans. His tactics of nonviolent passive resistance remained the major tool of the Civil Rights movement until the mid-1960's. Shortly after the boycott's conclusion, King was instrumental in founding the Southern Christian Leadership Conference, which applied the Montgomery formula to other southern cities. African American leaders tried nonviolent resistance and economic protests in Birmingham, Alabama, and Albany, Georgia. The Montgomery bus boycott was an important harbinger of the most profound social changes in the United States during the 1960's, in that it marked a change in the attitudes and strategies of African Americans to confront racial indignity.

Courtney B. Ross, updated by Edward R. Crowther

Core Resources

David J. Garrow's *Bearing the Cross: Martin Luther King, Jr., and the Southern Christian Leadership Conference* (New York: William Morrow, 1986) is a thorough, detailed biography of King that provides an excellent account of King's Montgomery days. Martin Luther King, Jr.'s *Stride Toward Freedom: The Montgomery Story* (New York: Harper & Row, 1958) is King's own account of the boycott. Jo Ann Gibson Robinson's *The Montgomery Bus Boycott and the Women Who Started It: The Memoir of Jo Ann Gibson Robinson* (Knoxville: University of Tennessee Press, 1987) provides a powerful portrait of the world of middle-class women in Montgomery and the essential role they played in the boycott strategy.

See also: *Brown v. Board of Education*; Civil Rights movement; King, Martin Luther, Jr., assassination; Little Rock school desegregation.

Moose Lodge No. 107 v. Irvis

In *Moose Lodge No. 107 v. Irvis,* the Supreme Court on June 12, 1972, ruled that a state did not deny the equal protection of the law when it granted a license to serve alcohol to a racially discriminatory private club.

Moose Lodge No. 107 was a private club in Harrisburg, Pennsylvania, that served both food and alcohol, the latter under a license granted by the Pennsylvania Liquor Control Board. The club was often used by members of the state legislature for lunch breaks and after-hours relaxation. A white member of the lodge brought an African American fellow legislator, K. Leroy Irvis, into the club's dining room and bar, where the pair were refused service on the grounds of Irvis's race.

The Fourteenth Amendment to the Constitution forbids state action in furtherance of racial discrimination. Since the lodge's refusal to serve Irvis amounted to racial discrimination, the Supreme Court was asked to determine whether Pennsylvania's granting of a liquor license constituted state action in furtherance of that discrimination.

The Court ruled in a 6-3 vote that mere state licensing of a private club on private land did not make every action of the club an action of the state. The majority noted that the impetus for discrimination did not have to originate with the state in order for there to be state action, so long as the state was involved in enforcing private discrimination in a significant way. If the lodge had been a tenant in a state-owned building and had opened its facilities to all members of the public except African Americans, the state would have been engaged in a joint venture with the club, and the club's discrimination would have been state action. In this case, however, the building was privately owned, it rested on privately owned land, and its facilities were open not to the public in general, but to members only. The Court observed that the state provided many services, among them water, electricity, licensing, and police and fire protection. The mere provision of such services was not enough to convert every action of the beneficiary into state action.

The dissenters argued that there was state action, since the liquor regulatory scheme was pervasive, regulating "virtually every detail of the operation of the licensee's business." They also observed that since the quota for liquor licenses had been exceeded in Harrisburg, the state's renewal of the Moose Lodge's license prevented a different facility with nondiscriminatory policies from opening.

This important case limited the reach of the Fourteenth Amendment by defining state action narrowly. It remained possible for victims of discrimination to find recourse in federal and state antidiscrimination statutes. Leroy Irvis was able to do just that when he brought suit against Moose Lodge No. 107 under Pennsylvania's public accommodations law. He eventually gained admission to the club's facilities and was later elected speaker of the Pennsylvania House of Representatives.

William H. Coogan

See also: Restrictive covenants; Segregation: de facto and de jure; *Shelley v. Kraemer.*

Morrill Land Grant Act of 1890

In 1862, the United States Congress passed the first Morrill Land Grant Act to authorize the establishment of a land-grant institution in each state to educate citizens in agriculture, mechanic arts, home economics, and other practical professions. Because of the emphasis on agriculture and mechanic arts, these institutions were referred to as A&M colleges. Because of the legal separation of the races in the South, African Americans were not permitted to attend these original land-grant institutions. This situation was rectified in 1890, when Congress passed the second Morrill Land Grant Act, expanding the 1862 system of land-grant colleges to provide support for the establishment of African American institutions of higher learning in states that lacked such facilities.

Each of the southern states that did not have an African American college by 1890 established one or more under the second Morrill Land Grant Act. The 1890 institutions evolved into a major educational resource for the United States. For more than a century, these institutions have provided the principal means of access to higher education for African Americans. They continue to be a major source of African American leaders who render valuable service to their communities, the nation, and the world.

Alvin K. Benson

See also: Black colleges and universities; College admissions; Desegregation: public schools; Education and African Americans.

Moynihan Report

One explanation for high levels of impoverishment in black communities was published in *The Negro Family* (1965), by Daniel Patrick Moynihan, a white social scientist of Irish descent who later became a U.S. senator. By postulating that "the family structure of the lower-class Negroes is highly unstable," the Moynihan Report argued that family deterioration was at the heart of high unemployment, welfare dependency, low achievement, and crime. In Moynihan's view, black communities were enmeshed in a "tangle of pathology." The report relied heavily on earlier observations by E. Franklin Frazier (1932), who conceptualized lower-class culture as disorganized and pathological. This thesis has since been used by others who contend that disadvantaged poor and minority groups encourage cultural practices that fuel their continued poverty.

Reaction to the Moynihan Report was generally negative on the part of leaders of the Civil Rights movement—especially clear when the report's conclusions were dismissed by those participating in the November, 1965, meeting of the White House Conference on Civil Rights. The idea that poverty is caused by subcultural patterns has implications for public policy. Instead of focusing on federal efforts to ensure good jobs, housing, education, health care, and income maintenance, those who hold this view focus on improving the character of individuals and families. Critics of the report said that this culture-of-poverty theory was a form of victim blaming that ignored societal and institutional structures—such as unequal access to jobs, segregated education, and unaffordable, deteriorating housing—that make groups who are discriminated against more susceptible to poverty and the problems it causes for families and communities. Poor and minority people have the same values as those in more advantaged sectors of society, but their barriers to achievement are much greater.

This perspective continues to offend and enrage many people, including African Americans, civil rights workers, and progressive community and government activists.

Eleanor A. LaPointe

See also: Culture of poverty; Economics and race; Poverty and race.

Mulattoes

Before the Civil Rights movement of the 1950's and 1960's, white supremacy was a prevalent concept in U.S. society. White supremacists held that Caucasians, or whites, were better than people of other races. Laws passed by white legislators usually discriminated equally against mulattoes (people of mixed white and black ancestry) and people of unmixed African ancestry. However, white leaders were generally more willing to interact with mulattoes than with darker-skinned African Americans. Consequently, blacks and whites alike saw having light skin as an asset; most African American leaders were mulattoes.

This began to change, however, during the Civil Rights movement. African Americans began to exhibit a new awareness of their racial identity and increased sense of self-worth—"black pride"—and to emphasize their African culture in their hairstyles, manner of dress, language, and artistic expression. Many African Americans began to think that mulattoes should be discriminated against because their physical characteristics were not more obviously African.

In time, however, as white supremacy became a thing of the past in U.S. society, African Americans began to view mulattoes the same way that whites had earlier—as simply African Americans with light skin. The U.S. Census Bureau, which had earlier counted blacks and mulattoes separately, combined the two designations. Consequently, the word "mulatto" lost both its social and legal significance and has slipped from general usage in the United States.

Roger D. Hardaway

See also: Biracialism; Blackness and whiteness: legal definitions; Passing.

Multiracial movement

The multiracial movement originated in the growing numbers of individuals in the United States who identify with more than one racial background. Its impact was most evident in challenges to official racial classifications, particularly on the decennial census, which have traditionally required individuals to identify with only one racial background.

In 1979, interracial couples in Berkeley, California, founded I-Pride (Interracial/Intercultural Pride) in order to provide general support for interracial families. However, its specific goal was to get the Berkeley public schools to reflect the identity of their offspring accurately by including a multiracial designator on school forms. During 1979-1980, the Berkeley public schools added "interracial" to school forms, the first time such a classification had been used in modern United States history. By the 1990's, I-Pride had become part of a coalition of more than fifty grassroots organizations that had come into existence since the 1970's. The coalition began pressuring for the addition of a multiracial identifier to the decennial census. These organizations included groups such as Multiracial Americans of Southern California in Los Angeles (MASC), the Biracial Family Network in Chicago (BFN), the Interracial Family Alliance in Atlanta (IFA), the Interracial Family Circle in Washington, D.C. (IFC), and a national umbrella organization called the Association of Multiethnic Americans (AMEA). This coalition also included A Place for Us/National, which is a national nondenominational religious support network for interracial families, organizations such as the Georgia-based activist, informational, and educational

Project RACE (Reclassify All Children Equally), and *Interracial Voice*, an advocacy journal on the Internet that provides a public forum for the discussion of issues related to multiracial-identified and interracially married individuals.

This network of organizations encompasses individuals from various racial backgrounds; however, it has attracted a significant number of black and white couples and their children, largely because of the one-drop rule of hypodescent, which designates everyone of African descent as black. The network also has attracted a smaller number of "multigenerational" individuals who have backgrounds that have been blended for several generations. Although they have been socially designated as members of the various traditional United States racial groups (European American, African American, Native American, Latino American, and so on), they have resisted identifying solely with those socially assigned communities.

The 1990 Census The controversy over the issue of multiracial identity became intense in 1988. On January 20 of that year, the Office of Management and Budget (OMB), the branch of the government responsible for implementing changes in federal statistical surveys, published in the Federal Register a notice soliciting public comment on potential revisions in Directive No. 15. This directive was implemented in May, 1978, as the government-wide guide for conducting racial/ethnic surveys. The revisions would permit individuals to identify themselves as "other" if they believed they did not fall into one of the four basic official racial categories—black, white, Asian/Pacific Islander, American Indian and Alaska Native—or in the so-called "ethnic" category, Hispanic. Heretofore, the OMB advised that the category that most closely reflected how the individual was recognized by the larger community should be used in cases where there was any uncertainty. (Although an "other" category has not been used on all statistical surveys, it has been provided on each census since 1910 to increase the response rate to the race question. However, write-in responses in the "other" category are reassigned to one of the traditional racial categories.)

Many interracial couples and multiracial-identified individuals requested that a multiracial or biracial identifier, instead of "other," be added to the five categories. (On the 1970 census, multiracial offspring were classified in terms of the father's racial identity; in 1980, the Census Bureau shifted to a formula relying on the identity of the mother. However, a "biracial" or "multiracial" designation was not permitted.) The OMB received overwhelmingly negative responses from the public to the proposed changes to Directive No. 15, particularly the addition of a multiracial identifier. This included some federal agencies, such as the Civil Rights Division of the Department of Justice, the Department of Health and Human Services, the Equal Employment Opportunity Commission, the Office of Personnel Management, and several large corporations. Some of this opposition was based on logistical and financial concerns about the increase in data collection, paperwork, changes in the format of forms and computer programs for data analysis, and data burden on respondents.

Various African American leaders and organizations in particular voiced their opposition to the change. They argued that most, if not all African Americans, have some European, and in many cases, Native American ancestry (although most identify solely with the black community). Consequently, they feared that many individuals would designate themselves as "multiracial" rather than black in order to escape the continuing negative social stigma associated with African Americans. Similar concerns were expressed by individuals and organizations representing other traditional communities of color, including Latinos, Native Americans, and Asian Americans. In addition, opponents argued that the rule of hypodescent, if originally oppressive, has also been a means of mobilizing communities of color in the struggle against white racial privilege. More important, this mechanism has prevented a reduction in the number of individuals who would be counted as members of the traditional communities of color. These numbers were needed to enforce and support civil rights legislation and claims aimed at tracking historical and contemporary patterns of discrimination. They were particularly important in arriving at goals for achieving social and economic equity in the manner of affirmative action.

On November 12, 1988, the AMEA was formed in Berkeley to serve as a national network for the various independent support groups. Its overall goal was to promote healthy images of interracial couples and multiracial individuals. More specifically, its purpose was to increase public awareness about the importance of adding a multiracial identifier to the decennial census. A flurry of telephone calls and correspondence between officials at the OMB and the Census Bureau and various individual groups affiliated with the AMEA ultimately resulted in some clarity as to how multiracial individuals might be accommodated on the 1990 census. Officials said they would specifically code write-in responses in the "other" category as "biracial," "multiracial," or some other designation that clearly indicated a blended identity. This would help determine what, if any, changes should be made on the year 2000 census. This was a departure from policy on previous censuses. However, none of the approximately 253,000 multiracial responses in the other category on the 1990 census can be used as a accurate estimate of the actual number of individuals who identify as multiracial. Also, vast numbers of individuals followed the tradition of circling one box because they were unaware of any other alternative.

The Year 2000 Census Efforts to get the U.S. Census Bureau to make "multiracial" an acceptable means of self-identification were unsuccessful for the 1990 census. Nevertheless, forms for the Operation Desert Shield/Storm Deployment Survey included a multiracial designator for the offspring of returning intermarried veterans. Under the guidance of Project RACE, several states included "multiracial" as an acceptable official means of self-identification. Georgia, Ohio, Illinois, Michigan, Indiana, and Maryland made this option available on all official state forms. Florida and North Carolina included a multiracial identifier on all school forms. A 1994 survey of eight hundred public school districts, conducted by the Education Office for Civil Rights, found that approximately 30 percent of the school districts use a special separate category. Other districts simply use the mother's racial designation; some use the father's. The American College Test (ACT), which is the alternative to the Scholastic Aptitude Test (SAT) college entrance exam, included "multiracial" as an acceptable means of identification. Most universities were resistant to any changes in the collection of racial data; however, Williams College in Williamstown, Massachusetts, included a multiracial identifier on its official forms. Beginning in 1989, reports prepared by the Center for Assessment and Demographic Studies at Gallaudet University in Washington, D.C., counted individuals who indicated identification with a multiracial background. Nevertheless, these data were reassigned at the federal level to one of the four official racial categories (along with the Hispanic identifier, when it was given as an option) or added into the figures for each of the racial groups with which multiracial individuals identified. This second method is especially useful when trying to track those whose background includes historically underrepresented groups of color for the purposes of affirmative action.

"Multiracial" was not accepted as a means of self-identification on federal forms during the early 1990's. However, the OMB began a comprehensive review process in 1993 to discuss possible changes in this direction on the year 2000 census. After extensive cognitive research and field testing of sample households, the OMB on October 30, 1997, approved changes that would allow multiracial individuals to identify themselves as such on official forms. (The key findings based on the comprehensive review were that between 1 percent and 1.5 percent of the public would select a multiracial identifier when offered an opportunity to do so.)

Most activists had hoped for a combined format that would include a separate multiracial box but would also allow individuals to check the other boxes representing the various components of their background. The OMB proposed a format that read: "What is this person's race? Mark[X] one or more races to indicate what this person considers herself/himself to be." This format was chosen partially in response to the unanimous support it received from the various federal agencies that require data on race and ethnicity. These agencies argued that the mark-one-or-more alternative—unlike the combined format—would require fewer changes in formatting on existing forms and allow for data continuity. More important, the data could be counted in each of the existing official racial categories with which multiracial individuals identified, thus including the historically underrepresented racial components in their background. This would be especially important for the purposes of the continued enforcement of civil rights legislation and in meeting affirmative action guidelines. This format is similar to the one that appears on the Canadian census. Since the 1980's, Canada has allowed individuals to check more than one box on the census race/ethnic ancestry question. In addition, Canadian census data have been used for the purposes of achieving "job equity" in a manner similar to affirmative action and other civil rights mandates in the United States.

The mark-one-or-more format also received strong support from traditional civil rights organizations such as the National Association for the Advancement of Colored People (NAACP), the National Urban League, the Congressional Black Caucus, and the Mexican American Legal Defense and Education Fund (MALDEF). These groups argued that a stand-alone multiracial identifier would lead to a decline in their numbers. (It should be noted, however, that the combined format would have prevented this loss. In addition, that format would have had the advantage of making it possible to count the data in each of the racial groups with which multiracial individuals identify as well as specifically acknowledging the identity of multiracial individuals.) Furthermore, the traditional communities of color expressed concerns about the potential divisiveness of even the appearance of a multiracial box, whether as a stand-alone identifier or in combination with checking multiple boxes. These concerns were very influential in prompting the OMB officials to chose the mark-one-or-more format. In addition, various representatives from traditional communities of color expressed concerns about how the data would actually be tabulated even though they supported the mark-one-or-more format. The OMB officials indicated that they would make recommendations and provide additional guidance with respect to this question before the year 2000 census after consulting with officials from various federal agencies, interested groups, demographers, planners, and social scientists.

G. Reginald Daniel

Core Resources

Racially Mixed People in America (Thousand Oaks, Calif.: Sage Publications, 1992) and *The Multiracial Experience: Racial Borders as the New Frontier* (Thousand Oaks, Calif.: Sage Publications, 1996), edited by psychologist Maria P. P. Root, are groundbreaking volumes that include research by scholars and other experts on the multiracial experience and movement in the United States. *American Mixed Race: The Culture of Microdiversity* (Lanham, Md.: Rowman & Littlefield, 1995), edited by Naomi Zack, includes several essays that discuss the multiracial movement and its impact on public policy. Jon Michael Spencer, in *The New Colored People: The Mixed-Race Movement in America* (New York: New York University Press, 1997), examines the potential dangers of the multiracial movement in the United States by comparing it with the multiracial identity of South African coloureds.

See also: Affirmative action; Biracialism; Censuses, U.S.; One-drop rule.

Naïveté explanation of racism

Paul Sniderman, professor of political science at Stanford University, concluded that most white Americans are not racists. Although Americans may sometimes express a simple-minded, naïve, prejudiced view of blacks, this disappears when researchers delve more deeply into their true beliefs concerning equality. Sniderman's views are found in *Reaching Beyond Race* (Cambridge, Mass.: Harvard University Press, 1997). Sniderman discovered that about as many white Americans believe in equality for blacks as are opposed to the concept. Sniderman's surveys led him to conclude that current conflicts over racial policies are driven as much by a white person's view of what the government should try to do as by any deep prejudice or racial hatred of African Americans. Sniderman finds that many Americans, white and black, share the basic values of liberalism: a belief in the equality of all human beings, a belief that government can be a positive force for social change, and a deep commitment to help those in society who are not well off. His surveys show that it is a mistake to believe that before equality can be achieved white values, based on prejudice, must be changed. It is not the prejudice of whites that prevents change because many whites no longer express or hold racist views of black inferiority. The overall impact of racial prejudice on political choices made by whites is very "modest," according to Sniderman.

Instead, Sniderman concluded, the programs advocated by civil rights groups are the biggest obstacles to equality because they seem to be opposed to another basic American value: fairness. Programs dedicated to creating equal opportunity, such as affirmative action, are seen as condoning unequal treatment under the law. Race-conscious policies aimed at overcoming prejudice blame people living now for crimes committed many years and generations ago. Many white Americans who are not prejudiced against African Americans see this as unfair. Similarly, laws outlawing hate speech bother many whites who see them as preventing free discussion and free speech.

Surveys of racial attitudes conducted by Sniderman show an increase, even since 1993, in the number of whites who bear goodwill toward blacks. He finds two forces at work in white America: a diminishing core of citizens who hate blacks fully and completely and a growing number who wish to see improvement in the quality of lives led by African Americans.

Sniderman suggests that it is no longer necessary to change the "hearts and minds" of whites to bring about full equality. What should be done is to change the terms of the debate. Political leaders who support programs aimed at helping impoverished black families should broaden their views to include help for all poor families. They should base their appeals for help on the moral principle of fairness, that all people who need help should get it, regardless of race. According to Sniderman, a platform calling for social justice, rather than racial justice, would end racial divisions in the United States and bring about a true biracial coalition that would change America forever.

Leslie V. Tischauser

See also: Affirmative action; Racism: changing nature of; Racism: history of the concept.

Nation of Islam

The Nation of Islam is a Muslim religious organization that inculcates black pride and helps elevate African Americans' social and economic status.

The Nation of Islam (NOI) is a religious organization that has successfully melded orthodox Islam, black nationalism, and a set of social and economic principles to produce a highly structured way of life for its African American membership. Founded in 1930 in Detroit, Michigan, the NOI crystallized around three leaders: W. D. Fard, Elijah Muhammad, and Malcolm X.

Beliefs The Nation of Islam embraces the essential teachings of orthodox Islam. Both groups stress cleanliness and a strict moral code, and shun alcohol, drug abuse, and eating pork. Early NOI leaders, however, expanded orthodox Islam because of the historic oppression of African Americans. The Nation of Islam is orthodox Islam customized for the African American experience, with solidarity and racial pride being key added features. Black Muslims are required to drop their European last names, associated with enslavement, and adopt the "X" until they earn an Islamic surname. Additional elements, such as advocating a separate nation for its members and teaching about the racist deeds of the "white man," were the source of much outside criticism and prevented the NOI's acceptance into the official fold of orthodox Islam.

History In the midst of Great Depression woes and the past specter of slavery, many African Americans were disillusioned and susceptible to philosophies and leaders who promised improvements. Consequently, a number of nationalistic and religious movements developed. In 1930, W. D. Fard formed the Nation of Islam, which espoused the political nationalism of Jamaican-born Marcus Garvey, who amassed thousands of followers in the United States from 1916 until his imprisonment in 1923 and subsequent deportation. Garvey advocated a separate African American nation, economic and political solidarity, and racial pride.

Fard, the first prophet of the Nation of Islam, is shrouded in mystery. Although believed to be from Mecca, his national origins, his real name, and the circumstances of his 1934 disappearance are not known. Fard's achievements, however, are well documented. In four years during the Great Depression, Fard established the church's basic philosophy, created a security force known as the Fruit of Islam, opened the University of Islam, built its first temple, and amassed about eight thousand followers. Many of his followers, including Elijah Muhammad, thought Fard to be an incarnation of Allah. After Fard's sudden disappearance Elijah Muhammad became the group's leader.

Elijah Muhammad was born Elijah Poole in Sandersville, Georgia. His parents had been slaves and sharecroppers. He married Clara Evans in 1919, and during the 1920's he and his family migrated to Detroit, where he met Fard and became one of his most devoted converts. He was rewarded by being chosen as Fard's successor, and he transformed Fard's sincere project into a thriving organization.

Elijah Muhammad After Fard's disappearance, rivalry caused some factionalism and a sharp decrease in NOI membership. Muhammad, often the victim of harassment and death threats, was imprisoned. Consequently, he moved the NOI headquarters from Detroit to Chicago, where he was able to rebuild and strengthen the organization. When Muhammad died in 1975, the Nation of Islam had temples and schools from coast to coast; owned a string of restaurants, apartments, and other businesses and real estate; operated a major printing press; and had a membership of more than one hundred thousand. Much of Muhammad's success, however, can be attributed to one of his ministers, Malcolm X.

Malcolm X Malcolm X was born Malcolm Little in Omaha, Nebraska. His parents, Earle and Louise Little, were organizers for Marcus Garvey's Universal Negro Improvement Association. Because of their views, the Littles were forced to move. They eventually settled in East Lansing, Michigan, where Earle apparently was murdered and Louise had a breakdown. Malcolm wandered between odd jobs and engaged in petty crime. He was imprisoned from 1946 to 1952, and he married Betty Shabazz in 1958. He was murdered in New York on February 21, 1965.

In prison, Malcolm became self-educated and converted to Islam. After his release, he met Elijah Muhammad, received his X, and trained for the NOI ministry. He headed temples in several cities before becoming the primary spokesperson for the Nation of Islam. His frank speeches and numerous public appearances catapulted the NOI into the national forefront. Membership swelled due to Malcolm's visibility, but his enemies increased also. For unauthorized remarks made about President John F. Kennedy's assassination, Malcolm was suspended from the NOI. Around that time, he changed his name to El Hajj Malik El-Shabazz. He left the NOI in March, 1964, and formed two new organizations, which were curtailed by his death.

After Elijah Muhammad's death, his son, Warith, also known as Wallace, became the NOI leader. Warith's changes forced another NOI split, spearheaded by Louis Farrakhan. The NOI expanded under Farrakhan, a controversial figure for some of his adamant and at times incendiary statements. His nondenominational Million Man March in October, 1995, immensely added to his visibility and to some extent mitigated his controversial image.

Linda Rochell Lane

Core Resources

Clayborne Carson's *Malcolm X: The FBI Files* (New York: Carroll & Graff, 1991) extracts data from Federal Bureau of Investigation files and provides information on Malcolm X, his family, and the Nation of Islam from 1919 to 1980. John Henrick Clark edited *Malcolm X: The Man and His Times* (Trenton, N.J.: African World Press, 1990), which contains essays by scholars and personal acquaintances and a chapter in Malcolm's own words. E. Franklin Frazier's *The Negro Church in America* (1963, reprint, New York: Schocken Books, 1974) and C. Eric Lincoln's *The Black Church Since Frazier* (New York: Schocken Books, 1974) provide critical background on African American religion. Lincoln's *The Black Muslims in America* (Boston: Beacon Press, 1961) is the first complete academic analysis of the Nation of Islam. Thomas W. Lippman, in *Understanding Islam* (New York: Signet Books, 1982), provides a good start for those with little knowledge of orthodox Islam. In *The Autobiography of Malcolm X* (New York: Ballantine Books, 1965), Malcolm X and Alex Haley tell the story of the African American revolutionary and Black Muslim leader. The beliefs of the Nation of Islam are explained by Elijah Muhammad in *The Supreme Wisdom* (2 vols., Brooklyn: Temple of Islam, 1957).

See also: Malcolm X assassination; Million Man March; Separatism; Universal Negro Improvement Association.

National Advisory Commission on Civil Disorders

The National Advisory Commission on Civil Disorders was created by executive order in 1967 with Governor Otto Kerner of Illinois as chairman and Mayor John V. Lindsay of New York City as vice chairman. The commission had eleven members, including four members of Congress as well as labor, civil rights, and law enforcement leaders. Other public officials and private citizens participated on advisory panels studying such things as private enterprise and insurance in riot-affected areas.

Racial violence had escalated with the riots in Watts in 1965 and, by the summer of 1967, was spreading to other American cities. After extensive study, the commission recommended new and expanded employment and educational opportunity programs, national standards for welfare programs, and increased access to housing. The commission's report stated that the United States was becoming "two societies, one black, one white—separate and unequal." It was the first major study to place the blame for creating black ghettos on white society.

The commission studied the major race riots, identified patterns in the violence, developed profiles of participants, and analyzed the conditions prior to and following the disorders. Despite concern among some officials that the violence was being encouraged by radical groups, the commission determined that the principal causes were widespread discrimination and segregation and the increasing concentration of the black population in inner-city ghettos offering little opportunity. These conditions, according to the report, led to pervasive frustration, the acceptance of violence as a means of retaliation, and growing feelings of powerlessness. A spark was all that was necessary to ignite violence, and the police often provided it.

The commission recommended new federal programs to address the problems of poverty, unemployment, education, and housing and the expansion of existing urban programs, such as the Model Cities Program, to provide economic opportunity to residents of the inner city. Guidance was also offered to state and local officials for identifying potentially violent conditions, reducing the likelihood of violence, providing training to police to lessen tensions in minority communities, and organizing emergency operations in response to escalating violence.

See also: Civil rights; Detroit riot; Kerner Report; Newark race riots; Race riots of the twentieth century; Watts riot.

National Association for the Advancement of Colored People

Founded in 1909, the NAACP has been at the center of the struggle for civil rights and social, political, and economic equality for African Americans.

The Niagara Movement, founded in 1905, was the forerunner to the National Association for the Advancement of Colored People (NAACP). A group of African American leaders headed by W. E. B. Du Bois and William Monroe Trotter met at Niagara Falls, Canada. Their chief purpose was to develop an aggressive campaign for the full citizenship of African Americans. They were dissatisfied with the approach of Booker T. Washington, who advocated black achievement while submitting to the injustice of segregation. Race riots, in which a number of African Americans were shot, beaten, burned, or hanged by lynch mobs in the early twentieth century, served as the backdrop for the meeting. Among the primary goals of the Niagara Movement were erasing all distinctions based on race, gaining respect for all working men, and attaining black suffrage. The Niagara Movement was the first attempt to organize African Americans after the Reconstruction Era (1863-1877).

Open-minded whites, moved to action by the race riots, called for a national conference on Lincoln's birthday in 1909 and invited Niagara Movement members. The NAACP was formally founded in May of 1910, and the Niagara Movement was incorporated into it. Most charter members were white rather than people of color. They had a wide range of expertise and resources. One of its most notable African American members was W. E. B. Du Bois, the great African American leader and scholar. The new organization vowed to fight de jure (legal) segregation and to work for equal education for white and black children, complete suffrage for African Americans, and the enforcement of the Fourteenth and Fifteenth Amendments. During its first year, the NAACP established programs for blacks in economic development and job opportunities. It pushed for more police protection in the South and for antilynching and lawlessness initiatives in the nation. *The Crisis*, the official publication of the NAACP, served as the "cutting edge" of critical thought regarding the "race question," publicizing injustices against African Americans. Du Bois served as editor.

Civil Rights or Economic Advancement? Early tension within the NAACP centered on the question of whether the budding organization should focus primarily on civil rights or should tackle economic issues as well. Noneconomic liberalism became the guiding light for the organization, since a consensus could not be reached over the importance of economic issues. The liberal white who served as president starting in 1930, Joel E. Spingarn, believed that once the racial issue in the United States had been resolved, African Americans would be able to compete on an equal footing in the economic and educational arenas. Future leaders of the NAACP would include Walter White, Roy Wilkins, Benjamin Hooks, and Benjamin Chavis.

There was considerable debate over whether African Americans should pursue a social agenda of equality and civil rights as opposed to economic development and independence. In its most acute form, this involved public debate between W. E. B. Du Bois and Booker T. Washington. Washington was renowned as the founder and president of Tuskegee Institute (now University) in Alabama. He was often consulted by presidents and invited to the White House. Washington argued that African Americans should focus on vocational education and training. He viewed politics as secondary and

Though associated mainly with African Americans, the NAACP has, since its inception, been an organization open to members of all racial and ethnic groups. *(Library of Congress)*

social equality for blacks as less important—a philosophy that pleased white southerners and presidents. Civil rights, to his way of thinking, would gradually evolve as African Americans developed their own business enterprises. Until then, African Americans should not be too pushy, for fear of alienating whites. In short, blacks should remain subservient to whites and, particularly in the South, reconcile with the prevalent racism.

Du Bois, on the other hand, argued that Washington's approach was inadequate and asked African Americans to give up too much. Du Bois held that African Americans needed higher education. He held that a "talented tenth," meaning those with higher education, would be in the position to lead the masses and working class. Unlike Washington, Du Bois maintained that economic progress was irrelevant without political participation and political power. To his way of thinking, political power would nurture economic development, not vice versa.

The failure of noneconomic liberalism can be seen in the results of the Great Depression. While the NAACP focused on social status and targeted race and racism, African Americans were devastated by the Depression. Already on the bottom of the economic ladder, many African Americans began to migrate to northern industrial cities in search of job opportunities and an improved standard of living relative to that in the South. The timing of their migration, however, collided with the Great Depression. African Americans in the South still survived at a subsistence level, trying to make a living as sharecroppers in an agricultural economy. The arrival on the political stage of Marcus Garvey in the early 1920's stirred the black masses. Preaching black nationalism and economic independence, Garvey urged African Americans to return to the Mother Country (Africa), emphasizing self-determination and independence. Garvey developed a large following in a short period of time between 1919 and 1925. Du Bois realized that the Garvey phenomenon, combined with the effects of the Depression of the 1930's, revealed a critical flaw in the thinking and philosophy of the NAACP. In 1934 Du Bois challenged the NAACP to question its organizational philosophy of noneconomic liberalism and to stress economic development and issues. The organization, still with Spingarn and a board of directors dominated by whites, failed to heed the call. Their agenda remained centered on racial equality. It was at this point that Du Bois broke with the NAACP.

Role in Justice and Equality A black and white team of lawyers of the NAACP, constituting its legal committee, won three significant legal cases during the first fifteen years of the NAACP's existence. In *Guinn v. United States* (1915) the Supreme Court invalidated the grandfather clause in Maryland and Oklahoma, ruling that it was unconstitutional under the Fifteenth Amendment. Two years later, in the case of *Buchanan v. Warley* (1917), the Court voided a Louisville ordinance requiring African Americans to live in certain sections of the city. In the case of *Moore v. Dempsey* (1923), the Court ordered a new trial in a case in which an African American had been convicted of murder in Arkansas. The poverty-stricken defendant had been tried before an all-white jury. As a result of these early victories, the NAACP soon realized that the court system could be a valuable ally in the fight against racial injustice and the struggle for equality.

In addition, the NAACP supported or provided the legal expertise in a number of cases that successfully challenged aspects of the "separate but equal" doctrine of racial segregation established in *Plessy v. Ferguson* (1896).

This doctrine was premised on the notion that it was legal to have separate facilities for blacks and whites as long as those facilities were equal. Successful challenges included restrictive covenants in the case of *Corrigan v. Buckley* (1926) and the legality of the white primary in *Nixon v. Condon* (1927, 1932). In the wake of *Smith v. Allwright* (1944), which finally sounded the death knell for the white primary, the NAACP began to organize local voter leagues in the South. Repression from local governments and the White Citizens' Council, however, led to the decrease of the NAACP's influence in the South in the 1950's, to be replaced by younger organizations such as the Southern Christian Leadership Conference.

The 1954 U.S. Supreme Court case of *Brown v. Board of Education* gained the greatest attention for the NAACP and its sister organization, the NAACP Legal Defense and Educational Fund. Thurgood Marshall argued this landmark case. In its decision, the Court ruled that the pernicious "separate but equal" doctrine of racial segregation in the public schools was unconstitutional, stating that separate schools for whites and blacks were inherently unequal. The *Brown* case served as the defining moment for the NAACP and the Civil Rights movement in the 1950's.

Legal Defense and Educational Fund The NAACP Legal Defense and Educational Fund (LDEF) was founded in 1939. It was designed to be the chief legal arm of the NAACP. It claimed to be a nonprofit entity, yet it had an interlocking membership with the NAACP. As a result of objections by the Internal Revenue Service in 1957, the legal and educational arm formally separated from the NAACP. Thus, the NAACP Legal Defense and Educational Fund developed its own staff, board of directors, budget, and

Meeting of the executive committee of the NAACP in 1963; seated at the left end of the rear table are Thurgood Marshall and Roy Wilkins. *(Library of Congress)*

policies. Thurgood Marshall became the first director-counsel until 1961, followed by Jack Greenberg, who served in this capacity until 1984, when Julius L. Chambers took over. The LDEF had represented thousands of cases in education, employment, prisoners' rights, housing, health care, voting rights, and other areas by the end of the 1980's.

The NAACP continued to push for civil rights and racial integration in the 1950's and 1960's as the Civil Rights movement intensified its efforts to overcome racial segregation in every phase of American society. Like other civil rights organizations of the time, the NAACP engaged in a number of nonviolent activities. The NAACP, along with a number of other organizations, was partly responsible for the Civil Rights Act of 1964. The NAACP, and the Civil Rights movement as a whole, reached its zenith in this decade, as the 1964 Civil Rights Act, the 1965 Voting Rights Act and the 1968 Civil Rights Act were passed. In the 1970's and 1980's, the organization became increasingly irrelevant, since constitutional civil rights guarantees were in place and had been upheld by the courts. At the same time, the social movement in African American communities switched increasingly toward community control, black nationalism, and separatism, which were diametrically opposed to the organizational goals of the NAACP. In the 1980's, as the federal government and the Reagan administration was less supportive of civil rights and previous black gains, the NAACP Legal Defense and Educational Fund continued to play an important role in the legal arena.

Mfanya D. Tryman

Core Resources

Informative sources include Gerald David Jaynes and Robin M. Williams, Jr., eds., *A Common Destiny: Blacks and American Society* (Washington, D.C.: National Academy Press, 1989); Harold Cruse, *Plural but Equal* (New York: William Morrow, 1987); John Hope Franklin, *From Slavery to Freedom* (New York: Alfred A. Knopf, 1967); Jack Greenberg's article "NAACP Legal Defense and Educational Fund," in *Civil Rights and Equality*, edited by Leonard W. Levy, Kenneth L. Karst, and Dennis J. Mahoney (New York: Collier Macmillan, 1989); Talcott Parsons and Kenneth B. Clark, eds., *The Negro American* (Boston: Houghton Mifflin, 1966). Additional information on the NAACP will be found in Mimmi Finch, *The NAACP: Its Fight for Justice* (Metuchen, N.J.: Scarecrow Press, 1981); Charles Flint Kellogg, *NAACP: A History of the National Association for the Advancement of Colored People* (Baltimore: Johns Hopkins University Press, 1964); and Robert Zangrando, *The NAACP Crusade Against Lynching, 1909-1950* (Philadelphia: Temple University Press, 1980).

See also: *Brown v. Board of Education*; Civil rights; Civil Rights Act of 1964; Civil Rights movement; Congress of Racial Equality; Equality of opportunity; National Association for the Advancement of Colored People Legal Defense and Educational Fund.

National Association for the Advancement of Colored People Legal Defense and Educational Fund

The National Association for the Advancement of Colored People Legal Defense and Educational Fund (LDF or LDEF) was established in 1939-1940 as a tax-exempt corporation by the National Association for the Advancement of Colored People. Its charter was handwritten in March, 1940, by Thurgood Marshall, who stated the new organization's dual purpose: to provide legal aid to African Americans "suffering legal injustices by reason of race or color" and to create education opportunities for African Americans that had been denied them by reason of race or color.

The LDF was founded to carry on litigation in the spirit of the social change agenda already established by the actions of NAACP attorneys in the American courts. It provides or supports legal representation on behalf of African Americans and other people of color in defending their legal and constitutional rights against discrimination in education, employment, land use, recreation, transportation, housing, voting, health care, and other areas. It has successfully argued against grandfather clauses, restrictive housing covenants in city ordinances, white primaries, white juries, capital punishment, and segregation of public facilities.

Since the 1950's the LDF has operated independently from its parent organization, which maintains its own legal department, and at times the relationship between the LDF and NAACP has involved some conflict. The LDF both represents individuals and brings suit on behalf of civil rights groups. It has been based in New York City since its formation and also maintains a center in Washington, D.C.

Barbara Bair

See also: *Brown v. Board of Education*; Civil Rights Act of 1964; Civil Rights movement; Little Rock school desegregation; National Association for the Advancement of Colored People; Voting Rights Act of 1965.

National Association of Colored Women

Near the end of the eighteenth century, grave concerns about African Americans being treated as second-class citizens compelled a group of

African American women to move beyond their local and state associations to devise plans for the formation of a national body that would systematically and professionally address the problems that they believed threatened the very survival of African Americans. Economic disparities, political disfranchisement, and social ostracism presented the greatest threats to African American aspirations for freedom and inclusion in the American system of democracy. Meeting at the Nineteenth Street Baptist Church in Washington, D.C., in July, 1896, the National Federation of Afro-American Women and the National League of Colored Women joined forces to form a national organization known as the National Association of Colored Women (NACW).

Operating through a series of departments and a strong executive cabinet, the NACW became an umbrella group for African American women's organizations at both state and local levels. The organization's official publication, *National Notes,* served as an instrument to unite the women and to educate them in the concepts and techniques of reform, advocating racial uplift, improved race relations, and protection of women. From its inception, the NACW has worked to improve the lives of African American people in the United States and to help them achieve full citizenship rights.

Alvin K. Benson

See also: African American women; Colored Women's League; National Council of Negro Women.

National Black Women's Political Leadership Caucus

Founded in 1971, the National Black Women's Leadership Political Caucus is committed to helping African American women work toward equality and increase their knowledge of the role of women in the political process. The organization has its headquarters in Washington, D.C., but it also has groups in three regions and thirty-three states throughout the United States. Aside from its primary members, the caucus has an auxiliary membership that includes men, senior citizens, and youth. The organization encourages African American women and youth to participate in the country's economic and political systems. In addition, the caucus enables women to familiarize themselves with the functions of city, state, and federal government. The group is also involved in research, conducting studies in the areas of African American families, politics, and economics. A variety of other services are provided by the National Black Women's Political Leadership Caucus, such as training in public speaking; legislative federal, state, and local workshops; children's services; charitable programs; awards for humanitarianism; and placement services. The organization publishes a semi-annual newsletter and has published election tabloids.

K. Sue Jewell

See also: African American women; Colored Women's League; National Council of Negro Women.

National Coalition of Blacks for Reparations in America

The National Coalition of Blacks for Reparations in America (N'COBRA) is a coalition of organizations across the United States that support reparations for African Americans. African Americans were supposed to receive "forty acres and a mule" from the U.S. government upon emancipation in reparation for the time they spent in slavery, but this proposal was never actually made law. The newly freed blacks lacked property, capital, education, and job experience, giving them a severely disadvantaged start. In addition, not long after slavery was made illegal, a system of segregation known as Jim Crow took effect. Segregation blocked equal access to home ownership, which is the main source of capital for most Americans, and this government-sanctioned inequality can be seen as the root cause of the wealth gap between black and white Americans in modern times, according to Melvin Oliver and Thomas Shapiro in *Black Wealth/White Wealth* (1995). N'COBRA supports and lobbies for HR 40, a congressional bill introduced every year since 1989 by John Conyers, a Democratic representative from Illinois, that demands reparations for blacks not unlike those received by Native Americans for land seized by the government and by Japanese Americans for time spent in internment camps during World War II.

Eileen O'Brien

See also: Emancipation Proclamation; Jim Crow laws; Slavery: history.

National Council of Colored People

The National Council of Colored People was one of the first groups concerned with the advancement of African Americans and the cause of abolition.

On July 6, 1853, more than one hundred delegates from around the country assembled in Rochester, New York, for a three-day convention to form the

National Council of Colored People. This organization was an outgrowth of the Negro Convention movement, which had begun during a meeting on September 20-24, 1830, in Philadelphia. Richard Allen formed the convention with the intention of improving the lives of African Americans by raising their social status through education and, possibly, emigration. The convention met many times in many cities, discussing plans for improvement, and the group thrived on the increasing solidarity among its members. It was at one of the convention meetings, in Rochester, New York, that the plan for the National Council of Colored People was adopted. The meeting in Rochester drew many prominent African American leaders, including Frederick Douglass, James McCune Smith, and James Pennington.

Formation of the Council At the meeting in 1853, a constitution was drawn up for the new organization, and a president and several vice presidents were chosen. The group discussed the rampant racial oppression of the African American people. Members of both the convention and the newly formed National Council of Colored People believed that, in order to increase the rate of improvement of the social status of African Americans, it was necessary to create a new institution for the education of African American youth. The new institution would be an industrial school that concentrated on agriculture and the mechanical arts. On the second day of the convention, the council elected to withdraw the proposed school plan because of the exclusive nature of the school. In the final hours of the last day of the convention, the council endorsed two seminaries as places for the education of African Americans—McGrawville College and Allegheny City College.

On November 15, 1853, elections were held in several cities to elect delegates for the formation of new state councils that would act in accordance with the National Council of Colored People. The leading delegates would attend the national council meetings as well as their own state council meetings. The first meeting of the National Council of Colored People was held November 23, 1853, in New York. At least one council member each from the states of New York, Connecticut, Rhode Island, and Ohio was missing, but because of the great distance the other council members had traveled, the meeting continued. After proceeding with the meeting, one delegate from Ohio appeared and demanded that all prior proceedings be nullified. This caused great distress among the council members and created a somewhat hostile working environment, which contributed to the short life of the council. Despite the bleak beginnings of the national council, the state councils operated much more smoothly and with enthusiasm.

Disagreements Continue In both the national and state councils, the idea of an African American school was revisited. Frederick Douglass defended the school plan unsuccessfully for two years. The country was experiencing an economic depression, which made it hard to fund the school.

There also was still concern over the exclusive nature of an African American school. The idea of a separate African American school brought many emotions to the forefront. Integrationists were wary of accepting such a school plan because of the isolation of the school and its students, yet even they saw benefits in an all African American school. Emigrationists considered the proposal and were much more willing to begin work on construction. Amid much opposition, in October, 1855, the convention elected to discontinue plans for the proposed school. The other committees set up by the first national convention and their ambitious plans to assist African Americans in business pursuits and the creation of a library and museum seemed to have stopped on paper.

The second meeting of the National Council of Colored People was scheduled for May 24, 1854, in Cleveland, but it was postponed in order to accommodate more delegates. Eventually, only a few delegates were able to attend. Among the members attending, a debate developed over the recognition of Ohio at the national level, creating a deadlock. A suggestion was made to dissolve the organization, but after a close vote, the National Council of Colored People continued to operate. Ohio, however, withdrew its participation.

At the meeting of May 8, 1855, nearly all the delegates were from New York, as most others had declined to participate. The issue of an African American school again was discussed and once again defeated. Another issue was discussed for the first time—emigration to Canada. Although most delegates at the convention were willing to remain in the United States, they expressed trepidation on the matter of the United States Constitution and the issue of slavery. The issue of emigration was the last to be discussed before the close of the final meeting of the National Council of Colored People. The state councils continued to operate and pursue social equality for African Americans for a few years longer, with councils in some states surviving longer than others.

Jeri Kurtzleben

Core Resources

Howard Holman Bell's *A Survey of the Negro Convention Movement, 1830-1861* (New York: Arno Press, 1969) contains substantial information on the Negro Convention Movement, from which the National Council of Colored People was formed. John W. Blassingame and John R. McKivigan edited the multivolume *Frederick Douglass Papers* (Series 1, *Speeches, Debates, and Interviews.* New Haven, Conn.: Yale University Press, 1991): Volume 2, *1847-1854,* includes several references to the industrial college proposed at the 1853 meeting in Rochester, New York; volume 3, *1855-1863,* includes an interview with President Andrew Johnson, in which the intent of the National Convention is discussed; and volume 4, *1864-1880,* contains a speech and several pages of notes from the National Council meeting in May, 1855. Alton Hornsby, Jr., in *Chronology of African-American History* (Detroit, Mich.: Gale

Research, 1991), places the National Council of Colored People in the context of relevant information on its foundation. Harry A. Ploski and James Williams are the editors of *The Negro Almanac: A Reference Work on the African American* (Detroit, Mich.: Gale Research, 1989), a beginning source of information on the Negro Convention movement.

See also: Abolition; AME Church; American Anti-Slavery Society; Free African Society; *Liberator, The*; Negro Conventions; Pennsylvania Society for the Abolition of Slavery; Underground Railroad.

National Council of Negro Women

The National Council of Negro Women (NCNW), founded in 1935, seeks to facilitate cooperation among women and act as an advocate for women's issues nationally and internationally. Founded by Mary McLeod Bethune (1875-1955), an African American educator and presidential adviser, the organization is composed of a coalition of thirty-one national organizations and individuals. It has local chapters throughout the United States, the Women's Center for Education and Career Advancement in New York City, and offices in western and southern Africa. The NCNW maintains a clearinghouse in which information that will improve the socioeconomic status of African American women and other women of color is compiled and disseminated. The organization also publishes *Black Woman's Voice*, a periodical, and *Sister's Magazine*, a quarterly. In addition, the council is responsible for an archive for black women's history and the Bethune Museum. One of the primary goals of the council is to assist women in developing leadership skills to be used on community, national, and international levels. One of its international projects is to improve social and economic conditions for rural women in Third World countries.

K. Sue Jewell

See also: African American women; Colored Women's League.

National Urban League

The National Urban League was founded in 1910 as the National League on Urban Conditions Among Negroes, an organization that helped black migrants coming from the rural South to find work and make transitions to living in northern cities. The league merged in 1911 with the Association for the Protection of Colored Women and the Committee for Improving the Industrial Conditions of Negroes in New York, both groups founded in 1906 to aid urban migrants, and adopted its shorter title. The emphasis of the organization has shifted over the years from serving black workers in northern cities to assisting the rural and urban poor in all regions of the country, and from an educational, service, and investigational association to one involved in political action. A nonmembership organization, it has a centralized structure, with a main headquarters in New York and local units in major cities; the local units have their own boards and budgets and adapt national policies to local needs. The league maintains regional bureaus in Washington, D.C.; Akron, Ohio; St. Louis, Missouri; and Atlanta, Georgia. The national governing board is, according to organization by-laws, interracial, and 25 percent of its members are under the age of thirty.

From 1923 until 1948 the National Urban League published the influential magazine *Opportunity*, which, along with the National Association for the Advancement of Colored People's *Crisis*, also based in New York, was a voice for black intellectuals, writers, and social reformers. From 1910 through the 1930's Depression, the league focused on services to those seeking jobs and housing, and lobbied to end discrimination in federal policies and the labor movement. The league grew in size and influence during World War II, when many thousands of blacks moved to northern industrial cities to do warrelated work. The organization was conservative in its approach until the 1960's, when the severity of the problems of segregated housing, ghetto conditions, and inferior education called for more activist policies.

The league emerged as a major advocate for civil rights under the leadership of Whitney M. Young, Jr., who became its executive director in 1961. Under the influence of the Civil Rights and Black Power movements, Young and the National Urban League pursued active protest politics, including a sponsorship role in the 1963 March on Washington. Young's successors, Vernon E. Jordan, Jr., and John Jacob, established several community-based improvement programs. These include street academies to aid high school dropouts in finishing school; job training and placement services in computer skills, law enforcement, and the construction industry; voter registration drives; a Business Development Program for black businesspersons; and a National Consumer Health Education Program to supply health workers to local neighborhoods.

Barbara Bair

See also: Civil rights; Civil Rights movement; Great Migration; National Association for the Advancement of Colored People.

Negro Conventions

Mass conventions were a popular means of protest among African Americans of the nineteenth century. Rooted in constitutional principles of free assembly and petition, these conventions were a product of the group consciousness that emerged among free blacks in northern urban areas following the American Revolution and were a reaction to a burgeoning institutional racism that legitimized slavery and stripped free African Americans of basic civil rights during the postrevolutionary period. The first great national Negro convention, held at Philadelphia in August, 1817, produced resolutions opposing slavery and denouncing a plan proposed by the United States Congress to colonize black Americans in Africa. Although largely symbolic, the convention of 1817 inspired the Negro Convention movement of the 1830's, which was to provide a forum for expressions of militancy and nationalism among the growing population of free northern blacks.

The Negro Convention movement of the 1830's was aided by the emergence of black leaders with national status and varied agendas. Although dominated by antislavery societies, the six national Negro Conventions held between 1830 and 1835 addressed a variety of issues, including the organization of economic boycotts and mass protests, the observance of national days of prayer and fasting, and the establishment of temperance societies and African missionary groups. The conventions exerted a considerable influence upon local black communities, chiefly through the encouragement of verbal agitation; yet the movement was cut short in mid-decade by white abolitionists who, fearing that the black separatism often advocated by convention delegates would damage the antislavery movement, infiltrated the conventions and split their leadership. The Negro Convention movement was briefly revived in the early 1840's, when young black militants in New York and Philadelphia called a convention of black leaders to protest slavery and racial inequality. However, this convention, which failed by one vote to endorse slave insurrection, proved a militant exception to a new spirit of gradualism among black abolitionists. The last notable antebellum Negro Convention, held in Cleveland, Ohio, in 1854, yielded compromise proposals for the repatriation of African Americans that early conventions had so vehemently opposed.

The end of the Civil War and the beginning of Reconstruction sparked a revival of Negro Conventions in the 1870's and 1880's, as southern freedmen and northern agitators sought vehicles to petition the government for civil rights and protection from mob violence. These conventions were chiefly local and regional in nature, designed to facilitate political organization and to appeal directly to legislators and state governors. Nevertheless, national conventions continued, the most notable being the National Colored Convention held in Louisville, Kentucky, in 1883, in which the delegates called for an end to economic peonage in the South, equal rights and suffrage for African Americans, and integration of schools and the military.

The Negro Convention movement died out in the 1890's as Jim Crow laws and mob violence swept the South and accommodationism replaced agitation and protest as a political strategy for black leaders. However, the tradition of assembly and militancy brought about by the convention movement survived in the black conferences of the early twentieth century (for example, the Niagara conference of 1909, which spawned the National Association for the Advancement of Colored People), in the mass protest marches of the Civil Rights movement during the 1960's, and in the Million Man and Million Woman Marches of the 1990's.

Michael H. Burchett

See also: Abolition; Accommodationism; Jim Crow laws; National Council of Colored People; Niagara Movement; Reconstruction.

New York City slave revolt

The New York City slave revolt of 1712 was an abortive uprising that shaped the institution of slavery in New York.

The New York City Slave Revolt of 1712 calls attention to the fact that slavery had become more firmly established in colonial New York than in any other British province north of Chesapeake Bay. Slaves were already an integral part of the labor force when England conquered Dutch New Netherland in 1664. As European immigration lagged, slave labor became increasingly important. Between 1703 and 1723, New York's total population almost doubled, increasing from 20,540 to 40,564, but its black population (slaves and free blacks were always lumped together and listed in the census as Negroes) almost tripled, jumping from 2,253 to 6,171.

Background As the number of bondsmen increased, so did the anxiety level of white New Yorkers. In 1708, following the grizzly murder of a Long Island planter and his family, four slaves were tried, convicted, and executed "with all the torment possible for a terror to others." Shortly thereafter, the provincial assembly passed An Act for Preventing the Conspiracy of Slaves, which defined the judicial proceedings and made death the penalty for any slave found guilty of murder or attempted murder. Fear of slave conspiracy led whites to look with ambivalence upon Anglican catechist Elias Neau's teaching among New York City blacks and Native Americans.

Small-scale slave owning prevailed in New York. Few white families owned more than a slave or two, so slave husbands, wives, and children might be scattered among several households. Regulations restricting their freedom of movement were bitterly resented by slaves, because they interfered with their domestic life. Such restrictions often were more apparent than real, because slavery in New York City and surrounding villages, where slaves were most heavily concentrated, was tied to a developing urban economy that demanded a flexible, if not free, labor supply. Slaves in New York City and Albany often hired themselves out, splitting the pay with their respective owners, but otherwise lived separately from their masters. The hustle and bustle of the urban economic scene afforded slaves considerable opportunity to meet, socialize, and discuss common grievances, despite the best efforts of whites to keep them under surveillance.

The slave uprising of 1712 apparently began as a conspiracy on March 25, then celebrated as New Year's Day. The ringleaders reportedly were of the Cormantine and Pawpaw peoples, Africans who had not been long in New York; a few Spanish Indian slaves; and at least one free black, a practitioner of African medicine and magic who reportedly supplied special powder to protect the rebels from the white man's weapons. Their motivation, according to both Governor Robert Hunter and Chaplain John Sharpe, was revenge for ill treatment at the hands of their respective masters. Their goal was freedom, which, claimed Hunter and Sharpe, was to be achieved by burning New York City and killing the white people on Manhattan.

The Revolt During the early morning hours of Sunday, April 6, 1712, about two dozen conspirators, armed with guns, swords, knives, and clubs, gathered in an orchard in the East Ward on the northeast edge of New York City. They set fire to several outbuildings and waited in ambush for the whites who came to put out the blaze, killing nine and wounding seven. Soldiers were dispatched from the fort, but when they arrived, the rebels had dispersed, taking refuge in the woods surrounding the town. The next day, local militiamen systematically searched Manhattan Island for the rebellious blacks. Rather than surrender, six slaves killed themselves, several cutting their own throats.

White New Yorkers were in full panic. "We have about 70 Negro's in Custody," read a dispatch from New York, dated April 14 but published in the *Boston News-Letter* on April 21, but it was "fear'd that most of the Negro's here (who are very numerous) knew of the Late Conspiracy to murder the Christians." Fear of another uprising drove the judicial proceedings. On April 9, a coroner's jury implicated thirty-eight slaves, identifying fourteen of them as murderers. In accordance with the 1708 Conspiracy Act, the coroner's findings were turned over to the Court of Quarter Sessions of the Peace, which convened on April 11. Attorney General May Bickley handled the prosecution, moving the trials on from the Quarter Sessions to the State Supreme Court on June 3.

The Trials Forty-two slaves and one free black were indicted and tried. Crucial to both the indictments and trials was the testimony of two slaves, Cuffee, who belonged to baker Peter Vantilborough, and Dick, a boy slave owned by Harmanus Burger, a blacksmith. The coroner's jury had found

Cuffee and Dick guilty of at least two murders, but Attorney General Bickley apparently promised them immunity, and they became the Crown's prime witnesses. Some whites, including such substantial citizens as former mayor David Provost, coroner Henry Wileman, and lawyers Jacob Regnier and David Jamison, testified for a few of the defendants. However, the general adequacy of defense counsel may well be doubted. Many of the convictions hinged upon the dubious testimony of Cuffee and young Dick, both of whom were manipulated by Attorney General Bickley, described by Governor Hunter as "a busy waspish man." Bickley also demonstrated considerable bias against certain slave defendants, depending upon who owned them. For example, Mars, belonging to Jacob Regnier, a rival attorney with whom Brickley had a private quarrel, was tried twice and acquitted before being found guilty in the third trial and sentenced to be hanged.

Most of the trials were over by early June. Twenty-three slaves were convicted of murder; fifteen slaves were acquitted, along with one free black. Two slaves were found guilty of assault with intent to kill, and two were acquitted of that charge. The twenty-five who were convicted were sentenced to death. Twenty were to be hanged; three were burned alive, one in a slow fire for eight to ten hours until consumed to ashes. Another was broken upon the wheel and left to die, and one was hung in chains and "so to continue without sustenance until death." Eleven were "executed at once," including those burned, broken at the wheel, and chained without food or water. These barbaric executions were defended by Governor Hunter as "the most exemplary that could be possibly thought of."

Yet even Hunter doubted the justice of it all. He postponed the execution of six slaves, including two Spanish American Indians taken during Queen Anne's War (1702-1713) and sold as slaves despite their claim of being free men, a pregnant slave woman, and the much tried and finally convicted Mars. At Hunter's request, the queen pardoned several of them, and perhaps all of those he had reprieved (the record is rather vague), despite the efforts of Bickley in New York and Lord Cornbury, a former governor of New York, in London to obstruct the pardons.

Impact of the Revolt There were other ramifications of the slave uprising. The provincial government passed laws making it impossible to free slaves without putting up a two-hundred-pound bond and paying the freed slave twenty pounds per year for life. Africans, American Indians, and mulattoes were prohibited from inheriting or otherwise owning property. Finally, due process rights were weakened for slaves accused of murder or conspiracy. In the wake of the revolt, Elias Neau, the preacher and catechist of Trinity Church, found it difficult to continue his school for blacks and Indians. Only two of his many pupils were implicated in the conspiracy, and Chaplain John Sharpe doubted that either was involved in the violence.

After the rebellion, New Yorkers were reluctant to import slaves directly from Africa or to purchase Spanish Indians as slaves. Black slaves from the

West Indies were preferred over the other two groups. Yet slavery remained a primary source of labor for both the province and city of New York, slaves constituting about 15 percent of the population. In 1730, other regulations were added to the slave code because "many Mischiefs had been Occasioned by the two great Liberty allowed to Negro and other Slaves." In 1741, white paranoia and slave discontent provoked a so-called slave conspiracy in which 150 slaves and 25 whites were jailed. Of that number, 18 slaves and 4 whites were hanged, 13 blacks burned alive, and 70 were sold and sent to the West Indies.

Ronald W. Howard

Core Resources

In Joyce D. Goodfriend's *Before the Melting Pot: Society and Culture in Colonial New York City, 1664-1730* (Princeton, N.J.: Princeton University Press, 1992), chapter 6 provides considerable insight into the life and labors of New York City slaves, both before and after the 1712 revolt. In Michael Kammen's *Colonial New York: A History* (New York: Charles Scribner's Sons, 1975), chapter 11 relates the slave revolts of 1712 and 1741 to larger social and economic problems in colonial New York society. Mary Lou Lustig's *Robert Hunter, 1666-1734* (Syracuse, N.Y.: Syracuse University Press, 1983) gives a brief but pertinent summary of the slave revolts and the persons most associated with the trials. Edgar J. McManus's *A History of Negro Slavery in New York* (Syracuse, N.Y.: Syracuse University Press, 1966) goes into considerable detail regarding the conditions that contributed to the 1712 uprising. Kenneth Scott's "The Slave Insurrection in New York in 1712," in *The New-York Historical Society Quarterly* (45, January, 1961), describes the revolt and the trials that followed. Peter Woods's "Slave Resistance," in *Encyclopedia of the North American Colonies*, vol. 2 (New York: Charles Scribner's Sons, 1993) relates the 1741 New York revolt to other examples of slave resistance in North America.

See also: Slave codes; Slave rebellions; Slavery: history; Turner's slave insurrection.

New York Times Co. v. Sullivan

This landmark 1964 Supreme Court ruling increased protections of the news media against libel charges made by public officials. The case began on March 20, 1960, when a group of African American ministers from Alabama published a full-page advertisement in *The New York Times* seeking support for the Civil Rights movement in the South, and for Dr. Martin Luther King, Jr., in particular. While accusing no one by name, the advertisement attacked the Montgomery, Alabama, police for performing a variety of illegal acts against black students. Some of the advertisement's allegations were subsequently found to be untrue.

L. B. Sullivan, an elected Montgomery city commissioner responsible for supervising the police, sued *The Times* and the Alabama ministers for libel in an Alabama court, claiming that the published attacks on the police were in effect attacks on him personally. The Alabama court ordered *The Times* to pay Sullivan a half million dollars in damages—at that time the largest libel judgment in Alabama history.

In the civil rights struggle of the 1950's and 1960's, the national media played a crucial role in informing the country as a whole about racial discrimination and injustice in the South. Sullivan's libel suit against *The Times* was considered by many journalists to be a ploy to censor the national media and discourage northern reporters from covering the struggle to end racial segregation in the South.

On appeal, Alabama's Supreme Court affirmed the decision against the newspaper. *The Times* then appealed the case to the U.S. Supreme Court which overturned the lower court decisions and created the "*New York Times* rule," or actual malice test. The *New York Times* rule states that under the constitutional guarantees of a free press it was necessary for a public official suing for defamation to prove malice by showing that the media defendants acted with malice in the publication of the allegedly libelous article. The court defined malice as "the publishing of material knowing it to be false, or with a reckless disregard of whether it is true or false."

The Court concluded that although some of the claims made in the advertisement published in *The Times* were untrue, they were not published with actual malice as defined under the law. The Court ruled that publication of editorial advertisements of the type in question was an important outlet for disseminating information and ideas by persons who did not have easy access to the media. The Court's decision immediately relieved *The Times* and the ministers of the half-million-dollar damage judgment. The decision also had broader implications by removing the threat of large libel judgments against those who criticized racial segregation.

Glenn Canyon

See also: Civil Rights movement; King, Martin Luther, Jr; Montgomery bus boycott.

Newark race riots

Race relations, already tense in much of the United States in 1967, were especially poor in Newark, New Jersey. In addition to high unemployment,

African Americans were angry about a proposal to relocate inner-city residents from their neighborhoods in order to build a medical and dental college. On July 12, 1967, rumors spread through the city that police had beaten an African American during an arrest. Protesters throwing bottles and shouting insults soon surrounded the police station, but the crowd dispersed in the early morning hours. The following night, a full-scale riot erupted, and the governor called out the National Guard. Despite the presence of troops, the rioting continued for several days. Twenty-three people died, and more than fifteen hundred people were injured. Police reported more than sixteen hundred arrests. Damage to buildings and property was estimated at more than ten million dollars. Although the Newark riot evidenced the frustration that many African Americans felt concerning the slow pace of economic and social change in the United States, the violence shocked many white Americans and diminished enthusiasm for continued government efforts in the area of civil rights.

Thomas Clarkin

See also: Detroit riots; Kerner Report.

Newberry v. United States

In 1918, Truman H. Newberry, Republican candidate for the U.S. Senate, was tried in Michigan, along with more than one hundred associates, for conspiring to violate the Federal Corrupt Practices Act of 1910. The statute violated had set a limit on campaign financing, and the indictment claimed that Newberry had exceeded this limit in primary and general election expenditures. Newberry and his associates were found guilty in the U.S. District Court for the Western District of Michigan.

The U.S. Supreme Court reversed the conviction and sent the case back to the lower court, finding that the statute on which Newberry's conviction rested had no constitutional authority. The Court argued that prior to the Seventeenth Amendment, the only part of the Constitution empowering Congress to regulate the election process was to be found in Article I, section 4, which pertained only to the time, place, and manner of holding general elections and failed to address such matters as party primaries and conventions, additions to the election process unforeseen by the framers of the Constitution. Consequently, the Court ruled that in the relevant section of the Corrupt Practices Act, Congress had exceeded its authority. The Court also maintained that because the statute antedated the ratification of the Seventeenth Amendment, which extended congressional authority, it was invalid at the time of its enactment. The Court held that a power later acquired could not, *ex proprio*, validate a law that was unconstitutional at the time of its passing. The Court did not question a state's right to regulate primaries and campaign financing, claiming that "the state may suppress whatever evils may be incident to primary or convention."

The *Newberry* ruling imposed an important barrier to the enfranchisement of black Americans in the single-party South. Although the Court would strike down laws expressly prohibiting African Americans from voting in primaries, as late as 1935, in *Grovey v. Townsend*, it upheld legal measures taken in Texas to bar blacks from participating in the state Democratic convention, arguing that such "private" discrimination did not come under constitutional purview. *Grovey* and *Newberry* were finally successfully challenged in *United States v. Classic* (1941), which held that Congress had the authority to regulate both primary and general elections for federal offices.

Three years later a final legal blow to de jure disfranchisement of African Americans was dealt in *Smith v. Allwright* (1944), which held that laws governing all elections—local, state, and federal—could be invalidated if they violated Article I, section 4 of the Constitution. Sponsored by the National Association for the Advancement of Colored People, the plaintiff argued that Texas Democratic Party officials had denied him a primary ballot because of his race. The Supreme Court concurred, noting that state laws regulated both primary and general elections and were therefore responsible for barriers to the ballot box erected on racial grounds.

John W. Fiero

See also: *Grovey v. Townsend*; Jim Crow laws; Poll tax; *Smith v. Allwright*; Voting Rights Act of 1965.

Niagara Movement

The Niagara Movement, a progenitor of the National Association for the Advancement of Colored People, was founded on July 11, 1905, and helped to lay the groundwork for the civil rights movement.

In the early years of the twentieth century, two major approaches to achieving African American progress were separated by their differing philosophies: Booker T. Washington was a pragmatist who acknowledged current policies toward blacks and wanted to make the lives of African Americans as easy as possible within that framework. Washington held that "it is important and right that all privileges of law be ours, but it is vastly more important that we be prepared for the exercise of those privileges." He assumed that as African Americans became productive workers who were not troublemakers, they would be seen as valuable assets to U.S. society. Then they would slowly but surely move up the economic and political ladder.

Beginnings The leaders of what came to be known as the Niagara Movement, by contrast, asserted that Washington's programs would keep African Americans at the bottom of the political, economic, and social ladder. One of the Niagara Movement's major leaders was W. E. B. Du Bois, a professor at Atlanta University at the beginning of the movement. Du Bois maintained that it was important for African Americans to press for the immediate implementation of their civil rights: "We want full manhood suffrage and we want it now. . . . We want the Constitution of the country enforced. . . . We want our children educated. . . . And we shall win!" The leaders of the Niagara Movement were convinced that as long as African Americans were not protected by law, economic and social advances would never come. They believed that the structures of United States society were developed in such a way that, without the force of law, other advances would never occur. These two different views of how to achieve progress for African Americans not only separated Washington and Du Bois throughout their lives but would remain at the heart of discord over how best to achieve freedom and progress for African Americans in the United States.

The Niagara Movement was formed on July 11, 1905, when twenty-nine radical African American intellectuals, headed by Du Bois, met at Niagara Falls, in Ontario, Canada. (Even though some organizational activities were held in Buffalo, New York, on the other side of the U.S.-Canadian border, most meetings were held in Canada because of the difficulty of finding places in the United States that would accommodate African Americans.) On nearly every issue, the Niagara Movement stood in direct contrast to Washington's approach. In sharp language, in a policy statement entitled the Negro Declaration of Independence, movement leaders placed full responsibility for the race problem on whites, denouncing the inequities of segregation and disfranchisement laws; they maintained that economic progress was not possible in a democratic society without the protection afforded by the ballot; and they insisted, above all, that African Americans could

One of the founders of the Niagara Movement, W. E. B. Du Bois was an uncompromising advocate of full rights for all Americans. *(Library of Congress)*

gain their rights only by agitation. Members of the Niagara Movement spoke out against an accommodationist approach at a time when almost all white and African American leaders believed that such policies were critical if blacks were to achieve equality in U.S. society and politics.

About five years after it had been established, the Niagara Movement had approximately four hundred members. Most were Northern, urban, upper-class college graduates. The movement never developed the wide following it wanted. Some assert that the movement did not reach a broad enough spectrum in the African American community, let alone create an appeal to the broader society of which it was part. At first women were excluded from the Niagara Movement, both as members and as a focus of emancipation. Some of the movement's organizers reasoned that fighting for women's rights along with rights for African American males would result in defeat of the movement's policies and goals. Du Bois, however, argued that African American civil rights would not be complete without women as well as men tasting the fruits of freedom. He argued that to obtain male suffrage on the backs of women was immoral and not in keeping with the solidarity that African Americans must maintain in the face of the hostility of the dominant white society. Du Bois's position finally prevailed.

The NAACP During its existence, the Niagara Movement held conferences in 1906, at Harpers Ferry, West Virginia; in 1907, at Boston, Massachusetts; and in 1908, at Oberlin, Ohio. Civil rights protests in cities across the nation were organized by the Niagara Movement, which gained a reputation for demanding recognition of the equality of all human beings through social protest and demonstrations. In the wake of a race riot in Springfield, Illinois, in 1908, the movement began to dissolve as members turned their attention to a new organization. On February 12, 1909, the ideas on which the Niagara Movement was founded were absorbed into the framework of the National Association for the Advancement of Colored People (NAACP), which not only developed a wider following but also addressed the broader issues of equality and civil rights that the Niagara Movement was not able to address effectively. Important members of the Niagara Movement, such as Du Bois, became instrumental in the NAACP as well. Du Bois, however, decided that even the NAACP was not forceful enough in addressing issues such as lynching, rape, and voting rights. He would end his life in exile in Africa.

Although the Niagara Movement survived only five years—formally disbanding in 1910—it had served as the foundation upon which later movements were built. It can be seen as both a negative reaction to Washington's accommodationist approach to African American equality and the progenitor of such later groups as the Student Nonviolent Coordinating Committee (SNCC), the Congress of Racial Equality (CORE), and the Black Panthers.

Paul Barton-Kriese

Core Resources

W. Haywood Burns's *The Voices of Negro Protest in America* (New York: Oxford University Press, 1963) discusses twentieth century protest movements, highlighting the NAACP. W. E. B. Du Bois's *The Souls of Black Folk* (1903; reprint, New York: Vintage Books, 1990) is Du Bois's powerful argument that black U.S. citizens will progress only via challenge, struggle, and political protest. Floyd B. McKissick's *Three-fifths of a Man* (New York: Macmillan, 1969) is an account of the racial basis of the Declaration of Independence, the Constitution, and the Emancipation Proclamation, with an examination of how these documents have influenced race relations. Donald G. Nieman's *Promises to Keep: African-Americans and the Constitutional Order, 1776 to the Present* (New York: Oxford University Press, 1991) is a constitutional history of the United States with special reference to charting the impact of the Constitution on U.S. social history. Booker T. Washington's *Up from Slavery* (1901; reprint, New York: Gramercy Books, 1993) describes his idea of the "talented tenth" and how black citizens of the United States will achieve full equality gradually, through hard work and demonstrating their worthiness; a direct contrast to the more aggressive platform of Du Bois.

See also: Atlanta Compromise; Congress of Racial Equality; Nation of Islam; National Association for the Advancement of Colored People; Southern Christian Leadership Conference; Talented Tenth; Universal Negro Improvement Association.

Nixon v. Herndon

In 1921, the U.S. Supreme Court ruled in *Newberry v. United States* that Congress lacked authority to regulate primary elections. Southern state legislatures immediately took advantage of this decision to prohibit black participation in state primary elections. "White primaries" were quickly adopted throughout the South. Texas, during the first half of the twentieth century, was part of the Democrat-dominated South. The only competition that mattered was within the Democratic Party, so if blacks were not allowed to participate in the Democratic primary they would effectively be denied any meaningful choice in the electoral process.

In 1924, the Texas legislature passed a law barring blacks from voting in the Democratic primary. L. A. Nixon, a black resident of El Paso, attempted to vote in the primary and was refused by Herndon, an election judge. Nixon and the National Association for the Advancement of Colored People (NAACP) claimed that the Texas law violated the Fourteenth and Fifteenth Amendments. The Supreme Court did not deal with the issue of the Fifteenth Amendment, but a unanimous Court found that the Texas white primary law violated the equal protection clause of the Fourteenth Amendment.

The NAACP won the battle but temporarily lost the war. Texas responded to the Court's decision by engaging in the strategy of "legislate and litigate." By passing a different white primary law after their defeat in *Nixon v. Herndon*, the Texas legislature forced the NAACP to institute another attack on the white primary. When the second law was declared unconstitutional in *Nixon v. Condon* in 1932, Texas came up with a third variation of the white primary. This time, in *Grovey v. Townsend* (1935), the U.S. Supreme Court upheld the Texas white primary, arguing that no state discrimination was present. According to the Court, the Texas Democratic Party, a private voluntary association, decided to exclude blacks from voting in the primary elections. It was not until *Smith v. Allwright* (1944) that a unanimous Supreme Court declared that the Fifteenth Amendment could be used as a shield to protect the right to vote in primary elections.

From the passage of the first white primary law in 1924 until the final abolition of white primaries in the *Smith* case in 1944, blacks were denied the right to vote in Democratic Party primaries, the only election of significance at that time. The white primary cases illustrate one of the dilemmas in using the federal courts—the fact that justice delayed is justice denied.

Darryl Paulson

See also: *Grovey v. Townsend*; National Association for the Advancement of Colored People; *Newberry v. United States*; *Smith v. Allwright*.

Nonviolent resistance

Nonviolence is a central method for expressing political dissent and marshaling the power necessary to bring about political change. In North American race relations, its most visible and effective proponents, including Martin Luther King, Jr., used it to advance the cause of civil rights.

Although the term "nonviolent resistance" is a twentieth century concept based on analysis of the strategies and conditions necessary for successful nonviolent action, its practice is deeply rooted in United States history. Religious groups from Europe such as the Amish and the Society of Friends (Quakers), who practiced a literal understanding of Jesus's teachings forbidding the use of violence, fled to North America to escape persecution. Their continued witness to principles of pacifism has influenced a tradition and philosophy of nonviolent protest. Additionally, the early colonists engaged in nonviolent resistance against British rule. In 1766, Britain passed an import tax, the Stamp Act. American merchants organized a boycott of goods, causing the repeal of the act. This action marked the first organized resistance to British rule and led to the establishment of the First Continental Congress in 1774. The legal basis for nonviolent action was established in the First Amendment to the Constitution, which protects the rights of persons to "freedom of speech," peaceful assembly, and petitioning the government "for a redress of grievances." The United States has a long history of expression of such rights.

Various Applications In 1845, Henry David Thoreau was jailed for refusing to pay a poll tax in protest of the Mexican-American War. In his essay "Civil Disobedience," Thoreau proclaimed the moral necessity of resistance in the face of immoral government action. Nonviolent protest has accompanied every war in which the United States has engaged, and it was so widespread during the Vietnam War that it became a central reason the United States withdrew from Vietnam in 1974. Nonviolent protest has also been central to various movements seeking to ban and limit nuclear weapons and in war tax resistance movements, in which members refuse to pay taxes to support the military budget. Strategies of nonviolent resistance were also employed by the women's rights movement, which culminated in the right to vote (1920) and in greater social and economic equality for women. The labor movement has used nonviolent tactics in the form of strikes, labor slowdowns, and boycotts to force improvement of working conditions and income. Despite strong, often violent responses by corporate owners, the Wagner Act, passed by Congress in 1935, recognized the legal right of workers to organize and use such methods. César Chávez effectively used consumer boycotts in the 1970's and 1980's to win better conditions for farmworkers. Nonviolent strategies have been used by environmental groups to block construction of nuclear power plants, stop the cutting of forests, or alter policies considered to be ecologically hazardous. They have also been employed since the 1980's by antiabortion groups attempting to close abortion clinics.

Race Relations The most prolonged, successful use of nonviolent resistance, however, came in the Civil Rights movement led by Martin Luther King, Jr., in the 1950's and 1960's. Drawing on the work of Mohandas Gandhi, the movement used marches, sit-ins, and boycotts to force an end to legal racial segregation in the South and informal (de facto) segregation in the North. This campaign demonstrated the ambiguity of governmental response to such tactics. Often participants were arrested and convicted under local statutes, only to have such laws ruled invalid by higher courts; this occurred during the Montgomery bus boycott. On the other hand, King and his followers were under constant surveillance by the Federal Bureau of Investigation and were considered threats to political stability by many government officials. The debate has also focused on what constitutes "freedom of expression" and "peaceful assembly." The "plowshares eight," in 1980, protesting nuclear weapons, entered a General Electric plant in Pennsylvania and dented the nose cone of a warhead. They were sentenced to prison on grounds of trespass and destruction of private property.

Theory and Strategy Nonviolent resistance has two distinct traditions. The religious tradition centers on the moral claim that it is always wrong to harm another and that only love of the "enemy" can transform persons and societies. Violence and hatred cannot solve social problems or end social conflict, for each act of violence generates new resentments. This spiral of violence can be ended only if some group absorbs the violence and returns only nonviolence and love. Central to this vision is a commitment to justice that requires adherents to engage injustice actively wherever they find it.

The political tradition focuses on strategies for organizing political and social power to force another, usually a political authority, to change policies. As Gene Sharp, a leading analyst, notes, government requires the consent of its citizens. In nonviolent resistance, dissenters organize forms of power including economic power, labor power, and the power of public opinion in order to undermine consent and force authorities to change policies.

The use of these theories and techniques remains important in stable, democratic societies as a way of resolving conflict, generating social change, and challenging power structures, especially on behalf of the powerless, whose rights are often ignored. Without the legal sanctions which permit such protest, the only recourse becomes open societal violence and conflict, even to the point of civil war.

Charles L. Kammer

Core Resources

Broad views of the topic are presented in Peter Ackerman and Christopher Kruegler's *Strategic Nonviolent Conflict: The Dynamics of People Power in the Twentieth Century* (Westport, Conn.: Praeger, 1994); David P. Barash's *Introduction to Peace Studies* (Belmont, Calif.: Wadsworth, 1991); *The Power of the People: Active Nonviolence in the United States* (Philadelphia: New Society, 1987), edited by Robert Conney and Helen Michalowski; and Gene Sharp's *The Politics of Nonviolent Action* (3 vols., Boston: Porter Sargent, 1973). A personal view is contained in Martin Luther King, Jr.'s *A Testament of Hope: The Essential Writings and Speeches of Martin Luther King, Jr.*, edited by James M. Washington (San Francisco: Harper, 1991).

See also: Civil Rights movement; Freedom Riders; Gandhi, Mohandas; King, Martin Luther, Jr.; Montgomery bus boycott; Southern Christian Leadership Conference; Student Nonviolent Coordinating Committee.

North Star, The

The North Star *was the vehicle for the first of Frederick Douglass's newspaper campaigns against slavery and for abolition.*

When the first issue of *The North Star* appeared on December 3, 1847, critics and readers discovered a newspaper that blended sardonic humor with moral urgency, written in a polished style. Some readers, however, were skeptical of editor Frederick Douglass's sophistication. Fathered by a white man and born to the slave Harriet Bailey in Talbot County, Maryland, Frederick Bailey had worked in bondage as a slave for Thomas Auld, witnessing the horrors of slavery, the brutal beatings, and even murder. In his teens, he had taught himself to read and write from a discarded speller and copybook, and learned public speaking by imitating orations appearing in *The Columbian Orator*, an abolitionist publication. *The Columbian Orator* led to his awareness of the abolitionist movement and influenced his writing style when he later published *The North Star*. Clashing with his master in 1838, Frederick escaped from Baltimore to New York with Anna Murray, a free African American domestic servant. Once married, they settled in New Bedford, Massachusetts, which offered sanctuary. To prevent recapture, Frederick changed his surname to Douglass, in honor of a character in Sir Walter Scott's poem *Lady of the Lake.*

Douglass and Garrison Douglass became active in local abolitionist gatherings, discovering his gift as a compelling speaker who provided first-hand examples of barbaric slavery. He became a favorite on the lecture circuit during the early 1840's; his autobiography, *Narrative of the Life of Frederick Douglass* (1845), sold more than thirty thousand copies over the next five years. Douglass came under the tutelage of the leading abolitionist of the times, a white man named William Lloyd Garrison. From Garrison's abolitionist newspaper, *The Liberator*, Douglass no doubt learned much about newspaper operations.

As Douglass's fame increased, so did his risk of capture as an escaped slave. In 1845, he sailed for England, then on to Scotland and Ireland, where he passionately lectured on the inhumane treatment of slaves. His newfound friends, moved by his personal plight, arranged to purchase Douglass's freedom for $711.66. Before returning to the United States in 1847, he also received $2,175 to bankroll his own antislavery newspaper.

When Garrison objected to Douglass's projected newspaper, the two close friends became estranged, then bitter enemies. Douglass believed that the white abolitionists thought him a child to be led. African Americans, he insisted, must lead to gain respect. He held that his newspaper could create that leadership and help increase self-respect among African Americans. Douglass knew of the hazards in starting an African American newspaper, because about one hundred such papers already existed in the United States, the first having been started in 1827. He located in Rochester, New York, because of the area's strong antislavery sentiments and because publishing there reduced the competition with *The Liberator* in Boston and the *National Anti-Slavery Standard* in New York City.

On December 3, 1847, the first issue of *The North Star* appeared—a four-page weekly with a subscription cost of two dollars per year, circulation of two to three thousand, and publishing costs of eighty dollars per week at the first print shop owned by an African American. Douglass chose journalist Martin Delaney as coeditor, but the two soon clashed over the issue of "colonization," by which freed slaves would seek a separate homeland in Africa rather than integrate within the United States white society. When a disgusted Delaney left in 1848 to found a colony in the Niger Valley, in Africa, Douglass became sole editor, vigorously espousing the principles of integration, as he did throughout his life.

Advocacy for All In the first issue of *The North Star*, Douglass urged African Americans to become politically active and pledged that his newspaper would aggressively attack slavery, work to free Southern slaves, and promote African American morality and progress. The lead article recounted the convention of "colored people" of 1847, with its primary objectives of abolishing slavery and elevating free African Americans. In subsequent years, *The North Star* dealt with a plethora of burning issues: injustice, inequality, racism, the avoidance of drink and dissipation, the benefits of integrated school systems, the elimination of segregated hotels and railroads, the folly of war and capital punishment, the worth of laborers, the imperative need for racial unity among African Americans, and the unfair voting practices leveled against African Americans in northern states. *The North Star* came to the defense not only of persecuted African Americans but also of American Indians, the Irish, and other immigrant groups.

Frederick Douglass, founder and editor of *The North Star*. *(Library of Congress)*

From its beginnings, *The North Star* lived up to its masthead: "Right Is Of No Sex—Truth Is Of No Color—God Is

The Father Of Us All, and All We Are Brethren." Douglass vigorously supported the women's rights movement, linking enslaved women to the abolition movement itself. At the Seneca Falls Convention in 1848, Douglass was the only one of the thirty-two men attending to speak and vote in favor of Elizabeth Cady Stanton's Declaration of Sentiments, which demanded equality for women. He effectively used *The North Star* to promote Stanton's feminist cause.

Subsequent Papers Financially, *The North Star* foundered after six months. Douglass mortgaged his house and used his lecture fees to keep the paper going. From time to time, he received financial gifts from Gerrit Smith, a philanthropist, reformer, and wealthy New York landowner. In 1851, the two men agreed to merge the financially troubled *North Star* with Smith's struggling *Liberty Party Paper.* Douglass maintained editorial control over the paper while including political news of the Liberty Party; he broadened his readership to four thousand; and he accepted a comfortable subsidy from Smith. The new effort, *Frederick Douglass' Paper,* appeared in June, 1851, and lasted until 1859. The paper continued Douglass's efforts in regard to abolition, equality, and women's rights. Douglass also dabbled in the Liberty Party campaigns, endorsing Smith and helping him win a seat in Congress. In 1852, Douglass himself became the first African American nominated for vice president on the Equal Rights Party ticket of 1852.

Recurring financial problems forced Douglass to reduce the size and frequency of his paper in 1859. His third effort, *Douglass' Monthly,* circulating in England as well as in the United States, lasted until the middle of the Civil War, 1863. Like the other two papers, *Douglass' Monthly* remained a magnet for African American writers and reformers and framed Douglass's own inimitable style and wit as well. He actively recruited African American soldiers for the war. He viewed Abraham Lincoln as the best hope for his race, pressing for the Emancipation Proclamation that Lincoln delivered in 1863. He proposed land reform, federally financed education, and a national association for African Americans. He believed that interracial marriages would someday eliminate racial hatred.

After the Civil War, Douglass moved to Washington, D.C. There he published the *New National Era,* focusing on the interests of the newly freed African Americans. During that paper's existence (1870-1873), Douglass editorialized on Reconstruction, the rise of mob lynchings in the South, race relations, politics, labor, and education. From 1873 until his death in 1895, Douglass continued to be heard on the lecture circuit and in leading newspapers. A self-made man, rising against great odds from slavery to publisher, race leader, prominent abolitionist, social reformer, and political activist, Douglass is one of the most important African Americans of the nineteenth century and became a powerful symbol in the Civil Rights movement throughout the twentieth century.

Richard Whitworth

Core Resources

Frederick Douglass's *The Frederick Douglass Papers,* edited by John W. Blassingame and John R. McKivigan (New Haven, Conn.: Yale University Press, 1979-1992), is a reconstruction of Douglass's thoughts and opinions from fragmentary newspapers, such as *The North Star,* and manuscript sources. Nathan I. Huggins's *Slave and Citizen: The Life of Frederick Douglass* (Boston: Little, Brown, 1980) portrays Douglass as troubled and self-contradictory at times. Waldo E. Martin's *The Mind of Frederick Douglass* (Chapel Hill: University of North Carolina Press, 1984) focuses on Douglass's formative years and the reworking of his views on slavery, inequality, and injustice. William B. Rogers's *"We Are All Together Now": Frederick Douglass, William Lloyd Garrison, and the Prophetic Tradition* (New York: Garland, 1995) juxtaposes the values, beliefs, and actions of Douglass and Garrison. Frederick S. Voss's *Majestic in His Wrath: A Pictorial Life of Frederick Douglass* (Washington, D.C.: Smithsonian Institution Press, 1995) brings together rare photos and commentary to commemorate the centennial of Douglass's death.

See also: Abolition; Emancipation Proclamation; *Liberator, The*; Underground Railroad.

Ole Miss desegregation

The October 1, 1962, enrollment of the first African American student at the University of Mississippi provoked a national controversy.

In January, 1961, James Meredith, a native Mississippian and an Air Force veteran attending Jackson State College, one of Mississippi's all-black colleges, decided to transfer to the University of Mississippi, affectionately called "Ole Miss." His application was rejected because, Ole Miss officials maintained, Jackson State was not an approved Southern Association Secondary School and because Meredith did not furnish letters of recommendation from University of Mississippi alumni. On May 31, 1961, he filed a lawsuit against the university, charging that he had been denied admission because of his race. In its 114-year history, the University of Mississippi had never admitted an African American student.

Meredith's Legal Victory A federal district court judge dismissed Meredith's suit, but in June, 1962, a U.S. court of appeals ruled that Meredith had been rejected from Ole Miss "solely because he was a Negro," a ruling based on the *Brown v. Board of Education* school desegregation case of 1954. The court ordered the university to admit Meredith, and the ruling was upheld by Justice Hugo L. Black of the United States Supreme Court. On

James Meredith on his first day as a student at the University of Mississippi. *(Library of Congress)*

September 13, Mississippi governor Ross Barnett delivered a televised speech and stated, "No school will be integrated in Mississippi while I'm governor." A week later, the board of trustees of Ole Miss appointed Governor Barnett as the university's registrar, and he personally blocked Meredith from registering for courses that same day.

Throughout Meredith's court appeals, the U.S. Department of Justice had been monitoring the case. Attorney General Robert F. Kennedy, the brother of President John F. Kennedy, made more than a dozen phone calls to Governor Barnett, hoping to persuade him to allow Meredith to matriculate and thereby avoid a confrontation between the state of Mississippi and the federal government. The attorney general had provided Meredith with federal marshals to protect him as he attempted to register.

On September 24, the court of appeals that initially had heard Meredith's case again ordered the Board of Higher Education of Mississippi to allow Meredith to register. The following day, Meredith reported to the registrar's office in the university's Lyceum Building, but again Governor Barnett was there to block his registration. During a phone conversation with Attorney General Kennedy that same day, Barnett declared that he would never agree to allow Meredith to attend the University of Mississippi. When Kennedy reminded Barnett that he was openly defying a court order and could be subject to penalty, Barnett told Kennedy that he would rather spend the rest of his life in prison than allow Meredith to enroll.

On September 26, Meredith again tried to register for courses, and for the third time, Governor Barnett turned him away. Two days later, the court of appeals warned Barnett that if he continued to block Meredith's admission to Ole Miss, the governor would be found in contempt of court, arrested, and fined ten thousand dollars per day. On Saturday, September 29, Governor Barnett appeared at an Ole Miss football game and proudly announced, "I love Mississippi, I love her people, her customs! And I love and respect her heritage. Ask us what we say, it's to hell with Bobby K!"

That evening, President Kennedy called Governor Barnett and told him that the federal government would continue to back Meredith until Ole Miss admitted him. Under direct pressure from the president, Barnett began to reconsider. Finally, he agreed to allow Meredith to register on Sunday, September 30, when, the governor surmised, few students and news reporters would be milling around the campus. On Sunday evening, Meredith arrived at the Lyceum Building protected by three hundred marshals, armed in riot gear and equipped with tear gas.

As Meredith and his escorts approached the campus, a group of twenty-five hundred students and other agitators attempted to block their passage. The crowd began to shout and throw bricks and bottles at the federal marshals, who retaliated with tear gas. Some of the protesters were armed with guns and began firing random shots. One federal marshal was seriously wounded by a bullet in the throat. Two onlookers, Paul Guihard, a French journalist, and Roy Gunter, a jukebox repairman, were shot and killed by rioters.

Kennedy's National Address On Sunday evening, while Mississippians rioted on the Ole Miss campus, President Kennedy addressed the nation on television. The Meredith crisis had captured the country's and news media's attention, and the president attempted to show Mississippians and other U.S. citizens that his administration's commitment to civil rights was serious and unwavering. He reminded his audience that "Americans are free . . . to disagree with the law but not to disobey it. For in a government of laws and not of men, no man, however prominent or powerful, and no mob, however unruly or boisterous, is entitled to defy a court of law." He told Mississippians, "The eyes of the nation and all the world are upon you and upon all of us. And the honor of your university—and state—are in the balance."

The situation at the University of Mississippi was deteriorating. The federal marshals, low on tear gas, requested additional help to control the unruly mob. President Kennedy federalized Mississippi National Guardsmen and ordered them to Oxford. At dawn on Monday morning, the first of five thousand troops began arriving at Oxford to restore order. During the evening's rioting, more than one hundred people were injured and about two hundred were arrested, only twenty-four of whom were Ole Miss students.

On Monday morning, October 1, at 8:30 A.M., Meredith again presented himself at the Lyceum Building to register. He was closely guarded by federal marshals, and National Guardsmen continued patrolling the Ole Miss campus and Oxford's streets. Meredith, dressed impeccably in a business suit, registered for classes and began his matriculation at the University of Mississippi. "I am intent on seeing that every citizen has an opportunity of being a first-class citizen," Meredith told a reporter the next day. "I am also intent on seeing that citizens have a right to be something if they work hard enough."

During his tenure at Ole Miss, Meredith was often the target of insults and threats. Federal marshals remained with him during his entire time at the university. On August 18, 1963, Meredith graduated from the University of Mississippi with a bachelor of arts degree in political science. After a year of study in Africa, Meredith enrolled at Columbia University of Law. In 1966, the year before he completed his law degree, Meredith was wounded by a sniper's gunshot during a voter registration march from Tennessee to Mississippi.

Meredith's Impact As a result of his successful effort to desegregate Ole Miss, Meredith became one of the heroes of the Civil Rights movement. In his "Letter from Birmingham Jail" (1963), Martin Luther King, Jr., states that "One day the South will recognize its real heroes. They will be the James Merediths, courageously and with a majestic sense of purpose facing jeering and hostile mobs and the agonizing loneliness that characterizes the life of the pioneer."

Meredith's victory at the University of Mississippi was a key triumph for the Civil Rights movement during the 1960's. Within two years, the University of Alabama, the University of Georgia, and other Southern colleges and universities that had prevented African Americans from enrolling were also desegregated, as the era of overt segregation in U.S. institutions of higher learning came to an end.

The Meredith case also convincingly demonstrated that the federal government would use its power to end racial segregation in the South. Despite Governor Barnett's defiance, President Kennedy and his attorney general were able to force the state of Mississippi to comply with a federal court order, signaling that the South would be unable to block the subsequent wave of federal legislation designed to void the region's segregation laws.

James Tackach

Core Resources

Russell H. Barrett's *Integration at Ole Miss* (Chicago: Quadrangle Press, 1965) discusses Meredith's attempt to integrate the University of Mississippi. James H. Meredith's *Three Years in Mississippi* (Bloomington: Indiana University Press, 1966) is Meredith's own story of his years at Ole Miss. Arthur M. Schlesinger, Jr.'s *Robert Kennedy and His Times* (Boston: Houghton Mifflin,

1978) details Kennedy's involvement in the Meredith case. Sanford Wexler's *The Civil Rights Movement: An Eyewitness History* (New York: Facts on File, 1993) devotes a chapter to Meredith's integration of Ole Miss.

See also: *Brown v. Board of Education*; Civil Rights movement; Little Rock school desegregation; Montgomery bus boycott; Southern Christian Leadership Conference.

One-drop rule

The one-drop rule is a definition of race that says that a person with any known amount of black ancestry is to be legally and socially classified as black. Although there is no "pure" race, some people believe otherwise and want to keep the dominant group racially "pure" and delegate all "impure" people to the subordinate or stigmatized group. The one-drop rule originated in the southern United States before the Civil War (1861-1865) but had not been rigidly conceptualized, and a few black-white mixed-race individuals (who physically appeared white) were accepted as white by the dominant white culture. White attitudes became more rigid at the time of the Civil War, and the one-drop rule became strictly enforced and largely accepted throughout the United States. In 1896, the United States Supreme Court (in *Plessy v. Ferguson*) approved the one-drop rule as a legal definition by defining it as "common knowledge." Although state laws against mixed-race marriages (miscegenation) were declared illegal by the Supreme Court in 1967, the one-drop rule still applies in some states. Socially, some whites support the rule to maintain "white racial purity," and some blacks support it to keep from losing members of their group to the dominant white group. The one-drop rule is unique to the United States.

Abraham D. Lavender

See also: Biracialism; Blackness and whiteness: legal definitions; Interracial and interethnic marriage; Miscegenation laws; Mulattoes; Passing; *Plessy v. Ferguson*; Race as a concept.

Orangeburg massacre

On Thursday night, February 8, 1968, three African Americans (two male college students and the teenage son of a college employee) were killed by police gunfire on the campus of almost entirely black South Carolina State College in Orangeburg. Twenty-seven other students were injured. Nearly all were shot in the back or side as they attempted to flee an unannounced fusillade of police gunfire. One police officer had been seriously injured by an object thrown at the police, but despite uncorrected false reports in the media, the students were unarmed. African American students had started protesting three nights earlier because the only bowling alley in Orangeburg continued to exclude African Americans despite pleas from local white and black leaders and students.

The Orangeburg massacre was the first incident of U.S. college students being killed by police because of protesting, but the killings received almost no national attention, largely because many white Americans had developed negative attitudes toward black protesters following a series of urban riots in 1967. Twenty-seven months later, the killing of four white students at Kent State University in Ohio during a Vietnam War protest received international publicity. Jack Bass and Jack Nelson's *The Orangeburg Massacre* (1970, revised 1984) is a detailed study of the massacre. A campus monument memorializes Henry Smith, Samuel Hammond, Jr., and Delano Middleton, whose lives were taken "in pursuit of human justice."

Abraham D. Lavender

See also: Civil Rights movement; Detroit riot; Race riots of the twentieth century.

Pan-Africanism

A broad movement aimed at the political unification of Africa through the destruction of European colonialism, Pan-Africanism includes the political independence and freedom of all peoples of African descent who live in the West Indies, the Americas, and other concentrated areas. Pan-African Congresses provide the forum at which movement members can disseminate ideas. The first Congress was held in London during the summer of 1990. W. E. B. Du Bois, credited as the father of the concept, and George Padmore, a West Indian intellectual, were both prolific advocates and key theoreticians of the Pan-African ideology.

Early post-colonial nation-states' leaders—Kwame Nkrumah (Ghana), Eric Williams (Trinidad/Tobago), Norman Manley (Jamaica), Gamal Abdel Nasser (Egypt), Jomo Kenyatta (Kenya)—were significantly influenced by Pan-Africanist philosophy and espoused and utilized its concepts in forming their own organizations to advance the liberation of peoples of African descent. Marcus Garvey's Back-to-Africa social movement in the 1920's was the largest and best approximation of this movement in the United States. Finally, this movement can also be regarded as the theoretical precursor to the black nationalism movement that swept the United States in the 1960's.

Aubrey W. Bonnett

See also: Black nationalism; Black Power movement; Universal Negro Improvement Association.

Pasadena City Board of Education v. Spangler

In 1968, several students and their parents filed suit against the Pasadena Unified School District in California, alleging that the district's schools were segregated as a result of official action on the part of the district. In 1970, the federal district court found for these plaintiffs, concluding that the district had engaged in segregation and ordering the district to adopt a plan to cure the racial imbalances in its schools. The federal court's order provided that no school was to have a majority of minority students. The district thereafter presented the court with a plan to eliminate segregation in the Pasadena schools; the court approved the plan, and the district subsequently implemented it.

Approximately four years later, the Pasadena Unified School District asked the district court to modify its original order and eliminate the requirement that no school have a majority of minority students. The district contended that though it had abandoned its racially segregative practices, changing racial demographics had created new racial imbalances in the district's schools. The federal district court refused to modify its original order, however, and the Ninth Circuit Court of Appeals upheld the district court's ruling.

Reviewing this decision, Justice William H. Rehnquist, joined by five other justices, concluded that the district court had abused its authority in refusing to remove the requirement that no district school have a majority of minority students. According to the Court, there had been no showing that changes in the racial mix of the Pasadena schools had been caused by the school district's policies. Since the school district had implemented a racially neutral attendance policy, the federal district court was not entitled to require a continual reshuffling of attendance zones to maintain an optimal racial mix. Justices Thurgood Marshall and William Brennan dissented from this holding, emphasizing the breadth of discretion normally allotted to federal district courts to remedy school segregation once a constitutional violation had been shown.

The majority's decision signaled that the broad discretion with which the Court previously had seemed to have invested federal district courts was not without limits. It had been widely thought that once officially sanctioned or de jure segregation had been shown, a federal court had great latitude in eliminating not only such de jure segregation but also de facto segregation—that is, segregation not necessarily tied to official conduct. The majority's decision in this case, however, signified otherwise.

Timothy L. Hall

See also: *Brown v. Board of Education*; Segregation: de facto and de jure; *Swann v. Charlotte-Mecklenburg Board of Education.*

Passing

Passing is the concealment of one's racial identity or ethnicity to gain access to another racial or ethnic group, usually to obtain social and economic benefits. Passing has been used by African Americans, Asian Americans, and Hispanic Americans as a means of transcending racial stigmatization and marginalization, especially during the period of segregation. Most commonly, individuals of biracial or multiracial descent who had certain characteristics associated with whiteness broke from their minority heritage and lived within the dominant white community. These characteristics included a light skin tone, "European" facial features, and a high level of acculturation to white society. Because the differences in skin tone and facial features are typically less dramatic, Asian Americans and Hispanic Americans generally had an easier time passing for white than did African Americans. Asian Americans and Hispanic Americans who wished to pass as white and have the necessary physical characteristics might only have had to anglicize their

Journalist John Howard Griffin undertook an unusual form of "passing" by traveling through the South as an African American; he described his experience in *Black Like Me* (1961), a book adapted to film in 1964 with James Whitmore (on stool) playing Griffin. *(Museum of Modern Art, Film Stills Archive)*

names or adopt white surnames. African Americans unable to pass as white often passed as Asian Americans or Native Americans to achieve a slightly higher status in society.

Passing could be temporary or permanent. It was a largely urban phenomenon, since individuals in rural areas were more likely to be recognized and hence were less able to escape their racial identities. The most common form of passing involved a temporary leave from one's racial identity, possibly to enter a white establishment or to hold a job; cases of individuals who permanently left their racial identities to assume lives within white society were probably less common.

There were drawbacks associated with both temporary and permanent acts of passing. For example, those who passed temporarily in order to hold jobs were faced with the constant pressure of operating in two different and antagonistic worlds while keeping their two identities separate. Those who chose to pass for white permanently were generally forced to leave behind their families and friends, and they lived with the constant fear that someone might learn their secret. Because of the secretive nature of the phenomenon, it is impossible to assess with any accuracy the number of individuals who have engaged in passing. It is also difficult to know whether passing has actually decreased in the era of desegregation, though the greater access that racial minorities have to all realms of society has probably removed the immediate impetus behind the act of passing.

The concept of passing is based on ideas of racial purity and the drawing of rigid racial boundaries by which individuals of biracial or multiracial descent are considered part of the minority group. An example of this is the "one-drop rule," which stipulated that any individual with even one drop of black blood was black. The idea of passing thus has meaning only within a society that defines race as mutually exclusive categories. Two important works that deal with the issue of passing are Paul R. Spickard's *Mixed Blood: Intermarriage and Ethnic Identity in Twentieth-Century America* (1989) and Maria P. P. Root's *Racially Mixed People in America* (1992).

Erica Childs

See also: Blackness and whiteness: legal definitions; Miscegenation laws; One-drop rule; Race as a concept.

Pennsylvania Society for the Abolition of Slavery

The Pennsylvania Society for the Abolition of Slavery was the first antislavery society in America.

On April 14, 1775, a group of men gathered at the Sun Tavern on Second Street in Philadelphia to establish the first antislavery society in America. After electing John Baldwin their president and adopting a constitution, they named their organization the Society for the Relief of Free Negroes Unlawfully Held in Bondage. Sixteen of the twenty-four founders were members of the Society of Friends, or Quakers. The creation of this antislavery society was instigated when Philadelphia Quakers Israel Pemberton and Thomas Harrison aided Native American Dinah Neville and her children, who were being detained in Philadelphia pending their shipment to the West Indies to be sold as slaves.

Harrison was fined in a Philadelphia court for giving protection to the Neville family. When this incident gained notoriety, members of the Quaker Philadelphia Meeting mobilized to form the antislavery society. At its first meeting, the antislavery society enlisted legal counsel to help the Nevilles and five other victims illegally held in bondage and to form a standing committee to investigate any conditions of slavery in the Philadelphia area.

The Revolutionary War interrupted regular meetings until 1784. At this time, Quaker abolitionist Anthony Benezet revived the antislavery society as members learned that two African Americans had committed suicide rather than be illegally enslaved. Benezet increased the membership to forty, including Benjamin Franklin, James Pemberton, and Dr. Benjamin Rush. The society renamed itself the Pennsylvania Society for Promoting the Abolition of Slavery, for the Relief of Free Negroes Unlawfully Held in Bondage, and for Improving the Condition of the African Race. Since the majority of the members were Friends, the group developed directly from Quaker religious beliefs and within the Quaker social structure. To explore the founding of the Pennsylvania Society for the Abolition of Slavery, it is critical to trace events and movements within the Society of Friends in seventeenth century colonial Pennsylvania.

Quaker Beginnings One of the basic principles espoused by Quaker founder George Fox was that all people are created equal. On a visit to the colonies in 1671, Fox spoke at Friends' meetings and encouraged Quaker slaveholders to free their slaves after a specified period of service. In 1676, Quaker William Edmundson, an associate of Fox, published the first antislavery literature in Rhode Island. While Quakers were formulating an antislavery position early in their movement, German Mennonites migrating to America had vowed that they would not own slaves. Several members of the Mennonite community and Dutch Pietists adopted Quakerism and became members of the Friends' Germantown Meeting. These German Quakers, their minister Pastorius, and other Friends of the Germantown Meeting delivered a petition to the Philadelphia Meeting in 1688 demanding that slavery and the slave trade be abolished. The protest addressed to slave owners of the Philadelphia Monthly Meeting challenged these Friends to explain why they had slaves and how such a practice could exist in a colony founded on the principles of liberty and equality.

Representing the radical leadership of Philadelphia Friends, George Keith published a tract entitled *An Exhortation and Caution to Friends Concerning Buying or Keeping of Negroes.* He gave several directives: that Friends should not purchase African slaves except for the express purpose of setting them free, that those already purchased should be set free after a time of reasonable service, and that, while in service, slaves should be given a Christian education and taught how to read.

During the early eighteenth century, the conservative, wealthy membership of the Philadelphia Meeting took a somewhat confusing position on slavery. Their inconsistent policies included a separate meeting for African Americans, a request that Quakers in the West Indies stop shipping slaves to Philadelphia, and disciplinary measures for members of the meeting who were engaged in antislavery activity. Many prominent Quakers, such as James Logan, Jonathan Dickinson, and Isaac Norris, continued to purchase and own slaves.

The customary procedure of resolving issues at Friends' meetings was to achieve a consensus. Thus, the Quaker drift toward an antislavery sentiment gained momentum with the efforts of a few radicals but achieved success only when the majority bowed to the principles of Quaker conscience.

Unpopular radical member Benjamin Lay was unwelcome at the Philadelphia Meeting because of his unorthodox promotion of the antislavery cause. For example, Lay once had kidnapped a Quaker youth in order to illustrate the tragedy of abduction of African children for the slave trade. In 1738, at the Philadelphia Yearly Meeting, he wore a military uniform to emphasize the connection between slavery and war and concealed under his cloak an animal bladder that he had filled with red juice. Delivering an inflamed speech on the evils of slavery, he concluded by saying that slavery took the very lifeblood out of the slave, simultaneously piercing the bladder and splashing the horrified audience with simulated blood.

By the 1730's, the effects of the antislavery movement were evident among Quakers as more Friends provided for the manumission of their slaves in their wills. In addition, the increased immigration of Germans in need of work eliminated the demand for slave labor in the Middle Colonies.

John Woolman Much of the credit for the success of the antislavery movement among Quakers must be given to New Jersey Quaker John Woolman. Known for his gentle, persuasive approach as a Quaker minister, he began a series of visitations to Quaker slaveholders in New England, the Middle Colonies, and the South in 1743. In 1754, he published *Some Considerations on the Keeping of Negroes,* which proclaimed the evils of slavery and the absolute necessity for Friends to free their slaves. Meetings throughout the colonies and England effectively used his visitations to pressure Quakers to free their slaves. By 1774, Quaker meetings in England, New England, and

Pennsylvania had adopted sanctions to disown any member for buying slaves or for serving as executor of an estate that included slaves. It also required slaveholders to treat their slaves humanely and to emancipate them as soon as possible.

Some have argued that Quakers were willing to emancipate their slaves because slavery was not profitable in Pennsylvania in the absence of labor-intensive agriculture. Others claim that Quaker sensitivity to antislavery was aroused not by their own religious ideals but rather by eighteenth century Enlightenment philosophy, which held that liberty is a natural human right. These may be considered arguments; nevertheless, it was the Quakers who first championed the antislavery cause and who organized the first antislavery group in America.

Spread of the Antislavery Movement The Pennsylvania Society for the Abolition of Slavery served as a model for other antislavery groups. As early as 1794, other states that had formed antislavery societies were asked to send representatives to Philadelphia for annual meetings. As new associations were formed, Friends constituted a majority of the membership. Statesmen such as Franklin, Rush, Alexander Hamilton, John Jay, and Thomas Paine believed that the institution of slavery contradicted the ideals of the Declaration of Independence and joined in support of the Friends' antislavery campaign.

Emily Teipe

Core Resources

David Brion Davis's *The Problem of Slavery in the Age of Revolution, 1770-1823* (Ithaca, N.Y.: Cornell University Press, 1975) is an exhaustive study of the slave question immediately before the American Revolution and in the succeeding federal period, which includes the pioneering efforts of the Quakers. *The Quaker Origins of Antislavery* (Norwood, Pa.: Norwood Editions, 1980), edited by J. William Frost, is a history of the Quaker antislavery cause that includes a comprehensive collection of Quaker documents. Sydney V. James's *A People Among Peoples: Quaker Benevolence in Eighteenth Century America* (Cambridge, Mass.: Harvard University Press, 1963) discusses antislavery as an outreach of Quaker religious piety, along with the Quakers' other efforts for the good of the social order. Gary B. Nash's *Quakers and Politics: Pennsylvania 1681-1726* (Princeton, N.J.: Princeton University Press, 1968) places the antislavery cause within the larger framework of troubled politics in colonial Pennsylvania. Jean R. Soderlund's *Quakers and Slavery: A Divided Spirit* (Princeton, N.J.: Princeton University Press, 1985) is a study of the Philadelphia Yearly Meeting and its progression to an antislavery philosophy.

See also: Abolition; American Anti-Slavery Society; Free African Society; Slavery: history.

Plessy v. Ferguson

The Supreme Court's 1896 decision in Plessy v. Ferguson *upheld American apartheid as constitutional if public facilities were "separate but equal."*

On July 10, 1890, the Louisiana General Assembly, over the objection of its eighteen African American members, enacted a law which read, in part:

> . . . all railway companies carrying passengers in their coaches in this state shall provide equal but separate accommodations for the white and colored races, by providing two or more passenger coaches for each passenger train, or by dividing the passenger coaches by a partition so as to secure separate accommodations.

The law empowered train officials to assign passengers to cars; passengers insisting on going into a car set aside for the other race were liable to a twenty-five-dollar fine and twenty days' imprisonment. In addition, the company could refuse to carry an obstreperous passenger and, if it were sued for doing so, was immune from damages in state courts. A third section outlined the penalties for noncomplying railroads and provided that "nothing in this act shall be construed as applying to nurses attending children of the other race."

Opposition to the Law The prominent black community of New Orleans organized to mount a legal attack on the new law. A group calling itself the Citizens' Committee to Test the Constitutionality of the Separate Car Law, led by Louis Martinet and Alexander A. Mary, organized to handle the litigation and enlisted the services of Albion W. Tourgée. Tourgée was to serve as chief counsel and devote his considerable talents to rallying public opposition to the Jim Crow system typified by the Louisiana law. Martinet engaged James Walker to assist in handling the Louisiana phase of the controversy. Before the first test of the Louisiana law (also featuring an African American who could "pass for white") could be settled, the Louisiana Supreme Court decided that the 1890 law could not be applied to interstate travelers since it was an unconstitutional regulation of interstate commerce (*State ex rel. Abbot v. Hicks*, 11 So. 74 in 1892). The *Plessy* case, then, relitigated the question raised in the 1890 Mississippi railroad case, but as a problem in the constitutional law of civil liberties rather than one of interstate commerce.

The person recruited to test the segregation law was Homer Adolph Plessy, a person of seven-eighths Caucasian and one-eighth African ancestry, in whom "the mixture of colored blood was not discernible." On June 7, 1892, holding a first-class ticket entitling him to travel on the East Louisiana Railway from New Orleans to Covington, Louisiana, Plessy took a seat in the car reserved for whites. The conductor, assisted by a policeman, forcibly removed Plessy and, charging him with violating the segregation law, placed him in the parish jail. The state prosecuted Plessy in the Orleans Parish criminal district court before Judge John H. Ferguson. Plessy's plea that the law was unconstitutional was overruled by Ferguson, who directed the defense to address itself to the questions of fact. Having no defense in the facts, Tourgée and Walker appealed Ferguson's ruling on the law's constitutionality to the Louisiana Supreme Court by asking that court to issue a writ of prohibition which in effect would have directed Ferguson to reverse his ruling on the constitutional question.

On December 19, 1892, Associate Judge Charles E. Fenner of the Louisiana Supreme Court ruled the law constitutional in an opinion which served as a model for that written later by Justice Henry Billings Brown of the U.S. Supreme Court. After a delay of almost four years—a delay that Tourgée encouraged on the grounds that it gave the opponents of segregation needed time—the United States Supreme Court heard the arguments in Plessy's case on April 13, 1896. On May 18, 1896, Justice Brown handed down the majority opinion, supported by six other justices (Justice David Brewer did not participate, and Justice John Marshall Harlan dissented).

Justice Brown first disposed of Tourgée's argument that the segregation law was a "badge of servitude," a vestige of slavery prohibited by the Thirteenth Amendment (1865). Decisions in 1873 (*Slaughterhouse* cases) and 1883 (*Civil Rights* cases), wrote Brown, indicated that it was because the Thirteenth Amendment barred only outright slavery and not laws merely imposing "onerous disabilities and burdens" that the movement for the Fourteenth Amendment was successful.

Brown in his opinion delivered a famous statement on the relationship between law, prejudice, and equality:

> The [plaintiff's] argument also assumes that social prejudice may be overcome by legislation, and that equal rights cannot be secured to the negro except by an enforced commingling of the two races. We cannot accept this proposition. If the two races are to meet on terms of social equality, it must be the result of natural affinities, a mutual appreciation of each other's merits and a voluntary consent of individuals.

The law in question, however, specifically interfered with the "voluntary consent of individuals."

Effects of the Decision The Court thus sanctioned Jim Crowism. What comfort blacks derived from the case had to be found in the strong dissenting opinion of Justice Harlan, who once again proved himself to be a staunch champion of a broad interpretation of the Reconstruction amendments. Harlan construed the ban on slavery to cover segregation laws; he insisted on Tourgée's thesis that a railroad was a public highway and that under the Fourteenth Amendment government could make no racial distinctions whether one considered the case under the privileges and immunities, due process, or equal protection clauses of that amendment. Harlan attacked the Court's reliance on pre-Fourteenth Amendment precedents; his most memorable language appeared in connection with his charge that the majority usurped constitutional power by assuming authority to decide on the "reasonableness" of state social legislation:

> The white race deems itself to be the dominant race in this country. And so it is, in prestige, in achievements, in education, in wealth, and in power. So, I doubt not that it will continue to be for all time, if it remains true to its great heritage and holds fast to the principles of constitutional liberty. But in view of the Constitution, in the eye of the law, there is in this country no superior, dominant, ruling class of citizens. There is no caste here. Our Constitution is color-blind, and neither knows nor tolerates classes among citizens. In respect of civil rights, all citizens are equal before the law.

Harlan turned out to be a competent soothsayer:

> The destinies of the two races in this country are indissolubly linked together, and the interests of both require that the common government of all shall not permit the seeds of race hate to be planted under the sanction of law.

It would, however, take the general public and the justices of the Supreme Court decades to adopt Harlan's views and interpretation of the Constitution. *Plessy*'s strong sanction of segregation in transportation lasted formally until 1950 *(Henderson v. United States)* and in education until 1954 *(Brown v. Board of Education)*. Antimiscegenation laws were not outlawed until 1967 *(Loving v. Virginia)*.

James J. Bolner, updated by Brian L. Fife

Core Resources

Paul G. Kauper's "Segregation in Public Education: The Decline of *Plessy v. Ferguson*" (*Michigan Law Review* 52, 1954) contends that the Court did not deal definitively with the validity of segregation legislation, relying instead on its view of "reasonableness." Charles A. Lofgren's *The Plessy Case: A Legal-Historical Interpretation* (New York: Oxford University Press, 1987) concludes that *Plessy* did not cause Jim Crow but instead confirmed the American racism of its era. John P. Roche's "*Plessy v. Ferguson:* Requiescat in Pace?" (*University of Pennsylvania Law Review* 103, 1954) asserts that the *Plessy* decision reflected the political climate of its time and was a judicial attempt to deal with a social and political problem. C. Vann Woodward's *American Counterpoint: Slavery and Racism in the North-South Dialogue* (Boston: Little, Brown, 1971) discusses the irony of Justice Brown's and Harlan's positions in the light of the origins of the two men.

See also: Black codes; *Brown v. Board of Education*; *Civil Rights* cases; Jim Crow laws; Segregation: de facto and de jure.

Police brutality

Police brutality includes the excessive use of force to compel a citizen to obey police orders or to arrest someone, the excessive use of force to compel an assembly of people to disperse, the physical maltreatment of someone who has already been taken into police custody (often for purposes of extracting a confession), and the use of deadly force against a fleeing suspect unless it is necessary to save the officer's own life or the lives of others.

Because of the stresses inherent in their work, some tendency toward brutality has probably always existed among police officers. In the second half of the twentieth century, however, the changing racial makeup of large cities has made the American public (and that of some other countries) more sensitive to the problem than ever before. Although urban riots triggered by allegations of police brutality made headlines in the 1960's, 1980's, and early 1990's, a less well publicized, peaceful struggle against police brutality has proceeded throughout the United States along several fronts: the push for civilian complaint review boards, civil suits and criminal prosecutions, Supreme Court decisions, and reforms within the police departments themselves.

Police Subculture and Police Brutality To do their job, police officers must be able to use physical force as a last resort to compel obedience, and they inevitably must be granted a certain amount of leeway, or discretion, as to when such force is to be used. The decision to use force, although it can easily be second-guessed at leisure, often must be made with great speed, and it is often difficult to know exactly how much force is "excessive" in any particular instance. The main protection that police officers believe they possess is the respect and fear that others have of them; if they encounter signs of defiance or disrespect on the part of a citizen, they may feel compelled to arrest the person—and to use force if the person resists. The possibility of death and maiming at the hands of criminals is, moreover, a hazard of the job. The trust that police officers must place in one another in order to survive sometimes produces an "us versus them" attitude of distrust of citizens. When the public at large demands that police crack down on crime at all costs, police officers are tempted to violate individual rights in order to get results. Moreover, police officers' need to make split-second decisions tempts them to stereotype citizens by age, sex, and race; hence, decisions regarding whom to stop and when to use force may be made, or seem to be made, in a discriminatory manner.

Urban Racial Change and Police Brutality From 1940 to 1990, the major cities of the northern and western United States, once overwhelmingly white, witnessed dramatic increases in their African American and Hispanic populations. Until the 1970's, however, the ranks of police officers consisted overwhelmingly of non-Hispanic whites. The tendency of big-city police officers, as time went on, to live in predominantly white suburbs further alienated them from many of those they policed, as did the replacement of foot patrols by two-person patrol cars. High unemployment among young urban blacks promoted petty crime and disorderly conduct, thereby making police-citizen confrontations more likely. The high physical identifiability of most African Americans, and the tendency of white Americans to stereotype them as potential criminals, made police brutality an issue with resonance for middle-class as well as poor blacks. In New York City, Chicago, Denver, and Los Angeles, complaints about police brutality frequently arose among Hispanics as well as blacks.

Although many controversial incidents of police use of force have elicited only peaceful protests, minority group anger over alleged police brutality has sometimes exploded into violence. For example, riots erupted in New York City in July, 1964 (after a police officer killed a black youth); in Los Angeles in 1965; in cities throughout the United States in 1967; in Miami in May, 1980 (after the police officers who had beaten to death a black motorcyclist were acquitted); in Miami again in January, 1989 (after a black motorcyclist was shot to death by a police officer); and in Los Angeles on April 29-May 1, 1992 (after the acquittal of police officers involved in the videotaped beating of black motorist Rodney King).

Police Brutality and Public Assembly Excessive use of force against people demonstrating publicly for particular causes was a common complaint in the 1960's, a decade of unusual political ferment in the United States; even after that era ended, such incidents sometimes occurred. Examples include the use of police dogs against blacks demanding desegregation in southern cities in the early 1960's, the clubbing of youthful (and mostly white) demonstrators against the Vietnam War in Chicago in August, 1968, and the use, in 1989, of painful restraint devices against predominantly white antiabortion demonstrators in Los Angeles.

Civilian Police Review Boards Handling citizen complaints about police brutality was the exclusive concern of police department internal affairs units until the late 1950's and early 1960's, when the American Civil Liberties Union joined minority civil rights activists in demanding the establishment of civilian review boards (bodies with at least half their members from outside the police department) to hear such complaints. A civilian review board was instituted in New York City in 1966 but was abolished after a referendum; it was not reestablished until 1993. By 1990, about half of the fifty largest American cities had some form of civilian oversight over the police.

Police officers who opposed civilian review boards feared that such bodies would be dominated by militant antipolice activists; on the other hand, it was also argued that civilian arbiters would accept excuses for brutality that would never pass muster with professional police officers. By the early 1990's, scholarly advocates of civilian review boards, while conceding their imperfections, viewed them as a necessary (although inefficient) way to assure citizens that complaints of brutality would be treated fairly.

Fighting Police Brutality Through the Courts Even though the beating of Rodney King by members of the Los Angeles Police Department on March 3, 1991, was recorded on videotape, the four officers who had beaten him were acquitted in their first jury trial, before a state court, on April 29, 1992. For a number of reasons, many police officers suspected of acts of brutality are never brought to trial at all. District attorneys, who need willing police cooperation to try cases, are usually reluctant to prosecute police; police officers are usually unwilling to testify against other officers; it is widely understood that jurors often sympathize with police officers; and victims of police brutality are not always entirely blameless individuals. One of the few cases in which a police officer was both prosecuted and convicted of brutality in a state criminal trial was that of New York City patrolman Thomas Ryan, sentenced in 1977 to four years in prison by a Bronx jury for beating Israel Rodriguez to death in 1975. Another was the sentencing of two white Detroit police officers to stiff prison terms in 1993 for the 1992 death of a black man, Malice Green.

Police officers can also be tried on federal criminal charges of having violated the brutality victim's civil rights. In April, 1993, two of the four officers who had beaten Rodney King were convicted of such charges. In *Monroe v. Pape* (1961), the Supreme Court laid the basis for such legal action by holding that the Civil Rights Acts of 1871 (originally passed to protect African Americans in the South) applied to abuses of power by local police officers anywhere in the country. As of the early 1990's, however, federal trials of local police officers were rare. The Department of Justice lacked the personnel to check up on police abuses throughout the country.

Two milestones made civil suits a more effective means of obtaining redress: the Supreme Court decision (unconnected with police brutality) in *Monell v. New York City Department of Social Services* (1978), holding local governments financially liable for the transgressions of their employees, and a 1976 act of Congress permitting judges to award attorneys' fees to a plaintiff if the plaintiff wins the case. In April, 1994, Rodney King was awarded $3.8 million in damages from the city of Los Angeles; other American cities have also paid out considerable sums. Brutality lawsuits have the best chance of success when the victim has suffered obvious physical harm.

The Supreme Court and Police Brutality In the decisions *Brown v. Mississippi* (1936) and *Rochin v. California* (1952), the Supreme Court voided criminal convictions based on confessions extracted by torture. Under Chief Justice Earl Warren (whose term lasted from 1953 to 1968), the Supreme Court increasingly imposed on state and local police forces the restrictions of the Bill of Rights, which had been formerly imposed only on federal authorities. In *Mapp v. Ohio* (1961), the Court ordered local police to obey the Fourth Amendment's ban on searches without warrant; in *Miranda v. Arizona* (1966), it ordered the police to inform those in custody of their rights to remain silent and to have legal counsel. The Court provided no guidelines for disciplining erring officers; it only stated that evidence obtained through torture or illegal searches could not be used in a trial.

After Warren's retirement, the Supreme Court no longer led the way in the fight against police brutality. In *Rizzo v. Goode* (1976), the justices, in a 5-4 decision, declined to interfere in the operations of the Philadelphia police department, which had been accused of systematic brutality toward minorities. In *Lyons v. Los Angeles* (1982), the Court refused to outlaw the use of chokeholds by the Los Angeles Police Department. In two cases decided in 1984, the Court allowed certain exceptions to the rules established in *Mapp* and *Miranda.* In 1985, in *Tennessee v. Garner,* the justices decreed that the police should no longer automatically have the right to shoot at a fleeing felony suspect, but this doctrine had already been adopted by many local police departments before the Supreme Court ratified it.

Police Chiefs' Efforts at Reform In the 1960's, critics of the police accused police chiefs of automatically defending any officer accused of brutality. During the 1970's and 1980's, however, chiefs of police in many American cities took measures to discipline officers guilty of brutality and to reduce the number of incidents in the future. Black and Hispanic police chiefs, becoming more common by the 1980's, made special efforts in this regard. In 1972, New York City police commissioner Patrick V. Murphy instituted strict new rules governing the use of deadly force; in 1985, New York City police commissioner Benjamin Ward punished officers who had used stun guns against suspects in their custody. In 1990, Kansas City police chief Steven Bishop summarily dismissed officers who had severely beaten a suspect involved in a high-speed car chase. Police departments in Oakland, California, and Miami, Florida, aided by social scientists, instituted programs to teach officers how to defuse potentially violent police-citizen confrontations. Some departments brought back foot patrols to enable officers to get to know people in minority neighborhoods better. Even in Los Angeles, where real reform began only after the 1992 riot and the subsequent retirement of police chief Daryl Gates, widespread public outcry in the early 1980's ended the use of chokeholds.

Minority Recruitment and Police Brutality Affirmative action has increased the percentage of minority officers in police departments and reduced somewhat the level of prejudice-motivated brutality, but it has not worked miracles. Minority police officers are sometimes guilty of brutality themselves. In 1994, in Detroit, Michigan, and Compton, California, black police officers were accused by Hispanic activists of brutality against Hispanics. The Miami police officer who shot to death a black motorcyclist in 1989 was Hispanic.

Progress in Controlling Brutality Although considerable progress in decreasing police brutality was made in the 1980's, the Rodney King beating brought home the fact that brutality was still a problem in the 1990's. Three examples of events that engendered protests from 1994 and 1995 illustrate the continued existence of the problem. Protests arose in New York City in April, 1994, after a black man died in police custody; in Paterson, New Jersey, in February, 1995, after police shot a black teenager; and in Cincinnati, Ohio, in April, 1995, after a white police officer was videotaped beating an eighteen-year-old black youth.

In spite of such examples, however, many scholars see a general trend toward stricter regulation of the police use of force. They view the actions and attitudes (and what was described by an investigative commission as the "siege mentality") of the pre-1992 Los Angeles Police Department, for example, as an exception rather than the rule. Although in 1990 civil libertarians in Chicago accused the police of torturing alleged police-killer Andrew Wilson while he was in custody, torture of suspects by the police was almost certainly much less common by the mid-1990's than it had been in 1931, when the federally appointed Wickersham Commission found such "third-degree" tactics to be widespread. Between 1970 and 1984, shooting deaths of fleeing suspects, although not completely eliminated, decreased in number, and the once yawning gap in police shooting deaths between blacks and whites had appreciably narrowed.

Paul D. Mageli

Core Resources

Jerry Bornstein's concise *Police Brutality: A National Debate* (Hillside, N.J.: Enslow, 1993) contains synopses of a wide range of brutality incidents of the 1980's and early 1990's. Chapters 8, 9, and 11 of Samuel Walker's *The Police in America: An Introduction* (2d ed., New York: McGraw-Hill, 1992) connect the brutality problem to the broader issues of police discretion, accountability, and police-minority group relations. *Above the Law: Police and the Excessive Use of Force* (New York: Free Press, 1993), by Jerome H. Skolnick and James J. Fyfe, ably combines grand theory with down-to-earth examples and offers both historical and comparative perspectives (including insights from the British experience). *The New Blue Line: Police Innovation in Six American Cities* (New York: Free Press, 1986), by Jerome H. Skolnick and David H. Bayley, is enlightening on efforts to curb police brutality in Houston, Texas, and Oakland, California. In the chapter on police discretion in *Taming the System: The Control of Discretion in Criminal Justice, 1950-1990* (New York: Oxford University Press, 1993), Samuel Walker provides a brief summary of two decades of effort to regulate the police use of deadly force. *Chief: My Life in the LAPD* (New York: Bantam, 1992), by Daryl Gates, exemplifies the "us versus them" mentality to which police officers are susceptible. Another retired police chief, Anthony V. Bouza, offers a more liberal viewpoint in *The Police Mystique: An Insider's Look at Cops, Crime, and the Criminal Justice System* (New York: Plenum Press, 1990).

See also: King, Rodney, case; Los Angeles riots of 1992; Miami riots of 1980; Race riots of the twentieth century; Watts riot.

Poll tax

Poll taxes existed in the United States from the earliest colonial times. They were usually quite small and did not act to discourage many people from voting. In the years following the Civil War (1861-1865), the poll tax system was refined in the southern states for the purpose of disfranchising black voters. The tax remained small, but it had to be paid during every election in which the potential voter might have voted. This tax effectively disfranchised nearly all black voters. Because the election laws in the United States are made by state governments, a constitutional amendment was needed to do away with poll taxes. In 1964, the Twenty-fourth Amendment abolished the payment of such taxes as a condition for voting in federal elections.

Robert Jacobs

See also: Disfranchisement laws in Mississippi; Jim Crow laws; Voting Rights Act of 1965.

Poverty and race

The poverty rate measures the fraction of families who do not have sufficient income and therefore lack a decent standard of living. When a large fraction of a particular racial or ethnic group finds itself in poverty, other people often place little value in that group.

When a large proportion of a particular racial, ethnic, or other minority group is poor, the group is generally looked down on by the majority of the population. This has negative consequences for race relations and for the entire society. This reaction perpetuates poverty and leads to feelings of resentment and hostility among the impoverished minority group. Aristotle, the ancient Greek philosopher, noted in his *Politics* that "poverty is the parent of revolution and crime." The 1968 Kerner Commission Report pointed to inner-city poverty amid general affluence as a major cause of urban violence and rioting in the United States during the late 1960's.

In the early 1960's, Mollie Orshansky of the Social Security Administration developed the methodology that is used to measure poverty in the United States. Using Department of Agriculture nutritional studies, Orshansky found the minimum food requirements for households of different sizes and types. She then estimated the cost of purchasing this food. From surveys, Orshansky knew that households spent around one-third of their income on food. To derive a poverty line for a family of a particular size, Orshansky multiplied the cost of that size household's minimum food requirements by three. Each year, poverty lines are raised to reflect the increase in prices during the prior year. The poverty rate is defined as the percentage of families or individuals who fall below the poverty line. Poverty rates have been calculated for different racial groups as well as the general population.

Estimates of Minority Poverty According to U.S. Census Bureau estimates, African Americans and Hispanics are around three times more likely to be poor than non-Hispanic whites. In 1996, 11.2 percent of whites were poor, yet nearly 30 percent of African Americans and almost 30 percent of Hispanics were poor. This nearly three-to-one ratio has changed very little over time. In 1980, 10.2 percent of whites were poor, compared with 32.5 percent of blacks and 25.7 percent of Hispanics. In 1970, 9.9 percent of whites were poor, and 33.5 percent of blacks were poor; and in 1959, 18.1 percent of whites were poor, and 55.1 percent of blacks were poor.

Native Americans have experienced some of the highest poverty rates in the United States. In the late 1960's, Native Americans had poverty rates of around 74 percent. However, federal antipoverty programs directed at Native Americans cut this figure to around 25 percent by the late 1970's, about the same as for African Americans and Hispanics.

Causes of High Poverty Among Minorities Many scholars have attempted to explain why minorities have such high poverty rates. Their answers have included prejudice and discrimination in the job market, cultural or behavioral traits, single-parent families and illegitimate children, urban ghettos, a lack of adequate education or business skills, and language barriers.

Prejudice and discrimination in the labor market is one prominent explanation. Because African Americans and members of other racial minorities cannot get good jobs, they are forced to accept low-wage, menial positions. Moreover, these jobs provide little opportunity for advancement and for workers to develop skills. Many of these jobs are unstable, which means the workers often lack a source of income for part of the year. Gunnar Myrdal's groundbreaking work *An American Dilemma: The Negro Problem and Modern Democracy* (1944) blamed high rates of African American poverty on a cumulative process in which prejudice and discrimination reinforced each other. Sociologist William J. Wilson updated Myrdal's cumulative analysis by arguing that discrimination also leads to feelings of inferiority and causes African Americans to adapt in dysfunctional ways.

A second explanation focuses primarily on cultural or behavioral traits. The cultural explanation for poverty was first set forth in Louis Wirth's *The Ghetto* (1929). Wirth considered the urban mode of life too difficult for people with rural backgrounds. Therefore, when rural southern African Americans migrated to the urban North, crime and alienation became more prevalent as employment diminished. A similar thesis appears in Nicholas Lehman's *The Promised Land* (1991).

A common view in the early twentieth century was that high rates of African American poverty were caused by the numerous single-parent families and large numbers of illegitimate children, which were usually blamed on African American racial characteristics. Edward Frazier's *The Negro Family in the United States* (1939) countered this view and argued that the overall status of the black family was shaped by prevailing economic and social conditions. Slavery destroyed African cultural patterns, and emancipation maintained the matriarchal system that developed under slavery. The migration of African Americans to the North further undermined communal institutions and community pressure that helped keep African American families intact.

Racial prejudice and discrimination have historically consigned poorly paying menial jobs to members of racial minorities, particularly African Americans. *(Library of Congress)*

More recent work has focused on the problem of African Americans living in urban ghettos. Wilson blames this problem partly on historical discrimination. However, the real blame, according to Wilson, lies with economics and demographics. When the U.S. economy shifted from manufacturing to services, it produced high unemployment rates in urban cities. This exacerbated the problems generated by the flow of African American migrants from the rural South and the rapid growth of young minorities in central cities. Sociologist John Kasarda, likewise, sees the decline of manufacturing and the rise of the service economy as causing the poverty of urban blacks. However, he notes another aspect to the problem: African Americans are less likely to move to areas experiencing job growth. In part, he says, this is caused by racial discrimination, which keeps African Americans from moving to the suburbs, and in part, it is because African Americans lack the skills and education required by the new service jobs.

Since the Coleman Report (1966) documented racial segregation in American schools and proclaimed that education in the United States was separate but unequal, differences in the quality of education have figured prominently in explanations of why racial minorities are more likely to be poor. If minority children receive a poor education, they are unlikely to leave school with the skills needed for high-paying jobs.

Another problem facing racial minorities is their lack of business experience and management skills. They also lack access to capital, making it hard for them to start their own businesses. Another problem is that businesses catering to racial minorities are less likely to be successful and make money when they cater primarily to low-income individuals.

Many Hispanics face additional problems involving language and culture. The inability to speak English well reduces some Hispanics' ability to get jobs and receive a decent education. Cultural differences make some Hispanics critical and distrustful of the values and interests of the dominant culture in the United States and suspicious of social institutions such as the government and schools. Their differences have led to discrimination against them in the job market. Native Americans, like Hispanics, have some cultural differences that may reduce their ability to obtain high-paying positions.

Policy Solutions There are probably as many suggestions for reducing the racial disparity in poverty as there are theories of why minority racial groups are more likely to be poor. Many scholars have looked to desegregation in education as a means of improving the incomes of minorities and thereby reducing their high poverty rates.

Another approach has focused on labor market policies to increase the wages of minorities, to help minorities get better or higher-paying jobs, and to improve the job training that they receive both before and after employment. This approach has supported affirmative action as a means of combating discrimination in the labor market. It has also supported raising the minimum wage so that those with jobs are more likely to earn wages above the poverty line.

A third approach has been to work on developing minority businesses and to teach minorities entrepreneurial skills. Another approach has focused on spurring economic growth, assuming that growth will lead to more jobs and higher incomes. Finally, beginning in the 1970's, a great deal of debate arose over government welfare programs and whether they can be made an effective antipoverty tool. Some experts argue that government benefits reduce work incentives and hurt the very people they are intended to help.

Others argue that government benefits have always been inadequate to bring families above the poverty line.

Steven Pressman

Core Resources

Mollie Orshansky's "Consumption, Work, and Poverty," in *Poverty as a Public Issue*, edited by Ben B. Seligman (New York: Free Press, 1965), explains how poverty is calculated in the United States. Poverty data can be found at the Census Bureau's Web site (www.census.gov). The Coleman Report, *Equality of Educational Opportunity* (Washington, D.C.: Government Printing Office, 1966), documents the separate and unequal education received by black and white children. Edward Frazier's *The Negro Family in the United States* (Chicago: University of Chicago Press, 1939) is a classic early study of African American poverty. *The New Urban Reality*, edited by Paul Peterson (Washington, D.C.: Brookings Institution, 1985), is one of the best contemporary studies of the causes of African American poverty and contains important articles by Kasarda and Wilson. *Inequality at Work: Hispanics in the U.S. Labor Force*, by Gregory DeFreitas (New York: Oxford University Press, 1991), provides a good description of the Hispanic poverty problem. *American Indians and Federal Aid*, by Alan Sorkin (Washington, D.C.: Brookings Institution, 1971), presents a great deal of information on Native American poverty, although some of it is a bit outdated. A more recent analysis is contained in Matthew Snipp and Gene Summers's "American Indians and Economic Poverty," in *Rural Poverty in America*, edited by Cynthia Duncan (New York: Auburn House, 1992). For additional information on antipoverty policies, see the collection *Fighting Poverty: What Works and What Doesn't*, edited by Sheldon Danziger and Daniel Weinberg (Cambridge, Mass.: Harvard University Press, 1986). The *Encyclopedia of Political Economy*, edited by Phil O'Hara et al. (New York: Routledge, 1998), contains several excellent introductory essays on race that are connected to the question of why certain groups of people are poor.

See also: Discrimination: racial and ethnic; Economics and race; Employment among African Americans; Welfare reform: impact on racial/ethnic relations.

President's Committee on Civil Rights

Like many white people of his time, U.S. president Harry S Truman inherited the racial attitudes of his southern ancestors. He attended segregated schools in Missouri and regarded segregation as normal and desirable. He used what people today consider offensive racial language and once claimed that blacks belonged in Africa, not America. Yet when he became president in 1945, Truman rose above his racist heritage and responded to African American demands. As a successful politician, he had learned to work with African American political groups and to understand the necessity of serving all his constituents. He disliked social mixing among people of different races, but he believed that African American people had the right to equality under the law and deserved equal opportunity.

At the end of World War II, racial tension rose as African Americans tried to cement economic and social gains they had made during the war. Racial violence increased. For example, in February, 1946, a South Carolina policeman blinded an African American veteran still in uniform, and in July, two more veterans were killed in Monroe, Georgia. In addition to domestic racial problems, the Cold War was beginning to destroy the wartime alliance between the United States and the Soviet Union. The two superpowers began to divide the world between them and to compete for the allegiance of Asian and African peoples. Truman, recognizing the negative image presented by American segregation, said, "The top dog in a world which is 90 percent colored ought to clean his own house."

On December 5, 1946, Truman issued Executive Order 9008 to create the President's Committee on Civil Rights and filled the fifteen-member committee with prominent Americans who were sympathetic to civil rights. It was a high-profile committee that included important businessmen, educators, labor leaders, and members of the African American community. On October 29, 1947, in a document entitled *To Secure These Rights*, the committee recommended establishment of a civil rights division in the Department of Justice, a commission on civil rights, and a fair employment practices committee. It urged Congress to strengthen existing civil rights statutes, pass an antilynching law, and provide new protection for voting rights. To move toward desegregation, the committee said, the government must discontinue federal funding to private and public bodies that practiced discrimination, prohibit discrimination in private employment and in health services, and seek court action to end restrictive covenants in housing.

These recommendations established the civil rights platform for Truman and his successors. In 1948, Truman issued Executive Order 9980 to forbid discrimination in federal government employment and Executive Order 9981 to integrate the armed forces. Under Truman's direction, the Justice Department entered *amici curiae* briefs in court cases to back the National Association for the Advancement of Colored People (NAACP) and others in their assaults on the legal edifice that supported segregation. It took many years before the vision expressed in *To Secure These Rights* started to become reality, but the report moved civil rights to the forefront of the national reform agenda.

William E. Pemberton

See also: Desegregation: defense; Discrimination: racial and ethnic; Military desegregation; Race riots of 1943.

Proposition 209

Proposition 209, the California Civil Rights Initiative (CCRI), was a measure to amend the California state constitution that appeared before California voters on the November, 1996, election ballot. Proposition 209 proposed that the state should "not discriminate against, or grant preferential treatment to, any individual or group on the basis of race, sex, color, ethnicity, or national origin in the operation of public employment, public education, or public contracting." This proposal did not affect preferential treatment practices of private firms or private educational institutions in the state.

In the weeks leading up to the election, a heated public debate developed over the CCRI. Ward Connerly, a black businessman from Sacramento who led the campaign for the CCRI, and other supporters claimed that the measure's intent in prohibiting discrimination and preferential treatment was in accord with the desires of those involved in the Civil Rights movement of the 1960's to create a society in which everyone, regardless of gender or skin color, would be guaranteed equal treatment under the law. The opposition to Proposition 209 included a wide variety of organizations, such as the state chapters of the National Association for the Advancement of Colored People and the American Civil Liberties Union (ACLU). Opponents argued that the CCRI was a deceptive measure whose true intent was not revealed by its language. As they saw it, although Proposition 209 did not explicitly mention the words "affirmative action," the purpose of the proposition was not to end discrimination or preferential treatment but rather to end state-supported affirmative action programs in California. This, they argued, would actually lead to increased, rather than decreased, discrimination against women and African American, Latino, and other California minorities, and cause setbacks in the educational and employment gains achieved by these groups as a result of affirmative action programs.

On election day, Proposition 209 passed by a vote of 54 percent to 46 percent. It was immediately challenged in the California courts, and an injunction was issued against its enforcement. Those who challenged the CCRI argued that it violated the equal protection clause of the Fourteenth Amendment by denying some groups, namely women and racial minorities, preferential treatment but not denying it to other groups, such as military veterans. In April, 1997, the U.S. Court of Appeals affirmed the constitutionality of the CCRI, and the injunction against the CCRI was lifted in August, 1997. In a "Save the Dream" march led by the Reverend Jesse Jackson, thousands rallied in the streets of San Francisco to protest the lifting of the injunction. Although the ACLU attempted to take the appellate court decision to the Supreme Court, toward the end of 1997, the Court declined to review the measure. Pete Wilson, the governor of California and a supporter of Proposition 209, took a major step toward implementing it in March, 1998, by officially ending the enforcement of preferential treatment for firms owned by women or minorities engaged in state contracting.

By mid-1998, the full impact of Proposition 209 had yet to be determined. At the University of California, Berkeley, for example, the number of African American and Latino students accepted for admission in the entering class of spring, 1998, declined by more than 50 percent, while the proportion of white and Asian American students accepted for admission rose. These changes followed decreases in the preceding year in African American and Latino admissions to the University of California law and business schools. To what extent these declines in minority enrollments were the direct result of the passage of Proposition 209 and to what extent they were brought about by the implementation of a 1995 decision by the University of California Board of Regents to discontinue gender and racial preferences in admissions is difficult to determine.

Diane P. Michelfelder

See also: Affirmative action; College admissions; Education and African Americans.

Proslavery argument

The proslavery argument served as an intellectual bond among Southerners who saw slavery as a moral institution.

In the quarter-century preceding the Civil War, Southerners advanced a wide range of arguments and theories—some old, some new—to justify the institution of chattel slavery. The distinctiveness of proslavery thinking during the years before the Civil War lay less in its content than in its tone or spirit. Defenders of the South's "peculiar institution" were no longer on the defensive; their mood was no longer apologetic. Unlike most of their predecessors, they did not merely tolerate slavery; they defined it as a moral institution and many glorified it. They took the offensive on behalf of slavery partly in response to the attacks of Northern abolitionists. Perhaps the primary objective of their aggressive proslavery campaign was to dispel the doubts of Southerners as to the justice of slavery and to offer compelling proof to nonslaveholders and slaveholders alike that slavery found sanction in religion, science, and morality, forming an essential part of a civilized economic and political order.

A southern U.S. senator once justified slavery by arguing that African Americans were the "mud-sill of society"—an inferior class of human beings, but one "eminently qualified in temper, in vigor, in docility" to work in a difficult climate. *(Library of Congress)*

Post-1830 proslavery discourse borrowed from a variety of sources, many of which had been used before immediate abolitionism posed a new threat to slavery. Proslavery apologists pointed to the existence of slavery in biblical times and throughout most of history, as well as to the notion of entailment, which blamed the introduction of slavery on the British and predicted social catastrophe should slavery be abolished. These arguments continued to dominate the thinking of most proslavery writers in the 1830's, as evidenced, for example, in Thomas R. Dew's *Review of the Debate in the Virginia Legislature of 1831 and 1832.* Although this was once treated as the first work of the new proslavery discourse, later historians have seen it as the culmination of the earlier, less affirmative phase of proslavery writing in the South. Dew's work, which was widely read, asserted that slavery was a preferred way of compelling efficient labor in the hot states of the lower South, the harbinger of the notions of perpetual slavery developed by later Southern apologists.

The Response to Garrison Traditionally, historians have understood post-1830 pro-slavery as a reaction to the publication of William Lloyd Garrison's journal *The Liberator* (1831-1865), which marks the onset of immediate abolitionism, and the fear spawned by Nat Turner's slave rebellion in Southampton County, Virginia. Both events occurred in 1831, but other issues intensified proslavery writing and abolitionist discourse during the 1830's.

Proslavery polemics seem to have escalated along a continuum, rather than suddenly appearing after 1831. Two interrelated themes characterized this escalation of Southern proslavery. The first was a reaction to the abolitionist mail campaign of 1835, in which Northern abolitionists attempted to flood the South with literature arguing that slavery was immoral. In response, Southern ministers and denominations took the lead in denouncing the moral foundations of abolitionists. Virulent anti-abolitionism became a major feature, perhaps the single constant, in Southern proslavery. Southerners denounced abolitionism as incendiary, a wanton and dangerous interference with Southern safety. Southerners construed abolitionists as intent upon fomenting rebellion among Southern slaves, and were also infuriated by the "Gag Rule" in Congress, which persuaded Northerners that Southerners would trample on the First Amendment or any other right to preserve slavery.

The second theme involved a defense of slavery more ideological in tone, which blended biblical literalism with conservative social theories, some of which were quite popular among New England Federalists during the early nineteenth century. This strain of thinking challenged industrial economics and modern reform movements, asserting that a stratified social order produced the best society possible. A heavy lace of paternal imagery, which threaded together honor and social responsibility, gave ornamentation to this new proslavery fabric. In the hands of John C. Calhoun, this two-pronged argument proved that slavery was not an evil, as the abolitionists claimed, but "a good—a positive good," "a great blessing to both races," and "the great stay of the Union and our free institutions, and one of the main sources of the unbounded prosperity of the whole."

Typical of thinkers who championed this phase of proslavery writing was Thornton Stringfellow, a Baptist minister of Culpepper County, Virginia, whose *Brief Examination of Scripture Testimony on the Institution of Slavery* argued that slavery enjoyed "the sanction of the Almighty in the Patriarchal Age . . . that its legality was recognized . . . by Jesus Christ in his kingdom; and that it is full of mercy." Godly Southerners, Stringfellow maintained, should withdraw from abolitionists, whose moral notions must originate from some other source than the Bible. In a speech before the U.S. Senate in 1858, James Henry Hammond of South Carolina held that African American slaves provided the "mud-sill" of society, whose labor was necessary but whose mean estate made essential their exclusion from the political process. Slavery was essential to free "that other class which leads progress, civilization and refinement" for more enlightened endeavors. Fortunately, the senator observed, the South had found African Americans perfectly adapted to serve as the "very mud-sill of society and of political government," "a race inferior to her own, but eminently qualified in temper, in vigor, in docility, in capacity to stand the climate, to answer all her purposes."

The Prewar Era During the 1850's, other Southern writers embraced more extreme proslavery theories, although these attracted more interest from historians in the twentieth century than from nineteenth century advocates. Henry Hughes, of Port Gibson, Mississippi, drew upon the infant discipline of sociology to buttress his proslavery views. He described slavery as "Ethical Warranteeism," in which the slave labored for a master in return for food, clothing, and shelter. Josiah Nott, of Mobile, Alabama, embraced the theory of polygenesis, holding in *Types of Mankind* that African Americans resulted from a separate creation and were not *Homo sapiens.* Others compared Southern slavery with free labor in the North. In *Sociology of the South* (1854) and *Cannibals All!* (1857), for example, Virginian George Fitzhugh suggested that the Northern states would have to adopt some form of slavery to control the immigrant working classes, or else face moral and social chaos. Free labor, he asserted, produced class warfare in the North, while slavery permitted social harmony in the South. Southern masters had moral obligations toward, and were predisposed to kind treatment of, their slaves; Northern factory owners discarded their laborers at whim.

Most Southerners adhered to the less extreme argument based on the Bible and Plato. The proslavery argument became a justification for the entire Southern way of life, whose culture, social structure, and economy were believed to depend upon the institution of slavery. Its ubiquity helped bind Southerners together and produced the remarkable degree of unity among them in the days following the election of Abraham Lincoln in 1860 and his call for troops in April, 1861. Undoubtedly, the intensity and unanimity with which Southerners defended slavery had much to do with the fact that they had come to identify the system of slavery with Southern society as a whole and with their place in the Union.

Anne C. Loveland, updated by Edward R. Crowther

Core Resources

William S. Jenkins's *Pro-Slavery Thought in the Old South* (Chapel Hill: University of North Carolina Press, 1935), the oldest monograph on proslavery thinking, remains a useful starting point. Drew Glipin Faust's *The Ideology of Slavery: Proslavery Thought in the Antebellum South, 1830-1860* (Baton Rouge: Louisiana State University Press, 1981) is an excellent anthology of proslavery writing augmented by a thoughtful introductory essay. William W. Freehling's *The Road to Disunion: Secessionists at Bay, 1776-1854* (New York: Oxford University Press, 1990) shows the complex uses Southerners made of proslavery thinking and why a degree of intellectual unity was vital in a South divided against itself. Larry E. Tise's *Proslavery: A History of the Defense of Slavery in America, 1701-1840* (Athens: University of Georgia Press, 1987) shows that proslavery thinking existed in both Northern and Southern states.

See also: Abolition; Bleeding Kansas; Compromise of 1850; Fugitive slave laws; Kansas-Nebraska Act; *Liberator, The;* Lincoln-Douglas debates; Missouri Compromise; *Scott v. Sandford*; Turner's slave insurrection.

Psychology of racism

Students of racism examine the phenomenon of negative attitudes and behavior by members of the majority toward those who belong to racial and ethnic minorities. The topic of racism, which straddles the boundaries between social psychology and sociology, is connected with the study of intergroup relations, cognition, and attitudes in general.

The social and psychological study of prejudice and discrimination, including prejudice and discrimination against African Americans, has a long history; the term "racism," however, did not enter the language of social psychology until the publication of the Kerner Report of 1968, which blamed all-pervasive "white racism" for widespread black rioting in American cities. Although usually applied to black-white relations in the United States, the term is also sometimes used with regard to white Americans' relations with other minority groups such as Asian Americans or Latinos, or to black-white relations outside the United States, for example, in Britain, Canada, or South Africa. Most of the studies and research on racism, however, have focused on white racism against blacks in the United States.

The Causes of Racism Racism is seen by many social psychologists not as mere hatred but as a deep-rooted habit that is hard to change; hence, subvarieties of racism are distinguished. Psychoanalyst Joel Kovel, in his book *White Racism: A Psychohistory* (1970), distinguishes between dominative racism, the desire to oppress blacks, and aversive racism, the desire to avoid contact with blacks. Aversive racism, Samuel L. Gaertner and John Dovidio find, exists among those whites who pride themselves on being unprejudiced. David O. Sears, looking at whites' voting behavior and their political opinions as expressed in survey responses, finds what he calls symbolic racism: a resentment of African Americans for making demands in the political realm that supposedly violate traditional American values. Social psychologist James M. Jones distinguishes three types of racism: individual racism, the prejudice and antiblack behavior deliberately manifested by individual whites; institutional racism, the social, economic, and political patterns that impersonally oppress blacks regardless of the prejudice or lack thereof of individuals; and cultural racism, the tendency of whites to ignore or denigrate the special characteristics of black culture.

Where Dovidio and Gaertner find aversive racism, Irwin Katz finds ambivalence. Many whites, he argues, simultaneously see African Americans as disadvantaged (which creates sympathy) and as deviating from mainstream social norms (which creates antipathy). Such ambivalence, Katz contends, leads to exaggeratedly negative reactions to negative behaviors by an African American, but also to exaggeratedly positive reactions to positive behaviors by an African American. He calls this phenomenon ambivalence-induced behavior amplification.

The reasons suggested for individual racism are many. John Dollard and others, in *Frustration and Aggression* (1939), see prejudice as the scapegoating of minorities in order to provide a release for aggression in the face of frustration; in this view, outbursts of bigotry are a natural response to hard economic times. Muzafer and Carolyn Sherif, in *Groups in Harmony and Tension* (1953) and later works, see prejudice of all sorts as the result of competition between groups. Theodor Adorno and others, in *The Authoritarian Personality* (1950), view prejudice, whether directed against blacks or against Jews, as reflective of a supposedly fascist type of personality produced by authoritarian child-rearing practices. In *Racially Separate or Together?* (1971), Thomas F. Pettigrew shows that discriminatory behavior toward blacks, and the verbal expression of prejudices against them, can sometimes flow simply from a white person's desire to fit in with his or her social group. Finally, both prejudice and discrimination, many psychologists argue, are rooted in those human cognitive processes involved in the formation of stereotypes.

Stereotyping Stereotypes are ideas, often rigidly held, concerning members of a group to which one does not belong. Social psychologists who follow the cognitive approach to the study of racism, such as David L. Hamilton, Walter G. Stephan, and Myron Rothbart, argue that racial stereotyping (the tendency of whites to see blacks in some roles and not in others) arises, like any other kind of stereotyping, from the need of every human being to create some sort of order out of his or her perceptions of the world. Although stereotypes are not entirely impervious to revision or even shattering in the face of disconfirming instances, information related to a stereotype is more efficiently retained than information unrelated to it. Whites, it has been found, tend to judge blacks to be more homogeneous than they really are, while being more aware of differences within their own group: This is called the out-group homogeneity hypothesis. Whites who are guided by stereotypes may act in such a way as to bring out worse behavior in blacks than would otherwise occur, thus creating a self-fulfilling prophecy.

Why is stereotypical thinking on the part of whites about African Americans so hard to eliminate? The history of race relations deserves some of the blame. Some mistakes in reasoning common to the tolerant and the intolerant alike, such as the tendency to remember spectacular events and to think of them as occurring more frequently than is really the case (the availability heuristic), also occur in whites' judgments about members of minority groups. In addition, the social and occupational roles one fills may reinforce stereotypical thinking.

Pettigrew contends that attribution errors in explaining the behavior of others may have an important role to play in reinforcing racial stereotypes. The same behavioral act, Pettigrew argues, is interpreted differently by whites depending on the race of the actor. A positive act by a black person might be ascribed to situational characteristics (for example, luck, affirmative action programs, or other circumstances beyond one's control) and thus discounted; a positive act by a white person might be ascribed to personality characteristics. Similarly, a negative act might be ascribed to situational characteristics in the case of a white person, but to personality characteristics in the case of a black person. The tendency of whites to view the greater extent of poverty among blacks as solely the result of lack of motivation can be seen as a form of attribution error.

The Study of Racism and Prejudice Although the study of racism per se began with the racial crisis of the 1960's, the study of prejudice in general goes back much further; as early as the 1920's, Emory Bogardus constructed a social distance scale measuring the degree of intimacy members of different racial and ethnic groups were willing to tolerate with one another. At first, psychologists tended to seek the roots of prejudice in the emotional makeup of the prejudiced individual rather than in the structure of society or the general patterns of human cognition. For many years, the study of antiblack prejudice was subsumed under the study of prejudice in general; those biased against blacks were thought to be biased against other groups such as Jews, as well.

In the years immediately following World War II, American social psychologists were optimistic about the possibilities for reducing or even eliminating racial and ethnic prejudices. Adorno's *The Authoritarian Personality* and *The Nature of Prejudice* (1954), by Gordon Allport, reflect the climate of opinion of the time. Allport, whose view of prejudice represented a mixture of the psychoanalytic and cognitive approaches, used the term "racism" to signify the doctrines preached by negrophobe political demagogues; he did not see it as a deeply ingrained bad habit pervading the entire society. Pettigrew, who wrote about antiblack prejudice from the late 1950's on, cast doubt on the notion that there was a specific type of personality or pattern of child rearing associated with prejudice. Nevertheless, he long remained in the optimistic tradition, arguing that changing white people's discriminatory behavior through the enactment of civil rights laws would ultimately change their prejudiced attitudes.

The more frequent use by social psychologists of the term "racism" from the late 1960's onward indicates a growing awareness that bias against blacks, a visible minority, might be harder to uproot than that directed against religious and ethnic minorities. Social psychologists studying racial prejudice shifted their research interest from the open and noisy bigotry most often found among political extremists (for example, the Ku Klux Klan) to the quiet, everyday prejudices of the average apolitical individual. Racial bias against blacks came to be seen as a central, rather than a peripheral, feature of American life.

Responses to surveys taken from the 1940's to the end of the 1970's indicated a steady decline in the percentage of white Americans willing to admit holding racist views. Yet in the 1970's, the sometimes violent white hostility to school busing for integration, and the continuing social and economic gap between black and white America, gave social psychologists reason to temper their earlier optimism. The contact hypothesis, the notion that contact between different racial groups would reduce prejudice, was subjected to greater skepticism and ever more careful qualification. Janet Ward Schofield, in her field study of a desegregated junior high school, detected a persistence of racial divisions among the pupils; reviewing a number of such studies, Walter Stephan similarly discerned a tendency toward increased interracial tension in schools following desegregation. The pessimism suggested by field studies among younger teenagers was confirmed by experiments conducted in the 1970's and 1980's on college students and adults; such studies demonstrated the existence even among supposedly nonprejudiced people of subtle racism and racial stereotyping.

Yet while social psychological experiments contribute to an understanding of the reasons for negative attitudes toward blacks by whites, and for discriminatory behavior toward blacks even by those whites who believe themselves to be tolerant, they do not by any means provide the complete answer to the riddle of racial prejudice and discrimination. Unlike many other topics in social psychology, racism has also been investigated by journalists, historians, economists, sociologists, political scientists, legal scholars, and even literary critics. The techniques of social psychology surveys, controlled experiments, and field studies provide only one window on this phenomenon.

Paul D. Mageli

Core Resources

Gordon W. Allport's *The Nature of Prejudice* (Cambridge, Mass.: Addison-Wesley, 1954) contains one of the earliest expositions of the contact hypothesis and one of the earliest treatments of the relationship between prejudice and stereotyping. *Prejudice, Discrimination, and Racism* (Orlando, Fla.: Academic Press, 1986), edited by John F. Dovidio and Samuel L. Gaertner, collects essays on aversive racism, racial ambivalence, stereotyping, symbolic racism, and cultural racism. Irwin Katz's *Stigma: A Social Psychological Analysis* (Hillsdale, N.J.: Lawrence Erlbaum, 1981) reports on subjects' reactions to both blacks and people with physical disabilities and develops the notion of ambivalence-induced behavior amplification. *Towards the Elimination of Racism* (New York: Pergamon Press, 1976), edited by Phyllis A. Katz, contains particularly good essays on racism in small children, psychological approaches to intergroup conflict, aversive racism experiments, and opposition to racial reform. *Prejudice*, by Thomas F. Pettigrew, George M. Frederickson, Dale T. Knobel, Nathan Glazer, and Reed Ueda (Cambridge, Mass.: The Belknap Press of Harvard University Press, 1982), presents a concise and clearly written review of the social psychological literature on prejudice and racism up to 1980. Walter G. Stephan and David Rosenfield's "Racial and Ethnic Stereotypes," in *In the Eye of the Beholder: Contemporary Issues in Stereotyping*, edited by Arthur G. Miller (New York: Praeger, 1982), is a good critical review of the social psychological literature on whites' and blacks' stereotyping of each other.

See also: Friendships, interracial/interethnic; Ideological racism; Individual racism; Racism: history of the concept; Symbolic racism.

Quotas

A "quota" is a minimum or maximum number allowable, such as the ceiling on the number of automobiles that Japanese manufacturers once agreed to export to the U.S. market. In ethnic and race relations in the United States, the term has acquired an odious reputation as a means to limit the selection of meritorious persons in personnel matters.

After World War II, many well-trained Jewish high school students applied for college with test scores so high that they were fully qualified for admission to the very best colleges. Parents of alumni from those same colleges, finding the competition exceedingly difficult for their children, pressured the colleges to establish quotas in order to limit the number of Jews admitted. These quotas were later rescinded under pressure from many quarters. However, in the 1980's, when well-qualified Asian students achieved very high test scores for admission to colleges in California, a similar informal quota system was established, only to be abolished when word leaked out that academic standards were being compromised.

In the 1970's, with the advent of affirmative action, federal enforcement agencies began to insist that employers work toward desegregating the workforce by becoming aware of the percentage of qualified workers of each race for each job category. Employers were asked to establish the goal of having their businesses ultimately mirror the hiring patterns of the labor market as a whole, based on such labor market surveys as are found in the decennial census. Timetables for accomplishing this desegregation were to be based on turnover statistics and estimates of business expansion. Federal agencies also encouraged educational institutions to follow the same process of establishing goals and timetables in admissions.

Although federal guidelines insisted that goals and timetables were not quotas, in practice employers and educational institutions implemented affirmative action in such a way that quotas resulted, infuriating qualified white job seekers and college aspirants. Litigation resulted, culminating in the definitive *Regents of the University of California v. Bakke* (1978), in which the Supreme Court of the United States declared quotas, unless rationally based, to be unconstitutional. Even though Congress adopted a provision of the Public Works Employment Act that set aside 10 percent of all federal construction contracts for minority firms, the Supreme Court struck down the concept of a rigid quota in *Adarand Constructors v. Peña* (1995), holding that strict scrutiny must be applied to all race-conscious decision making, even that undertaken by Congress, and therefore a rational basis must be demonstrated in selecting 10 percent rather than some other figure.

In the late 1990's, affirmative action quotas were allowable when there was a logical basis. If specific harm to an ethnic or racial group is demonstrable, a court-approved remedy involving a quota must be tailored to the precise quantitative extent of that harm.

Michael Haas

See also: *Adarand Constructors v. Peña*; Affirmative action; *Bakke* case; Censuses, U.S.; College admissions; Set-asides.

Race as a concept

Eighteenth century racial concepts, with little if any scientific basis, molded modern racial classification and gave rise to stereotypes of superior and inferior peoples. Distortions of Charles Darwin's theory of evolution were used to justify imperialism as well as genocide. Today, ethnicity, not race, is used in understanding the complex phenomenon of human variation.

Although human societies from earliest times were aware of differences between themselves and other societies, the concept of race is a relatively modern construct, first developed in the late eighteenth century. The ancient Greeks had no word even remotely resembling race. Aristotle's classification system of Genus, Species, Difference, Property, Accident (which helped earn him the title of father of biology) contributed to the founding of racial classification systems. Aristotle himself believed that climate caused physical differences in humans. Like other ancient Greeks, he also believed in slavery. However, for Aristotle, slavery was a matter of virtue, not race. The most virtuous had leisure time for active involvement in politics.

Medieval and Early Modern Concepts The Middle Ages in Europe was a land-locked age, with little reason to speculate on race. Yet, much ethnocentrism existed. Prussians, Irish, Lombards, and a host of others were portrayed in unflattering ways. By 1100 and the era of the Crusades, particularly venomous language was used to describe the followers of Islam. Jews also were subject to verbal and physical attacks, increasing with a vengeance after the bubonic plague epidemic in 1348. Yet when the word "race" was used in the Middle Ages, it was to refer to the pure lineage of some noble family. Racial theory itself did not emerge in the Middle Ages.

The age of exploration opened Europeans to a world of other human types, causing a debate about whether Indians and black Africans were men or beasts. The famous chemist and physician, Paracelsus, described Europeans as children of Adam, and found blacks and other races to have separate origins. Such separate origin theories were cut short when the papacy, in the mid-sixteenth century, condemned the separate origin of humanity theory as heretical. In 1565, French historian and political theorist Jean Bodin divided the world into Scythian, German, African, and Middler, according to skin color and basic body features. Bodin's primitive classification scheme was still far more advanced than that of Cambridge historian Raphael Holinshed, who wrote in 1578 about races of giants as well as races devoted to sorcery and witchcraft. During the age of the Counter-Reformation and witch-hunting (1550-1650), references to evil races grew, and at least in popular literature, black became viewed as a sign of the devil. With the beginning of the scientific revolution, classification became more in line with Bodin's schema. In 1684, François Bernier described four human races: European, Asian, African, and Lapp.

Racial Taxonomies The term "race" was first used to classify humanity in 1775, when Johann Friedrich Blumenbach, a German professor of medicine, created a taxonomy dividing humanity into five separate races: Caucasian, Mongolian, American, African, and Malay. Each was described in terms of skin color, cranial size and shape, and other physical characteristics. Blumenbach used the term Caucasian for European, and he believed that the most beautiful people in the world lived in the Caucasus region. Devoting much attention to skull size, Blumenbach founded what would later be the pseudoscience of craniology and phrenology. In his classification system, Blumenbach built on the earlier work of Swedish botanist Linnaeus (Carl von Linné). In his *Systema Naturae* (1758), Linnaeus divided humans into four groups defined by skin color, personality, and moral traits. Hence Europeans were "fair, gentle, acute, and inventive," while Asiatics were "haughty and covetous." Although Blumenbach and Linnaeus were early scientists, writing long before evolution or genetics were concepts, their classification systems became firmly embedded in scientific taxonomies and accepted as gospel in the public mind—despite the fact that Blumenbach used "race" as a convenient label and nothing more.

Blumenbach and Linnaeus were writing during the Enlightenment, when philosophers, historians, and political scientists were also toying with human classification themes. In 1749, the Count de Buffon defined six separate groupings of men, viewing all other races as variations of what he termed the "White Race." In 1775, the famous philosopher Immanuel Kant defined four races—Hunnic, White, Negro, Hindu—but viewed all races as having a common origin. Yet ten years later, Kant was further speculating about special powers of each race that could be evoked or suppressed as new conditions demanded.

Romantic Pseudoscientific Concept Enlightenment thought generally dealt with universals. As a whole, the eighteenth century racial theorists viewed humanity as one distinct species. Their taxonomies were subdivisions of related peoples. It was the nineteenth century Romantics, with their stress on the unique and particular, who transformed taxonomies of race into vitriolic concepts of racism.

Johann Fichte (1762-1814), a student of Kant, argued that Germans inherited superior biological qualities through their blood. Fichte believed that these blood characteristics destined Germany to produce a nation unsurpassed in moral and social order. Similarly Johann Gottfried von Herder (1744-1803) pointed to different races having different inner qualities, and historian Barthold Niebuhr in his *History of Rome* (1828) viewed the German tribes as being powerful enough to conquer Rome because they, unlike the Romans, had maintained their racial purity. German racial concepts also influenced contemporaneous English and American thought. In 1850, English historian Robert Knox published a series of lectures entitled *The Races of Man,* in which he attempted to show that all scientific and cultural advances, and even civilization itself, were a manifestation of race. Similarly, American historian William H. Prescott extolled the Anglo-Saxon virtues that shaped the American character, and Francis Parkman praised the German race for its masculine qualities.

Many nineteenth century scientists joined the Romantics in identifying culture with race. Georges Cuvier, a leading French zoologist, argued that Caucasians created the highest civilization and, by right, dominated all others. For him, Mongolian peoples could only create static empires, and blacks remained in a state of barbarism. Cuvier introduced the concept of "fixity of type" to explain why different races were predestined to follow different developmental paths. In *Natural History of the Human Species* (1848), Charles H. Smith, an anatomist and a friend of Cuvier, classified three racial types based on the size of the brain. In the United States, Samuel George Morton collected hundreds of skulls and poured mustard seeds into each skull to calculate the skull's volume. He called this new science craniometry and published his conclusions in the influential *Crania Americana* (1839), which listed brain capacity from most (Caucasian) to least (black), with Amer-Indians falling somewhere in between.

The most powerful pre-Darwinistic racial theorist was Joseph-Arthur de Gobineau, called the father of racist ideology because of his stress on the inferiority and superiority of certain races. His *Essay on the Inequality of the Human Races,* published between 1853 and 1855, stressed that the races were physically, mentally, and morally different. For him, the white race was unsurpassed in beauty, intelligence, and strength. It was a natural aristocracy. Of the peoples in the white race, he found the Aryan to be the most advanced, and the German to be the foremost developed of the Aryans. Gobineau, interested also in the decline of civilizations, found race mixing to be a major cause. It is not surprising that the young Adolf Hitler found Gobineau fascinating.

Darwinism and Race The advent of Charles Darwin's theory of evolution in 1859 shattered old racial concepts but opened the way for new ones. Darwin viewed all humans as belonging to the same species and had little to say about race except that all species change over time and that human subspecies had crossed repeatedly. If anything, he found that the similarities among humans far outweighed any differences.

However, the social and racial Darwinists who adapted Darwin's ideas had a lot to say. Francis Galton, a cousin of Darwin, coined the term "eugenics." He concluded that there are grades of races and grades of humans in each race. By 1883, Galton was popularizing the idea that social agencies were responsible for improving the racial qualities of future generations.

The Herculean mind of Herbert Spencer used evolution, natural selection, and survival of the fittest to explain practically everything in the universe, including race. In his travels he viewed Papuans, Australian aborigines, and African tribesmen, all of whom were classified as primitive, childlike, and of little intelligence. Spencer had a tremendous impact on other scholars and on the educated public. By the end of the century, Rudyard Kipling would write his famous poem "The White Man's Burden," classifying colonial peoples as "half-devil and half-child."

Another famous Darwinist was Henrik Hackle, who traced life from an organic broth in the oceans to the emergence of humankind. In his *Riddle of the Universe* (1899), Hackle found racial differences to be of paramount importance. He found "lower" races such as the Hottentots destined for extinction, while Negroes were labeled as incapable of higher mental thoughts. Hackle taught at the University of Jena. One of his students, Joseph Chamberlain, was destined to be British Secretary of State for Colonies.

A powerful writer, Chamberlain synthesized nineteenth century trends in his works on race. He found race to be everything; the germ of the culture, art, and genius of a people ran in its blood. Therefore, any race that al-

British naturalist Charles Darwin (1809-1882) developed a scientific theory of evolution that others distorted to support their own pseudoscientific theories about race. *(Library of Congress)*

lowed its blood to be mixed with that of others was destined to fall. In his own time, Chamberlain saw a major battle taking place between Teutons and Jews. However, the awakening of the Teutonic spirit in this battle was a great turning point in history that would lead to a new Europe and a new future world order. Hitler honored Chamberlain as a great world thinker and acted on many of his conclusions. The carnage that resulted made overt racial concepts unfashionable in the post-1945 world.

Counterattack Against Racial Classification Racial taxonomies should have been greeted with skepticism from the beginning. Scientist Chevalier Lamarck had shown that species change over time as their living environments change; however, the implications of his conclusions were ignored. The noted anthropologist Franz Boas challenged the rampant Darwinism of his time and demanded proof from his colleagues that race determines mentality and temperament. During the 1940's, Ashley Montagu claimed race was invented by anthropologists as an artificial concept and did not make sense in light of the hybridization of humanity over many millennia. Finally in 1964, the United Nations Educational, Scientific, and Cultural Organization (UNESCO), using the worldwide work of anthropologists and scientists, concluded that there is no such thing as a pure race, making it difficult to place humanity into clear-cut categories. UNESCO stated that because of the great mobility of humanity over time, no national, religious, geographical, linguistic, or cultural group in the modern world constitutes a race.

The majority of anthropologists find "race" to be a mystical and imprecise term that does not come close to explaining the tremendous biodiversity in humanity. They prefer, instead, "ethnicity," a term that encompasses people's language, religion, and geography and recognizes the existence of several hundred ethnic groups. The old divisions of Asian, African, European, American (Amer-Indian) have come to be viewed as mainly geographic terms. As populations continue to intersperse, even these geographic terms for humanity are becoming increasingly obsolete.

Irwin Halfond

Core Resources

Ivan Hannaford's *Race: The History of an Idea in the West* (Baltimore, Md.: Johns Hopkins University Press, 1996) provides a thorough analysis of racial concepts from the ancients to the Renaissance and a detailed view of the racialization of the West from 1684 to 1996 in part II. Michael Banton's *Race Relations* (New York: Basic Books, 1967) presents a clear picture of the development of racial concepts in world societies. Two chapters are devoted to racial concepts in the United States. Banton's study *The Idea of Race* (London: Tavistock Publications, 1977) should also be consulted for a topical approach to racial concepts. Thomas Gossett's *Race: The History of an Idea in America* (New York: Oxford University Press, 1997) analyzes how racial concepts affected and were affected by developments in the United States. The concluding chapter provides an analysis of the counter-theorists who fought against rigid racial classifications. *The Concept of Race*, edited by Ashley Montagu (New York: Free Press, 1964), provides essays by ten leading anthropologists. Many of the essays, although dated, are still of value.

See also: Ideological racism; Individual racism; Psychology of racism; Racism: history of the concept.

Race card

The term "race card" refers to the practice of bringing up the issue of race or racial identity—usually African American—as an explanation or motivation for a certain circumstance or situation. To "play the race card" is to claim that an individual's race is the reason the person has been treated a certain way or has ended up in a particular situation.

The race card forces issues to be drawn along racial lines. Many minority members, especially African Americans, believe that it is erroneous to discuss a "race card" as if race were significant only in certain cases and could be "played" to gain an advantage. Others maintain that minority members use the issue of racism to win support or simply to evade responsibility for their actions. These critics view the race card as an excuse or negotiating ploy that people of color use when they find themselves in an unfavorable situation. They believe that race is being conveniently brought up at certain times to maximize support even if race is irrelevant to the issue at hand.

Whether playing the race card is a legitimate move is a matter of perspective and often depends on the situation. During the O. J. Simpson trial, defense lawyer Johnnie Cochran was accused of playing the race card when he implied that Simpson was wrongfully accused of murder and set up simply because he is African American.

Erica Childs

See also: Crime and race/ethnicity; Criminal justice system; Psychology of racism; Simpson, O. J., trial.

Race relations cycle

Park developed his theory of the race relations cycle in the early twentieth century to explain the process by which societies incorporate racially and ethnically diverse peoples into one social entity. Park's cycle consists of four progressive stages: contact, competition, accommodation, and assimilation.

In the 1920's, Robert E. Park's theory of the race relations cycle provided a new direction away from pseudo-scientific racialist theories and toward more scientific views of race and race relations. The theory hinges on an assumption that assimilation of minorities into a society's dominant culture is desirable—both for the minorities and for the dominant culture—and that it is also inevitable, proceeding through four consistent, irreversible stages: contact, competition, accommodation, and assimilation.

Park's Four Stages Park describes the first stage of race relations, *contact*, from the vantage point of Europeans who, as they migrated into new territories, came into contact with peoples who seemed alien in their appearance and behavior. Contact and conquest, according to Park, form a natural part of the process of building a civilization. Park admitted that, as European peoples migrated into areas inhabited by other societies, they disrupted the sociocultural organization of those societies. They then replaced the indigenous social institutions with their own. He describes the processes accompanying the formation of the new social order as the unavoidable outgrowth of the migration, expansion, and amalgamation (intermarriage and reproduction) of peoples. As Park saw it, race relations develop as the natural product of migration and conquest; in this view, society is like a living organism that struggles to maintain balance, or "equilibrium." The absorption of new groups, then, is merely part of the society's attempt to reestablish this social equilibrium.

Park defined the second stage, *competition*, as the struggle of a racial group to perpetuate itself, or to continue to exist. Competition can be cooperative when it is based upon a division of labor that provides people with roles that suit them. Competition can also be accompanied by conflict, however, when different races or ethnic groups are first brought together. This conflict can be lessened through time as the different peoples come to have greater contact with each other and become attached to the moral order of the larger society.

Park defined the third stage, *accommodation*, as the inevitable result of the isolation felt by immigrants or racial minorities. They respond to this isolation by desiring to play an active role in the larger society. They also become aware of the "social distance" (the lack of intimacy, understanding, or influence between individuals and groups in society) that prevents their acceptance into that society. Driven to achieve higher social status, they become self-conscious of their differences from members of the dominant society. This social distance, according to Park, may last a long time, reinforced by established social customs and forming equilibrium. Eventually, however, social distance dwindles, making assimilation possible.

To Park, the final stage, *assimilation*, was a natural feature of what he called "civilized" society. In fact, he believed that a civilization is formed through the process of absorbing outside groups. Like other European and Euro-American sociologists, Park assumed that urbanization and modernization would break down ties based on family, race, and ethnicity. The breakdown of these ties, he believed, would free the individual to participate in modern civilization. Park believed that the United States was a democratic meritocracy—a society in which individuals could achieve upward mobility based on their innate abilities and in which caste and race distinctions would ultimately disappear.

Park on Prejudice Nevertheless, Park acknowledged that for people of color, assimilation, while inevitable, would take time to achieve. Although he held the dominant society to be a meritocracy, he believed that prejudice would hinder assimilation. He did not consider the difference between white ethnic groups and racial ethnic groups highly significant. Rather, he believed that, to the extent that there was difference, it was attributable to the race *prejudice* confronting people of color because of their "racial uniform," the physical appearance that they could not alter. Park saw prejudice against intermarriage as a particular problem, because his theory required assimilation not only in a cultural sense but in a physical, biological sense as well, through intermarriage and reproduction (what Park termed "amalgamation"). Ultimately, then—especially for African and Asian Americans—the major barrier to assimilation was whites' prejudiced attitudes rather than the inability or lack of desire of African and Asian Americans to assimilate. This hypothesis became a major premise of assimilationist theories and led to an emphasis on the study of attitudes.

The "Marginal Man" Another concept credited to Park is that of the "marginal man"—the person caught between two cultures. According to Park, this marginal person is produced in the process of building civilization, as new peoples are incorporated into one society. Often racially or ethnically mixed, this person assumes the role of the stranger, fitting into neither of the two cultures that produced him or her. Rather, the "marginal man" embodies a new personality type, created by the processes of acculturation that accompany the race relations cycle. He understands both cultures or groups that produced him, but he is neither at home in, nor accepted by, either group.

Impact on Theories of Race Relations Park's theory of the race relations cycle laid the groundwork for a major trend in sociology: assimilationist theories of race relations, which assume the possibility of a harmonious "melting pot" society in which race and ethnicity are not significant determinants of social status. The melting pot theory influenced many of the sociologists who followed Park, including Louis Wirth and Gunnar Myrdal. These sociologists shared Park's analysis of ethnicity and race, arguing that the assimilation difficulties faced by African Americans constituted an aberration—or, as Myrdal put it in his seminal 1944 study of the same name, an "American dilemma." Even assimilationists who took issue with Parks, such as Milton Gordon—who argued that minorities were not expected to join in the melting pot so much as to meet the demands of "Anglo-conformity"—can trace their intellectual roots to Park. Elements of the race relations cycle theory have been applied to race relations in many areas, including studies of social distance; measurement of racial prejudice and changes in those attitudes over time; studies of cultural differences among those who have not been assimilated; and studies of the extent to which society remains segregated.

Today, Park's theory of the race relations cycle is generally criticized for assuming that assimilation is inevitable. Assumptions implicit in Park's theory remained rooted in later assimilationist theories: an assumption that the United States is an open, meritocratic society; an assumption that discrimination is caused by prejudice; the view that, upon their enslavement, African Americans lost any culture they once had and that they should therefore embrace acculturation; the belief in the inherent superiority (or, at least, desirability) of the dominant culture; the belief that racial inequality is abnormal in what is otherwise an egalitarian society; and an assumption of the assimilative effects of urbanization and industrialization. Spearheaded by the work of Park assimilationist theories remained predominant until the latter twentieth century, when the Black Power movement and subsequent ethnic movements signaled that racial and ethnic minorities exist who neither embrace the dominant culture nor seek inclusion in it.

Impact on Public Policy Park's premise that society, to achieve assimilation, must minimize social distance and racial prejudice has been instrumental in the promotion of racial integration in education, housing, and work. For example, Jonathan Kozol, in his book *Savage Inequalities: Children in America's Schools* (1991), detailed the social costs of segregation and promoted the concept that only when members of different races minimize their social distance by early contact with one another, as children in schools, will Americans reach accord through mutual understanding. Such studies helped give rise to the busing of African American children from predominantly black to predominantly white schools during the 1970's. Likewise, public and private universities across North America have adopted policies intended to end racial strife by minimizing racial prejudice through mutual exposure and appreciation. A more controversial policy adopted by some institutions involves punishment for the verbal expression of racial hatred ("hate speech"), critics claiming that such policies impinge on the constitutional protection of free speech.

Numerous studies measuring social distance have polled American citizens on whether they would tolerate the presence of people with different racial backgrounds in their neighborhoods, in their churches, in their schools, and as members of their families. Results indicating that whites have minimized their social distance from people of color are taken as evidence that racial prejudice has declined and that, therefore, the United States is moving toward an assimilated society. A number of sociologists, however, including Joe R. Feagin, have argued that racism is driven more by discrimination, which can be unintentional, than by prejudiced attitudes. Feagin and others question the validity of a focus on racial prejudice as the underlying basis of racial conflict in society.

More negative, even punitive, consequences of a belief in the value of assimilation can be seen in examples in which acculturation—the process by which culturally distinct groups understand, adapt to, and influence each another—was forced on people of color in order to minimize their differences from the dominant white society. For example, many schools for American Indian children in the nineteenth and early twentieth centuries (some run by missionaries, some by the federal government's Bureau of Indian Affairs) aimed to "civilize" the children by removing them from their parents and placing them in boarding schools where teachers worked to eliminate all vestiges of traditional culture. This pattern of forced acculturation is a good example of how government policy toward immigrants and racial minorities both drove, and was driven by, assimilationist assumptions. Park's theory of assimilation, articulated in the wake of such government policies, echoed the status quo in American society, assuming that the dominant Euro-American society is an open society in which racial and ethnic divisions will inevitably be eroded and replaced by a true meritocracy.

Assimilationist assumptions in the educational system have also invested schools with the responsibility of teaching both the English language and the values of citizenship, important tools in the acculturation process. Feagin notes, as evidence of society's emphasis on acculturation, the development of nativist citizen groups that promote "English-only" schooling. These groups insist that all children must learn the language of the land if they wish to participate as full members of society.

Assimilationist scholars have found ready partners in government policymakers as well. In the 1960's, for example, a report issued by Daniel P. Moynihan entitled *Report on the Negro Family: A Case for National Action* cited the "peculiar" structure of many African American families—dominated or headed by a female—as responsible for the failure of blacks to be fully assimilated into American society. This family structure, Moynihan held, promoted values alien to those needed for successful integration into the dominant society. Some scholars followed this report by emphasizing that blacks who have moved into the middle class have done so by virtue of their acculturation to the dominant culture; they claimed that racial prejudice is not the true barrier to assimilation but rather that failure to acculturate is the problem. In the 1990's, such applications of Park's pioneering theory of assimilation were common among those who sought to end what they believed were "preferential" programs for assimilation, such as affirmative action in hiring and in admissions to colleges and universities.

Sharon Elise, adapted by Chris Moose

Core Resources

Robert Park's *Race and Culture* (Glencoe, Ill.: Free Press, 1950) collects the essays in which Park developed his theory of the race relations cycle. E. Franklin Frazier's *Black Bourgeoisie* (Glencoe, Ill.: Free Press, 1957) is a classic study of the "marginal man" dilemma applied to the black middle class. Perhaps the most famous heir to the Park tradition was Gunnar Myrdal, whose classic *An American Dilemma: The Negro Problem and Modern Democracy* (New York: Harper Brothers, 1944) grappled with the "aberration" of the African American experience. Robert Blauner, in *Racial Oppression in America* (New York: Harper & Row, 1972), criticizes assimilationist theories and counters their focus on racial prejudice with an analysis of racial privilege as embedded in a system of internal colonialism. Stanford M. Lyman, *The Black American in Sociological Thought* (New York: Putnam, 1972), reveals some of the racial biases in the development of the sociology of race and ethnic relations. Michael Omi and Howard Winant, in *Racial Formation in the United States* (New York: Routledge & Kegan Paul, 1986), examine the major paradigms of race relations—the dominant ethnic model, the class model, and the nation model—followed by their own "racial formation" thesis. Joe R. Feagin, in his textbook *Racial and Ethnic Relations* (5th ed., Englewood Cliffs, N.J.: Prentice-Hall, 1996), offers an introductory survey of race relations theories, analyzing each of the United States' major ethnic and racial groups against the background of competing sociological explanations.

See also: Psychology of racism; Race as a concept; Racism as an ideology; Racism: changing nature of; Racism: history of the concept.

Race riots of 1866

Economic and social disparities between the races, along with a continuing military presence, led to violence during Reconstruction.

Racial disturbances in Memphis and New Orleans in 1866 were the result of economic, social, and political issues that troubled the nation during Reconstruction. Given the upheaval in the lives of Southerners after the Civil War, the racial disturbances are hardly surprising. In the simplest terms, one of the major tasks of Reconstruction was to assimilate the more than four million former slaves into U.S. society. A more complex view must consider the problems faced by the newly freed African Americans who had to achieve a new identity in a society that had allowed them no control over their own lives. White Southerners had to live with the economic, social, and political consequences of defeat. The military occupation of the South by federal troops after the Civil War angered Southern whites, who believed in their right to rebuild and rule their own society without interference from the North. The presence of federal troops (many of them African Americans), an armed citizenry, and the psychological difficulty of accepting the end of the world they had known created explosive conditions that erupted into violence.

The Black Codes The Memphis and New Orleans riots were one result of this upheaval. Soon after the surrender of the Confederate army at Appomattox in April, 1865, legislatures in the South acted to pass a series of black codes. These laws were intended to maintain control over the lives of the newly freed African Americans and, in effect, keep them enslaved. For example, harsh vagrancy laws allowed police to arrest black people without cause and force them to work for white employers. President Abraham Lincoln's Emancipation Proclamation, on January 1, 1863, had freed the slaves in the Confederate states. The United States Congress, having abolished slavery throughout the nation with the Thirteenth Amendment to the Constitution in 1865, founded the Freedmen's Bureau to assist the former slaves and was in the process of enacting, over the strong opposition of President Andrew Johnson, a series of Reconstruction Acts intended to repeal the South's black codes. President Johnson resisted congressional attempts to admit African Americans to full citizenship, but Congress ultimately overrode his veto and took control of the Reconstruction program in the South.

Many former slaves, rejecting the life they had known on the plantation, moved to the cities of the South. Most African Americans were refugees without any economic resources, competing with Irish and German immigrants for scarce jobs in the war-torn South. Southern white Protestants feared both the immigrants and the African Americans as threats to the social order.

Conditions in Memphis were especially volatile in May, 1866. The city was a rowdy river town known for heavy drinking, gambling, prostitution, and fighting. In 1865, the black population of Memphis had increased to between twenty and twenty-five thousand, many of them living in a run-down district near Fort Pickering. The white citizens were alarmed by incendiary newspaper accounts of crime and disorder.

The Memphis police, mostly Irish immigrants, were corrupt and ill-trained and had a record of brutality toward black people. Added to this already explosive mixture was a body of federal troops, four thousand of whom were black soldiers stationed at Fort Pickering waiting to be mustered out of the army. The violence began on April 29, with a street confrontation between black soldiers and white policemen. On May 1, the violence escalated, with fights breaking out between groups of black soldiers and the city police. By May 2, the mob included a number of people from the surrounding countryside as well as white citizens of Memphis. The mob rampaged through the black district, attacking families, raping women, and burning homes. Civil authorities took no steps to curb the disturbance.

After considerable delay, Major General George Stoneman, commanding the federal troops, brought the city under control. The three days of mob violence resulted in the deaths of forty-six African Americans and two white people. An estimated seventy to eighty other people were injured, and some ninety homes of black people, along with several African American churches and schools, were destroyed. Southern newspapers and civic officials blamed the black soldiers for the outbreak. A committee appointed by Congress, however, attributed the disturbances to the hatred of white people for the "colored race."

The New Orleans Riots Although the Memphis riots were the result of local conditions, the New Orleans disturbance of July 30 was caused by state politics and had national significance. Louisiana governor James Madison Wells, a Union sympathizer who needed to consolidate his power over the Confederates in New Orleans and the state, supported a plan to reassemble the state constitutional convention that had been disbanded in 1864. This convention, supported by Unionists, planned to gain votes by enfranchising African Americans. The city, sympathetic to Confederate politics, was armed, and the corrupt police force had a record of false arrests and mistreatment of free African Americans. The local newspapers, using highly emotional language, incited the fear of white citizens that African Americans would gain political control.

The commander of the federal troops, General Absalom Baird, should have foreseen the impending violence but apparently ignored the problem. When the delegates to the state convention began to assemble on July 30, fighting broke out between the city police and African American marchers supporting the right to vote. Delegates were dragged from the convention hall and assaulted by people in the street and by the police, who joined in the mob violence. The attacks on African Americans were savage; the wounded were dragged to the city jail and beaten, and the bodies of the dead were mistreated. As the violence escalated, fueled by the drunkenness of the mob, African Americans were dragged from their homes and beaten.

The death toll in the one-day riot included 34 African Americans and 3 white people; approximately 136 people were injured. Although General Baird declared martial law, his action was too late. Several observers, including General Philip H. Sheridan, who was called in to restore order, described the mob violence as a "slaughter." As in the case of the Memphis riots, nearly all the dead and injured were African Americans.

Although the Memphis riots were caused by local conditions, the disturbances in New Orleans had state and national political consequences. The Republican Party lost power, paving the way for Democratic control of the state. Precedents for the racial violence that would mark the years of Reconstruction and beyond had been established.

Marjorie Podolsky

Core Resources

Eric Foner's "The Meaning of Freedom" and "The Making of Radical Reconstruction," in *Reconstruction: America's Unfinished Revolution, 1863-1877* (New York: Harper & Row, 1988), interprets the scholarly history of Reconstruction and combines older views with newer scholarship. John Hope Franklin's *Reconstruction: After the Civil War* (Chicago: University of Chicago Press, 1961) presents a revised view that rejects the carpetbagger stereotype and argues for a more positive representation of African Americans during Reconstruction. John Hope Franklin and Alfred A. Moss, Jr.'s "The Effort to Attain Peace," in *From Slavery to Freedom: A History of African Americans* (7th ed., New York: McGraw-Hill, 1994), is a widely accepted record of the role of African Americans in U.S. history. Leon F. Litwack's "How Free Is Free?" in *Been in the Storm So Long: The Aftermath of Slavery* (New York: Vintage Books, 1980), is based on the accounts of former slaves interviewed by the Federal Writers' Project in the 1930's. George C. Rable's "The Memphis Race Riot" and "New Orleans and the Emergence of Political Violence," in *But There Was No Peace: The Role of Violence in the Politics of Reconstruction* (Athens: University of Georgia Press, 1984), uses contemporary newspaper articles to bring the riots to life and connect the disturbances with similar events in the twentieth century. Kenneth R. Stampp's "The Tragic Legend of Reconstruction," in *The Era of Reconstruction, 1865-1877* (New York: Alfred A. Knopf, 1969), uses research on race from social scientists to counteract previous historians.

See also: Black codes; Civil Rights Acts of 1866-1875; *Civil Rights* cases; Emancipation Proclamation; Fourteenth Amendment; Freedmen's Bureau; Ku Klux Klan; Race riots of 1943; Race riots of the twentieth century; Reconstruction; Thirteenth Amendment.

Race riots of 1943

Racial tensions peaked as minorities and whites competed for jobs and social services during World War II.

The urban race riots in the summer of 1943 did not occur spontaneously. A pattern of violence throughout the nation, similar to the racial conflicts that occurred during World War I, had been escalating since 1940, as urban areas swelled with workers drawn to wartime industries. The lack of interracial communication, the failure of local, state, and federal agencies to comprehend the severity of the racial environment, challenges against established southern racial traditions, and extreme shortages of housing and social services created frustration, which manifested itself in racial violence.

The Mobile Riots Tremendous growth in the population of Mobile, Alabama, caused severe problems in housing and city services. These shortages, combined with the competition for jobs, created racial tension. Whites jealously protected what they considered to be white-only, high-paying, skilled jobs. The largest wartime contractor in Mobile was ADDSCO, the Alabama Dry Dock and Shipbuilding Company. ADDSCO, like numerous other industries, employed African Americans only for unskilled or semiskilled positions. Unable to find enough skilled welders and to appease the local National Association for the Advancement of Colored People (NAACP), led by John LeFlore and Burton R. Morley of the War Manpower Commission, ADDSCO agreed to employ African American welders. On May 24, 1943, black welders reported for work on the third shift at the Pinto Island Yard. No racial incidents occurred during the night, but the next morning, after additional black welders reported for work, violence erupted.

Between five hundred and one thousand whites attacked black workers and drove them from the yards. Governor Chauncey Sparks ordered the Alabama State Guard to intervene, and by noon the rioting had ended. Federal troops occupied the shipyards, and local city and county government ordered all bars and liquor stores closed until the tension eased. Mobile police eventually charged three whites with felony assault, intent to murder, and inciting a riot. On June 5, 1943, the Alabama State Guard pulled out and on June 10, 1943, federal troops returned to their base at Brookley Field.

The Zoot-Suit Riots As emotions in Mobile calmed, racial tensions in Los Angeles exploded. On June 3, 1943, servicemen from area bases began attacking Mexican American youths known as "zoot-suiters" in response to rumors that the youths had assaulted female relatives of military personnel. Servicemen, accompanied by civilians, roamed the streets, sometimes in taxicabs, in search of zoot-suiters. Streetcars and buses were stopped and searched, and zoot-suiters found in stores and theaters were disrobed and beaten.

In retaliation, gangs of Mexican American adolescents attacked military personnel. Police arrested reported zoot-suit leaders Frank H. Tellez and Luis "the Chief" Verdusco in an effort to stop Mexican American violence against whites. Fighting reached a climax on June 7, 1943, when a mob of more than a thousand servicemen and civilians moved down Main Street in downtown Los Angeles to the African American neighborhood at Twelfth and Central, and then through the Mexican American neighborhood on the east side, looking for zoot-suiters. The Mexican ambassador to the United States lodged a formal complaint with Secretary of State Cordell Hull, and California governor Earl Warren appointed Attorney General Robert Kenny to investigate the riots. While the riots officially ended on June 7, violent incidents continued throughout the city for the rest of the summer.

As rioting in Los Angeles subsided, racial violence returned to the South. Beaumont, Texas, located between Houston and the Louisiana border, had experienced tremendous wartime growth because of its petroleum production facilities and shipbuilding operations. With emotions already frayed from an earlier suspected rape of a white woman by a black ex-convict, the reported rape of a young white woman by a black man on June 15, 1943, set off a violent reaction among white workers at the Pennsylvania Shipyards. In the early evening, approximately two thousand workers marched on downtown Beaumont. Police Chief Ross Dickey convinced the mob not to lynch any black prisoners.

Around midnight, mobs converged on black neighborhoods in north Beaumont and along Forsythe Street. At the Greyhound bus station, about three hundred whites assaulted fifty-two African American army draftees. Whites looted and burned local businesses and assaulted African Americans until the next morning. Killed during the evening's violence were Alex Mouton and John Johnson, African Americans, and Ellis C. Brown, a white man. Local law enforcement tried diligently to stop the rioting. More than two hundred whites and six African Americans were arrested during the rioting. Martial law was declared on June 16 and lifted on June 20. Although calm had been restored to Beaumont, the violence compelled approximately twenty-five hundred blacks to leave soon after the riots.

Detroit and Harlem One of the worst riots in the summer of 1943 occurred in Detroit. On Sunday, June 20, 1943, more than one hundred thousand Detroiters, a large percentage of them African American, had gone to the Belle Isle Amusement Park. A group of black teenagers led by Charles "Little Willie" Lyon began attacking whites. A fight broke out between white sailors and young African Americans on the bridge connecting Belle Isle with the city. The fighting spread, and by 11:00 P.M., an estimated five thousand people were fighting on and around the Belle Isle Bridge.

Rumors of atrocities against African Americans circulated in the Paradise Valley ghetto. Black rioters stoned passing cars of whites and destroyed white-owned businesses. By early morning, whites along Woodward Avenue had retaliated by beating African Americans. Mayor Edward J. Jeffries asked Governor Harry F. Kelly to request federal troops, but Kelly hesitated until Monday evening, and federal troops did not arrive until Tuesday morning. As African Americans rioted along the east side of Woodward Avenue, whites continued congregating along Woodward Avenue. Detroit remained under a curfew and martial law for the following week, and federal troops remained for two weeks. After two days of intense rioting, the Detroit riots were over. Authorities reported thirty-four people, mostly African Americans, killed and more than seven hundred injured. Property damage estimates were around two million dollars.

As the situation calmed in Detroit, tensions were mounting in Harlem, New York. On August 1, 1943, in the late afternoon, Robert Bandy, an African American soldier on leave from the army, argued with James Collins, a white policeman, over the arrest of a black woman at the Braddock Hotel on West

126th Street. A fight ensued, and Collins shot Bandy, inflicting a superficial wound. Rumors quickly spread that a black soldier trying to protect his mother had been killed by a white policeman. Crowds of angry African Americans gathered at the Braddock Hotel and the twenty-eighth police precinct, and by midnight, rioting had started.

The rioting centered in Harlem and never directly involved confrontations between blacks and whites. Mayor Fiorello H. La Guardia acted swiftly to confine the violence by using extra police, firefighters, black Office of Civilian Defense volunteers, and National Guardsmen. African American civic leaders such as Walter White worked alongside city officials to calm Harlem residents. The all-night looting and burning of white-owned businesses left Harlem looking like a war zone. By the time peace was restored, after twelve hours of rioting, six African Americans had been killed by police and National Guard troops, and almost two hundred people reported injuries. Property damage was estimated to be as high as five million dollars. The racial violence of the summer of 1943 had ended, but the problems that triggered riots and violence across the nation remained.

Craig S. Pascoe

Core Resources

John Morton Blum's *V Was for Victory: Politics and American Culture During World War II* (New York: Harcourt Brace Jovanovich, 1976) examines established segregation and prejudice in the United States during World War II. Dominic J. Capeci, Jr.'s *The Harlem Riot of 1943* (Philadelphia: Temple University Press, 1977) argues that African Americans became disillusioned with social gains that were meager compared with their contributions to the war effort. Alfred McClung Lee's *Race Riot, Detroit 1943* (1943; reprint, New York: Octagon Books, 1968) is a firsthand account of the Detroit riots.

See also: Detroit riot; Los Angeles riots of 1992; Miami riots of 1980; Newark race riots; Race riots of 1866; Race riots of the twentieth century; Watts riot.

Race riots of the twentieth century

Race riots both threaten the stability of society and, by their very occurrence, call into question the fundamental fairness of society.

Referring to racial violence in the United States as "race riots" is often misleading. Many race riots were actually one-sided white massacres of blacks; this was particularly true of those prior to 1921. Nineteenth century race riots were often called "slave revolts" or "slave insurrections." These slave revolts were most frequent in the areas of the South where blacks constituted at least 40 percent of the population. Fearing that slave revolts in one part of the South would trigger similar revolts throughout the South, slaveholders quelled such rebellions quickly and viciously.

Twentieth century race riots differ from nineteenth century riots in both motive and location. Whereas nineteenth century riots were primarily concerned with maintaining the institution of slavery, twentieth century riots—particularly those in the years before World War II—were often designed to maintain white supremacy over urban blacks. Also, where nineteenth century race riots were almost exclusively a southern phenomenon, twentieth century race riots took place in almost every major urban area of America.

1900-1945 Race riots prior to World War II often followed a consistent pattern. In almost all cases, the riots were initiated by whites against blacks. In only two of the major riots—Harlem, New York, in 1935 and again in 1943—did African Americans initiate the riots. Second, most riots were caused by a white fear of blacks competing for jobs that previously were held by whites. The rapid movement of blacks from the South to the urban industrial areas of the North contributed to this fear. Third, most riots took place during the hot and humid summer months when young people were out of school. Finally, the riots were often fueled by rumors—allegations of police brutality against blacks or allegations of black violence against whites heightened racial tensions.

One of the major race riots during this period occurred in East St. Louis, Illinois, in 1917. An automobile occupied by four whites drove through black areas firing shots. When a similar car was seen, blacks opened fire and killed two occupants, both of whom were police officers. Whites invaded the black community, burning three hundred homes and killing fifty blacks. The summer of 1919 saw twenty riots in communities such as Charleston, South Carolina; Washington, D.C.; Knoxville, Tennessee; and Chicago. The riots of 1919 were so bloody that the period was called the "Red Summer."

Post-World War II Riots Although post-World War II riots were fueled by rumor and also took place during the summer months, they differed from pre-World War II riots in two important ways. First, a majority of the riots were initiated by blacks, not whites. Second, many of the post-World War II riots were not confined to the black community. In several cases, whites were singled out as victims of black violence.

The race riots of the 1960's threatened to destroy the fabric of American society. The 1964 Harlem riot in New York City and the 1965 Watts riot in Los Angeles were both triggered by police incidents. The Watts riot lasted six days and resulted in thirty-four deaths and four thousand arrests. "Burn, baby, burn" became a battle cry in black ghettos throughout the United States.

Aftermath of racially motivated rioting in New York City in the summer of 1964. *(Library of Congress)*

The year 1967 brought major riots to Newark, New Jersey, and to Tampa, Cincinnati, Atlanta, and Detroit. Newark's riot was the most severe, resulting in twenty-six deaths and $30 million in property damage. The assassination of Martin Luther King, Jr., on April 4, 1968, triggered racial violence in more than one hundred cities. In response to the urban racial violence, President Lyndon B. Johnson appointed the National Advisory Commission on Civil Disorders, better known as the Kerner Commission. After investigating the causes of the rioting the commission presented a series of recommendations. According to the Kerner Commission, the most important grievances of the black community were police practices, lack of employment opportunities, and inadequate housing. The ominous conclusion of the Kerner Commission was that unless the causes of urban violence were addressed, the United States would continue to become two societies, one black, one white—separate and unequal.

1980's and 1990's Although there was a lull in race riots during the 1970's, the Miami riots in May of 1980 signaled a renewal of urban racial unrest. On December 17, 1979, a black insurance agent, Arthur McDuffie, was stopped by Miami police officers after a high-speed chase. A fight ensued, and McDuffie was beaten to death. The police officers engaged in a cover-up and reported that McDuffie died as a result of a motorcycle crash. When the cover-up unraveled, five Miami police officers were arrested. Four were charged with manslaughter, and one was charged with tampering with evidence. After deliberating less than three hours, an all-white jury found all defendants not guilty. Within hours of the verdict, the Liberty City section of Miami exploded in violence. Before order was restored three days later, eighteen people were dead, including eight whites who had the misfortune to be driving through Liberty City when the riot began.

The riot that took place in Los Angeles in May of 1992 was triggered by a similar event. Almost immediately after four white police officers were acquitted of assault in the videotaped beating of Rodney King, a black man, one of the most violent race riots in American history broke out. Before it was over, more than sixty people had died, more than four thousand fires had been set, and Los Angeles had suffered property damage totaling more than a billion dollars.

Although the patterns of racial violence may have altered over the decades, the fact remains that race riots continue to occur. Once a southern phenomenon, they have become a national problem in search of a solution.

Darryl Paulson

Core Resources

See James W. Button, *Black Violence: Political Impact of the 1960's Riots* (Princeton, N.J.: Princeton University Press, 1978); Robert Connery, ed., *Urban Riots* (New York: Vintage Books, 1969); Bruce Porter and Marvin Dunn, *The Miami Riot of 1980* (Lexington, Mass.: Lexington Books, 1984); *Report of the National Advisory Commission on Civil Disorders* (New York: Bantam Books, 1968); and Elliott Rudwick, *Race Riot at East St. Louis* (New York: Atheneum, 1972).

See also: Black Power movement; Civil Rights movement; Commission on Civil Rights, U.S.; Detroit riot; Kerner Report; King, Rodney, case; Los Angeles riots of 1992; Miami riots of 1980; National Advisory Commission on Civil Disorders; Newark race riots; Race riots of 1866; Race riots of 1943; Watts riot.

Racial and ethnic demographics: trends

The demographic makeup of the United States has changed greatly over the years, affecting the relations between and relative power and dominance of the various racial and ethnic groups that live in this nation of immigrants.

The United States, Canada, and Australia are the three most important "receiving" countries for immigrants worldwide. The United States and Canada, as a result of their immigration policies, have become two of the world's most ethnically diverse geographical areas. Two centuries ago, the population of these two nations was predominantly of white European heritage, but in the twenty-first century, nonwhites and people whose heritage is not European are expected to become an increasingly large part of their populations. Because the United States and Canada both possess a strong democratic ethos and high standard of living, they are likely to attract many more people, especially oppressed ethnic minorities.

Historical Changes Since 1790, as required by the U.S. Constitution, a census has been conducted every ten years. The initial purpose of the census was to enable the U.S. government to determine an equitable apportionment of tax dollars and the number of representatives each area would send to Congress. During its early history, the census was executed by temporary workers in nonpermanent facilities. It was not until March, 1902, that the government created the Bureau of the Census with a full-time staff and permanent facilities.

A perennial issue for the bureau has been the underreporting of certain subpopulations, including the very young, the poor, immigrants, and nonwhites. The resulting lower numbers have often resulted in those populations having less government representation and, unfortunately, fewer benefits. In the latter part of the twentieth century, the bureau made great efforts to correct these shortcomings by making questionnaires available in Spanish and developing methods for assessing the undocumented immigrant population.

During its first hundred years, the United States had an open immigration policy. It was not until 1882 that Congress passed the Chinese Exclusion Act, which outlawed Chinese immigration for ten years. This anti-Chinese legislation followed thirty years of heavy Chinese immigration during which more than two hundred thousand Chinese came to the United States to escape overpopulation, poverty, and warfare in China.

The history of legal immigration to the United States between 1820 and 1985 exhibits dramatic changes in the regions of the world from which immigrants came. Examination of the table "Regional Background of U.S. Immigrants (1820-1985)" reveals these changes. Most striking is the decline of European immigrants, largely whites, and the significant increase in immigrants from Latin America and Asia, mostly Hispanics and nonwhites. Experts have projected population changes that suggest that by 2080, the U.S. population will consist of 49.8 percent white non-Hispanics, 23.4 percent Hispanics, 14.7 percent blacks, and 12 percent Asians and other persons.

African Americans With about 30 million African Americans, the United States has the third-largest black population in the world (only Brazil and Nigeria have larger black populations). By contrast, Canada has fewer than 1 million blacks, mostly of West Indian descent. Contrary to popular belief, the first blacks in North America were not slaves. In 1619, twenty black men became indentured servants to wealthy Virginian white men. Unfortunately, most of the other blacks who landed in the United States came as slaves. From the beginning of the American slave trade in the 1600's to the

Emancipation Proclamation in 1863, almost 90 percent of all blacks in what is now the United States were slaves. The first U.S. census in 1790 reported 757,000 blacks. By 1800, they numbered 1 million. In the 1860 census, there were about 4,442,000 blacks. The 1990 U.S. census reported almost 30 million blacks, or about 12.1 percent of the total U.S. population of almost 250 million. By 2080, it is projected that blacks will reach around 14.7 percent of the U.S. population. Although blacks have made tremendous progress in the second half of the twentieth century, many serious problems still need to be addressed and solved.

Future Trends For the last five hundred years, the United States and Canada have been dominated by white European peoples and cultures. However, in the last fifty years, non-Europeans, nonwhites, Hispanics, and Asians have become the fastest-growing populations in these nations. By 2080, experts predict that more than 50 percent of the U.S. population will be non-European and nonwhite and that the largest ethnic group will be Hispanic. In Canada, although the makeup of the population is changing, it is not likely that the U.S. population patterns will be duplicated. However, the proportion of British, French, and European people in the overall population is projected to fall. In the face of these trends, the power and influence of the dominant white group in the United States and Canada will probably diminish somewhat, and the two nations will continue to be pluralistic and democratic societies that attract refugees and immigrants.

R. M. Frumkin

Core Resources

Some helpful books on the racial and ethnic demographics of the United States include the *Statistical Abstracts of the United States: 1997* (117th ed., Washington, D.C.: U.S. Bureau of the Census, 1997), L. F. Bouvier and R. W. Gardner's *Immigration to the U.S.* (Washington, D.C.: Population Reference Bureau, 1986), and R. T. Schaefer's *Racial and Ethnic Groups* (4th ed., Glenview, Ill.: Scott, Foresman/Little, Brown Higher Education, 1990). Information on Canadian demographics can be obtained from the government agency Statistics Canada, Statistical Reference Center, in Ottawa, Canada.

See also: Censuses, U.S.; Minority voting districts; Redistricting.

Racial formation theory

Racial formation theory was the outcome of a process of introspection by social scientists who had been frustrated by both academic attempts to explain race and racism and political ideologies that attempted to collapse race into other social categories such as nationality or economic class. The theory was developed principally by sociologists Michael Omi and Howard Winant in their book *Racial Formation in the United States* (1986, 2d ed. 1994).

Racial formation theory avoids two mistakes in analyzing race in the United States. The first mistake is the tendency to view race and races as fixed social or biological facts, which is not plausible. Attempts to develop biological classifications that match social definitions of the races have failed. Different societies have defined race and races very differently, and all definitions have changed over time, often over the course of a single lifetime.

The second mistake attempts to correct for the first but overcompensates. In this view race is wholly illusory, a fictional product of cultural representation. Omi and Winant argued that this perspective, however appealing to those who would rather live in a "color-blind" society, unrealistically suggests the remedy of merely ignoring or eliminating race and races—as if society could simply learn to do without race. The problem with this view is that race is such a fixture of American political, cultural, and economic reality that to pretend it does not exist would be to ignore all of its serious consequences for society, such as racial discrimination and segregation.

Race and racism have in fact been at the core of the American experience since the nation's inception, and Omi and Winant argue that they always will be, although race is impossible to pin down as a fixed concept. The theory handles this contradiction by defining racial formation as the process that both creates the racial categories with which people identify and transforms these categories over time.

By this reasoning, race exists as both social structure and symbolic representation. Historically, the racial projects that seek to allocate various resources one way or another along racial lines are the same movements that create, impose, or change racial definitions. At any one point in time, these categories seem to most participants to be fixed and normal, a sort of common sense of race. However, that static appearance masks a turbulent undercurrent of racial projects. These projects take place at the macro level of society in the struggles of social movements and state policies and at the micro level in the daily social interactions and private battles of identity that all Americans face.

While describing race as a fluid concept reflecting the outcome of centuries of social struggle, racial formation theory defines racism more simply. Racism is a racial project that perpetuates domination based on categories of race. The theory thus allows for the ever-changing nature of race as a social construction while simultaneously establishing criteria for identifying and challenging racism as a problem to be combated.

Philip N. Cohen

See also: Race as a concept; Racism: history of the concept.

Racism as an ideology

Racism can be described as an ideology—a belief that helps to maintain the status quo. More specifically, "racism" refers to the belief that one race is superior to other races in significant ways and that the superior race is entitled, by virtue of its superiority, to dominate other races and to enjoy a larger share of society's wealth and status.

Race, according to almost all scientists, is a socially defined concept rather than a biologically determined reality. "Race" is therefore real only in the sense that certain groups have, for whatever reason, decided to categorize people according to certain aspects (arbitrary and even superficial aspects) of their physical appearance. Terms such as "black" and "white," then, must also be viewed as socially, rather than biologically, meaningful distinctions.

Sociologist Howard Schuman has defined racism as the belief that there are clearly distinguishable human races, that these races differ not only in superficial physical characteristics but also innately in important psychological traits, and that the differences are such that one race (almost always one's own) can be said to be superior to another. According to this view, it follows that the advantages which the superior race enjoys with respect to health care, housing, employment, education, income and wealth, and status and power are attributable to its superiority rather than to discriminatory social structures. Consequently, according to this view, racial inequality is no reason to change any of society's institutionalized ways of doing things; the social structure can be maintained. Racism is, then, an ideology: a belief that rationalizes the status quo.

"White racism," Schuman says, "is the belief that 'white' people are inherently superior to ['black'] people in significant ways, but that the reverse is not true." Prior to the mid-twentieth century, the prevailing form of white racism was the belief that blacks were genetically inferior, especially with respect to intelligence. Since that time the view that blacks are inferior to whites has persisted, but racist whites have changed their minds about the cause of the inferiority. Schuman cites a helpful statistic: In 1942, 42 percent of a national sample of whites said they believed that blacks were as intelligent as whites; by 1956, 78 percent of whites agreed that blacks were as intelligent.

The National Opinion Research Center (NORC) found, in 1991, that 14 percent agreed that blacks were disadvantaged in housing, income, and education because they have less inborn ability. The remaining 86 percent, however, did not all believe that blacks and whites were biologically and psychologically equal and that the differences in housing, income, and education were attributable to discriminatory social structures. Only 40 percent said the differences were attributable "mainly to discrimination." Fifty-five percent said that the difference existed "because most blacks just don't have the motivation or will power to pull themselves up out of poverty." If racism is the belief that one race is superior in significant ways to other races, and if "free will" is considered to be a significant trait (and it is if differences in education and income are attributable to differences in free will) then such a belief is an example of racism. Schuman, analyzing similar data prior to the 1970's, concluded that "the phrase 'white racism' appears wholly appropriate."

Psychologist William Ryan (1976) concurs. The old-fashioned ideology was that blacks were genetically defective. The modern ideology is that they are environmentally defective, that the defects are caused by "the malignant nature of poverty, injustice, slum life, and racial difficulties." Ryan notes that "the stigma, the defect, the fatal difference—though derived in the past from environmental forces—is still located *within* the victim, inside his skin."

The ideology of racism has injured not only those in "nonwhite races" but those in certain white ethnic groups as well. The historian John Higham (*Strangers in the Land: Patterns of American Nativism 1860-1925*, 1955) traced the history of "race thinking" about European immigrants to the United States:

> Several generations of intellectuals took part in transforming the vague and somewhat benign racial concepts of romantic nationalism into doctrines that were precise, malicious, and plausibly applicable to European immigration. The task was far from simple; at every point, the race-thinkers confronted the liberal and cosmopolitan barriers of Christianity and American democracy.

Challenges to the Ideology The most direct attack on the ideology of racism has been challenges to the very concept of race. If there are not in fact different "races" of people, then obviously all arguments about the superiority and inferiority of various races are false. Science has challenged the concept of race. The sociologist James W. Vander Zanden (1983) has traced the progress of science's views from the "fixed type school" to the "breeding population school" and ultimately to the "no-race school." The fixed type school held the view that "races are relatively fixed and immutable hereditary groupings that reach back into antiquity." The breeding population school held the view that races start with a common genetic heritage and that geographic and social isolation (breeding barriers), mutation, natural selection, and genetic drift gave rise to "more or less stable, differentiated gene pools among humankind"—populations that differ with respect to the frequency of certain genetic traits. The "no-race school" denies that races, as discrete biological entities, are real.

Race nevertheless remains a social reality. People are socially defined as belonging to different races, and they are treated differently based upon these social definitions. The differences in treatment produce differences in outcomes for the different races, and these different outcomes are then used as evidence to support the ideology of racism. Consequently, the ideology of racism can also be challenged by examining the way any social institution functions. If the institutions of education, health care, religion, the family, the polity, or the economy treats all races equally, then differences among races with respect to that institution might be attributable to racial differences. If those institutions treat people in different races unequally, then these differences in treatment may be sufficient to explain any differences among groups, and any racial explanation would more likely be an expression of the ideology of racism.

History of the Ideology The ideology that one race is superior to others, particularly with respect to intelligence, has existed for thousands of years. The sociologists Brewton Berry and Henry L. Tischler quote a letter from Cicero, the Roman statesman and orator, to Atticus (c. 100 B.C.E.): "Do not obtain your slaves from Britain because they are so stupid and so utterly incapable of being taught that they are not fit to form a part of the household of Athens." Almost two thousand years later, Count de Gobineau returned the insult, complaining about the Italians, as well as the Irish and "cross-bred Germans and French" who were immigrating to the United States. They were, in de Gobineau's opinion, "the human flotsam of all ages . . . decadent ethnic varieties."

Just as de Gobineau was not deterred by Cicero's low opinion of northwestern Europeans, so are many of the descendants of those Italians, Irish, Germans, French (and others) not deterred by de Gobineau's opinion from thinking that they constitute a superior race. Consequently, one of these descendants, psychologist R. Meade Bache, in an 1895 study entitled "Reaction Time with Reference to Race," reached the conclusion that whites were intellectually superior to blacks and American Indians, even though whites had the slowest reaction times of the three groups. Bache interpreted the results to mean that whites "were slower because they belonged to a more deliberate and reflective race."

Bache was the first of a long line of so-called scientists who managed to confirm the superiority of their own race. After him came the famous psychologist Robert Yerkes, who developed intelligence tests for World War I recruits and concluded that the tests proved the intellectual inferiority of blacks. Then Carl Brigham used the Yerkes data to prove that more recent European immigrants were genetically intellectually inferior to earlier European immigrants. This ideology of racism has continued to the present day, when many are still convinced that whites are intellectually superior to other races because they average higher scores on IQ tests.

During the last four centuries, prejudices toward blacks have changed, but such prejudices still exist. As scientific research slowly convinces many people that a particular prejudice is factually incorrect, informed people begin to laugh and scorn when it is expressed, and others become ashamed to express it. Yet as that particular prejudice falls into disuse, another is invented, often by respected and influential people, to take its place. This occurs because continuing discrimination requires prejudice to rationalize it. In the future, if racial discrimination continues, so will racism as an ideology.

Donald M. Hayes

Core Resources

Stephen Jay Gould's *The Mismeasure of Man* (New York: W. W. Norton, 1981) challenges the concept of intelligence as a single entity that can be quantified by one number (as an IQ score) that can then be used to rank order according to worthiness—invariably to find that oppressed groups are innately inferior and least worthy. William Ryan's *Blaming the Victim* (rev. ed., New York: Vintage Books, 1976) is an excellent rebuttal of racism as an ideology. James W. Vander Zanden's *American Minority Relations* (4th ed., New York: Alfred A. Knopf, 1983) includes a discussion of the concept of race in chapter 2.

See also: Intelligence and race; Race as a concept; Racism: changing nature of; Racism: history of the concept.

Racism: changing nature of

Overt racism—such as legal discrimination and open use of derogatory language—largely disappeared in the 1960's and 1970's but racism lingers on in the form of covert racism, often manifest through the use of "code words" and in subtly, even unconsciously, racist attitudes and policies.

Various ethnic groups have experienced racism—both overt and covert—since the colonization of the Americas by European explorers in the 1500's. Although some of the worst forms of discrimination, including slavery, have been abolished, racism still exists in the United States. Recent U.S. history contains numerous examples: During World War II, Japanese Americans were incarcerated in concentration camps, and until the 1950's and 1960's, African Americans were legally segregated from whites in residential areas and public facilities, including schools, buses, and restaurants.

Decline of Overt Racism Some of the events and legislation that contributed to a climate of reform and the gradual demise of overt racism include the 1954 U.S. Supreme Court decision in *Brown v. Board of Education*, which legally ended discriminatory "separate but equal" policies for whites and blacks, and Rosa Parks's 1955 refusal to give up her bus seat to a white woman and the subsequent Montgomery bus boycott. The 1963 civil rights marches in Birmingham, Alabama, and the Freedom March on Washington, D.C., where Martin Luther King, Jr., gave his famous "I Have a Dream" speech, helped bring about the passage of the Civil Rights Act of 1964, which prohibited discrimination on the grounds of race or sex. Another important piece of legislation was the Voting Rights Act of 1965, which banned barriers to free exercise of the right to vote and led to a dramatic increase in black voter registration.

In most parts of the United States, using racial epithets and engaging in racist activities is socially unacceptable, and throughout the nation, denying someone housing, employment, education, or opportunity on the basis of race is illegal; however, racism has not disappeared from American culture. Some examples of overt racism can still be found, such as the 1998 murder of a black hitchhiker, James Byrd, Jr., in Jasper County, Texas. Byrd died after being picked up by three white men, tied to the back of their truck, and dragged. However, for the most part, racism has gone underground, becoming either covert or unconscious.

Covert Racism Covert, or what has been called inferential, racism is the form of racism that develops in a society that declares itself to be free of racism despite abundant evidence to the contrary. Such racism, according to researcher Stuart Hall, is actually more dangerous and difficult to combat than overt racism simply because it is harder to pinpoint and because it is often expressed unconsciously by "well-meaning liberals" with seemingly antiracist intent.

One way that covert racism operates is by recoding race into what appears to be a nonracial discourse. In this way, race "can be spoken silently, its power can be exerted invisibly," according to John Fiske in *Media Matters* (1994). Some people believe that race was recoded as a discourse on "family values" in Republican politics in the early 1990's. For example, in a May, 1992, address at the Commonwealth Club of California in San Francisco, former vice president Dan Quayle commented on a "poverty of values" in the African

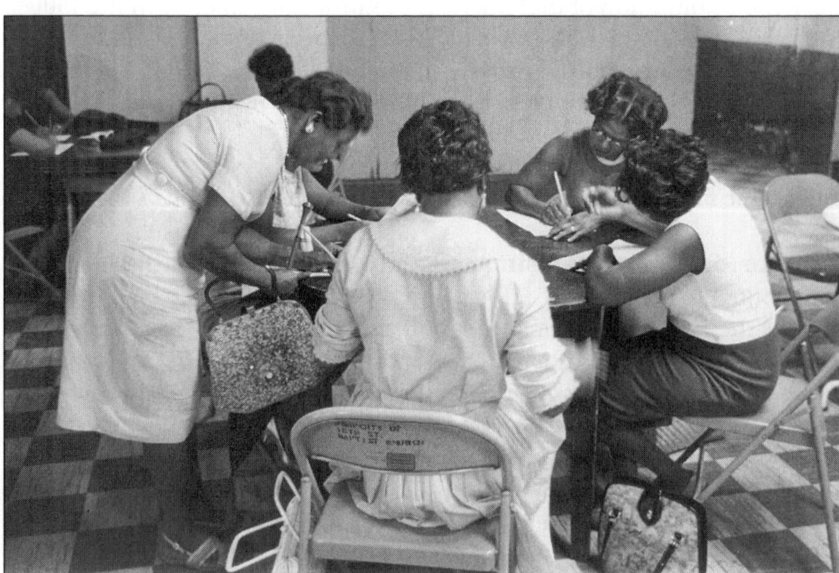

Women participating in a May, 1963, voter education meeting in the basement of Birmingham's Sixteenth Street Baptist Church, where four young girls were killed by a bomb attack four months later. *(Library of Congress)*

American community. More specifically, he attributed the 1992 uprisings in South Central Los Angeles, a predominantly minority area, to a "breakdown of family structure, personal responsibility, and social order." He went on to discuss the formation of a new underclass "dependent on welfare for very long stretches" and said that "the intergenerational poverty that troubles us so much is predominantly a poverty of values." Many people believe that his statements imply that poverty and welfare problems in the United States are a black problem, not a white problem, and that African Americans do not have the appropriate values (those held by the white majority) to avoid or escape poverty.

Another example of recoding race into a "nonracial" discourse—in this case, law and order—is a campaign advertisement produced in support of Republican George Bush's bid for the U.S. presidency in 1988. The advertisement featured African American and convicted felon Willie Horton, who, upon his release from jail on a "weekend pass" in Massachusetts, raped and stabbed a white woman and stabbed a white man. Designed explicitly to convince people that Michael Dukakis, Bush's opponent and governor of Massachusetts, was soft on crime, the campaign spot played on white Americans' stereotypical view of black men as violent and hypersexual.

A second type of inferential racism, according to Fiske, is denial. This occurs when the racial intent or impact of an action or comment is denied, despite protestations of racism by the offended group or others. For example, the videotaped 1991 beating of African American Rodney King during an arrest by Los Angeles Police Department officers is regarded by many people as a racially motivated incident. However, a white juror in the 1992 trial of four white police officers accused of excessive force in the beating of King, commenting on the not-guilty verdict, said of the prosecution, "They kept trying to bring race into it, but race had nothing to do with it."

Although the denial of racism is a common strategy used by conservatives, Fiske argues that liberals who claim to be nonracist "are more likely to exert a form of nonracist racism unintentionally by marginalizing or silencing any explicit references to the topic." As an example, he cites the white liberal senators who supported Anita Hill's sexual harassment accusations against Clarence Thomas, the black conservative judge appointed by George Bush to the U.S. Supreme Court. In supporting Hill, these senators emphasized her gender and ignored or marginalized her blackness, although many black and white Americans believed that race was a central factor in the culture's prurient fascination with both Thomas's and Hill's sex lives.

A final way in which inferential racism exerts itself is through American culture's assumption that whiteness is the default value, the norm or the "natural" state of being. Whiteness is never examined or dissected, but what is instead open for discussion and debate is blackness or race in general. Therefore, any problems created by racism or relations between races are termed "the race problem"—situations or difficulties occurring within the black community and largely that community's responsibility. What is not addressed is the need for whites to examine their own racist values and practices.

Susan Mackey-Kallis

Core Resources

Books and articles on the changing nature of racism include John Fiske's *Media Matters: Everyday Culture and Political Change* (Minneapolis: University of Minnesota Press, 1994), Ruth Frankenberg's *White Women, Race Matters: The Social Construction of Whiteness* (Minneapolis: University of Minnesota Press, 1993), Toni Morrison's *Playing in the Dark: Whiteness and the Literary Imagination* (New York: Vintage, 1993), and Stuart Hall's "The Whites of Their Eyes: Racist Ideologies and the Media," in *The Media Reader*, edited by Manual Alvarado and John Thompson (London: BFI, 1990).

See also: King, Rodney, case; Race as a concept; Race relations cycle; Racism as an ideology; Racism: history of the concept.

Racism: history of the concept

Racism as a widespread social phenomenon rose in the late fifteenth and early sixteenth centuries as European explorers encountered the indigenous peoples of unknown lands, who looked, spoke, and lived so differently that it was easy to deny their humanity.

The concept of race is an invention of the early modern world. The ancient and medieval worlds did not identify persons by race. Individuals were recognized during these earlier periods in geographic terms. Hence, an African would be called Ethiopian or Egyptian as opposed to being called black or Negro.

Origins Racial emphasis came into use as a support for imperialism and its accompanying institution of slavery. Although the origin of the word "race" is obscure, experts believe that it began as a loose description of similar groups. This description originally was not restricted to biologically similar people. For example, in 1678, John Bunyan in *Pilgrim's Progress* wrote of a "race of saints."

The first English record of the use of the word "race" was in 1508. In that year, William Dunbar in a poem spoke of "bakbyttaris if sindry racis" (backbiters of sundry races).

It was not until 1684 that the term "race" was used to designate skin color and other distinguishable physical features. It was then used by the Frenchman François Bernier, who used his experiences as a traveler and physician to employ such an application.

It appears, however, that such classifications did not become commonplace immediately. It was only after science adopted the concept of race as an explanation for human variation that it became a broadly accepted tenet.

Citations of Earlier Prejudices Some scholars, such as Winthrop Jordan and Joseph Harris, have documented evidence of racial prejudice all the way back to the earliest contact between whites and nonwhites. These actions appear to be based more on geographic differences than on color differences. For example, fantastic fables about Africans circulated among Europeans. Equally preposterous stories about Europeans, however, circulated in the ancient and medieval world among Europeans. Thus, such views seem to be the products of encounters between different peoples in an age that was characterized by superstition and fear of the unknown.

Scientific Racism The year 1798 has been cited as marking the beginning of scientific racism. This later form of racism was not restricted to skin color alone. It was used to slight Jews and Catholics as well as nonwhite people. In its earliest use, scientific racism was employed mainly as a justification of economic inertia. Thus, it was said that human deprivation could not be relieved through charitable donations. According to the proponents of scientific racism, government volunteer agencies or individuals would simply be throwing money away if they were to invest it in the segment of humanity that was hopelessly and irretrievably at the bottom of the social and economic ladder.

This employment of a pseudoscientific justification for racism was expanded with the introduction of Social Darwinism in the late nineteenth century. Purveyors of this doctrine imported Charles Darwin's theory of evolution from biology and applied it to a social context. Whereas Darwin himself had only theorized about species, the Social Darwinists declared that one race was superior to another because it had evolved further and faster than had the inferior group. A chain of evolutionary progress was created that placed the black race at the bottom and whites of the Nordic pedigree at the summit of humanity. Thus, black people were portrayed as animalistic, subhuman, and therefore incapable of higher thought, while Nordic Europeans were said to be natural leaders.

The use of science to prop up racism has probably been the most pernicious development in the history of racism. When zoology, anatomy, and other fields of scientific study advanced explanations of human differences, they were given serious hearings. Consequently, the layperson accepted the scientist's word as authoritative in spite of its theoretical and unproved claims.

Religious Influences From the beginning of the European enslavement of Africans, religion was an element in the process. As early as 1442, Pope Eugenia IV granted absolution to Portuguese seamen who, under the direction of Prince Henry the Navigator, took African "souls" and sold them. Within ten years, however, it became unnecessary to ask for absolution, because Pope Nicholas V gave the king of Spain his blessing to enslave "pagans." Christopher Columbus's writings show that he used this same justification for the enslavement of Native Americans. Chapels were included in most of the slave factories, also known as "castles," which were erected along the west coast of Africa. Their presence was indicative of organized Christianity's approval of slavery.

At first, the Spanish provided for enslaved Africans to be manumitted upon their conversion to Christianity, since it was considered wrong for one Christian to hold another Christian in bondage regardless of the bondsman's race. As conversions to Christianity became commonplace among African slaves, however, manumissions became uncommon. By the middle of the seventeenth century, Europeans began to identify black skin with a lifetime of slavery.

The Bible was used to "prove" that blacks were a cursed people. A favorite scriptural citation for this purpose was Noah's curse upon his grandson Canaan because his father Ham had mocked his own father (Genesis 9:20-27). This scripture was given a racial interpretation by the slavocracy's hermeneutists. They declared that Ham was the father of the black race and that Noah's specific condemnation of Canaan should be expanded to include all black people. Thus, religious justification for the enslavement of blacks evolved from the belief that it was immoral for a Christian to enslave another Christian, regardless of race, to the nineteenth century idea that the African was eternally condemned to be a servant of others. By the nineteenth century, proponents of slavery declared that it simply was the natural order for the African to be "a hewer of wood and drawer of water" for the more advanced races. As the "peculiar institution" of slavery became more prevalent, the argument to legitimate it—especially from a religious perspective—became more vindictive toward nonwhite lands.

Cultural Racism Both slavery and imperialism used cultural arguments to control other races. The doctrine of the "white man's burden" said that Europeans had a moral responsibility to expose deprived nonwhites to the superior culture of the whites. Thus, Africans who were kept on a plantation were thought to benefit from their close association with their masters. It was said that Africans, if left alone, would languish in retrogressive ignorance and backwardness.

This paternalistic view was not unique to American slavery. Both Europe and the United States used the concept of the white man's burden to justify the usurpation of the lands of nonwhite people. In each territory, the indigenous people were characterized as savage and uncivilized. Only exposure to the white man's superior culture would save such people. This attitude of superiority legitimated the takeover of other peoples and lands.

This view reflected the belief that many whites held during the age of imperialism. They saw themselves as God's gift to humanity. Officially, this concept came to be known as Manifest Destiny. The imperialists believed that they had a mission to expand beyond others' borders to uplift those people to the imperialists' level. This attitude was arrogant and discriminatory. Anything of note that had been done by nonwhite people was ignored, while every important aspect of human civilization was always in some way considered a product of white genius. Such a polemical view of culture helped to solidify white supremacy and the existence of racism.

Economic Racism During slavery, the argument was advanced that the institution was necessary for the benefit of black people. It was declared that they were childlike and incapable of self-support. As long as they remained on the plantation, they had a haven that protected them from want. Slavery's defenders used this argument to portray slavery as advantageous to the slaves. Even after the Civil War, many southern historians continued to use the economic argument to show that slavery was an economic boon to blacks. They pointed to postbellum vagabondage and government dependency among freed slaves as proofs that black people were better off on the plantation, where they were given food, clothing, and shelter.

Those who advanced these "proslavery arguments" failed to acknowledge that it was the years of exploitation and neglect on the plantation that had contributed to the freed slaves' deplorable condition. Also, they never addressed the freed slaves and antebellum free blacks who, in the face of tremendous difficulties, still managed not only to support themselves and their families but also to become entrepreneurs, landowners, and employers, sometimes even of whites.

Even in the twentieth century, economics was used as a defense for racism: South Africa's apartheid policy and business transactions carried on there were justified by American and European corporations. In the wake of an international call for divestiture, these companies argued that their continued operation in South Africa was for the good of the blacks and colored people at the bottom of the economic ladder. Divestiture would deprive these two groups of a livable wage. Therefore, it was prudent for nonwhite people to continue to work for these corporations while the corporations used their influence to effect change.

Social Segregation After the American Civil War and Reconstruction, Jim Crow laws were instituted throughout the southern United States. These laws segregated society on the basis of race in practically every area of life. Except in menial jobs, blacks could not enter white restaurants, hotels, schools, or any other "whites only" public facility. When they were allowed in the same buildings as whites, African Americans had separate, well-defined places such as balconies or basements to occupy.

Most southern states reinforced their segregation policies with laws that prohibited interracial marriages. Propagandists repeatedly warned that having one drop of Negro blood meant that one was a Negro. To the racist, amalgamation was a deadly sin.

Resulting from such hysteria was a Negrophobia that frequently manifested itself in the worst imaginable forms of brutalization. In the late nineteenth century and the first half of the twentieth century, it was common for African Americans to be lynched at the hands of white gangs without due process of law. The most common offense was the rape, real or imagined, of white women. Frequently, it was the latter. A celebrated case of this sort occurred when fourteen-year-old Emmett Till was murdered in Money, Mississippi, in 1955. Apparently, his only offense was that he called a white woman "baby."

Institutional Racism With the massive urbanization of African Americans in the United States in the twentieth century and the resulting residential segregation in cities, the stage was set for the emergence of institutional racism. This form of racism was more covert than was individual racism, which was person-to-person, emotional and blunt. Institutional racism resulted in a denial of equal access to goods and services by predominantly black sections of the cities. For example, higher prices and less desirable products were more often found in the predominantly black and Hispanic inner cities than in the white suburbs.

Since this type of discrimination manifested itself through institutions and was not conducted by individuals, many people were simply oblivious to its existence. In addition, because of diminished interracial contact in urban areas, many suburbanites, as a result of ignorance of the ways in which societal institutions discriminate, were prone to blame deplorable living conditions within inner cities on the residents' lack of initiative and concern rather than on institutional biases.

Institutional racism can explain a disproportionate number of nonwhites being unemployed, underemployed, and incarcerated in prisons. Despite affirmative action policies and legal gains during the twentieth century, African Americans and other minorities were excluded and ignored by many institutions, such as employers, lenders, and investment agencies. A prime example is the absence of stockbrokers' and other investment advertisements in African American-oriented media.

New Conflicts Many African American leaders have argued that it is impossible for black people to be racist. They believe that they can be prejudiced, but not racist, because they lack the power to enforce their prejudice.

While this position has been advanced by the African American left, the white right has charged that group with "reverse" racism. Many conservatives contended that government affirmative action programs and the preferential treatment accorded minorities since the passage of civil rights legislation victimize whites in the same way that nonwhites previously experienced discrimination. Even black neoconservatives have argued that "race preferences" victimize blacks and other people of color by minimizing their achievements.

Efforts to Eradicate Racism Persons of goodwill have seen the wisdom in freeing humanity of racial bigotry. Although racism has been opposed since its inception, the most celebrated and concentrated efforts began with the modern Civil Rights movement, which began with the bus boycott in Montgomery, Alabama, in 1955. Under the nonviolent leadership of Martin Luther King, Jr., racism was exposed as morally wrong. King's philosophy accentuated the brotherhood of humanity and love for one's neighbor, regardless of race, nationality, or ethnicity.

By developing an integrated coalition and marching peacefully under King's leadership, King's followers erected a workable model of human cooperation that could be emulated throughout the world. Ironically, those who brutalized these nonviolent protesters with police dogs and fire hoses convinced many people throughout the world that racism was an insidious evil that should be stamped out.

As a result, people have become more reluctant to be known as racists. Therefore, racially sensitive issues have become increasingly difficult to discuss openly, and instead such discussions have adopted code words or centered on peripheral issues such as socioeconomic class. Racism continues to flourish, but it has become more covert and institutional than overt and individual.

Randolph Meade Walker

Core Resources

Michael Banton and Jonathan Harwood's *The Race Concept* (New York: Praeger, 1975) is a general discussion of the evolution of the idea of race. Jacques Barzun's *Race: A Study in Superstition* (rev. ed., New York: Harper & Row, 1965) is an interesting refutation of Nazi teachings that addresses the expanded use of race beyond color applications. Allan Chase's *The Legacy of Malthus: The Social Costs of the New Scientific Racism* (New York: Alfred A. Knopf, 1977) is a thorough treatment of scientific racism. Earl Conrad's *The Invention of the Negro* (New York: Paul S. Eriksson, 1967) contends that black Africans did not suffer extreme degradation until the slave trade became big business in the Americas. Winthrop D. Jordan's *White over Black: American Attitudes Toward the Negro, 1550-1812* (New York: W. W. Norton, 1977) contends that racism produced slavery, providing an interesting contrast to Conrad's thesis.

See also: Civil Rights movement; Economics and race; Employment among African Americans; Individual racism; Institutional racism; Lynchings; Proslavery argument; Race as a concept; Racism as an ideology; "Reverse" racism; Sexual fears and racism; Slavery: history.

Rainbow Coalition

The Rainbow Coalition, a multicultural effort to unify racial and ethnic groups that have been marginalized in the U.S. political process, was founded in 1983 under the leadership of the Reverend Jesse Jackson.

Historically, racial and ethnic groups in the United States have experienced differing levels of participation in formal political institutions, leading to substantial inequalities in the distribution of political power among various groups. African Americans, for example, were historically excluded from participation in political processes through such legal and extralegal means as poll taxes, intimidation, and gerrymandering.

What political power African Americans did acquire was often symbolic, achieved through appointments of black leaders to high-profile positions. This tradition led to the development of a black elite that accepted the role of junior partner in the process of achieving racial integration. Most of this leadership came from minority group members in nonelected positions and from extrapolitical movements such as strikes, boycotts, and acts of civil disobedience.

In the early 1980's, Jackson organized a united front of liberal integrationists, socialists, trade unionists, feminists, gays, and racial minority constituencies to work together in the 1984 presidential campaign. The Rainbow Coalition platform was based on four premises: that Jackson had a base among the "black masses," that he was an important figure in southern black politics, that the campaign would stimulate registration of black voters, and that Jackson's presidential candidacy would create "coattail" effects that would propel other outsiders into the electoral process. None of these premises was supported by subsequent events.

To appeal to a broad range of voters, Jackson moved the left-leaning Rainbow platform toward the political center for the time of the 1988 presidential campaign. Jackson purged the coalition of its activists by blocking democratic elections of local Rainbow leadership and by placing gag orders on radical dissenters. In 1989, Jackson asserted the right to appoint all coalition leaders at the congressional district rank. In response, thousands of activists left the coalition, and several splinter groups were organized.

In the 1990's, Democratic leaders including Bill Clinton effectively undermined Jackson's leadership role in the African American community, severely diminishing the power of the Rainbow Coalition. Clinton's 1992 presidential victory was followed by the political rise of Ron Brown, one of Jackson's protégés, who had become the chair of the Democratic National Committee and was appointed secretary of commerce. Such developments led many members to leave the Rainbow Coalition and to adhere to Clinton's policies.

Glenn Canyon

See also: Civil Rights movement; Vote, right to.

R.A.V. v. City of St. Paul

During the early morning hours of June 21, 1990, "R.A.V."—an unnamed, male seventeen-year-old, self-described as a white supremacist—and several other teenagers burned a makeshift wooden cross on the front lawn of the only African American family in their St. Paul, Minnesota, neighborhood. They were prosecuted for disorderly conduct in juvenile court under the city's "bias-motivated crime ordinance," which prohibited cross burning along with other symbolic displays that "one knows" or should know are likely to arouse "anger, alarm or resentment in others on the basis of race, color, creed, religion, or gender."

The state trial court ruled that this ordinance was unconstitutionally overbroad because it indiscriminately prohibited protected First Amendment speech as well as unprotected activity. The Supreme Court of Minnesota reversed the lower court's decision and upheld the ordinance, which it interpreted to prohibit only unprotected "fighting words," face-to-face insults that are likely to cause the person to whom the words are addressed to attack the speaker physically.

The U.S. Supreme Court ruled unanimously in favor of R.A.V. and invalidated the ordinance, but the justices did not agree in their reasoning. Stating that they found the cross burning reprehensible, Justice Antonin Scalia, writing for the majority, nevertheless concluded that the ordinance was unconstitutional because it criminalized only specified "fighting words" based on the content of the hate message and, consequently, the government was choosing sides. He noted that the ordinance would prohibit a sign that attacked Roman Catholics but would not prohibit a second sign that attacked those who displayed such an anti-Catholic bias.

Four justices concurred in the ruling of unconstitutionality, but Justice Byron White's opinion sharply criticized the majority opinion for going too far to protect racist speech. He reasoned that the ordinance was overbroad because it made it a crime to cause another person offense, hurt feelings, or resentment and because these harms could be caused by protected First Amendment speech. Justices Harry A. Blackmun and John Paul Stevens also wrote separate opinions complaining that hate speech did not deserve constitutional protection.

The ruling called into question numerous similar state laws designed to protect women and minorities from harassment and discrimination. Some of these individuals and groups may still invoke long-standing federal civil rights statutes, however, which carry severe criminal penalties of fines and imprisonment. In 1993, *R.A.V.*'s significance was called into question by the *Wisconsin v. Mitchell* decision upholding a state statute that increased a sentence for a crime of violence if the defendant targeted the victim because of the victim's race or other specified status.

Thomas E. Baker

See also: Crime and race/ethnicity; Psychology of racism; Racism: changing nature of; Racism: history of the concept; *Wisconsin v. Mitchell.*

Reconstruction

Reconstruction denotes both the period and the process after the Civil War in which the Union attempted to solve the problems, and restore the status, of the southern secessionist states. During this period, formerly enslaved African Americans both enjoyed new freedoms and suffered new atrocities at the hands of segregationists and white supremacists intent on preserving the old racial hierarchy.

Soon after the Civil War commenced in 1861, northern leaders began to debate how the Confederate states should be readmitted to the Union and the many attendant problems to be resolved. For example, how should punishment for secession (withdrawing from the Union) be meted out, and against whom? What human and civil rights should be extended to the approximately four million freed slaves, and how could those rights be protected? In 1863 President Abraham Lincoln announced his plan for Reconstruction, but it was countered a year later by a proposal from Congress which touched off a national debate over who should establish Reconstruction policy.

Status of Blacks After the Civil War ended on April 9, 1865, the status of blacks quickly became the most critical issue of Reconstruction. In January, 1865, Congress had proposed the Thirteenth Amendment to the U.S. Constitution, which called for the abolition of slavery. By March, Congress had created the Freedmen's Bureau to protect the rights of southern blacks, most of whom had no private homes, money, or formal education because southern laws had relegated slaves to subhuman status. The Freedmen's Bureau obtained jobs and set up hospitals and schools for blacks. In December, 1865, the Thirteenth Amendment was ratified. Most northerners hoped that the United States could be quickly reunited and the rights of blacks protected. Tragically, however, vicious attacks on former slaves increased in 1865 and 1866. Some were accompanied by race riots. Whites murdered about five thousand blacks in the South. By December, 1865, a secret organization called the Ku Klux Klan had been founded in Tennessee. It grew rapidly, spreading terror by murder and intimidation.

Johnson's Plan After Andrew Johnson became president following Lincoln's assassination in April, 1865, he announced his own Reconstruction plan. It did not offer blacks a role in the process of Reconstruction—a prerogative left to the southern states themselves. During the summer and fall, new state governments were organized under Johnson's plan, but they began passing a series of restrictive laws against blacks called the black codes. These laws did little more than put a new face on the old practices of slavery. As a result, Republicans in Congress, both moderates and radicals, became convinced that President Johnson's plan was a failure and that the rights of both blacks and whites needed greater protection. The radicals also thought that giving blacks the right to vote was the only way to ensure the establishment of southern state governments that would remain loyal to the Union and administer uniform justice.

Civil Rights Legislation Early in 1866, Congress passed the Civil Rights Act, which guaranteed basic legal rights to former slaves. Though Johnson vetoed the bill because he did not think that the federal government should protect the rights of blacks, Congress overrode the veto, making the 1866

These turn-of-the-twentieth-century Mississippi political figures represented a generation of African American elected officials in the South whose careers were made possible by Reconstruction. *(Library of Congress)*

Civil Rights Act the first major law in U.S. history to be passed over the official objection of the president.

In June, 1866, Congress proposed the Fourteenth Amendment to the Constitution, which gave citizenship to blacks and mandated that all federal and state laws apply equally to blacks and whites. Though President Johnson urged the states to reject it (which all the Confederate states except Tennessee did), the Fourteenth Amendment was finally ratified in 1868. A third Reconstruction amendment to the Constitution, the Fifteenth, was proposed in 1869. Ratified by the states in 1870, this amendment made it illegal to deny any citizen the right to vote because of race.

Reconstruction Governments In 1867, Congress passed a series of laws called the Reconstruction Acts. These enactments abolished the newly formed state governments and placed every secessionist state (excluding Tennessee) into one of five military districts. Federal troops stationed in each district enforced martial law. By 1870 all southern states had been readmitted to the Union, and new state governments were reestablished.

Southern whites (the majority of whom were Democrats) protested the Reconstruction Acts by refusing to vote in elections which established the new state governments. Thousands of blacks (who were Republicans) did vote, and as a result Republicans won control of every new state administration. Most whites in the South refused to support the Reconstruction governments because they could not accept the idea of former slaves voting and holding elected positions. Many whites turned to violence despite military attempts to halt attacks on blacks. Army troops had little success in preventing the Ku Klux Klan and similar groups from terrorizing people and controlling the outcome of elections.

The Legacy of Reconstruction As white Democrats began regaining control of state governments in the South during the early 1870's, northerners lost interest in Reconstruction. The 1876 presidential election led to the end of Reconstruction when the Republicans agreed to a compromise with three southern states. Their disputed election returns were resolved in favor of Republican candidate Rutherford B. Hayes in exchange for the complete withdrawal of U.S. troops.

Reconstruction produced mixed results. The Union was restored, some rebuilding of the South did occur, and some blacks did get a taste of basic human and civil rights. In the end, however, most things scarcely changed at all. Many blacks remained enslaved by poverty and lack of education. Most continued to pick cotton on land owned by whites. Some scholars have suggested that the most fundamental flaw of Reconstruction was its failure to redistribute land, which would have provided an economic base to support the newly acquired political rights of black citizens.

The most important indicator of the impact of Reconstruction on American justice is the way blacks were treated after 1877. Ending slavery did not, and could not, end discrimination. The southern states continued to violate the rights of blacks for many decades afterward. It was only in the mid-1950's that black Americans inaugurated the intense struggle for complete legal equality known as the Civil Rights movement. This movement was based on the most significant judicial legacy of the Reconstruction period—the Fourteenth and Fifteenth Amendments to the Constitution. Eventually these amendments were used to establish a national system of protecting equality before the law.

Andrew C. Skinner

Core Resources

Of the many books on Reconstruction, two are classics. Eric Foner's *Reconstruction: America's Unfinished Revolution, 1863-1877* (New York: Harper & Row, 1988) is the most comprehensive; an abridged version is available as *A Short History of Reconstruction, 1863-1877* (New York: Harper & Row, 1990). The other classic is James M. McPherson's *Ordeal by Fire: The Civil War and Reconstruction* (New York: Alfred A. Knopf, 1982). Other important works include Leon F. Litwack's *Been in the Storm So Long: The Aftermath of Slavery* (New York: Alfred A. Knopf, 1979); Richard W. Murphy's *The Nation Reunited: War's Aftermath* (Alexandria, Va.: Time-Life Books, 1987), which is copiously illustrated; and Kenneth M. Stampp's *The Era of Reconstruction, 1865-1877* (New York: Alfred A. Knopf, 1965).

See also: Black codes; Civil rights; Civil Rights Acts of 1866-1875; Freedmen's Bureau; Jim Crow laws; Ku Klux Klan; Slavery: history.

Redemption period

Redemption refers to the reestablishment of conservative Democratic political dominance in the post-Reconstruction South. During the post-Civil War Reconstruction period, northern forces rebuilt the governments in the southern states after the South's defeat in the Civil War. The seeds of redemption were sown in the late 1860's as Union troops began gradually withdrawing from the South and Democrats organized locally to reclaim state legislatures and governorships. By 1877, all eleven states of the former Confederacy were controlled by conservative political interests. The chief political goals of these redeemer Democrats were reduction of government, debt repudiation, expansion of the rights of landlords, encouragement of northern capital investment, and the promotion of white supremacy.

Under redeemer state governments, the paltry advances that African Americans had made under Reconstruction were systematically reversed. Black suffrage was first nullified through electoral fraud and later circumscribed through poll taxes, literacy tests, and "grandfather clauses" that prevented all but a handful of southern blacks from voting. Sharecropping defined economic life for increasing numbers of blacks and poor whites. Violence against African Americans escalated throughout the redemption period; by the 1890's, lynchings of black men had become commonplace in many southern localities. By the turn of the century, Jim Crow legislation inspired by the Supreme Court's *Plessy v. Ferguson* (1896) decision had given legal sanction to segregation and a racial caste system that would dominate southern society well into the twentieth century.

Michael H. Burchett

See also: Jim Crow laws; Lynchings; *Plessy v. Ferguson*; Reconstruction.

Redistricting

The racial or ethnic makeup of various voting blocs can be a significant consideration when drawing electoral district boundaries. Once established, multiethnic districts may also experience intense political competition among different groups.

Redistricting is a procedure that has tremendous significance for the way that the individual votes cast by U.S. citizens are translated into the selection of legislative representatives. Racial and ethnic groups, as well as any number of other groups, may be either concentrated in particular districts or divided among many districts.

The Process The citizens of the United States are divided into 435 congressional districts, with each district electing one legislator to the U.S. House of Representatives. Each state is allocated a certain number of districts based on its relative population. Every ten years, after the census is completed, the 435 congressional seats are "reapportioned" among the states based on the new population figures.

The states then draw new district boundaries, both to permit an increase or decrease in their allotment of congressional seats and to ensure that all districts include approximately the same number of voters. These objectives derive from prevailing voting rights standards. In *Wesberry v. Sanders* in 1964, the U.S. Supreme Court decreed that congressional representation must be based on the one man, one vote principle; that is, districts must be created "as nearly as practicable" with roughly equal numbers of voters.

Gerrymandering Simply creating districts with numerically comparable populations does not ensure that the one-person, one-vote principle is observed. With knowledge of certain voting indicators (such as party affiliation), a district can be drawn that is heavily weighted toward a particular political party or group. This practice is known as "gerrymandering." Gerrymandering has a long tradition in U.S. politics, having been observed in reapportionment efforts since the late eighteenth century. In the latter half of the twentieth century, however, various redistricting plans were rejected for their overt skewing in favor of a particular party. In *Davis v. Bandemer* in 1986, the U.S. Supreme Court held that gerrymandering could be considered a violation of the equal protection clause of the Fourteenth Amendment.

Yet at the same time, gerrymandering based on race or ethnicity (rather than party affiliation) seems to have the support of institutions such as the U.S. Department of Justice and the Supreme Court. Beginning in the 1970's and 1980's, districts intentionally created to include a large percentage of racial minorities officially were seen as an appropriate corrective to address the small number of minority legislators in the U.S. Congress and in various state and local legislatures. In other words, it was assumed that the voting strength of racial and ethnic groups could be increased by concentrating their votes in individual districts. Such a procedure was understood to fulfill the objectives of the 1965 Voting Rights Act and was bolstered by a 1982 amendment to the act that upheld the right of African Americans and Hispanics "to elect representatives of their choice."

Early nineteenth century political cartoon satirizing Massachusetts governor Elbridge Gerry's plan to create a voting district shaped like a salamander. *(Library of Congress)*

This reasoning implies that racial and ethnic groups have unique, shared interests; that those interests can be represented only by a member of the group; that the members of a racial and ethnic group tend to vote in the same way; and that "outsiders" will tend not to vote for a member of the group. If all of these suppositions are true, then dividing a racial group between two districts may indeed dilute the voting strength of the bloc. Yet critics claim this reasoning conflicts with the traditional principles of U.S. liberalism, which place individual interests above group interests, and which hold ascriptive characteristics such as race to be irrelevant to the awarding of political benefits.

Legal Challenges to Majority-Minority Districts In the 1990's, the notion of "majority-minority" districts came under increasing, powerful attack. Although many leaders of minority groups continued to defend such districts as a necessary mechanism for increasing minority representation, the public mood and the U.S. Supreme Court turned against the idea.

A watershed occurred with the *Shaw v. Reno* decision in 1993. In this case, two predominantly African American districts in North Carolina were at issue. Under pressure from the U.S. Department of Justice, the North Carolina legislature had created the districts in an attempt to ensure that the state, whose population was 22 percent African American, would elect its first black congressional representatives in more than a century. Both districts did indeed elect African Americans in 1992. However, five white voters in one of the districts sued the state, claiming that they had been effectively disfranchised by the reapportionment plan. The case reached the Supreme Court, whose 5-4 majority decision instructed the lower courts to reconsider the constitutionality of the district lines, which created a "bizarre" shape and had an "uncomfortable resemblance to political apartheid." Although the lower courts again upheld the district (while making findings to satisfy the Supreme Court), *Shaw* opened the door for more legal challenges to majority-minority districts. In the ensuing court and policy battles, minority groups that stood to "lose" districts created expressly for them were pitted against whites. The National Association for the Advancement of Colored People (NAACP), the Southern Christian Leadership Conference, the Congressional Black Caucus, and various other groups associated with minority issues expressed their support of the concept of majority-minority districts. Some claimed the trend would lead to the "ultimate bleaching of the U.S. Congress."

In 1995, the Supreme Court more definitively rejected the notion of race-based districts in *Miller v. Johnson.* In this case, the Court rejected redistricting plans in which "race was the predominant factor motivating the legislature's decision to place a significant number of voters within or without a particular district." *Miller* forced the Georgia legislature to amend its reapportionment plan, and subsequent decisions forced other states to do the same. A number of incumbent minority legislatures found themselves running for reelection in districts that no longer had a high proportion of minority voters. Many minority groups saw this as a reversal in their quest for greater representation. Some even claimed that *Miller* was akin to the 1857 *Scott v. Sandford* decision, which held that blacks "had no rights which the white man was bound to respect." However, many of these incumbent legislators were reelected in their newly white-dominated districts. The relationship between race and redistricting was being rethought once again.

Steve D. Boilard

Core Resources

An outline of legal and political developments concerning race and redistricting is provided in David G. Savage's "The Redistricting Tangle," in *State Legislatures* (September, 1995). Mark F. Bernstein offers a strong defense of majority-minority districts in "Racial Gerrymandering," in *The Public Interest* (Winter, 1996). A more optimistic assessment of developments during the 1990's is offered by Carol M. Swain in "Limiting Racial Gerrymandering," in *Current* (January, 1996).

See also: Representation: gerrymandering, malapportionment, and reapportionment; "Reverse" racism; *Shaw v. Reno.*

Redlining

Redlining is a broad term, denoting the discriminatory treatment of people living in certain neighborhoods by mortgage lenders, insurance agencies, and other businesses. In effect, a "red line" is drawn around certain areas on a community map, and these areas are either excluded as potential clients or are subjected to more stringent conditions. Perceptions of redlining have triggered charges of racism by various minority groups.

Redlining arises when business decisions are made not with regard to particular individuals but with regard to particular neighborhoods. Automobile insurance, homeowner's insurance, mortgage insurance, business loans, and other risk-sensitive financial products are often priced based on conditions in a particular neighborhood or region. For example, an insurance policy for a home in a floodplain might reasonably be priced higher than the same home on higher ground because of the increased risk. Similarly, homes, automobiles, and businesses in areas with high levels of crime, fires, and other risks might be treated differently by insurance agencies and lenders. This is the most neutral definition of redlining. In itself, this practice has sometimes been the target of criticism, since it treats people as groups rather than individuals. For example, some people have objected to automobile insurance rates being set on the basis of a person's zip code rather than strictly on the basis of the individual's driving record.

The issue of redlining therefore turns on how people are categorized. Businesses such as insurance underwriting usually require that distinctions be made about different types of policyholders (smokers versus nonsmokers, young versus old, urban versus rural, brick dwelling versus wood-frame dwelling). Various laws and court decisions have established that race (as well as other characteristics) cannot be a basis for such business decisions. However, racial issues emerge when it is suspected that certain criteria (such as a person's neighborhood) are used as surrogates for race.

The issue of race becomes especially relevant when high-risk areas also happen to have high concentrations of minority households and businesses. Because many predominantly minority neighborhoods also happen to be poor, the housing stock can be older and in worse repair than the average. Further, these poorer minority neighborhoods can be more likely to experience problems with gangs, vandalism, and other forms of criminal activity. The racial issues emerge from differing perceptions about the linkage between risk, race, and business practices. The question is whether white mortgage lenders and insurance agents are motivated strictly by a color-blind analysis of risk potential or if they make unfair and unsubstantiated risk assumptions about minority neighborhoods and minority households.

Redlining on the basis of race is prohibited by federal law as well as by many state and local laws. In addition, the 1977 Community Reinvestment Act (CRA) requires financial institutions to serve all segments of the community, irrespective of race, income, and other factors. However, the CRA does not require that all applicants must be afforded the same loan conditions and terms. Instead, lenders may consider risk in issuing loans and policies. The central racial issue with regard to redlining is whether race and ethnicity are considered in evaluating risk.

Steve D. Boilard

See also: Banking practices; Discrimination: racial and ethnic; Housing; Restrictive covenants.

Reitman v. Mulkey

In the May 29, 1967, *Reitman v. Mulkey* decision, California's adoption of Proposition 14, which repealed the state's fair housing laws, was struck down by the U.S. Supreme Court.

In 1959 and 1963, California established fair housing laws. These statutes banned racial discrimination in the sale or rental of private housing. In 1964, acting under the initiative process, the California electorate passed Proposition 14. This measure amended the state constitution so as to prohibit the state government from denying the right of any person to sell, lease, or refuse to sell or lease his or her property to another at his or her sole discretion. The fair housing laws were effectively repealed. Mr. and Mrs. Lincoln Mulkey sued Neil Reitman in a state court, claiming that he had refused to rent them an apartment because of their race. They claimed that Proposition 14 was invalid because it violated the equal protection clause of the Fourteenth Amendment. If Proposition 14 was unconstitutional, the fair housing laws would still be in force. The Mulkeys won in the California Supreme Court, and Reitman appealed to the Supreme Court of the United States.

Justice Byron White's opinion for the five-justice majority admitted that mere repeal of an antidiscrimination statute would not be unconstitutional. In this case, however, the California Supreme Court had held that the intent of Proposition 14 was to encourage and authorize private racial discrimination. This encouragement amounted to "state action" that violated the equal protection clause of the Fourteenth Amendment.

The four dissenters in the case agreed on an opinion by Justice John M. Harlan. Harlan argued that California's mere repeal of its fair housing laws did not amount to encouraging and authorizing discrimination. If the repeal were to be seen that way, then a state could never rid itself of a statute whose purpose was to protect a constitutional right, whether of racial equality or some other. Harlan also suggested that opponents of antidiscrimination laws would later be able to argue that such laws not be passed because they would be unrepealable. Indeed, several ballot measures which have reversed or repealed civil rights laws protecting gays and lesbians have been struck down on the basis of *Reitman v. Mulkey*.

Reitman v. Mulkey has not had a major effect on American civil rights law. The Supreme Court has not been disposed to expand the "authorization" and "encouragement" strands of constitutional thought. The principle of "state action"—which is all that the Fourteenth Amendment equal protection rules can reach—has not been further broadened. Nevertheless, the precedent remains, with its suggestion that there is an affirmative federal constitutional duty on state governments to prevent private racial discrimination.

Robert Jacobs

See also: Discrimination; Fair Housing Act; Fourteenth Amendment; Housing.

Representation: gerrymandering, malapportionment, and reapportionment

As of 1995, the citizens of the United States were divided into 435 congressional districts, with each district electing one representative. Every ten years the congressional seats are "reapportioned" through a process of drawing new districts based on the latest census data. In *Wesberry v. Sanders* in 1964, the Supreme Court decreed that congressional representation must be based on the "one man, one vote" principle; that is, districts must be created "as nearly as practicable" with roughly equal numbers of voters. Reapportionment thus is necessary to account for population shifts over each ten-year period. Malapportionment describes the situation that results when districts are not fairly drawn.

Simply ensuring roughly equal population does not necessarily ensure that the "one man, one vote" principle is observed. With knowledge of the patterns of party affiliation within a region, a district can be drawn which gives an advantage to one particular political party. This practice is known as "gerrymandering," after Massachusetts governor Elbridge Gerry, who oversaw the creation of contorted districts, one of which was said to resemble a salamander. Gerrymandering has a long tradition in American politics, having been observed in reapportionment efforts since the late eighteenth century. Gerrymandered districts ensured continued control by party "machines" and were blamed for various political ills. In *Davis v. Bandemer* (1986), the U.S. Supreme Court held that gerrymandering could be considered a violation of the equal protection clause of the Fourteenth Amendment. To avoid charges of gerrymandering, districts must be reasonably and compactly drawn.

More recently the issue of representation has been subjected to another justice claim. Some see the incongruity between the racial makeup of the population and the racial makeup of elected bodies as evidence that racial voting strength has been "diluted." This reasoning implies that (1) racial and ethnic groups have unique, shared interests, (2) those interests can be represented only by a member of the group, (3) the members of such a group tend to vote in the same way, and (4) outsiders will tend not to vote for a member of the group. If all these suppositions are true, then dividing a racial group between two districts may indeed dilute the voting strength of the bloc. Critics, however, claim that this reasoning conflicts with the traditional principles of American liberalism, which place individual interests above group interests and hold ascriptive characteristics such as race to be irrelevant to the awarding of political benefits.

By the early 1990's some districts, such as supervisorial districts in Los Angeles County, had been designed specifically to include a significant proportion of minority citizens, presumably giving those groups more weight in the outcome of an election. The issue remains controversial, however, with some claiming that this government-sanctioned "racial gerrymandering" amounts to creating districts that isolate minority votes. The U.S. Supreme Court supported that charge by holding racially gerrymandered districts unconstitutional in *Shaw v. Reno* in 1993. The Court's 1995 *Miller v. Johnson* decision reaffirmed the unconstitutionality of districts drawn with race as the dominant factor in their design.

Steve D. Boilard

See also: Discrimination: racial and ethnic; Redistricting; *Shaw v. Reno*; Voting Rights Act of 1965.

Republic of New Africa

The Republic of New Africa (RNA) is a revolutionary black nationalist organization that was founded in 1968. Its objectives included territorial separation of African Americans from the dominant white society in the area of the five southern states considered the "Black Belt" (Mississippi, Louisiana, Alabama, Georgia, and South Carolina); cooperative economics and community self-sufficiency (as defined by the Tanzanian principles of "Ujamaa"); and the collection of reparations from the U.S. government in the amount of ten thousand dollars per person to compensate for retrenchment of the Reconstruction promise of "forty acres and a mule" to freed slaves.

The Republic of New Africa formed a government for the "non-self-governing Blacks held captive within the United States." "Consulates" were established in New York, Baltimore, Pittsburgh, Philadelphia, Washington, D.C., and Jackson, Mississippi. The RNA was seen as an internal threat to the security of the United States and targeted for attack by the U.S. federal government.

M. Bahati Kuumba

See also: Black Power movement; National Coalition of Blacks for Reparations in America.

Restrictive covenants

Restrictive covenants, sometimes called racial covenants, were agreements that barred specific racial, ethnic, and religious minorities from owning or renting certain properties. These "covenants," sometimes contracts but more often clauses placed in deeds by developers, became popular in the early twentieth century with the advent of mass black migration to northern urban areas. Restrictive covenants prevented the integration of many urban and suburban neighborhoods by denying entry to minority groups, encouraging the formation of inner-city ghettos and precipitating shortages of housing available to minorities.

Restrictive covenants proliferated after the U.S. Supreme Court upheld their constitutionality in the case of *Corrigan v. Buckley* (1926). Civil rights attorneys subsequently targeted restrictive covenants as part of their legal strategy, winning a major victory before the Supreme Court in *Shelley v. Kraemer* (1948). The Court ruled in *Shelley* that state courts, by enforcing the covenants, had violated the Fourteenth Amendment by denying minorities equal protection of the law. Yet residential segregation through covenants continued virtually unabated as few of its victims could afford to challenge these private contracts in court. In 1968, the Supreme Court, in the case of

Jones v. Alfred H. Mayer Company, outlawed restrictive covenants by upholding the Civil Rights Act of 1968, which banned racial discrimination in the sale or rental of real estate.

Michael H. Burchett

See also: Civil Rights Act of 1968; Housing; *Jones v. Alfred H. Mayer Company*; *Shelley v. Kraemer*.

"Reverse" racism

"Reverse" racism is a term applied to government-supported programs designed to remedy past injustices caused by racial discrimination. Remedies such as hiring quotas and affirmative action favor one race at the expense of random members of another race to make up for privileges that the second race once enjoyed at the expense of the first. In the simplest terms, such policies have been questioned on the basis of whether two wrongs can make a right. The term "reverse" racism has also been applied to racial consciousness-raising methods among minority groups that use the denigration of the majority racial group as a means of attaining intraracial solidarity. These methods are practiced by minority political and religious figures such as the Nation of Islam's Louis Farrakhan and academics such as Leonard Jeffries, head of the African-American Studies Department of City College of New York, who has told his classes that the lack of melanin in the skin of whites has rendered them inferior to blacks.

William L. Howard

See also: Affirmative action; Quotas; Racism: changing nature of.

Reynolds v. Sims

The 1960's witnessed a significant change in the apportionment of state legislative and congressional delegations. For the first time, the U.S. Supreme Court interfered with the apportionment practices of the states. The Court's action was an attempt to rectify what it deemed to be the malapportionment of a great majority of American state legislatures and of state delegations to the national House of Representatives

This situation had developed over the years because predominantly rural state legislatures continually ignored the population shifts that produced the tremendous growth of the country's cities in the twentieth century. In many cases, state legislatures, out of a fear that equitable redistricting would shift the rural-urban balance of power, deliberately ignored the provisions within their own state constitutions for periodic redistricting. The result was a constitutional abnormality that was distorting the democratic political process.

In a series of cases brought before the Court in the 1960's, the malapportionment problems were judicially corrected when the Court applied a "one man, one vote" principle. In 1964, a federal district court ordered the state of Alabama to reapportion but nullified two plans that did not apportion the legislative districts solely on the basis of population. The state appealed to the Supreme Court, which held that the equal protection clause of the Fourteenth Amendment requires that the seats in both houses be equally apportioned. The existing apportionment of the Alabama state legislature was struck down when the Court, in an 8-1 majority, applied the one person, one vote principle in the case. Writing for the majority, Chief Justice Earl Warren declared that restrictions on the right to vote "strike at the heart of representative government." The Court, he added, had "clearly established that the fundamental principle of representative government in this country is one of equal representation for equal numbers of people, without regard to race, sex, economic status, or place of residence within the state." The concept of one person, one vote was virtually a pure and intractable rule.

In his dissent, Justice John M. Harlan argued that the decision had the "effect of placing basic aspects of state political systems under the pervasive overlordship of the federal judiciary." This type of "judicial legislation" frightened not only Harlan but a number of conservatives who did not want to see the Supreme Court become more active in producing equal voting rights.

The legacy of this case is clear: In *Reynolds* and several companion cases decided the same day, the Supreme Court determined that it had an obligation to interfere in the apportionment practices of the states in order to guarantee that no person was deprived of the right to vote. By guaranteeing those individual rights, the legislatures as well as the House of Representatives would more properly reflect the genuine complexion of American society.

Kevin F. Sims

See also: Redistricting; Representation: gerrymandering, malapportionment, and reapportionment; Voting Rights Act of 1965.

Richmond v. J. A. Croson Company

In 1983, the City Council of Richmond, Virginia, adopted a minority set-aside program for city contracting. Under the plan, 30 percent of all city construction subcontracts were to be granted to (or "set aside" for) minority-owned business enterprises. The J. A. Croson Company, a contracting firm which had been the low bidder on a city project, sued the city when its bid was rejected in favor of a higher bid submitted by a minority-owned firm. Croson's position was that the minority set-aside violated the equal protection clause of the Fourteenth Amendment by establishing a racial classification. Richmond argued that the minority set-aside was valid as an attempt to remedy past discriminations. An earlier case, *Fullilove v. Klutznick* (1980), had approved a similar set-aside program for federal government contracts. The city pointed out that only 0.67 percent of its prime construction contracts had gone to minority firms between 1978 and 1983.

By a vote of 6 to 3 the Supreme Court decided for the Croson Company. The opinion of the Court was written by Justice Sandra Day O'Connor. Justice O'Connor argued that the earlier federal case was not relevant because the federal government has legislative authority to enforce the Fourteenth Amendment. State governments are limited by it. Race-conscious affirmative action programs are valid only where there is a showing of past discrimination by the state government itself. In the case of the Richmond statute, there was no such showing. It was undeniable that there had been discrimination against minority contractors, but that discrimination was by private firms, not by the city itself. While the city has the power to remedy private discriminations, she argued, it may not do so by setting up a quota system which is itself racially biased.

Justice Thurgood Marshall wrote the major dissenting opinion. He argued that the majority's view of the facts was too narrow. The extraordinary disparity between contracts let to minority and nonminority firms showed that there was systematic and pervasive discrimination which could be remedied in practice only by a set-aside or quota program of the kind passed in Richmond. He pointed out, as he had in earlier cases, the irony of a constitutional rule which forbids racial classifications for benign purposes, given the long history of constitutionally permitted racial classifications for discriminatory purposes. Justice Marshall insisted that the court should not scrutinize racial classifications strictly so long as the purpose of the classification is benign. Justices William J. Brennan and Harry A. Blackmun joined Marshall in his dissent.

Richmond v. J. A. Croson Company cast doubt on the future of race-conscious programs designed to remedy past discriminations. At the very least it meant that racial quotas, however well-intentioned, were likely to be held unconstitutional.

Robert Jacobs

See also: *Adarand Constructors v. Peña*; Affirmative action; *Bakke* case; *Fullilove v. Klutznick*; Quotas; Set-asides.

Roosevelt coalition

The Roosevelt coalition was an electoral bloc that supported the candidacy of President Franklin D. Roosevelt, who won office four times between 1932 and 1944. It consisted of a number of racial and ethnic minority groups that rallied around Roosevelt's New Deal policies. The programs that Roosevelt implemented as part of his New Deal had not only eased the privations of the Great Depression but, to some voters, also seemed to promise economic opportunity and the possibility of a racially just society. The Roosevelt coalition included African American, Jewish, Irish American, Italian American, and Polish American voters.

Maintaining this coalition was a difficult balancing act, particularly after the outbreak of World War II. Roosevelt had to reconcile the demands of Polish Americans and Jewish Americans that U.S. foreign policy engage Nazi Germany (which was persecuting Poles and Jews in Europe) with the isolationist sentiments of the majority of the American public. A. Philip Randolph, president of the Brotherhood of Sleeping Car Porters, threatened to lead a march on Washington, D.C., in 1941 to protest discrimination against African Americans in defense industries and the armed forces. Roosevelt responded by establishing the Fair Employment Practices Committee to address these concerns. The coalition of minority voters and solid Democratic supporters that Roosevelt created laid the foundation for the dominance of the Democratic Party through the middle of the twentieth century.

Aristide Sechandice

See also: Brotherhood of Sleeping Car Porters; Desegregation: defense; Employment among African Americans; Fair Employment Practices Committee; Labor movement.

Runyon v. McCrary

In this 1976 case, the U.S. Supreme Court broadened the meaning of Title 42, section 1981 of the 1866 Civil Rights Act to outlaw discrimination in all contracts.

Parents of African American children brought suit in federal court against private schools in Virginia that had denied their children admission. Disregarding the defendant schools' argument that a government-imposed obligation to admit black students to their unintegrated student bodies would violate constitutionally protected rights of free association and privacy, the district and appellate courts both ruled in the parents' favor, enjoining the schools from discriminating on the basis of race.

The parents had based their case on a section of the 1866 Civil Rights Act that was still in effect. In 1968, the Supreme Court had held in *Jones v. Alfred*

H. Mayer Company that section 1982 of the act prohibited racial discrimination among private parties in housing. In *Runyon,* the Court broadened this holding to imply that section 1981, the act's right-to-contract provision, outlawed all discriminatory contracts, whether involving public or private parties—including one between private schools and the parents of student applicants.

In the wake of *Runyon,* lower federal courts employed section 1981 to outlaw racial discrimination in a wide variety of areas, including banking, security deposit regulations, admissions to amusement parks, insurance, and mortuaries. The breadth of the Court's interpretation in *Runyon* of section 1981 also caused it to overlap with Title VII of the Civil Rights Act of 1964, governing employment contracts. This overlap, together with ongoing concern about the extensiveness of the interpretation of section 1981, caused the Court to consider overruling *Runyon* in *Patterson v. McLean Credit Union* (1989). Instead, *Patterson* severely restricted *Runyon* by declaring that section 1981 did not apply to postcontractual employer discrimination. *Patterson* went so far as to declare that although section 1981 protected the right to enter into employment contracts, it did not extend to future breaches of that contract or to the imposition of discriminatory working conditions. Congress in turn overruled this narrow reading of section 1981 in the Civil Rights Act of 1991, which includes explicit language permitting courts to prohibit employment discrimination that takes place after hiring.

The reason for the Court's about-face with regard to section 1981 can be found in its changing political composition. *Runyon* was decided midway through Chief Justice Warren Burger's tenure, when the Court was dominated by justices who occupied the middle of the political spectrum. In 1986, however, one of two dissenters in *Runyon,* Justice William H. Rehnquist, had succeeded Burger. Rehnquist, who had always been outspoken in his criticism of what he regarded as the Court's excess of liberalism under Chief Justice Earl Warren, dissented in *Runyon* on grounds that the Warren-era *Jones* case had been improperly decided. By 1989, when the Court handed down its decision in *Patterson,* Rehnquist had been joined by enough fellow conservative thinkers to overrule *Runyon*'s interpretation of section 1981 by one vote.

Lisa Paddock

See also: Civil Rights Act of 1991; Civil Rights Acts of 1866-1875; *Jones v. Alfred H. Mayer Company.*

Scott *v.* Sandford

In the March 6, 1857, Scott v. Sandford *decision, the U.S. Supreme Court ruled that Congress could not limit slavery in the territories, nullifying the Missouri Compromise.*

In 1834, Dred Scott, a slave of African descent, was taken by his owner, John Emerson, an army surgeon, to the free state of Illinois and then to Wisconsin Territory, which was free by the provisions of the Missouri Compromise of 1820. Emerson returned to Missouri with Scott in 1838. After Emerson's death in 1846, Scott sued his widow in the Missouri courts for his freedom, on the grounds of his having resided in a free state and later in a free territory. Although he won in the lower court, the state supreme court reversed the decision in 1852 and declared that Scott was still a slave because of his voluntary return to Missouri. During this litigation, Emerson's widow remarried and, under Missouri law, the administration of her first husband's estate passed to her brother, John F. A. Sanford. (Sanford's name was misspelled when the suit was filed.) Because Sanford was a citizen of New York, Scott's lawyer, acting on the grounds that the litigants were residents of different states, sued for Scott's freedom in the U.S. circuit court in Missouri. The verdict there also went against Scott.

The Supreme Court's Ruling The case was appealed to the U.S. Supreme Court, where it was argued in February, 1856, and reargued in January, 1857. For a variety of reasons, the Supreme Court justices determined to deal with the controversial questions of African American citizenship and congressional power over slavery in the territories. The Supreme Court announced its decision on March 6, 1857.

Although each of the nine justices issued a separate opinion, a majority of the Supreme Court held that African Americans who were descendants of slaves could not belong to the political community created by the Constitution and enjoy the right of federal citizenship; and that the Missouri Compromise of 1820, forbidding slavery in the part of the Louisiana Purchase territory north of 36°30′ north latitude, was unconstitutional. According to the opinion of Chief Justice Roger B. Taney, African Americans were "beings of an inferior order" who "had no rights which the white man was bound to respect." Taney's comments established a perception of African Americans that transcended their status as slaves. In considering the issue of equality, Justice Taney did not limit his assessment of African Americans to those who were slaves, but also included African Americans who were free. Taney's opinion raises questions about the extent to which this precept of the inferiority of African Americans helped to establish conditions for the future of race relations in the United States.

Although individual states might grant citizenship to African Americans, state action did not give blacks citizenship under the federal Constitution. Therefore, concluded Taney, "Dred Scott was not a citizen of Missouri within the meaning of the Constitution of the United States, and not entitled as such to sue in its courts."

Taney also declared that, since slaves were property, under the Fifth Amendment to the Constitution—which prohibited Congress from taking property without due process of law—Congress had only the power and duty to protect the slaveholders' rights. Therefore, the Missouri Compromise law was unconstitutional. This part of Taney's opinion was unnecessary, an *obiter dictum,* for, having decided that no African American could become a citizen within the meaning of the Constitution, there was no need for the Supreme Court to consider the question of whether Congress could exclude slavery from the territories of the United States.

Reaction The nation reacted strongly to the Supreme Court's decision. The South was delighted, for a majority of the justices had supported the extreme southern position. All federal territories were now legally opened to slavery, and Congress was obliged to protect the slaveholders' possession of their chattel. The free-soil platform of the Republicans was unconstitutional. The Republicans denounced the decision in the most violent terms, as the product of an incompetent and partisan body. They declared that when they obtained control of the national government, they would change the membership of the Supreme Court and secure reversal of the decision. Northern Democrats, while not attacking the Supreme Court, were discouraged by the decision, for if Congress could not prohibit slavery in any territory, neither could a territorial legislature, a mere creation of Congress. Therefore, popular sovereignty also would cease to be a valid way of deciding whether a federal territory should be slave or free.

John G. Clark, updated by K. Sue Jewell

Core Resources

Paul Finkelman's *Dred Scott v. Sandford: A Brief History with Documents* (Boston: Bedford Books, 1997), Don Edward Fehrenbacher's *The Dred Scott Case: Its Significance in American Law and Politics* (New York: Oxford University Press, 1978), and Walter Ehrlich's *They Have No Rights: Dred Scott's Struggle for Freedom* (Westport, Conn.: Greenwood Press, 1979) take a closer look at the famous case. Charles Morrow Wilson's *The Dred Scott Decision* (Philadelphia: Auerbach, 1973) combines a biography of Dred Scott with descriptions of the court cases and appeals. Derrick Bell's *Faces at the Bottom of the Well: The Permanence of Racism* (New York: Basic Books, 1992) employs literary models in addressing the issue of how African Americans experience racial injustice in the judicial system in the United States. Bell's *Race, Racism, and American Law* (2d ed., Boston: Little, Brown, 1980), presents a comprehensive analysis of U.S. law that asserts that racial inequality is integrated into the legislative and judicial system in the United States. K. Sue Jewell's *From Mammy to Miss America and Beyond: Cultural Images and the Shaping of U.S. Social Policy* (New York: Routledge, 1993) discusses how institutional policies and practices in the United States contribute to social inequality for African Americans in general, and African American women in particular. *Black Americans and the Supreme Court Since Emancipation: Betrayal or Protection?* (New York: Holt, Rinehart and Winston, 1972), edited by Arnold Paul, explores precedent-setting Supreme Court cases that reveal the Court's failure to ensure equal rights for African Americans.

See also: Fourteenth Amendment; Missouri Compromise; Slavery: history.

Scottsboro trials

The 1930's trials of nine young African Americans for rape mirrored both entrenched southern bigotry and antiliberal sentiments.

On March 25, 1931, nine African American boys were pulled off a freight train in Scottsboro, Alabama, after an alleged fight with a group of white youths. As the African Americans were being rounded up by sheriff's deputies, two women riders told onlookers that they had been raped by the entire group. Within a month, the boys were tried in Scottsboro, and eight of them were convicted and sentenced to death; the case of the youngest boy, only thirteen years of age, was declared a mistrial. Because of the speed of the convictions, the questionable nature of much of the testimony, and the hostile atmosphere in which the trial had been held, the case soon attracted widespread attention. Both the International Labor Defense (ILD), an arm of the Communist Party, and the National Association for the Advancement of Colored People (NAACP) expressed concern about the possibility of injustice and launched an appeal for a new trial. The boys and their parents chose the ILD to manage their defense.

The Retrials In *Powell v. Alabama* (1932), the U.S. Supreme Court overruled the convictions and sent the cases back to a lower court. There followed another series of trials in Decatur, Alabama, beginning in March, 1933, and lasting until December. This time, only three of the boys were tried, all of whom received convictions and death sentences, but the Supreme Court sustained an appeal that irregularities in the selection of jurors invalidated the verdicts. The specific irregularity was that the voting rolls showed no African Americans registered to vote in that county, in spite of a large population of qualified African Americans.

In January, 1936, a third group of trials, held in Decatur, resulted in the conviction of Haywood Patterson, who was sentenced to seventy-five years' imprisonment. After more than a year of delay and behind-the-scenes negotiations between Alabama officials and a group of the defendants' supporters, the remaining eight were tried in the summer of 1937. One received the death penalty, three were sentenced to long prison terms, and the four others were released without charges. Although the one death

The repeated convictions of nine young African Americans, known as the "Scottsboro Boys," on unsubstantiated rape charges raised questions about the fairness of the American criminal justice system. *(National Archives)*

sentence was later commuted to life imprisonment, the five convicted Scottsboro boys were unable to obtain a reversal. One was paroled in 1943, two more in 1946, and a fourth in 1950. The final prisoner escaped from a work gang in 1948 and managed to reach Michigan, from where the governor refused to extradite him. The former defendant quickly found himself in trouble, committing a murder and being sentenced to Michigan's worst prison.

Most observers outside Alabama and an increasingly large number of people within the state came to believe that the defendants were innocent and were, therefore, the victims of southern racial injustice. One of the two women accusers, Ruby Bates, had retracted her testimony by 1934 and admitted that she had lied in her original accusations. The other, a prostitute named Victoria Price, presented testimony so full of contradictions that one of the judges in the 1933 trials, Alabamian James E. Horton, overruled the jury's guilty verdict and declared a mistrial. At least one of the defendants was ruled physically incapable of rape, and a physician testified that a medical examination of Bates and Price, performed shortly after the presumed attack, did not support their claims. Although both women were found to have had recent sexual intercourse, there were no contusions or other injuries that would have matched their stories about brutality at the hands of the nine men. None of this had any appreciable effect on the juries, the prosecutors, or Judge William W. Callahan, who presided after Horton was removed from the case. Even the milder sentences meted out in 1937 resulted as much from a desire to end the unfavorable publicity surrounding the trials as from any reevaluation of the evidence.

Repercussions Besides serving as a symbol of southern bigotry, the Scottsboro trials attracted attention because of the efforts of the Communist Party to identify the cause of the defendants with their own. Working through the ILD, the Communist Party was one of the first groups to protest the verdicts in the 1931 trials, and it was the only group to offer direct aid at that time. For several years, it engaged in a running battle with the NAACP and an "American Scottsboro Committee" over the right to manage the boys' defense. The effect of these struggles was to unite many Alabamians against all "reds and foreigners" and make it more difficult to revise the verdicts. The chief defense counsel after 1931 was Samuel Leibowitz, a Jewish attorney from New York who became the target of attacks from the prosecutors. Even he, along with Judge Callahan and part of the Alabama press, came to regard the communist support as a liability and sought to dissociate the ILD from the case. In 1935, the NAACP, the American Civil Liberties Union, and the ILD joined to form the Scottsboro Defense Committee (SDC), designed to coordinate support for the defendants and to seek cooperation from moderate Alabamians. Although the ILD played a much smaller role in the case from that point on, there remained enough hostility toward outside interference in Alabama to frustrate the SDC's efforts.

The Scottsboro case mirrored many of the important social currents of the 1930's. While illustrating the extent to which white southerners would go to defend a system of white supremacy, it also marked a change from the not too distant era when the defendants might well have been summarily lynched. The hysterical attitude with which many Alabamians reacted to outside interest in the case underlined a regional insecurity that had been intensified by the unsettled conditions of the Depression. It was common for both men and women to hop onto freight trains, which the nine men had done, as had the two alleged victims. The Scottsboro boys had gotten into a fight with several white men. In Scottsboro and Decatur, race was on trial, not nine boys and men, much to the lasting chagrin of the state of Alabama. In 1976, the Alabama Board of Pardons and Paroles granted Clarence Norris a full pardon.

Courtney B. Ross, updated by John Jacob

Core Resources

Dan T. Carter's *Scottsboro: A Tragedy of the American South*, rev. ed. (Baton Rouge: Louisiana State University Press, 1979) analyzes the trials and treatment of the nine African Americans and discusses the impact of the events on the South. Allan Knight Chalmers's *They Shall Be Free* (Garden City, N.Y.: Doubleday, 1951) is an account of the Scottsboro trials from the perspective of one of the defense attorneys who also argued before the Supreme Court. In Clarence Norris and Sybil D. Washington's *The Last of the Scottsboro Boys* (New York: Putnam, 1979), the last and most literate of the defendants presents his case. Haywood Patterson and Earl Conrad's *Scottsboro Boy* (Garden City, N.Y.: Doubleday, 1950) is the first book to shed personal light on the plight of the nine.

See also: Crime and race/ethnicity; Criminal justice system; Jury selection; Lynchings.

Segregation

Segregation of minorities in the United States was a negative social and economic practice that kept the country from achieving "liberty, freedom, and equality," promises upon which the nation was founded; the practice consigned millions of people to second-class citizenship.

American segregation was born in the colonial era, when the "majority" practiced de facto segregation. When most blacks were slaves, free blacks suffered de facto segregation in housing and social segregation based on custom and folkways. As the northern colonies abolished slavery, de facto segregation sometimes became de jure separation supported by local ordinances and/or state law.

As long as the South maintained slavery, that institution regulated race relations, and de jure segregation was not needed. In 1865, however, the southern slaves were set free and legal segregation made its appearance. After the Civil War, most southern states passed legislation known as black codes, which resembled the old slave codes. Under the new codes, social segregation was often spelled out. For example, most states moved immediately to segregate public transportation lines. By the end of Reconstruction (1863-1877), race lines had hardened, and social segregation was the rule rather than the exception.

Unsuccessful Challenges Some African Americans challenged segregationist laws. In 1896, blacks from Louisiana sued a public transportation company (railroad) that operated segregated passenger cars, as stipulated by Louisiana's state laws. Black leaders argued that the state laws and the railroad's actions violated the Thirteenth and Fourteenth Amendments to the Constitution. The case, *Plessy v. Ferguson,* reached the United States Supreme Court, which ruled that segregation was legal as long as "separate but equal" facilities were made available for minorities. A lone dissenter, Justice John M. Harlan, who happened to be a white southerner, rejected the majority opinion, saying that the Constitution should be "color-blind" and that it should not tolerate "classes" among the citizens, who were all equal.

Despite Harlan's dissent, the *Plessy* decision gave absolute legal sanction to a practice that many states, including some in the North, were already practicing by custom and tradition—*Plessy* froze segregation into the highest law of the land. Thereafter, segregationists, especially those in the South, used their legislatures to pass a host of new laws that extended the supposed "separate but equal" doctrine to all areas of life. For example, restaurants, hotels, and theaters became segregated by law, not only by custom. Railroad cars and railroad stations divided the races; hospitals, doctors' offices, and even cemeteries became segregated. Some southern state laws called for segregated prisons, while prisons in other states took criminals from both races but separated them within the facility. At least one state passed a law that forbade a white and a black prisoner to look out the same prison window at the same time. If the prisoners were physically close enough to look out at the same time, they were too close to please segregationists.

As the United States matured during the twentieth century, segregation was extended whenever technology made it seem necessary. For example, in 1915, Oklahoma became the first state in the Union to require segregated public pay telephone booths. When motor cars were first used as a taxi service, taxi companies were segregated—a "white" taxi serving whites only and a "black" taxi serving African Americans only. Public water fountains became segregated, as did public restroom facilities.

Another problem became associated with segregation. Often, there was no separate facility for blacks, who were denied service altogether. For example, as late as the 1960's, President Lyndon B. Johnson's personal maid and butler-handyman experienced difficulty traveling by car from Washington, D.C., back to Johnson's Texas home. There were few if any motels along the way that would rent rooms to African Americans.

Successful Challenges Eventually, the National Association for the Advancement of Colored People (NAACP) launched new attacks against segregationist laws—especially in circumstances in which no separate facilities existed for African Americans.

Signs such as "White Ladies Only" on a public restroom were common during the days of Jim Crow, especially—but not only—in the South. *(Library of Congress)*

For example, in *Gaines v. Missouri* (1938) and *Sweatt v. Painter* (1949; a Texas case), the Supreme Court ruled that blacks could attend white law schools because no separate school was available in state for African Americans. In 1950, in *McLaurin v. Oklahoma,* the NAACP tested the same concept and won another court battle. As *McLaurin* showed, the University of Oklahoma had admitted a black student to its graduate program but then had segregated him on campus. After the Supreme Court ruled that such segregation was unfair and illegal because it denied equal education, Thurgood Marshall of the NAACP became even more determined to challenge segregation. He did so successfully when, in *Brown v. Board of Education* (1954), the Court declared segregated public education illegal.

If segregation was unjust and unconstitutional in education, it seemed clear that it was also unjust in other areas of life. In 1955, under the leadership of Martin Luther King, Jr., and others, a nonviolent protest movement took to the streets and eventually won victories that included new laws such as the Civil Rights Act of 1964 and the Voter Registration Act of 1965. Ultimately, a limited social and economic revolution occurred that condemned segregation and, in part, created a new American society.

James Smallwood

Core Resources

Segregation and its consequences are discussed in Bob Blauner's *Racial Oppression in America* (New York: Harper & Row, 1972); Taylor Branch's *Parting the Waters: America in the King Years, 1954-1963* (New York: Simon & Schuster, 1988); Joe R. Feagin and Clairece B. Feagin's *Racial and Ethnic Relations* (5th ed., Englewood Cliffs, N.J.: Prentice-Hall, 1996); James Forman's *The Making of Black Revolutionaries* (2d ed., Washington, D.C.: Open Hand, 1985); Fred Powledge's *Free at Last? The Civil Rights Movement and the People Who Made It* (Boston: Little, Brown, 1991); and Harvard Sitkoff's *The Struggle for Black Equality, 1954-1992* (New York: Hill & Wang, 1993).

See also: Bigotry; Black codes; Integration; *Plessy v. Ferguson*; Racism: history of the concept; Segregation: de facto and de jure; Segregation vs. integration; Slavery: history; *Sweatt v. Painter.*

Segregation: de facto and de jure

When used in reference to American history, *de jure* segregation (separation of races "by law") most often refers to the system of segregation that existed in the South between the 1870's and the mid-1950's. *De facto* segregation (separation "in fact" or in practice) most often refers to the continuation of segregation after legally mandated segregation was declared unconstitutional in 1954. Yet it is somewhat misleading to pigeonhole segregation with such definitions, as both types may exist simultaneously. Moreover, de facto segregation existed before the Jim Crow laws of the late nineteenth century as well as after the end of legal segregation. Both types testify to a refusal to admit various categories of Americans to full membership in American civic culture.

De jure segregation's constitutionality was upheld by the U.S. Supreme Court in *Plessy v. Ferguson* (1896). Only with the Supreme Court's unanimous decision in *Brown v. Board of Education* (1954) did de jure segregation end in the United States. The ruling specifically concerned segregated schools, but it spelled the beginning of the end for all forms of legally mandated segregation. The persistence of de facto segregation in American cities largely results from white outmigration from urban areas to suburbs.

Malcolm B. Campbell

See also: Black codes; *Brown v. Board of Education*; Civil Rights movement; Jim Crow laws; *Plessy v. Ferguson*; Segregation vs. integration.

Segregation on the frontier

Several thousand African Americans moved to the American West in the late nineteenth and early twentieth centuries in an effort to escape the racism that existed in the eastern United States. Once on the frontier, blacks established segregated communities that allowed them to live apart from whites who would discriminate against them.

Most people who have studied the western frontier have concluded that racial discrimination existed there, but that it was different from that found in the former slave states in the southeastern United States. For example, some western territories and states passed statutes requiring segregation of the races in schools and other public facilities, but these laws were not enforced as vigorously as in the South. Incidents of racial violence (such as white mobs lynching African Americans) were less numerous on the frontier than they were east of the Mississippi River.

Still, racism did exist on the frontier, and African Americans sought to avoid it. Even before the Civil War (1861-1865), free blacks established segregated communities in isolated areas of Arkansas, Louisiana, and Texas. After the war, blacks who had been slaves to Native Americans created several all-black towns and agricultural colonies in Indian Territory. Other African Americans availed themselves of the provisions of the Homestead Act (1862), which allowed them to claim a 160-acre parcel of public land on the frontier.

Members of the Shores family, who became famous as musicians in Nebraska in the late nineteenth century. *(Nebraska State Historical Society)*

Many of these black homesteaders created segregated communities where they could live by their own rules rather than those imposed upon them by white Americans.

All-Black Communities Several of the all-black settlements were towns in which all of the businesses were owned by African Americans. Others were agricultural colonies whose residents expected to earn their living primarily by farming. In reality, however, the distinction between the two types of communities often became blurred. The farmers needed businesses to supply some of their needs, and the business owners often farmed to make extra money. Consequently, many of the segregated frontier communities were small urban areas surrounded by farms.

Perhaps the most famous all-black frontier settlement was Nicodemus, Kansas. A few promoters of an all-black settlement chose a spot on the western Kansas prairie to establish Nicodemus. They filed homestead claims and mapped out town lots on part of their land. They then went back East to make speeches and distribute brochures encouraging people to move to the proposed town. The promoters then charged the recruits fees for helping them move to Kansas and for filing their homestead papers.

The Nicodemus settlers established churches, schools, and various social organizations to improve their quality of life. This attempt to create a sense of community was essential in making the colonists feel content in strange surroundings. As the people became friends with their neighbors and worked to help one another succeed, the sense of community began to grow and to become stronger. This sense of community was one of the main reasons that African Americans chose to live in segregated settlements on the frontier. However, while the sense of community was strong in Nicodemus and other all-black frontier colonies, other factors caused most of them to fail.

The frontier environment was such that droughts often led to crop failures, which sometimes caused residents to grow disillusioned and move elsewhere to farm. A second problem was that many of the settlers lacked the capital to obtain enough animals, supplies, and equipment to make farming successful. This, of course, had an adverse effect on the businesses that relied on the farmers' patronage. Many businesses went broke, and African American farmers often had to work for nearby whites in order to eke out a living from the harsh frontier land. Eventually, many inhabitants of all-black communities abandoned their claims and moved into or near towns where whites also lived.

Black Neighborhoods in White Communities Even in these larger, predominantly white settlements, African Americans usually segregated themselves. Many frontier towns had a neighborhood where African Americans lived and socialized, creating a black community within the larger, white-controlled community. In these situations, African Americans experienced social segregation while participating in an integrated business environment that allowed them to benefit from their more prosperous white neighbors. Some blacks worked as hired hands and domestic servants for white families, and others ran restaurants, hotels, barbershops, laundries, repair shops, and other businesses that catered to customers of all races.

Laws and customs of the late nineteenth and early twentieth centuries dictated that the social contact between blacks and whites be limited. This was true in the American West just as it was in the older eastern sections of the country. However, a relatively low level of prejudice on the western frontier allowed for much business activity between the races. Thus, although African Americans on the western frontier usually lived in segregated communities, their lives were more prosperous and successful when they engaged in commerce with their white neighbors.

Roger D. Hardaway

Core Resources

Norman L. Crockett discusses four all-black frontier towns (Nicodemus, Kansas, and Boley, Clearview, and Langston, Oklahoma) in *The Black Towns* (Lawrence: Regents Press of Kansas, 1979). Kenneth Marvin Hamilton examines Nicodemus, Boley, Langston, and Allensworth, California, in *Black Towns and Profit: Promotion and Development in the Trans-Appalachian West, 1877-1915* (Urbana: University of Illinois Press, 1991). Black communities in predominantly white towns are the subject of Thomas C. Cox's *Blacks in Topeka, Kansas, 1865-1915: A Social History* (Baton Rouge: Louisiana State University Press, 1982) and of William L. Lang's "The Nearly Forgotten

Blacks on Last Chance Gulch, 1900-1912," in *Pacific Northwest Quarterly* (70, 1979). A general survey of the various types of western black settlements is Roger D. Hardaway's "African American Communities on the Western Frontier," in *Communities in the American West,* edited by Stephen Tchudi (Reno: Nevada Humanities Committee and University of Nevada Press, 1999).

See also: African American-American Indian relations; African American cowboys; Segregation.

Segregation vs. integration

Segregation is the separation of groups of people, either by law or because of custom or economic disparities. Integration means that all people and groups in a society are considered equal under the law and are allowed to move freely and live without unequal restrictions.

Examples of segregation may be found throughout history, as groups considered inferior or subordinate have been forced to live in specific areas of a city or town. Jews in Europe were forced into separate communities, called ghettos, in the Middle Ages by Christians who believed the Jews were "unclean" and racially inferior. The caste systems in India and Southeast Asia forced persons born into "inferior" castes to live in separate areas of a community. Some people, considered so unclean that merely breathing the same air they breathed would contaminate a higher caste member's body, were forced to live outside the walls surrounding many Indian villages. These "untouchables" suffered miserably, but their status was defined by Hindu religious beliefs, and they could do little to improve their living standards. Though the caste system has been outlawed by the Indian government and all citizens are considered equal in the eyes of the law, beliefs die hard, and Indians considered lower caste are still victims of discrimination and segregation. Other examples of segregation include the apartheid system that existed in South Africa and the Jim Crow system that existed in the southern part of the United States. South Africa officially repudiated its system of separate racial communities in 1992, and, since 1964, discrimination based on race has been illegal in the United States. Yet segregation is still found in both countries. Though legal (or de jure) segregation has largely disappeared, de facto segregation resulting from attitudes and customs, can be found almost everywhere in those two countries.

School Segregation In 1954, the U.S. Supreme Court outlawed racial segregation in public schools in *Brown v. Board of Education.* Separating children by race, the Court found, created a feeling of inferiority among African American students. Segregation made them feel unwanted by the white majority, and this feeling prevented them from getting an equal educational opportunity. The Court ordered school districts to desegregate "with all deliberate speed." White reaction, however, which turned violent in many southern communities, prevented rapid compliance with the Court's ruling. By 1966, only 15 percent of southern school districts were desegregated. In an effort to push integration forward, the Office of Civil Rights in the Department of Health, Education, and Welfare began to withhold federal money from segregated districts. These financial sanctions encouraged fuller compliance with the *Brown* ruling so that by 1973 almost half of the districts in the South had desegregated. In the North and West, on the other hand, where the government did not threaten to withhold money, almost 70 percent of school districts remained highly segregated.

In 1990, racially integrated schools (defined as those with some black students but with white students in the majority) remained a distant goal. More than 63 percent of African American children attended segregated schools.

Housing Segregation Housing patterns and neighborhood segregation were the primary reasons for this racial division. Segregation in the American school system has also resulted directly from the attitudes and actions of white parents who refused to send their children to schools attended by blacks.

Many white Americans, according to studies of public opinion, hold beliefs that help prevent integration. Generally, whites say that they believe in equality for all, but when it comes to action that would make that principle possible, they reject any changes. For example, many white Americans fear that once a few black people move into a neighborhood, more will quickly follow, and the racial change will greatly lower the value of their property. They also fear that crime rates will increase—even if many, or most, of the newcomers are middle class—and that educational quality will decline. White residents flee, and neighborhoods quickly become resegregated. Unlike most whites, a majority of African Americans (more than 70 percent) in the late 1980's support and say they would choose to live in mixed communities. The ideal neighborhood, according to polls of African Americans, would be 55 percent white and 45 percent black. Whites polled, on the other hand, have said they would probably move if the black population reached more than 20 percent.

White Attitudes Many white Americans do not believe that racism and racial discrimination are major problems. These whites believe that integration and affirmative action programs have all but ended inequality and that blacks exaggerate the negative effects of inequality on their educational and employment opportunities. Only 26 percent of white Americans in a national poll in the late 1980's thought that African Americans faced any "significant" discrimination in their daily lives. More than twice as many blacks (53 percent) responded that they faced significant amounts of prejudice and discrimination in their day-to-day affairs. Many white Americans believe that African Americans deserve the rejection they receive in American society, believing that it is "their" fault they are economically and socially unequal. If "they" simply worked a little harder, drank less, made a greater effort to find better jobs, and took firmer control of their own lives, this argument goes, they would be accepted as equal by whites. Other surveys of white attitudes, however, show that this belief is not borne out in reality. Many whites want little or no contact with blacks and will, in fact, go to great expense and move considerable distances to maintain racial isolation and separation. This type of de facto segregation is the norm in American society, and it is very difficult to change.

Remedial Efforts Before the Civil War (1861-1865), slavery was the principal system of maintaining white supremacy in the United States. The slave system rigidly segregated African Americans into an inferior status; under the laws of most slave states, slaves were not even considered human beings. With the abolition of slavery in the aftermath of the bloodiest war in American history, southern whites constructed a system of legal segregation to maintain white supremacy and keep blacks in an inferior economic and social status. That system of legal segregation, called Jim Crow, in which it was a violation of state law for black and white Americans to attend school or church together, or to eat together, lasted until the 1960's.

Officially the Civil Rights Act of 1964 barred discrimination in education, employment, or housing based on race, religion, ethnicity, or gender. Still, the attitudes of white superiority remained dominant in the minds of most whites, and actual integration in schools, employment, and housing, occurred very slowly, if at all. In the 1980's in Illinois, for example, African Americans composed 18.7 percent of the student population, and 83.2 percent of them attended totally segregated schools. In Mississippi, African Americans totaled 55.5 percent of school enrollments, with 80.3 percent going to segregated classrooms. Such numbers reflect the continuing segregation of American society.

Even within integrated schools some observers find an internal system of student segregation. Black students make up about 16 percent of all public school students in the United States but 40 percent of all pupils considered to be retarded, to have a disability, or to be deficient. Black students are therefore further segregated by "tracking," in which students are separated by scores on standardized tests and according to their "potential." Black students are found in overwhelming numbers in the lowest track. African American children enter school with great disadvantages in socioeconomic backgrounds and cultural opportunities; those two factors, especially the first (which refers to family income), are directly related to doing well in school and on achievement tests. Unless economic opportunities for black families greatly improve, it is likely that the large gap in educational outcomes will not be significantly reduced. Disparities in family income account for most of the differences among white students on these same tests, so it should not be surprising that, given the large income gap between white and black families, with median wealth for black families ($6,837 in 1984) being less than 25 percent of white family wealth ($32,667 in 1984), African Americans would do less well in schools.

Some American communities have achieved a degree of integration, but usually it requires some restrictions and positive actions on the part of local leaders. In one study in the 1980's, it was noted that the number of black residents could not be allowed to become more than 16 to 20 percent of any neighborhood, or whites would begin to move. Citizens interested in integration must take charge of their own communities and not allow real estate interests to take advantage of racial fears through "blockbusting" tactics. Oak Park, Illinois, has shown that a carefully controlled housing market can promote racial integration. It has been shown in this Chicago suburb that white citizens will remain in an integrated community as long as black residents make up less than half of the population. White anxieties about crime are significantly reduced in these circumstances.

In other areas and communities, desegregation of public schools could be accomplished only by an extensive busing program that took students out of their neighborhoods and transported them to integrated school facilities. Although such programs met with mixed success, they did help to jump start school integration during the 1970's. Other ideas, such as freedom-of-choice plans (whereby students can voluntarily attend any school in the district), and so-called "magnet schools," offering special programs for selected students, have done little to reduce segregation.

Leslie V. Tischauser

Core Resources

John Hope Franklin's *The Color Line: Legacy for the Twenty-first Century* (Columbia: University of Missouri Press, 1993) is a series of lectures delivered by an eminent African American historian looking into the past and the future of race relations in the United States. Andrew Hacker's *Two Nations: Black and White, Separate, Hostile, Unequal* (New York: Charles Scribner's Sons, 1992) provides direct statistical evidence from polls bearing witness to the deteriorating state of race relations in the United States. Gunnar Myrdal's *An American Dilemma: The Negro Problem and Modern Democracy* (New York: Harper & Row, 1962), originally published in 1944, is a classic study of race relations in the United States.

See also: *Brown v. Board of Education*; Busing and integration; Integration; Jim Crow laws; *Plessy v. Ferguson*; Segregation; Segregation: de facto and de jure.

Self-segregation

The racial integration of American institutions was an important part of the 1960's Civil Rights movement. However, many neighborhoods, schools, and social and religious organizations continued to be segregated even after laws enforcing segregation disappeared. Some observers have maintained that this is largely a result of self-segregation by minority group members, sparking debates over the extent and desirability of self-segregation.

Racial segregation by law, also known as de jure segregation, was common in the United States until the Civil Rights movement. Since the passage of the 1964 Civil Rights Act, the integration of American institutions has been a major goal for many governmental organizations and concerned citizens. However, the end of segregation by law did not produce the end of actual segregation. In their influential book *American Apartheid: Segregation and the Making of the Underclass* (1993), sociologists Douglas S. Massey and Nancy A. Denton offered evidence that American neighborhoods were becoming more racially segregated over the course of the twentieth century. The National School Boards Association reported in 1989 that a majority of African American schoolchildren were attending racially segregated schools. Even when residential areas and institutions were integrated, many whites and African Americans associated primarily with members of their own racial groups.

Given this continuing racial separation, the issue of self-segregation became a topic of debate on several points. First, observers have disagreed as to what extent continuing segregation was a product of self-segregation rather than of continuing racial discrimination. Second, it is often unclear whether minority group members are more likely than whites to avoid social contacts with outsiders. Third, some commentators have argued that self-segregation is undesirable and destructive for minority group members and for American society in general, while others have held that voluntary segregation can often be beneficial.

In *American Apartheid*, Massey and Denton pointed to residentially segregated neighborhoods as evidence of continuing systematic discrimination in American housing. However, sociologist Orlando Patterson responded that African Americans tended to live in majority black neighborhoods as a matter of choice. Because school districts are based on residential areas, if Patterson is correct, segregated schools, as well as segregated neighborhoods, would be largely a product of voluntary self-segregation.

Some of those who object to the continuing segregation of American society have criticized minority group members for clustering in their own neighborhoods or friendship groups. However, according to a study of college students by University of Michigan scholar Sylvia Hurtado, white students are more likely than African Americans, Mexican Americans, or Asian Americans to voluntarily segregate themselves. Therefore, minority self-segregation may be a response to a real or perceived lack of complete acceptance by whites. When minority members do engage in self-segregation, they often do so in order to overcome disadvantages. In her book *Blacks in College* (1984), for example, Jacqueline Fleming reported that African Americans in majority black colleges showed more academic progress and higher graduation rates than did African Americans in majority white colleges.

Carl L. Bankston III

See also: Black colleges and universities; Hypersegregation; Integration; Segregation vs. integration.

Selma-Montgomery march

During 1964, with civil rights upheavals reaching crisis proportions, leaders in the Southern Christian Leadership Conference (SCLC) realized the urgency of forcing the enactment of a voting rights act to enfranchise southern blacks. The SCLC selected Selma, Alabama, seventy-three miles west of Montgomery, as the place to organize voter registration demonstrations. Early in 1965, Martin Luther King, Jr., announced that the SCLC would lead blacks to the courthouse in Selma to register them to vote. During January, more than two thousand blacks were arrested for trying to register, leading to demonstrations in which blacks and their white supporters, who poured in from across the nation, were also arrested.

King scheduled a march from Selma to Montgomery, culminating in the marchers' handing Governor George Wallace a petition demanding enfranchisement for blacks. State troopers attacked the marchers, beating them with nightsticks and shocking them with cattle prods. This brutality attracted national attention and led President Lyndon B. Johnson to support the Voting Rights Act of 1965, the passage of which, along with Supreme Court decisions upholding the Twenty-fourth Amendment, which outlawed the poll tax in federal elections, enfranchised southern blacks and changed forever the course of politics in the South.

R. Baird Shuman

See also: Civil Rights movement; Southern Christian Leadership Conference; Voting Rights Act of 1965.

Separatism

As a conception, separatism may be defined as the goal or policy of a group of people—usually united by ethnic or racial, linguistic, geographical, and/or religious bonds—that wishes to free itself from the rule of a different people and to establish an independent form of self-government or that, lacking the capacity to free itself from the government of an existing state, attempts to establish exclusive or segregated social mechanisms in which to express and to preserve the group's common identity and to insulate the group from wider cultural influences. Full-blown separatism can lead to revolution and civil war. Less extreme versions of separatism can lead to localized violence.

In the United States, white and black separatist movements exist, often in opposition to one another. The militia and survivalist movements reflect a similar mentality. Separatism of these sorts does not appeal to the majority of Americans. Moreover, owing to the distinctive pluralism of American society, the U.S. government tolerates such group expressions as long as they do not threaten public order or safety. Because most Americans are members of many groups with cross-cutting interests, separatist movements have a difficult time winning wider public participation or support.

Robert F. Gorman

See also: Black nationalism; Segregation.

Set-asides

In the Public Works Employment Act of 1977, Congress legislated a 10 percent set-aside of federal grants awarded by the Department of Commerce to minority-owned businesses, intending to remedy lingering discrimination. White contractors who felt discriminated against brought suit. The U.S. Supreme Court, in *Fullilove v. Klutznick* (1980), upheld the legislation's constitutionality. Concurring justices argued that Congress has a unique role to play in eradicating discrimination; dissenting justices contended that *Fullilove* reinstated race-based preferences and, therefore, was unconstitutional. Subsequently, in *Richmond v. J. A. Croson Company* (1989), the Supreme Court declared a Richmond, Virginia, plan that required primary contractors to subcontract 30 percent of contract dollars to minority contractors a violation of the equal protection clause of the Fourteenth Amendment. All state and local governmental racial classifications, the Court held, must be strictly scrutinized. In *Metro Broadcasting v. Federal Communications Commission* (1990), however, the Supreme Court upheld a policy of the Federal Communications Commission (FCC) to increase broadcast licenses to minority groups, affirming proportional representation as a societal goal, even absent past or present discrimination. At the time, strict scrutiny was not yet applicable to the FCC, a federal agency. Later, in *Adarand Constructors v. Peña* (1995), the Supreme Court declared that a Department of Transportation policy requiring primary contractors to subcontract to certified disadvantaged businesses violated the equal protection component of the Fifth Amendment's due process clause. Following *Adarand,* strict scrutiny of racial classification by any governmental agency necessitates demonstrating a compelling governmental interest.

Gil Richard Musolf

See also: *Adarand Constructors v. Peña*; Affirmative action; *Fullilove v. Klutznick*; *Richmond v. J. A. Croson Company*.

Sexual fears and racism

The connection between sexual fears and racism has been discussed by historians, sociologists, and novelists, notably historian Lillian Smith and novelist and essayist James Baldwin. This connection is a metaphor for the interplay in American society between sex, race, gender, and power.

The mingling of sex and race has characterized racial relations since Africans were forcibly brought to North America in 1619, throughout the period of slavery, and beyond. This simultaneous hatred of and fascination with black male sexuality in particular, originates in the rape of black women by white men. Social mores of the seventeenth, eighteenth, and nineteenth centuries placed white women on a pedestal, too pure for white men to let lose their sexual passion. Though some sexual contact was necessary for procreation, white men created the myth of lustful, insatiable black women to justify raping them.

The rape of black women was not simply a brutal form of social control and a reaffirmation of white power. The violation also signified for black men their powerlessness to protect their wives, mothers, sisters, and daughters. Nevertheless, the threat of revenge by black men for these atrocities was real for white men. English colonists believed in the supposed hypervirility, promiscuity, and aggression of black men, which psychologists today might see as a projection of their own sexual aggression and guilt. If black women were perceived as by nature lascivious, attitudes about black men were further exaggerated by this fear of retribution.

Lynching and Sexual Fears The white man's fear of black male sexual aggression manifested itself in the use of lynching as "punishment" and social control. Exact numbers are impossible to verify, but according to historian Lillian Smith in her seminal history of the south, *Killers of the Dream* (1949), approximately 3,148 lynchings took place in the South from 1882 to 1946, and during that time, no member of a lynch mob was given a death sentence or life imprisonment, and only 135 people in the United States were convicted of being members of lynch mobs. Although the desire to prevent insurrection is sometimes given as a reason for the lynchings, the most socially compelling "rationale" for the murders was to avenge black men's alleged sexual assaults upon white women.

Castration and Homoeroticism Castration of black men, though a frequent element of lynching, is often neglected in the scholarly literature. When castration is referenced, as in Winthrop Jordan's *White Over Black* (1968) or in W. J. Cash's *The Mind of the South* (1941), it is usually offered as further evidence of unspeakable cruelty or of white males' feelings of sexual inadequacy in the light of cultural myths of black male sexual prowess.

Novelist and essayist James Baldwin expands the connection between sex and racism in the novel *Another Country* (1960) and the short story "Going to Meet the Man" (1966). In these works, the white sheriff participates in his first lynching, and the castration reads like a sexualized rite of passage: "The man with the knife took the nigger's privates in his hand, one hand, still smiling, as though he were weighing them. . . . Jesse felt his scrotum tighten; and huge, huge, much bigger than his father's flaccid, hairless, the largest thing he had ever seen till then, and the blackest. The white hand stretched them, cradled them, caressed them." An undeniable but often unmentionable aspect of the history of race relations, Baldwin suggests, is an obsession with black male sexuality that is rooted in "a secret desire mingled with fear and guilt."

Chalis Holton

Core Resources

Gerda Lerner's *Black Women in White America: A Documentary History* (New York: Vintage Books, 1972) surveys the literature of protest by black women against lynching, rape as social control, and against the myths of the "bad" black woman. Lerner's text also reprints journalist and activist Ida B. Wells's pamphlet *A Red Record* (1895), which is probably the most well-regarded antilynching document of the nineteenth century. Wells was one of the first to openly protest the habitual rape of black women by white men, and she contradicted the myth that all sexual contact between white women and black men was based on rape. W. J. Cash openly explores the sexual nature of American racism in *The Mind of the South* (New York: Alfred Knopf, 1941), and Lillian Smith's *Killers of the Dream* (New York: W. W. Norton, 1949) is recognized as a seminal history of southern race relations. The early history of racism in the United States and the West Indies and the sexual link are discussed by Winthrop Jordan in *White Over Black: American Attitudes Toward the Negro, 1550-1812* (Durham: University of North Carolina Press, 1968). James Baldwin is perhaps the only novelist to explore the history of racism and sexual desire so overtly, in both the interracial and homosexual contexts. See Baldwin's *Another Country* (New York: Dell, 1960) and "Going to Meet the Man" (New York: Dell, 1966). Sociologist Calvin Hernton's *Sex and Racism in America* (New York: Grove Press, 1965) is a now classic study of the psychology of racism and the intersecting myths of sex and race.

See also: Friendships, interracial/interethnic; Interracial and interethnic marriage; Lynchings; Psychology of racism.

Sharecropping

In the aftermath of the American Civil War (1861-1865), the South faced many difficulties. Its cities, factories, and railroads had been shattered, and its valuable agricultural industry had been turned upside down. Many large planters lost their entire workforce when the Thirteenth Amendment to the U.S. Constitution freed southern slaves. Newly freed slaves, most of whom were farmworkers, had no land to cultivate. Landowners, former slaves, and small farmers negotiated a compromise: sharecropping. The system they created would eventually lead to a steady decline in southern agriculture during the twentieth century.

Deeply in debt after the war, many southern landowners were forced to give up all or fragments of their property to local merchants, banks, and corporations. By the end of Reconstruction (1866-1877), large portions of southern farmland were controlled by absentee landlords who neither lived on nor worked their land but managed it from afar. Southern landowners had a large number of acres to be planted and not enough money to hire farm laborers. At the same time, thousands of African Americans were free from slavery but without the homes, land, or tools they needed to support themselves.

A black sharecropper and his family returning home after spending their morning working on a North Carolina tobacco farm in 1939. *(Library of Congress)*

To earn a living, agricultural laborers agreed to become tenants on farmland.

Landlords provided tenants with land, a small house, and tools to grow a crop. Tenants worked the land and promised a percentage of their annual crop yield, usually between 20 percent and 50 percent, to the landlord. Landlords frequently arranged credit for tenants with local merchants to help them establish a household and buy seed. Storekeepers and landowners, who sometimes were the same person, placed liens on the farmers' crops to protect their interests. Tenants hoped to yield enough profit from their labor not only to pay off their liens but also to eventually purchase the land they worked.

A bad year or depressed cotton prices could easily leave many farmers in debt at the end of the season. Sharecroppers frequently promised an additional percentage of their crop to local merchants to purchase the next year's seed and feed their families through the winter. Year after year, sharecroppers became more indebted. Forced to work until liens were paid, tenants became bound to their land, continually impoverished and with little hope of becoming property owners.

Sharecropping in the South increased steadily in the latter half of the nineteenth century until approximately 75 percent of all southern farmers were sharecroppers. Cotton prices began to drop after the turn of the century and then fell drastically during the Great Depression of the 1930's. These conditions forced thousands of tenants to leave the land and move to northern cities in search of employment. Others were forced to leave when landlords decided farming was no longer profitable. As a result of this loss of labor and increases in technology, sharecropping represented only a small percentage of farming in the South by the end of the twentieth century.

Leslie Stricker

See also: Great Migration; Poverty and race; Reconstruction.

Shaw v. Reno

By calling for close scrutiny of a predominantly black congressional district whose shape it considered "bizarre," the Supreme Court in *Shaw v. Reno* (1993) struck a blow against the practice of drawing district boundaries to create "majority-minority" electoral districts.

After the 1990 census, the state legislature of North Carolina began the task of "reapportionment," or redrawing its electoral districts. Although about 22 percent of the state's population was African American, no blacks had been elected to Congress for almost a century. To remedy this, and ostensibly to meet provisions of the Voting Rights Act, the legislature created two majority-nonwhite districts. In order to avoid disturbing incumbents' districts, the legislature drew one of the two districts largely along an interstate highway, snaking 160 miles through the north-central part of the state. The resulting district was 53 percent black.

Five voters filed suit against the reapportionment plan, objecting that the race-based district violated their right to participate in a nonracial electoral process. The case reached the Supreme Court, whose 5-4 majority instructed the lower courts to reconsider the constitutionality of such a district in light of its "bizarre" shape and its "uncomfortable resemblance to political apartheid." In essence, the majority expressed its concern about the practice of creating districts on the basis of race and of establishing contorted geographical boundaries. The coupling of the two practices presumably could result in districts that patently violated the Constitution's equal protection clause, unless a compelling state interest could be demonstrated.

When the *Shaw* case was subsequently returned to North Carolina, a federal panel upheld the reapportionment plan after finding that the state did indeed have a compelling interest in complying with the Voting Rights Act. Nevertheless, the Supreme Court's *Shaw* decision has been the basis for other important decisions concerning racially defined districts. In 1994, for example, a majority-black district in Louisiana was rejected by a federal district court invoking *Shaw*. The court expressed particular concern that the district was intentionally created on the basis of the voters' race. More significant, in 1995 the U.S. Supreme Court extended *Shaw*'s admonitions about racial reapportionment to argue that voters' rights are violated whenever "race was the predominant factor motivating the legislature's decision to place a significant number of voters within or without a particular district," irrespective of shape.

Shaw served as a watershed in the contest between advocates of racial representation and those who champion a "color-blind" electoral system. It came at a time when various racial issues that had for years remained largely outside sharp political debate—affirmative action, welfare reform, and so forth—had been thrust into the center stage of American political discourse. Although *Shaw* by no means resolved these debates, it helped to delineate the battle lines.

Steve D. Boilard

See also: Redistricting; Representation: gerrymandering, malapportionment, and reapportionment; Voting Rights Act of 1965.

Shelley v. Kraemer

In the 1948 *Shelley v. Kraemer* decision, the Supreme Court acknowledged the right of private individuals to make racially restrictive covenants but ruled that state action to enforce such covenants was a violation of the Fourteenth Amendment.

After J. D. Shelley, an African American, purchased a house in a predominantly white neighborhood of St. Louis, Missouri, one of the neighbors, Louis Kraemer, sought and obtained an injunction preventing Shelley from taking possession of the property. Unknown to Shelley, the neighboring landowners had signed a contractual agreement barring owners from selling their property to members of "the Negro or Mongolian race." Supported by the National Association for the Advancement of Colored People (NAACP), Shelley challenged the constitutionality of the contract in state court, but the Missouri Supreme Court upheld its legality. Appealing to the U.S. Supreme Court, Shelley's case was argued by the NAACP's leading counsels, Charles Houston and Thurgood Marshall. President Harry S Truman put the weight of the executive branch in favor of the NAACP's position.

This was not the first time that the issue of residential segregation had appeared before the Court. In *Buchanan v. Warley* (1917), the Court had struck down state statutes that limited the right of property owners to sell property to a person of another race, but in *Corrigan v. Buckley* (1926) the Court upheld the right of individuals to make "private" contracts to maintain segregation. *Corrigan* was based on the establishment principle that the first section of the Fourteenth Amendment inhibited the actions of state governments, not those of individuals.

The Court refused to declare restrictive contracts unconstitutional, but it held 6-0 that the Fourteenth Amendment's equal protection clause prohibited state courts from enforcing the contracts, meaning that the contracts were not enforceable. The decision, written by Chief Justice Fred Vinson, emphasized that one of the basic objectives of the Fourteenth Amendment was to prohibit the states from using race to discriminate "in the enjoyment of property rights." The decision did not directly overturn *Corrigan,* but it interpreted the precedent as involving only the validity of private contracts, not their legal enforcement. In a companion case five years later, *Barrows v. Jackson* (1953), Chief Justice Vinson dissented when the majority used the *Shelley* rationale to block enforcement of restrictive covenants through private damage suits against covenant violators.

Eliminating the last direct method for legally barring African Americans from neighborhoods, *Shelley* was an important early victory in the struggle against state-supported segregation. Civil rights proponents hoped that a logical extension of the case would lead to an abolition of the distinction between private and state action in matters of equal protection, but in later decisions such as *Moose Lodge No. 107 v. Irvis* (1972), the majority of judges were not ready to rule against private conduct that was simply tolerated by the state.

Thomas T. Lewis

See also: *Buchanan v. Warley*; Civil Rights Act of 1968; Civil Rights movement; Fair Housing Act; *Heart of Atlanta Motel v. United States*; *Moose Lodge No. 107 v. Irvis*; Restrictive covenants; Segregation: de facto and de jure.

Simpson, O. J., trial

The murder trial and acquittal of former football star Orenthal James "O. J." Simpson in 1995 polarized racial attitudes about American criminal justice and police racism. Both before and after the trial, most whites thought Simpson was guilty, and most African Americans thought he was innocent.

On the night of June 12-13, 1994, the slashed and stabbed bodies of Nicole Brown Simpson and her friend Ronald Goldman, both white, were discovered at the Los Angeles condominium of Nicole Simpson. After making a preliminary investigation, police left the crime scene and went to the nearby Brentwood estate of Nicole Simpson's former husband, O. J. Simpson, the African American former football star. Finding blood on the door of a white Ford Bronco parked askew on the street in front of the house, Los Angeles Police Department detective Mark Fuhrman climbed the fence without a warrant, allegedly to protect Simpson from any possible danger, and admitted other detectives to the premises.

Simpson was not at home, but Fuhrman, who had been at the Simpson residence five years earlier to answer a domestic violence complaint, used the opportunity to search for evidence linking Simpson to the murder. A bloody glove he allegedly found behind the guest quarters later became a key factor in the trial.

When Simpson returned from Chicago, where he had flown the evening of the murder, he quickly became the only suspect in the case. After a bizarre low-speed vehicle chase watched by millions on live television, Simpson surrendered to police on June 17. Denied bail, he remained in jail during the lengthy trial. He used his wealth to hire a "dream team" of famous attorneys. Jury selection began in September, 1994, and took most of the fall.

The Trial What the media dubbed the "trial of the century" began in late January, 1995, under Judge Lance Ito with a heavily sequestered jury of mostly African Americans. Shortly afterward, O. J. Simpson's self-exonerating book *I Want to Tell You* was published, the first of dozens of books about the case. Gavel-to-gavel coverage on Cable News Network (CNN) guaranteed continuous public attention, and the rest of the electronic and print media rapidly followed suit.

Prosecutors Marcia Clark and Christopher Darden began with a case emphasizing the history of domestic violence in the Simpsons' stormy marriage, but they soon shifted to an emphasis on DNA (deoxyribonucleic acid) evidence linking the blood of O. J. Simpson and both victims to physical evidence found at the crime scene and the Brentwood estate. This made Detective Fuhrman a key witness, along with his partner Detective Philip Vannatter. Another key witness from the Los Angeles Police Department was Dennis Fung from the crime lab, who admitted under cross-examination that some of the blood evidence had been processed by a trainee, Andrea Mazzola. The most damaging cross-examination was that of Fuhrman by defense attorney F. Lee Bailey, who scathingly portrayed Fuhrman as a bigoted racist and perjurer who denied his own racist statements and actions despite several witnesses to the contrary. Vannatter was also portrayed as a racist because of his association with Fuhrman and was accused of mishandling blood samples before turning them over to the crime lab.

These and various other defense accusations of police misconduct and conspiracy left sufficient doubts in the minds of jurors, and they acquitted Simpson of both murders after only a brief deliberation on October 3, 1995. The passionate summation by defense attorney Johnnie Cochran made it quite clear to both the jury and the general public that the alleged racism and misbehavior of Fuhrman and the rest of the Los Angeles Police Department were more important elements in the case than either DNA evidence or domestic violence, thus alienating Cochran from Simpson's other principal attorney, Robert Shapiro.

The cast of characters made race an obvious factor in the trial from the very beginning. Simpson, Darden, and Cochran were African Americans, as were nine of the jurors. The detectives, the other attorneys, and both victims were white. Judge Ito was a Japanese American married to a white police captain.

Near the end of the trial, surveys conducted by CBS News found that 64 percent of whites surveyed thought that Simpson was guilty, while 59 percent of African Americans thought that he was not guilty. Only 11 percent of whites surveyed thought Simpson was not guilty, and only 12 percent of African Americans thought he was guilty. Only about one-fourth of each group was undecided, and the disparity of perceptions between the races had actually increased during the trial.

Reactions to the Trial After the verdict was announced, many African Americans rejoiced and treated the outcome as if it were a conviction of the Los Angeles Police Department on charges of racism and conspiracy to frame Simpson. This response should be viewed in the light of the highly publicized 1991 Los Angeles beating of African American motorist Rodney King by white police officers, four of whom were acquitted of state criminal charges, leading to massive racially motivated rioting in Los Angeles, but two of whom were later convicted of federal criminal charges.

Meanwhile many white people expressed their dismay at the Simpson acquittal and asserted that a combination of Simpson's money and reverse jury bias had led to a serious miscarriage of justice. These feelings were not greatly diminished sixteen months later when Simpson was held liable for the deaths of the two victims in a civil lawsuit and assessed punitive damages of $25 million, which compares interestingly with the nearly $20 million that the criminal trial cost both sides.

The prosecution's case against Simpson suffered a severe setback when a bloody glove it produced as evidence against him proved to be too small for his hand. *(Reuters/Sam Mircovich/Archive Photos)*

Explanations of the Verdict Various explanations have been put forward to account for Simpson's acquittal in the criminal trial. They include reasonable doubt, the lack of a specific theory of the crime, jury nullification, and "evidence" of a police conspiracy.

The simplest explanation is that the jurors did not find persuasive evidence of Simpson's guilt and followed the judge's instructions to acquit the defendant if there was not proof beyond a reasonable doubt. Many African Americans hold this view and give the jury credit for a job well done despite the brevity of their deliberations.

A somewhat more complex version of this explanation is that the prosecution never advanced a specific theory of the crime. For example, they asserted throughout the trial that Simpson committed the entire crime by himself despite circumstantial evidence that an unknown accomplice may have been involved before, after, or during the murders. Some African Americans may have felt that this was condescending or patronizing to the jury and therefore have given jury members credit for realizing that a more complex theory might make better sense of the known facts. Simpson's DNA fairly clearly placed him at the crime scene on the night in question, but to this day, there is no specific scenario for the crime.

Many whites feel that some jury nullification of crucial evidence must have occurred to produce such a speedy acquittal. Very little of the evidence handled by Fuhrman and Vannatter was formally excluded by Judge Ito, and it was left up to the jurors to decide what weight to give each item of evidence. In the belief that evidence obtained through biased procedures by racist police officers ought not to count against the African American defendant, it would be quite conceivable for nullificationist jurors to neglect the entirety of the evidence found at the Brentwood estate and some of the evidence found at the crime scene. Many whites clearly felt that this was exactly what happened, so the jury may have neglected part of its job.

A further twist on this argument is that a police conspiracy was involved and that key pieces of evidence such as a bloody glove and a bloody sock found in the bedroom were planted by overzealous officers to incriminate Simpson. Cochran's very controversial summation encouraged this viewpoint, and many African Americans, including some of the jurors, may have agreed. However, most whites did not agree even if they thought Simpson was not guilty. This was probably the most divisive outcome of the trial, because despite Simpson's acquittal, it tended to reaffirm racially polarized opinions about the extent of previously alleged inequities toward minorities in the U.S. criminal justice system.

Unresolved Questions The entire jury system was called into question by the Simpson trial. Its cost and its fairness, both to defendants and to victims or their families, are still hotly debated. The fairness of televising criminal trials was also called into question, though the public clearly has an immense appetite for such events. However, only a few people still have any doubts as to the verdict itself, and only a few people have changed their minds. Despite his lost wealth and status, after the trial Simpson still golfed at public courses and professed his love for his former wife, Nicole. In 1998 he was fighting for custody of the two children.

Tom Cook

Core Resources

Tapes from the Cable News Network (CNN) are crucial to a thorough study of the trial. However, more succinct analyses can be found in Vincent Bugliosi's *Outrage: The Five Reasons Why O. J. Simpson Got Away with Murder* (New York: W. W. Norton, 1996), Alan M. Dershowitz's *Reasonable Doubts: The O. J. Simpson Case and the Criminal Justice System* (New York: Simon & Schuster, 1996), Frank Schmalleger's *The Trial of the Century: The People of the State of California vs. Orenthal James Simpson* (Englewood Cliffs, N.J.: Prentice-Hall, 1996).

See also: Crime and race/ethnicity; Criminal justice system; King, Rodney, case; Los Angeles riots of 1992; Race card.

Slave codes

Slave codes were colonial and state laws dealing with slavery. In Virginia, these codes were used to make slavery an institution; in Ohio, they were used to discourage blacks from moving to the state.

The first colonial laws recognizing and institutionalizing slavery were enacted in Virginia in the mid-seventeenth century. A similar series of Ohio laws denying civil rights to African Americans were enacted to discourage black immigration to that state in the early nineteenth century.

Virginia In March, 1661, the Virginia General Assembly declared that "all children borne in this country shalbe held bond or free only according to the condition of the mother." Enacted to alleviate confusion about the status of children with English fathers and African mothers, this law was the first in a series of laws recognizing perpetual slavery in Virginia and equating "freedom" with "white" and "enslaved" with "black." This law is especially indicative of the hardening of race relations in mid-seventeenth century Virginia society, as status in the patriarchal society of England traditionally was inherited from the father. By reversing this legal concept, perpetuation of enslavement for blacks was ensured for their children, whether of black or white ancestry.

Despite the extent to which the 1661 law narrowed the options for defining Africans' status, this act did not in itself establish slavery. Africans had two available windows through which they could obtain freedom—conversion to Christianity and manumission (formal emancipation). In 1655, mulatto Elizabeth Key brought a successful suit for her freedom, using as her main argument the fact that she had been baptized. In 1667, a slave named Fernando contended that he ought to be freed because he was a Christian and had lived in England for several years. Not only did the court deny Fernando's appeal, but also that same year the General Assembly took another step toward more clearly defining blacks' status, by declaring "that the conferring of baptisme doth not alter the condition of the person as to his bondage or freedome." Planters felt that if baptism led to freedom, they would be without any assurance that they could retain their slave property. The 1667 law thereby built on the earlier one to define who would be a slave, and was clarified in 1670 and again in 1682, when the Assembly declared that any non-Christian brought into the colony, either by land or by sea, would be a slave for life, even if he or she later converted.

In 1691, colonial leaders provided a negative incentive to masters wishing to free their slaves by declaring that anyone who set free any "negro or mulatto" would be required to pay the costs of transporting the freedmen out of the colony within six months. Although manumissions still occurred and some free blacks managed to remain in the colony, the primary status for African Americans in Virginia was that of chattel.

Although who was to be a slave in Virginia had now been defined, it had yet to be determined precisely what being a slave meant on a daily basis for Africans and their descendants. Between 1661 and 1705, nearly twenty separate laws were passed limiting, defining, and prescribing the rights, status, and treatment of blacks. In general, these laws were designed to protect planters' slave property and to protect the order and stability of white society from an "alien and savage race."

The piecemeal establishment of slavery in these separate laws culminated in 1705 in a comprehensive slave code in Virginia. This code reenacted and strengthened a number of earlier slave laws, added further restrictions and harsher punishments, and permanently drew the color line that placed blacks at the bottom of Virginia society. Whites were prohibited from trading with, having sexual relations with, and marrying blacks. Blacks were forbidden to own Christian servants "except of their own complexion," leave their home plantation without a pass, own a gun or other weapon, or resist whites in any way.

Slaves chained together while being relocated. *(Library of Congress)*

Many of the harsher penalties for slave crimes, for example, the death penalty and maiming, were not carried out nearly as frequently as the laws suggest, because doing so would harm or destroy the master's property. Laws prohibiting slaves from trading or hiring themselves out were disregarded almost routinely. The disadvantage for slaves of this lack of enforcement was that laws prohibiting cruel treatment or defining acceptable levels of correction often were ignored as well. Where abuse was blatant, action against white offenders was taken only reluctantly, and punishments were insignificant and rare. Generally, laws in the economic and political interest of the white planter elite were enforced and respected; laws that restrained planters' pursuits were not.

Ohio and the Northwest Territory The Northwest Territory was established in 1787 and ultimately became the states of Ohio, Indiana, Michigan, Illinois, and Wisconsin. In 1800, what was to become the state of Ohio separated from the rest of the territory. Two years later, Ohio elected delegates to a constitutional convention in preparation for a statehood petition, which was approved in 1803.

Although the Northwest Ordinance prohibited slavery in that territory, Ohio's constitutional convention debated the issue during its sessions. With the slaveholding states of Virginia on Ohio's eastern boundary and Kentucky on its southern boundary, there was considerable pressure for Ohio to recognize slavery. Many of the immigrants to Ohio came from slave states and saw nothing evil in the system. While many southern Ohioans did not object to slavery, persons in the northern part of the state were more likely to oppose it.

Delegates at the 1802 constitutional convention debated several questions that focused on African Americans. There was no strong feeling for instituting slavery in Ohio; there was, however, strong opinion in favor of limited rights for African Americans. After a major debate over allowing African Americans to vote, it was decided not to delete the word "white" from the qualifications for the franchise. Nevertheless, the African American population grew from five hundred in 1800 to nearly two thousand by 1810. In 1804, the legislature debated and passed the first of the "Black Laws," statutes intended to discourage African Americans from moving into Ohio and to encourage those already there to leave.

A few years later, an even stronger bill to restrict African Americans was presented in the Senate. In its final version, it forbade African Americans from settling in Ohio unless they could present a five-hundred-dollar bond and an affidavit signed by two white men that attested to their good character. Fines for helping a fugitive slave were doubled. Finally, no African American could testify against a white in court.

However restrictive the original Black Laws were, the new law was far worse. African Americans were stripped of legal protection and placed at the mercy of whites. Whites did not need to fear being tried for offenses against

African Americans unless there was a white witness who would testify. There is evidence of at least one African American being murdered by whites, with only African American witnesses to the crime. African American witnesses could not provide evidence against a white assailant. Even if a case went to court, it would be heard by an all-white jury before a white judge. African American victims could not testify on their own behalf, because of the restrictions against providing testimony against whites. Because they could not vote, African Americans could neither change nor protest these laws.

While the Black Codes of 1804 and 1807 were enforced only infrequently, they still were the law and were a constant reminder that African Americans in Ohio had only the barest minimum of human and civil rights—and those rights existed only at the whim of white society. The laws fell into disuse and finally were repealed in 1849, long after the abolitionist movement, with its western center located in Oberlin, Ohio, was well under way, and long after the Underground Railroad had opened several stations in Ohio.

Laura A. Croghan and Duncan R. Jamieson

Core Resources

Joseph Boskin's *Into Slavery: Racial Decisions in the Virginia Colony* (Philadelphia: J. B. Lippincott, 1976) provides an account of the evolution of perpetual slavery and a representative selection of relevant primary documents. *In the Matter of Color: Race and the American Legal Process, the Colonial Period* (New York: Oxford University Press, 1978), by A. Leon Higginbotham, Jr., recounts the events culminating in the legal recognition of slavery in the British mainland colonies. Philip J. Schwartz's *Twice Condemned: Slaves and the Criminal Laws of Virginia, 1705-1865* (Baton Rouge: Louisiana State University Press, 1988) uses criminal trial records to examine slave resistance and whites' efforts to control threatening slave behavior. Robert B. Shaw's *A Legal History of Slavery in the United States* (Potsdam, N.Y.: Northern Press, 1991) illustrates the history of slavery in terms of its legislative and judicial background, from settlement through emancipation. Charles Jay Wilson's "The Negro in Early Ohio" (*Ohio Archeological and Historical Quarterly* 39, 1930) is the most complete analysis of Ohio's Black Laws.

See also: Abolition; Black codes; Fugitive slave laws; Missouri Compromise; Slavery: North American beginnings; Underground Railroad.

Slave rebellions

Slave rebellions were attempts by African slaves to resist oppression by the white, slave-owning population of North America. In the southern United States, where the slave population was the greatest, blacks made up more

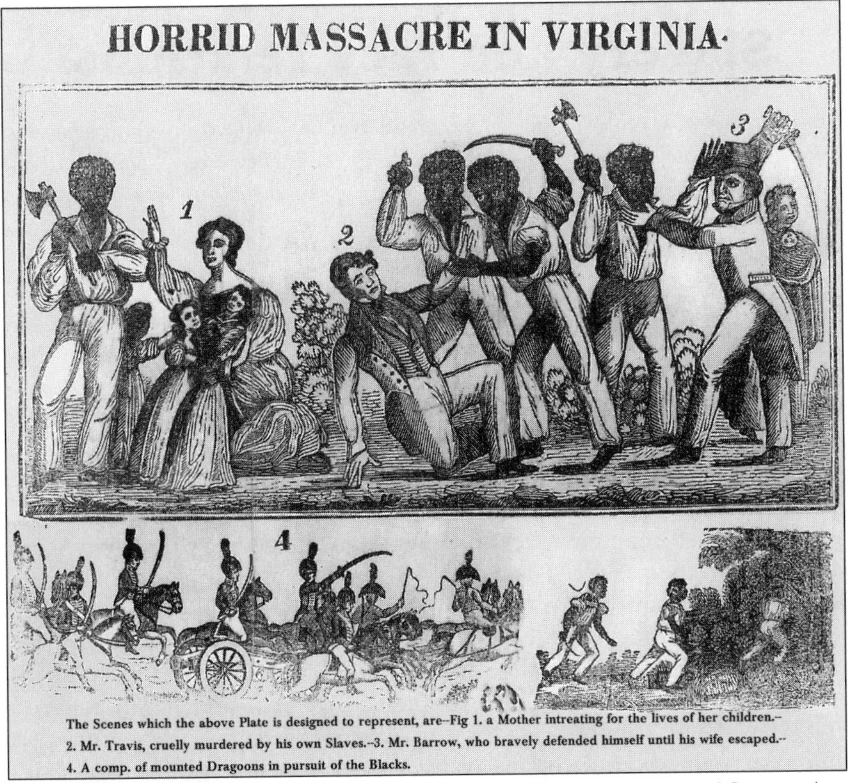

Contemporary illustration of a slave rebellion in colonial Virginia. *(Library of Congress)*

than half of the population. In order to guarantee their way of life, white southern plantation owners used terror to control their slave populations. Despite the harsh treatment of African Americans, slaves developed a number of methods of resisting their masters' orders. Running away was always a popular alternative to work in the field and was punished through torture or, in repeat cases, amputation of a foot. Slaves also engaged in work slowdowns; slaves would purposely work more slowly or break and lose tools.

The most serious response to slavery, however, was the slave uprising. Despite harsh repression in most slave nations to discourage such occurrences, several slave uprisings occurred in the seventeenth, eighteenth, and early nineteenth centuries. Most slave revolts were unsuccessful and were met by extreme repression by armed whites fearing a takeover by black slaves. There were successful slave uprisings, however. One successful slave revolt, the Haitian Revolution, freed the French colony of Haiti and created the first nation of freed slaves in the Western Hemisphere.

Jason Pasch

See also: *Amistad* slave revolt; John Brown's raid; Slavery: history; Turner's slave insurrection.

Slavery and race relations

The enslavement of people of African ancestry was closely connected to the development of both racial prejudice and racial inequality in the United States. The heritage of slavery prevented African Americans from entering into the mainstream of American life even after slavery was abolished. Debates over responsibility for slavery and the legacy of slavery have complicated relations between African Americans and whites.

One of the theoretical points debated by historians is whether Europeans and Euro-Americans imposed slavery on people from Africa because they viewed Africans as inferior or whether racism came into existence as a justification for slavery. Some historians have suggested that as Europeans expanded their control over much of the world, they came into contact with many who were unlike themselves in appearance and in culture. Ethnocentrism, the tendency to see one's own group as the standard by which all others are to be judged, may have led Europeans to see the people of Asia and Africa as inferior to themselves. Thus, people from China, as well as people from Africa, were brought to the Americas as forced labor at various times.

Historians such as George Frederickson, however, have maintained that racism was a consequence rather than a cause of slavery. From this point of view, the growth of plantation economies in North and South America encouraged the importation of slave labor because these economies required large numbers of workers. Native Americans did not make good slaves because they were in their homeland and could easily escape.

Slave owners needed to justify holding other humans in bondage, according to this theory, so they argued that their slaves were childlike and needed the protection of their masters. Thus, the influential apologist for slavery Henry Hughes argued in his *Treatise on Sociology* (1854) that the simple slaves as well as the masters benefited from the arrangement.

To some extent, the relationship between slavery and racism is similar to the ancient question of whether the chicken or the egg came first. The European enslavement of Africans was probably encouraged by feelings of European superiority. Once slavery became established, though, it was necessary to justify it, and the American descendants of Europeans could comfort themselves with claims that their slaves were inferior beings.

Many of the stereotypes of African Americans developed during slavery continued to flourish well into the twentieth century. The racism of slavery outlived slavery itself; films, radio programs, and books before the Civil Rights era often portrayed black Americans as childlike, comic, servile, or dangerously unable to control themselves. The sociologist Stanford M. Lyman has observed that popular American films ranging from *Birth of a Nation* (1915) to *Gone with the Wind* (1939) drew on the racial images of slavery to portray "good" blacks as humorous, loyal, obedient family servants and "bad" blacks as rebellious and violent.

Consequences of Master-Slave Relations Economist Raymond S. Franklin has noted that one of the debates regarding consequences of master-slave relations concerns whether slaves and their descendants were in some way damaged by being owned and controlled. A number of historians, including Kenneth Stampp, Stanley Elkins, and William Styron, have held that being slaves left psychological scars on the slaves and damaged social institutions that slaves passed on to free black Americans. Along these lines, in 1966, Daniel Patrick Moynihan published a controversial report on the black family, in which he maintained that the experience of slavery contributed to the weakness of the black family. More recently, Harvard sociologist Orlando Patterson has claimed that the slave status undermined the roles of husband and father for black men and reinforced the central role of women in families.

Franklin observes that some historians and social thinkers have argued that the master-slave relationship actually strengthened many black social institutions by promoting the need to resist slavery. Historian Herbert Gutman, for example, offered evidence that slavery had actually strengthened black families. The historian Eric Foner has traced the origins of the black church, a central institution in African American history, to the religious activities of slaves who organized themselves into churches after emancipation.

Geographical Consequences of Slavery Slaves were heavily concentrated in the southern part of the United States. Even after the end of slavery, African Americans continued to be a southern population. In 1860, on the eve of the Civil War, 94 percent of the people of African ancestry in the United States were concentrated in the slave-owning states of the South. This percentage did decline notably in the years following World War I, and the descendants of slaves did move to other regions over the course of the twentieth century. Nevertheless, at the end of the century, the geographical legacy of slavery was still evident; the 1990 U.S. census showed a majority of the American black population residing in the South.

In many areas of the South, working as sharecroppers or low-paid wage laborers during the years following slavery, African Americans continued to do much the same sort of agricultural labor that they had performed as slaves. In order to maintain white domination, in regions with large black populations, southern whites sought to replace slavery with segregation, which placed blacks in a separate and disadvantaged position. This kept African Americans dependent on whites and subservient to whites in a manner that was similar in many ways to the old master-slave relationship. These patterns may have even survived the years following the Civil Rights movement. As recently as the 1990's, sociologist Ruth Kornfield, looking at a rural community in Tennessee, found that patron-client relationships between white employers and black employees continued to mirror master-slave relationships.

The continuing concentration of African Americans in the South was one of the reasons that early actions of the Civil Rights movement concentrated primarily on this region. Despite the stubborn survival of many old patterns of racial inequality in this region, numbers have given African Americans in this part of the country some measure of power. In 1993, two-thirds of the black-elected officials in the United States were from the southern states. Furthermore, the major southern cities of Atlanta, Georgia; New Orleans, Louisiana; Birmingham, Alabama; and Richmond, Virginia, all had black mayors.

The Legacy of Slavery and Urbanization Although the South did not cease to be home to the largest proportion of African Americans, the group did shift from being heavily rural to being heavily urban. Over the course of the twentieth century, the agricultural jobs that black Americans continued to perform after slavery became increasingly unavailable as farms mechanized. In the years following World War II, African Americans moved to cities. They tended to settle in central urban areas because the U.S. government built housing projects reserved for the poor in these urban areas, and the heritage of slavery and of the system of segregation that had emerged from slavery left African Americans disproportionately poor. During the same years, whites were moving from cities to suburbs. Racism, an ideology with roots in America's centuries of slavery, contributed to the

African Americans marching through Richmond, Virginia, around the turn of the twentieth century to commemorate Emancipation Day. *(Library of Congress)*

unwillingness of homeowners, real estate companies, and mortgage lenders to allow blacks to move into homes in the suburbs.

As a result of the movement of whites to suburbs and African Americans to cities, the two groups came to live in separate places. Although schools and other public facilities ceased to be legally segregated after the 1960's, many urban neighborhoods and schools contained virtually no whites. This not only limited contact between members of the different races, but it also separated African Americans from the jobs and opportunities that became much more abundant in the suburbs. Further, even after it became easier for middle-class blacks to move into suburban neighborhoods, the poorest were left isolated in inner cities.

Questions of Responsibility Professor and social commentator Shelby Steele has observed that the question of innocence is central to race relations in the United States. Many African Americans maintain that they are innocent victims of the aftermath of slavery. The problem of race relations, from this perspective, is one of achieving equality of condition for people who suffer disadvantages as a group through no fault of their own.

White Americans also frequently put forward claims of innocence. They maintain that white people alive at the end of the twentieth century, well more than a century after the end of slavery, cannot be held responsible for the legacy of slavery. Therefore, programs such as affirmative action that aim at increasing African Americans' share of positions in employment and education seek to benefit the descendants of slaves at the expense of whites who are innocent of responsibility for slavery. In discussing issues of historical responsibility, whites will often become defensive, and any assertions of black disadvantage will sometimes be seen by whites as moral accusations.

Reparations The issue of reparations is one of the most controversial consequences of the thorny ethical issue of historical responsibility. The term "reparations" refers to compensation paid by one nation or group of people to another for damages or losses. The United States government, for example, has made some payments to Japanese Americans for violating their civil rights by imprisoning them during World War II.

Advocates of reparation payments for African Americans, such as the scholar Manning Marable, have argued that slavery was a massive denial of civil rights to this group. These advocates point out that slave labor built up much of the nation's wealth, allowing it to industrialize and therefore making it possible for the United States to achieve its current level of development. They point out that the descendants of slaves continue to suffer damages from slavery because African Americans have lower incomes, on average, than other Americans and tend to hold much less of the country's wealth.

Opponents of reparations maintain that while slavery is a historical source of contemporary disadvantages of African Americans, reparations would attempt to right a past injustice by penalizing present-day whites. Further, if reparations were paid to all African Americans, some rich African Americans would be receiving tax money taken from middle-class or even poor whites. Finally, opponents of reparations suggest that payments of this sort would be enormously unpopular politically and might increase racial hatred and conflict.

Carl L. Bankston III

Core Resources

George M. Frederickson's *White Supremacy: A Comparative Study in American and South African History* (New York: Oxford University Press, 1981) is a classic work on the development of racism and racial exploitation. The second chapter of Raymond S. Franklin's *Shadows of Race and Class* (Minneapolis: University of Minnesota Press, 1991) gives an excellent summary of major debates regarding the legacy of slavery. Ira Berlin's *Many Thousands Gone: The First Two Centuries of Slavery in North America* (Cambridge, Mass.: Belknap Press, 1998) is a comprehensive study of the history of American slavery and of how slavery shaped racial identities. Edward Ball considers the impact of slavery both on his own family of former slave owners and on the descendants of his family's slaves in *Slaves in the Family* (New York: Farrar, Straus & Giroux, 1998). The last work looks not only at the lingering resentment and suspicion toward local whites of the descendants of the slaves but also at the feelings of ill-defined guilt and defensiveness among the descendants of the slave owners. Clarence J. Munford gives arguments for the payment of reparations for slavery to African Americans in *Race and Reparations: A Black Perspective for the Twenty-first Century* (Trenton, N.J.: Africa World Press, 1996). On the other hand, Dinesh D'Souza's highly controversial book *The End of Racism: Principles for a Multiracial Society* (New York: Free Press, 1995) claims that whites bear no responsibility at all for contemporary racial inequality. D'Souza also denies that the history of slavery gives African Americans any moral claims as a group.

See also: Black conservatism; Great Migration; Moynihan Report; National Coalition of Blacks for Reparations in America; Slavery and the justice system; Slavery: history; Slavery: North American beginnings.

Slavery and the justice system

Slavery defined the legal treatment of African Americans for two and one-half centuries, and the crusade against slavery gave rise to modern concepts of citizenship and civil rights.

The first African laborers in the English colonies of North America arrived in Virginia in 1619. By the 1770's, slaves made up one-fifth of the population of the English colonies. At this time, slave labor was used in every colony, including those in the North. Only in the South, however, did slavery dominate economic life. Slaves were used primarily to grow staple crops such as tobacco and rice for exportation to Europe and the Caribbean.

Slavery and the Territories As Americans moved westward, the issue of whether slavery should expand into the new territories became increasingly important. Americans realized that new western states would determine the balance of political power between North and South. Congress initially divided the new territories between North and South. In the Northwest Ordinance (1787), Congress banned slavery in the lands north of the Ohio River while implicitly accepting slavery south of the Ohio. In regard to the Louisiana Purchase, the Missouri Compromise of 1820 banned slavery north of the line 36° 30′ latitude while allowing slavery to exist south of the line.

The Missouri Compromise resolved the issue of slavery in the territories until the Mexican-American War of 1846-1848 added new western lands to the United States. Subsequently, four positions emerged regarding the issue. Many northerners favored the Wilmot Proviso, a proposal to ban slavery in the territories. Other Americans favored popular sovereignty, which would allow the people of the territories to decide the issue for themselves. Some Americans favored extending the Missouri Compromise line to the Pacific coast. Many southerners believed the federal government should protect slavery in the territories.

In the 1850's, the popular sovereignty approach gained ascendancy. The Compromise of 1850 applied popular sovereignty to California, New Mexico, and Utah. The Kansas-Nebraska Act (1854) repealed the old Missouri Compromise boundary and enacted popular sovereignty for the Louisiana Purchase. The Kansas-Nebraska Act created such great controversy that the existing political alignment was shattered. Opponents of the act created a new antislavery political party, the Republican Party, while supporters of the act reconstructed the Democratic Party as a proslavery party.

Disagreements regarding slavery-related issues and sectional competition for political power led ultimately to the outbreak of the Civil War in 1861. During the war, northern military officials increasingly believed that freeing the South's slaves would severely injure the Confederacy. President Abraham Lincoln issued the Emancipation Proclamation in 1863, proclaiming that the Union Army would henceforth liberate the Confederacy's slaves. In 1865, the Thirteenth Amendment to the U.S. Constitution freed all remaining slaves belonging to American citizens.

Slavery and the U.S. Constitution Slavery significantly influenced the writing of the U.S. Constitution. The Constitutional Convention of 1787 nearly broke up because of disagreements regarding sectional issues. Ultimately the sectional impasse was resolved with the Compromise of 1787. Direct taxes and representation in the House of Representatives were to be apportioned according to the three-fifths rule: All free people and three-fifths of the slaves were to be counted in determining a state's tax burden and congressional representation. Congress could prohibit the importation of slaves into the United States after the lapse of twenty years. States were prohibited from freeing fugitive slaves, and slaveholders were given the right to cross state boundaries to recapture fugitives. Congress was prevented from taxing exports so that slavery would not be injured by excessive taxes on the products of slave labor. Finally, to ensure that the compromise would not be abrogated, the clauses regarding the international slave trade and the three-fifths rule were declared by the Constitution to be unamendable.

As the Civil War approached, Americans debated the significance of these actions. What was the relationship between the U.S. Constitution and slavery? Before 1860, most Americans believed that the Constitution did not establish a federal right to own slaves. Slavery was thought to exist as a result of state laws, and the federal government was thought to have few constitutional powers regarding slavery. Northerners and southerners disagreed regarding the practical application of this idea. Southerners believed the federal government was increasingly intruding into matters related to slavery. They called for an end to federal interference with slavery. Northerners argued that the federal government had been indirectly providing protection to slavery for years. They called for the withdrawal of this protection.

In the 1840's and 1850's, militants on both sides developed new constitutional theories regarding slavery. Some southerners claimed that there was a federal right to own slaves, established in the fugitive slave clause and the privileges and immunities clause of the U.S. Constitution. The federal government, they said, must protect the right of citizens to own slaves in the territories. Some southern extremists argued that the federal right to own slaves was so comprehensive that even northern states could not outlaw slavery within their own boundaries. Ironically, the branch of the abolitionist movement led by William Lloyd Garrison agreed with this argument, claiming that the Constitution protected slavery and arguing that northern states should abandon this corrupt document by withdrawing from the Union.

Another branch of the abolitionist movement, led by Gerrit Smith and William Goodell, argued to the contrary that the Constitution was best read as an antislavery document. They claimed that citizenship was based on residence in the United States and that slaves therefore were citizens. The privileges and immunities clause of the Constitution, they claimed, prevented both the states and the federal government from giving unequal treatment to citizens. The due process clause of the Fifth Amendment prevented citizens from losing their liberty without due process of law. Slavery violated these principles, and judges therefore ought to declare slavery unconstitutional. While this interpretation of the Constitution seemed extreme and utopian at the time, after the Civil War, the abolitionists' constitutional ideas were incorporated into the Fourteenth Amendment.

Fugitive Slave Laws One of the most significant controversies regarding slavery involved fugitive slave laws. In 1793, Congress adopted legislation to enforce the fugitive slave clause of the U.S. Constitution. The Fugitive Slave Act of 1793 allowed slaveholders to obtain warrants from either state or federal courts for the rendition of fugitive slaves. In the 1820's and 1830's, several states passed personal liberty laws to prevent state officials from assisting in the recapture process. In *Prigg v. Pennsylvania* (1842), the U.S. Supreme Court upheld the constitutionality of personal liberty laws by ruling that the enforcement of fugitive slave laws rested entirely in the hands of the federal government.

Without the assistance of state officials, slaveholders found that it was difficult to recapture their slaves. Southerners clamored for federal assistance. Congress responded by passing a new Fugitive Slave Act as a part of the Compromise of 1850. A new group of federal officials was created for the sole purpose of assisting slaveholders recapture slaves. State officials were forbidden to resist the rendition of fugitives. Even ordinary citizens could be compelled to serve in posses for the purpose of capturing fugitives. To prevent blacks who were seized as fugitives from challenging their seizure, their legal rights, including the right of *habeas corpus*, were abolished.

The Fugitive Slave Act of 1850 was met with strong opposition in the North. Hundreds of fugitives, and even some free blacks, migrated to Canada to avoid seizure under the new law. Many northern communities formed vigilance committees to assist fugitives, and in a few cases northern mobs tried to rescue fugitives from the hands of government officials.

One rescue in 1854 led to a conflict between Wisconsin and the federal government. This case is notable because Wisconsin, a northern state, used states' rights arguments to challenge federal authority, a ploy normally used by southerners to defend slavery. Sherman M. Booth, an abolitionist, was arrested by federal marshals for participating in the rescue of a fugitive slave. The Wisconsin State Supreme Court twice issued writs of *habeas corpus* to free Booth from federal imprisonment and declared the federal Fugitive Slave Act to be unconstitutional. The U.S. Supreme Court in *Ableman v. Booth* (1859) reasserted the primacy of federal over state law and the right of the federal government to enforce its own laws through its own courts. The Wisconsin court accepted this decision, now believing that it did not help the antislavery cause to promote the idea of states' rights and nullification of federal law.

Legal Treatment of Slaves African laborers occupied an ambiguous status in the American colonies before 1660 because English law did not recognize the status of slavery. Some Africans were held as slaves; others were held as indentured servants, persons whose term of labor expired after several years. Indentured servants enjoyed certain additional legal protections since, unlike slaves, their physical bodies were not owned by their masters. After 1660, Virginia and Maryland constructed elaborate slave codes

The value of slaves as laborers made their execution or imprisonment uneconomic forms of punishment for wrongdoing; as a consequence, corporal punishments—such as flogging—were common. *(Library of Congress)*

to establish the legal status of slavery. For the next two centuries, the vast majority of blacks in America were slaves.

In making and enforcing slave codes, Americans recognized slaves as both people and property. As property, slaves generally had few legal rights as independent beings. Slaves could not own property, enter into contracts, sue or be sued, or marry legally. Slaves had no freedom of movement. Masters could sell their slaves without restriction, and there was no legal protection for slave families against forced separation through sale. The status of slave children was inherited from their mothers, a departure from the traditional common-law doctrine that children inherited the status of their fathers.

In some ways, the masters' property rights in slaves were limited by compelling public interest. Most southern states made it difficult for masters to free their slaves on the theory that free blacks were a nuisance to society. Most southern states also tried to prevent slaves from becoming a threat to society. State laws often required slaves to carry passes when traveling away from their masters' homes. Laws in several states prohibited slaves from living alone without the supervision of whites. In all but two states, it was illegal for anyone to teach slaves to read or write. Some states banned the use of alcohol and firearms by slaves; others outlawed trading and gambling by slaves. Although these laws were primarily a burden to the slave population, they also restricted the manner in which masters could manage and use their property.

Southern law codes occasionally recognized slaves as people as well as property. By the mid-nineteenth century, most states provided slaves with a minimal degree of protection against physical assaults by whites, although these laws were generally poorly enforced. All states outlawed the murder and harsh treatment of slaves. Although masters were occasionally put on trial for murder of their slaves, evidence suggests that most homicidal masters either received light sentences or were not punished. Laws protecting slaves against other forms of inhumane treatment (such as excessive beatings or starvation diets) were almost never enforced. In practice, masters could beat or starve their slaves with impunity. Battery of slaves by strangers was illegal and was often punished by southern courts. Rape of slaves by whites, however, was not illegal. Masters had the full legal right to rape their own slaves, although masters could charge other whites with criminal trespass for an act of rape without the master's permission.

Under the law, blacks were assumed to be slaves unless they could prove otherwise, meaning that free blacks were forced always to carry legal documents certifying their freedom. Many actions, including the use of alcohol and firearms, were illegal for slaves but not for whites. Penalties for crimes were generally more severe for slaves than for whites. For slaves, capital crimes—those for which death was the penalty—included not only murder but also manslaughter, rape, arson, insurrection, and robbery. Even attempted murders, insurrections, and rapes were subject to the death penalty.

Despite the harshness of the law, actual executions of slaves were rare because even slave criminals were valuable property. State laws generally required governments to pay compensation to the masters of executed slaves. The fact that the labor of slaves was valuable meant that, in all states except Louisiana, imprisonment was rarely used as punishment for slave criminals. Instead, most penalties involved physical punishments such as whipping, branding, or ear-cropping, punishments which were rarely used against whites after the early nineteenth century. While southern courts did not give blacks and whites equal treatment, the courts made some effort to be fair to slaves, probably because of the influence of wealthy slaveholders with an economic interest in the acquittal of their property. The proportion of slaves among those people accused of crime was about equal to the proportion of slaves in the population. Slaves appear to have been convicted at nearly the same rate as whites. Southern law codes also reflected the slaveholders' interests. Many states required that slaves have access to counsel and protected them against self-incrimination and double jeopardy. Slaves, however, could not testify in court against whites, meaning that it was nearly impossible to prosecute crimes against slaves when blacks were the only available witnesses.

Harold D. Tallant

Core Resources

The most readable and comprehensive survey of slavery and the law is Harold M. Hyman and William M. Wiecek's *Equal Justice Under Law: Constitutional Development, 1835-1875* (New York: Harper & Row, 1982). Alan Watson's *Slave Law in the Americas* (Athens: University of Georgia Press, 1989) offers a succinct comparison of the law of slavery in several Western Hemisphere societies. Mark V. Tushnet's *The American Law of Slavery, 1810-1860: Considerations of Humanity and Interest* (Princeton, N.J.: Princeton University Press, 1981) discusses the tension within American law regarding the slaves' dual role as both property and people. The best survey of the legal treatment of slaves is Philip J. Schwarz's *Twice Condemned: Slaves and the Criminal Laws of Virginia, 1705-1865* (Baton Rouge: Louisiana State University Press, 1988).

See also: Abolition; Emancipation Proclamation; Free-Soil Party; Fugitive slave laws; Kansas-Nebraska Act; Missouri Compromise; Reconstruction; *Scott v. Sandford*; Slave codes.

Slavery: history

Slavery has historically constituted a significant denial of human rights and, as practiced in the United States, laid the foundations for conflict between whites and blacks for generations to come.

Slavery is one of the oldest institutions of human society. Slavery was present in the earliest human civilizations, those of ancient Mesopotamia and Egypt, and continued to exist in several parts of the world through the late twentieth century.

Definitions Despite the near universality of slavery, there is no consensus regarding what distinctive practices constitute slavery. In Western society, a slave typically was a person who was owned as property by another person and forced to perform labor for the owner. This definition, however, breaks down when applied to non-Western forms of slavery. In some African societies, slaves were not owned as property by an individual but were thought of as belonging to a kinship group. The slave could be sold, but so too could nonslave members of the kinship group. In certain African societies, slaves were exempted from labor and were used solely to bring honor to the master by demonstrating his absolute power over another person.

The sociologist Orlando Patterson suggested that slavery is best understood as an institution designed to increase the power of the master or the ruling group. Slaves can fulfill this role by laboring to make the master rich, but they can also do so by bringing honor to the master. One of the defining, universal characteristics of slavery is that the slave ceases to exist as a socially meaningful person. The slave relates to society only through the master. Slavery includes many mechanisms to remove the slave from membership in any groups, such as the family, through which the slave might derive an independent sense of identity. By placing the master in a dominant position over another individual, slavery is believed to increase the honor and power of the master. The slave's status is permanent and it is typically passed down to the slave's children.

History The use of slavery was widespread in the ancient world, especially in Greece and Italy. During the classical ages of Greek and Roman society, slaves constituted about one-third of the population. Following the collapse of the Roman Empire in Western Europe during the fifth and sixth centuries, declining economic conditions destroyed the profitability of slavery and provided employers with large numbers of impoverished peasants who could be employed more cheaply than slaves. Over the next seven hundred years, slavery slowly gave way to serfdom. Although serfs, like slaves, were unfree laborers, serfs generally had more legal rights and a higher social standing than slaves.

Familiarity with the institution of slavery did not, however, disappear in Western Europe. A trickle of slaves from Eastern Europe and even from Africa continued to flow into England, France, and Germany. Western Europeans retained their familiarity with large-scale slave systems through contacts with southern Italy, Spain, and Portugal, and with the Byzantine Empire and the Muslim world, where slavery flourished. Western Europeans also inherited from their Roman forebears the corpus of Roman law, with its elaborate slave code. During the later Middle Ages, Europeans who were familiar with Muslim sugar plantations in the Near East sought to begin sugar production with slave labor on the islands of the Mediterranean.

Thus, as Western Europe entered the age of exploration and colonization, Europeans had an intimate knowledge of slavery and a ready-made code of laws to govern slaves. During the sixteenth century, as European nations sought to establish silver mines and sugar plantations in their new colonies in the Western Hemisphere, heavy labor demands led to efforts to enslave Native Americans. This supply of laborers was inadequate because of the rapid decline of the Indian population following the introduction of European diseases into the Western Hemisphere. The Spanish and Portuguese then turned to Africa, the next most readily available source of slave laborers.

Between 1500 and 1900, European slave traders imported perhaps 10 million African laborers into the Western Hemisphere. Every European colony eventually used slave labor, which became the principal form of labor in the Western Hemisphere. Because the wealth of several modern nations was created by slave labor, some contemporary African Americans have claimed the right to receive reparations payments from nations such as the United States, which continue to enjoy the wealth accumulated originally by the use of slave laborers.

Slavery and Race The large-scale use of African slaves by European masters raised new moral issues regarding race. There is no necessary connection between slavery and race. A massive survey by Orlando Patterson of slave societies throughout history found that in three-quarters of slave societies, masters and slaves were of the same race. Slavery in the Western Hemisphere was unusual in human history because slaves were drawn almost exclusively from the black race.

In most colonies of the Western Hemisphere, the use of African slaves was accompanied by the rise of racism, which some scholars claim was a new, unprecedented phenomenon caused by slavery. Scholars seeking to understand contemporary race relations in the United States have been intrigued by the rise of prejudice in new slave societies. Did Europeans enslave Africans merely because they needed slaves and Africa was the most accessible source of slaves? If so, then prejudice probably originated as a learned association between race and subservience. Modern prejudice might be broken down through integration and affirmative action programs aimed at helping whites to witness the success of blacks in positions of authority. Did Europeans enslave Africans because the Europeans saw Africans as inferior persons ideally suited for slavery? If so, then contemporary racism is a deeply rooted cultural phenomenon that is not likely to disappear for generations to come. African Americans will receive justice only if the government establishes permanent compensatory programs aimed at equalizing power between the races.

Historical research has not resolved these issues. Sixteenth century Europeans apparently did view Africans as inferior beings, even before the colonization of the Western Hemisphere. These racial antipathies were minor, however, in comparison to modern racism. Emancipated slaves in recently settled colonies experienced little racial discrimination. The experience of slavery apparently increased the European settlers' sense of racial superiority over Africans.

After the slave systems of the Western Hemisphere became fully developed, racial arguments became the foundation of the proslavery argument. Supporters of slavery claimed that persons of African descent were so degraded and inferior to whites that it would be dangerous for society to release the slaves from the control of a master. In the United States, some proslavery theorists pushed the racial argument to extreme levels. In explain-

Contemporary drawings of slaves working a rice plantation in North Carolina. *(Library of Congress)*

ing the contradiction between slavery and the American ideal that all persons should be free, writers such as Josiah Nott and Samuel Cartwright claimed that blacks were not fully human and, therefore, did not deserve all the rights belonging to humanity.

A minority of proslavery writers rejected the racial argument and the effort to reconcile slavery and American egalitarian ideals. Writers such as George Fitzhugh claimed that all societies were organized hierarchically by classes and that slavery was the most benevolent system for organizing an unequal class structure. Slavery bound together masters and slaves through a system of mutual rights and obligations. Unlike the "wage slaves" of industrial society, chattel slaves had certain access to food, clothing, shelter, and medical care, all because the master's ownership of the slaves' bodies made him diligent in caring for his property. Slavery was depicted by some proslavery theorists as the ideal condition for the white working class.

The Antislavery Movement From the dawning of human history until the middle of the eighteenth century, few persons appear to have questioned the morality of slavery as an institution. Although some persons had earlier raised moral objections to certain features of slavery, almost no one appears to have questioned the overall morality of slavery as a system before the middle of the eighteenth century. Around 1750, however, an antislavery movement began to appear in Britain, France, and America.

The sudden rise of antislavery opinion appears to be related to the rise of a humanitarian ethos during the Enlightenment that encouraged people to consider the welfare of humans beyond their kin groups. The rise of the antislavery movement was also related to the growing popularity of new forms of evangelical and pietistic religious sects such as the Baptists, Methodists, and Quakers, which tended to view slaveholding as sinful materialism and slaves as persons worthy of God's love. The rise of the antislavery movement was encouraged by the American and French Revolutions, whose democratic political philosophies promoted a belief in the equality of individuals. The rise of antislavery opinion also coincided in time with the rise of industrial capitalism. The historian Eric Williams argued in *Capitalism and Slavery* (1944) that the economic and class interests of industrial capitalists rather than the moral scruples of humanitarians gave rise to the antislavery movement.

Antislavery activism initially focused on the abolition of the Atlantic slave trade. Reformers succeeded in prompting Britain and the United States to abolish the slave trade in 1807. Other nations followed this lead over the next half century until the Atlantic slave trade was virtually eliminated.

The campaign to abolish the slave trade achieved early success because it joined together moral concerns and self-interest. Many persons in the late eighteenth and early nineteenth centuries were prepared to accept the end of the slave trade while opposing the end of slavery itself. Even slaveholders were angered by the living conditions endured by slaves on crowded, disease-infested slave ships. Some masters, in fact, attempted to justify their ownership of slaves by claiming that the conditions on their plantations were more humane than the conditions on slave-trading ships or in allegedly primitive Africa. Some slaveholders supported the abolition of the slave trade because they realized that limiting the supply of new slaves from Africa would increase the value of the existing slave population. Finally, many persons believed that it was wrong for slave traders to deny liberty to freeborn Africans, but that it was not wrong for slave masters to exercise control over persons who were born into the status of slavery. Indeed, supporters of slavery argued that the well-being of society required masters to exercise control over persons who had no preparation for freedom and might be a threat to society if emancipated.

The campaign to eradicate slavery itself was more difficult and was accompanied by significant political upheavals and, in the case of Haiti and the United States, revolution and warfare. British reformers such as William Wilberforce, Thomas Clarkson, and Granville Sharp made, perhaps, the most significant contributions to the organization of a worldwide antislavery movement. In 1823, British activists formed the London Antislavery Committee, soon to be renamed the British and Foreign Antislavery Society. The society spearheaded a successful campaign to abolish slavery in the British Empire and, eventually, worldwide. It remained in existence in the 1990's. Known by the name Antislavery International, the society had the distinction of being the world's oldest human rights organization. Antislavery reformers were also active in the United States. From the 1830's through the 1860's, abolitionists such as William Lloyd Garrison, Wendell Phillips, and Frederick Douglass sought to arouse the moral anger of Americans against slavery. More effective, however, were politicians such as Abraham Lincoln, Charles Sumner, and Salmon P. Chase, whose antislavery message was a mixture of idealism, self-interest, and expedience.

Emancipation of Slaves Beginning in the late eighteenth century and accelerating through the nineteenth century, slavery was abolished throughout the Western Hemisphere. This was followed in the late nineteenth and twentieth centuries by the legal abolition of slavery in Africa and Asia.

In evaluating the success of abolition in any society, it is necessary to distinguish between legal and de facto emancipation. Changing the legal status of a slave to that of a free person is not the same thing as freeing the slave from the control of a master. Legal emancipation often has little impact on persons held as slaves if governments fail to enforce the abolition of slavery. For example, Britain in the nineteenth century outlawed slavery in its colonies in India, the Gold Coast, Kenya, and Zanzibar. Yet, fearing a disruption of economic production in these colonies, the British government simply abstained from enforcing its own abolition laws until pressure from reformers put an end to slavery. A similar situation existed in Mauritania, where slavery was prohibited by law three separate times, in 1905, 1960, and 1980, yet the government of Mauritania enacted no penalties against masters who kept slaves in violation of the emancipation law, and the government waged no campaign to inform the slaves of their freedom. As a result, journalists and investigators for the International Labor Organisation found slavery still flourishing in Mauritania in the 1990's.

Even in societies that vigorously enforced their acts of abolition, legal emancipation was usually followed by a period of transition in which former slaves were held in a state resembling that of slavery. The Abolition of Slavery Act of 1833, which outlawed slavery in most colonies of the British Empire, provided that slaves would serve as apprentices to their former masters for a period of four to six years. In the American South after the Civil War, former slaves were subject for a time to black codes that greatly reduced the freedom of movement of African Americans and required them to work on the plantations of former slave masters. After the Civil Rights Act of 1866 and the Fourteenth Amendment outlawed such practices, southerners created the sharecropping and crop-lien systems, which allowed planters to control the labor of many blacks through a form of debt bondage.

The efforts of former masters to control the labor of former slaves were a part of a larger effort by postemancipation societies to determine what rights freedpeople should exercise. In the United States, for instance, emancipation raised many questions regarding the general rights of citizens, the answers to which often remained elusive more than a century after the abolition of slavery. Should freedpeople be considered citizens with basic rights equal to other citizens? How far should equality of citizenship rights extend? Should equality of rights be kept at a minimum level, perhaps limited to freedom of movement, the right to own property, and the right to make contracts and enforce them in a court of law? Should citizenship rights be extended to the political realm, with guarantees of the right to vote, serve on juries, and hold political office? Should citizenship rights be extended to the social realm, with the protection for the right to live wherever one wanted, to use public spaces without discrimination, and to marry persons of another race?

Antislavery and Imperialism Ironically, the international effort to abolish slavery raised troubling new moral issues. During the last quarter of the nineteenth century, in the name of suppressing the African slave trade at its source, Britain and other European nations demanded of African rulers certain police powers within African kingdoms. The Europeans also organized new African industries to encourage the shift from the slave trade to the "legitimate trade" in other commodities. In this manner, the humanitarian impulse of antislavery combined with less humane motives to produce the New Imperialism of the 1880's through the 1910's. During this thirty-year period, nearly all of Africa fell under European domination. Time and again, the campaign to suppress the slave trade became a cloak for the imperialist ambitions of the European powers. It is worth remembering that the two international conferences in which the European powers agreed to carve up

Africa among themselves, the Berlin Conference of 1884-1885 and the Brussels Conference of 1889-1890, both devised significant agreements for ending the African slave trade.

Harold D. Tallant

Core Resources

The Antislavery Debate: Capitalism and Abolitionism as a Problem in Historical Interpretation (Berkeley: University of California Press, 1992), edited by Thomas Bender, is a collection of essays that debate the question of whether the rise of industrial capitalism caused the emergence of the antislavery movement. David Brion Davis's *The Problem of Slavery in the Age of Revolution, 1770-1823* (Ithaca, N.Y.: Cornell University Press, 1975) is a Pulitzer Prize-winning study of the intellectual background of the rise of the antislavery movement. Davis's *Slavery and Human Progress* (New York: Oxford University Press, 1984) is an excellent introduction to many of the ethical issues regarding slavery organized around a discussion of changing concepts of progress. Moses I. Finley's *Ancient Slavery and Modern Ideology* (New York: Viking Press, 1980) is a study of the moral, intellectual, and social foundations of slavery by the leading expert on ancient slavery. Eric Foner's *Nothing But Freedom: Emancipation and Its Legacy* (Baton Rouge: Louisiana State University Press, 1983) is a brief but thought-provoking study of the problems associated with emancipation in several countries. Orlando Patterson's *Slavery and Social Death: A Comparative Study* (Cambridge, Mass.: Harvard University Press, 1982), the most important study of slavery in its various forms, is based on a massive survey of slave societies on all continents from the beginning of history. William D. Phillips's *Slavery from Roman Times to the Early Transatlantic Trade* (Minneapolis: University of Minnesota Press, 1985) is a highly readable historical survey of the transition from ancient slavery to modern slavery.

See also: Abolition; Civil rights; Emancipation Proclamation; Racism: history of the concept; Slavery and race relations; Slavery: North American beginnings.

Slavery: North American beginnings

The establishment of institutionalized slavery in the British colonies of North America would have untold consequences for the history of the continent.

In August of 1619, a Dutch warship carrying "20 and odd" Africans landed at Point Comfort, Virginia. These Africans, the first to arrive in the British

Alexandra, Virginia, slave dealer's headquarters, around the 1850's. *(National Archives)*

colonies, were probably put to work not as slaves but as servants. Neither the laws of the mother country nor the charter of the colony established the institution of slavery, although the system was developing in the British West Indies at the same time and was almost one hundred years old in the Spanish and Portuguese colonies. To be sure, African servants were discriminated against early on—their terms of service were usually longer than those of white servants, and they were the object of certain prohibitions that were not imposed on white servants—but in the early seventeenth century, at least some black servants, like their white counterparts, gained their freedom and even acquired some property. Anthony Johnson, who labored on Richard Bennett's Virginia plantation for almost twenty years after he arrived in Virginia in 1621, imported five servants in his first decade of freedom, receiving 250 acres on their headrights. Another former servant, Richard Johnson, obtained one hundred acres for importing two white servants in 1654. These two men were part of the small class of free blacks that existed in Virginia throughout the colonial period.

Such cases as the two Johnsons were rare by midcentury. As early as the 1640's, some African Americans were in servitude for life, and their numbers increased throughout the decade. In 1640, for example, in a court decision involving three runaway servants, the two who were white were sentenced to an additional four years of service, while the other, an African named John Punch, was ordered to serve his master "for the time of his natural Life." In the 1650's, some African servants were being sold for life, and the bills of sale indicated that their offspring would inherit slave status. Thus, slavery developed according to custom before it was legally established in Virginia.

Slave Codes Not until 1661 was chattel slavery recognized by statute in Virginia, and then only indirectly. The House of Burgesses passed a law declaring that children followed the status of their mothers, thereby rendering the system of slavery self-perpetuating. In 1667, the Virginia Assembly strengthened the system by declaring that in the case of children that were slaves by birth "the conferring of baptisme doth not alter the condition of a person as to his bondage or freedome; that divers masters, freed from this doubt, may more carefully endeavor the propagation of christianity." Until this time, Americans had justified enslavement of Africans on the grounds that they were "heathen" and had recognized conversion as a way to freedom. This act closed the last avenue to freedom, apart from formal emancipation, available to African American slaves. In 1705, Virginia established a comprehensive slave code that completed the gradual process by which most African Americans were reduced to the status of chattel. Slaves could not bear arms or own property, nor could they leave the plantation without written permission from the master. Capital punishment was provided for murder and rape; lesser crimes were punished by maiming, whipping, or branding. Special courts were established for the trials of slaves, who were barred from serving as witnesses, except in the cases in which slaves were being tried for capital offenses.

In the other British colonies, the pattern was similar to that of Virginia. African racial slavery existed early in both Maryland and the Carolinas. Georgia attempted to exclude slavery at the time of settlement, but yielding to the protests of the colonists and the pressure of South Carolinians, the trustees repealed the prohibition in 1750. The Dutch brought slavery to the Middle Colonies early in the seventeenth century. The advent of British rule in 1664 proved to be a stimulus to the system in New York and New Jersey; but in Pennsylvania and Delaware, the religious objections of the Quakers delayed its growth somewhat and postponed legal recognition of slavery until the early eighteenth century. In seventeenth century New England, the status of Africans was ambiguous, as it was in Virginia. There were slaves in Massachusetts as early as 1638, possibly before, although slavery was not recognized by statute until 1641, which was the first enactment legalizing slavery anywhere in the British colonies. New England became heavily involved in the African slave trade, particularly after the monopoly of the Royal African Company was revoked in 1698. Like Virginia, all the colonies enacted slave codes in the late seventeenth century or early eighteenth century, although the New England codes were less harsh than those of the Middle or Southern Colonies. In all the colonies, a small class of free blacks developed alongside the institution of slavery, despite the fact that formal emancipation was restricted.

Slavery grew slowly in the first half of the seventeenth century. In 1625, there were twenty-three Africans in Virginia, most of whom probably were servants, not slaves. By midcentury, a decade before the statutory recognition of slavery, the black population was only three hundred, or 2 percent of the overall population of fifteen thousand. In 1708, there were twelve thousand African Americans and sixty-eight thousand whites. In a little more than fifty years, the black population had jumped from 2 percent to 15 percent of the total Virginia population. In the Carolinas, blacks initially made up 30 percent of the population, but within one generation outnumbered whites, making South Carolina the only mainland colony characterized by a black majority. In New England, blacks numbered only about one thousand out of a total population of ninety thousand. The eighteenth century would see the rapid development of the system of African racial slavery, particularly in the Southern colonies, where it became an integral part of the emerging plantation economy.

Anne C. Loveland, updated by Laura A. Croghan

Core Resources

Slavery's North Amercian beginnings are examined in David Brion Davis's *The Problem of Slavery in Western Culture* (Ithaca, N.Y.: Cornell University Press, 1966); Lorenzo J. Greene's *The Negro in Colonial New England, 1620-1776* (New York: Columbia University Press, 1942); Winthrop D. Jordan's *White over Black: American Attitudes Toward the Negro, 1550-1812* (New York: W. W. Norton, 1968); Edmund S. Morgan's *American Slavery, American Freedom: The Ordeal of Colonial Virginia* (New York: W. W. Norton, 1975); and Peter B. Wood's *Black Majority: Negroes in Colonial South Carolina from 1670 Through the Stono Rebellion* (New York: Alfred A. Knopf, 1974).

See also: Abolition; American Anti-Slavery Society; Slave codes; Slavery and race relations; Slavery: history.

Smith v. Allwright

In Smith v. Allwright, *the U.S. Supreme Court in 1944 ruled that disfranchisement of African Americans in state primary elections was unconstitutional.*

In 1923, the Texas legislature sought to disfranchise African American voters in the state by passing a resolution that "in no event shall a Negro be eligible to participate in a Democratic primary. . . ." Since the 1890's, in Texas as in all other southern states, nomination in the Democratic primary was tantamount to election; therefore, while African Americans would be permitted to vote in the general election, they would have no meaningful role in the political process.

The NAACP's Challenges Almost immediately after the Texas legislature barred African Americans from participating in the Democratic primary, the National Association for the Advancement of Colored People (NAACP) secured a plaintiff, Dr. L. A. Nixon, to test the constitutionality of the legislative act. In *Nixon v. Herndon* (1927), the U.S. Supreme Court, in an opinion written by Justice Oliver Wendell Holmes, Jr., held that the Texas statute violated the equal protection clause of the Fourteenth Amendment to the U.S. Constitution by discriminating against African Americans on the basis of race. He also ruled, however, that it was unnecessary to strike down the white primary as a denial of suffrage "on account of race[or] color" repugnant to the Fifteenth Amendment.

The Texas legislature reacted defiantly to the Supreme Court decision. On June 7, 1927, the legislature passed a new resolution granting to the state executive committees of every political party the authority to establish the qualifications of their members and to determine who was qualified to vote or otherwise participate in the party. In turn, the Democratic Party State Executive Committee limited participation in its primary to white voters in Texas.

Once again Nixon filed suit, this time against James Condon, the election officer who refused to give him a ballot in the 1928 Democratic primary. In *Nixon v. Condon* (1932), the Supreme Court struck down this new Texas statute as a violation of the equal protection clause.

The Democratic Party State Executive Committee immediately rescinded its resolution prohibiting African Americans from voting in its primary, but the state party convention voted to limit participation in its deliberations to whites. In July, 1934, Richard Randolph Grovey in Houston, Texas, was refused a ballot to vote in the Democratic primary. On April 1, 1935, in *Grovey v. Townsend,* Justice Owen J. Roberts ruled that the Democratic Party was a private organization, and that its primary, although held under state law, was a party matter paid for by the Democrats. Since Roberts could find no state action in the process by which Democrats nominated their candidates, there was, he said, no violation of the Fourteenth Amendment. Because the Democratic Party was a private organization, it was free to establish membership qualifications, and there was not sufficient state involvement to invoke the guarantees of the Fourteenth Amendment.

In 1941, however, in *United States v. Classic,* a case that ostensibly had nothing to do with African Americans or the white primary, the Supreme Court held for the first time that the right to vote was protected in a primary as well as in the general election, "where the state law has made the primary an integral part of the process of choice or where in fact the primary effectively controls the choice."

United States v. Classic dealt with a Louisiana primary in which there had been fraudulent returns, but otherwise there was no way to distinguish the Texas primary from the one held in the neighboring southern state. In Texas, as in Louisiana, in 1941 as in 1923, Democratic Party nomination in its primary was a virtual guarantee of election, and the general election was a mere formality.

The *Smith* Case The NAACP was back in action. Lonnie Smith, a Houston dentist and NAACP member, sued a Texas election official for five thousand dollars for refusing to give him a ballot to vote in the 1940 Democratic congressional primaries. The NAACP's legal counsel, Thurgood Marshall, and William Hastie, dean of the Howard Law School, brought *Smith v. Allwright* to the United States Supreme Court.

In April, 1944, mindful of southern sensibilities but intent upon overruling the nine-year-old precedent in *Grovey*, the Court chose Stanley Reed, a Democrat from Kentucky, to write its opinion. Justice Reed's opinion made it clear that the Court, except for Justice Roberts (the author of the *Grovey* decision), had concluded that the primary was an integral part of a general election, particularly in the southern states. The *Classic* decision, wrote Justice Reed, raised the issue of whether excluding African Americans from participation in the Democratic Party primary in Texas violated the Fifteenth Amendment. The answer was in the affirmative, and *Grovey v. Townsend* was expressly overruled.

The long litigative battle against the Texas white primary seemed to be over—but it was not. In Fort Bend County, Texas, the Jaybird Democratic Party, organized after the Civil War, held primaries closed to African American voters; its candidates consistently won county offices. In spite of *Smith v. Allwright*, the Jaybirds refused to open their primary to African Americans, arguing that they did not operate under state law or use state officers or funds. Nevertheless, in *Terry v. Adams* (1953), the Supreme Court held that the Jaybird primary violated the Fifteenth Amendment, because it controlled the electoral process in Fort Bend County.

It took twenty-one years for the United States Supreme Court to rule that the Texas white primary violated the right to vote guaranteed by the Fifteenth Amendment. It would take another twenty-one years before the Voting Rights Act of 1965 finally secured the ballot for African Americans in the South. In the interim, the fall of the white primary had the practical effect of increasing African American registrants in the southern states from approximately 250,000 in 1940 to 775,000 seven years later. African Americans were still intimidated and defrauded of their suffrage rights, but *Smith v. Allwright* was an important landmark on the road to uninhibited enfranchisement. It also was a symbol that the Supreme Court would examine the reality behind the subterfuge and act to protect African Americans in the enjoyment of their civil rights.

David L. Sterling

Core Resources

John D. Fassett's *New Deal Justice: The Life of Stanley Reed of Kentucky* (New York: Vantage Press, 1994) is a biography of the conservative Democratic justice who wrote the majority opinion in *Smith v. Allwright.* Darlene Clark Hine's *Black Victory: The Rise and Fall of the White Primary in Texas* (Millwood, N.Y.: KTO Press, 1979) is an examination of the background of the white primary and the struggle to bring about its demise. Steven F. Lawson's *Black Ballots: Voting Rights in the South, 1944-1969* (New York: Columbia University Press, 1976) traces the development of African American enfranchisement from *Smith v. Allwright* to the Voting Rights Act of 1965 and its aftermath. Includes a chapter on the white primary.

See also: Disfranchisement laws in Mississippi; Fourteenth Amendment; *Grovey v. Townsend*; *Nixon v. Herndon*; Voting Rights Act of 1965.

Social identity theory

Social identity theory examines the relationship between group membership and self-esteem. It has provided insights into intergroup conflict, ethnocentrism, cultural affirmation, and self-hatred, predicting both individual and group responses to an unfavorable self-concept.

Social identity theory maintains that all individuals are motivated to achieve and maintain a positive self-concept. A person's self-concept derives from two principal sources: personal identity and social identity. Personal identity includes one's individual traits, achievements, and qualities. Social identity includes the group affiliations that are recognized as being part of the self, such as one's image of oneself as a Protestant, a blue-collar worker, or a conservative. Some individuals emphasize the personal aspects in their quest for a favorable self-image, while others emphasize their social identities. Social identity theory focuses on the latter. It attempts to explain when and how individuals transform their group affiliations to secure a favorable self-concept.

Psychologist Henri Tajfel introduced social identity theory in 1978. The theory maintains that a person's social identity emerges from the natural process of social categorization. People categorize, or classify, themselves and other people by many criteria, including occupation, religious affiliation, political orientation, ethnicity, economic class, and gender. An individual automatically identifies with some categories and rejects others. This creates a distinction between "in-groups," with which one identifies, and "out-groups," with which one does not identify. A person who identifies himself or herself as a Democrat, for example, would consider other Democrats members of the in-group and would view Republicans as members of the out-group. Individuals inevitably compare their groups with other groups; the goal of the comparisons is to establish the superiority of one's own group, or the group's "positive distinctiveness," on some level, such as affluence, cultural heritage, or spirituality. If the comparison shows that the individual's group memberships are positive and valuable, the social identities become an important part of the self. If, however, one's group appears inferior, one's self-image acquires "negative distinctiveness." The individual is then motivated to acquire a more satisfactory self-concept.

Enhancing the Self-Concept Tajfel and John Turner proposed three strategies that can be used to enhance one's self-concept: "exit," "pass," and "voice." The first two strategies represent attempts to validate the self. Both involve rejecting or distancing oneself from the devalued group to improve identity; both presume that social mobility exists. Exit involves simply leaving the group. This response is possible only within flexible social systems that permit individual mobility. Although individuals cannot usually shed affiliations such as race or gender, they can openly discard other affiliations, such as "Buick owner" or "public school advocate." If dissatisfied with an automobile, one trades it in for another; if unhappy with the public school system, one may exit and move one's children into a private school. Pass, a more private response, occurs when individuals with unfavorable group memberships are not recognized as belonging to that group. A Jew may pass as a Gentile, for example, or a fair-skinned black person may pass as a Caucasian. Typically in such cases, the objective features that link the individual to the devalued group are absent or unnoticeable.

Voice, the final strategy for identity improvement, is a collective response: Group members act together to alter the group's image and elevate its social value. Also called the "social change" approach, it is common in rigid social systems in which individual movement away from the disparaged group is impossible. It also occurs when psychological forces such as cultural and personal values bind the individual to the group. Members of such physically identifiable groups as women, blacks, or Asians might adopt the social change strategy, for example, as might such cultural or religious group members as Irish Catholics or Orthodox Jews.

Voice is a complex response. Simply recognizing that social mobility is blocked for members of one's own group is insufficient to prompt social change activity. Two additional perceptions of the overall social structure are important: its stability and its legitimacy. Stability is concerned with how fixed or secure the social hierarchy seems. Theoretically, no group is completely secure in its relative superiority; even groups that historically have been considered superior must work to maintain their favored position. If members of a denigrated group believe that alternatives to the current social hierarchy are possible, they are encouraged to reassess their own value. Legitimacy, in contrast, involves the bases for a group's negative distinctiveness. If a group believes that its social inferiority is attributable to illegitimate causes such as discrimination in hiring practices or educational opportunities, group members will be more likely to challenge their inferior position.

Voice challenges to negative distinctiveness take two general forms: social creativity and direct competition. Social creativity involves altering or redefining the elements of comparison. The group's social positions and resources, however, need not be altered. In one approach, a group may simply limit the groups with which it compares itself, focusing on groups that are similar. A group of factory workers may choose to compare itself with warehouse workers or postal employees rather than with a group of advertising executives. This approach increases the chances that the outcome of the comparison will be favorable to one's own group. The group might also identify a new area of comparison, such as bilingual fluency, in its effort to enhance group distinctiveness.

Finally, the group might recast some of its denigrated attributes so that its value is reassessed. A new appreciation for group history and culture often emerges from this process. The Civil Rights movement, an important force for social change in the 1960's, caused such a recasting to occur. In the context of that movement, the label "Negro" was replaced by "black," which was recast by African Americans to symbolize group pride. Under the slogan "Black is beautiful," the natural look became more valued than the traditional Euro-American model. African Americans were less likely to lighten or straighten their hair or use makeup to make their skin appear lighter.

Direct competition, in contrast, involves altering the group's social position. It is often an institutional response; consequently, it encourages competition among groups. Displaced groups target institutions and policies, demanding resources in an effort to empower the group politically and economically. In the 1960's, for example, black students demonstrated for curricular changes at colleges and universities. They demanded greater relevance in existing courses and the development of black studies programs to highlight the group's social and political contributions. In the 1970's, the women's movement demanded economic and political changes, including equal pay for equal work, and greater individual rights for women, such as abortion rights and institutionalized child care.

In-Group Bias Social identity theory has been used to explain several intergroup processes. Among these are the phenomenon known as in-group bias (observed in laboratory experiments) and the actions of some subordinate groups to challenge their relative inferiority through collective (voice) approaches. The response of African Americans in the 1950's and 1960's to negative perceptions of their group illustrates the latter process.

In-group bias is the tendency to favor one's own group over other groups. In laboratory experiments, young subjects have been put in groups according to simple and fairly arbitrary criteria, such as the type of artwork they preferred. The goal was to establish a "minimal group situation": an artificial social order in which subjects could be easily differentiated but which was free of any already existing conflicts. Once categorized, subjects were asked to perform one of several tasks, such as distributing money, assigning points, evaluating the different groups, or interpreting group members' behavior. In all the tasks, subjects repeatedly showed a preference for their own groups. They gave to in-group members significantly more points and money than they gave to out-group members despite a lack of previous interaction among the subjects. When describing in-group members, they attributed altruistic behavior to the persons' innate virtuous and admirable qualities rather than to outside causes. When describing out-group members, however, they reversed the pattern, attributing altruistic behavior to situational factors and hostile behavior to personal character. Thus, even without any history of competition, ideological differences, or hostility over scarce resources, subjects consistently demonstrate a preference for their in-group.

Social identity theory predicts this pattern. The powerful need to achieve a positive self-image motivates a person to establish the value of his or her group memberships. Since groups strongly contribute to an individual's self-image, the individual works to enhance the group's image. Group successes are, by extension, the individual's successes. Daily life offers many examples of group allegiance, ranging from identification with one's country to support of one's hometown baseball team. Experiments in social identity suggest that ethnocentrism, the belief in the superiority of one's own ethnic group, serves important psychological needs.

Working for Change Social identity theory also explains why some subordinate groups challenge their relative inferiority through rebellion or social change while others do not. The theory predicts that individuals who are objectively bound to negatively distinct groups by gender or skin color, for example, will have fewer options for self-enhancement. Because they are driven by the powerful need to obtain a worthy self-image, however, they are unlikely to engage in self-hatred by accepting the denigrated image imposed on them by others. Instead, they will engage in some form of voice, the collective approach to image improvement.

Black Self-Images Psychologists studying social identity do not directly explore the historical background of a group's negative self-image. Rather, they perform laboratory experiments and field studies designed to determine individuals' actual perceptions of groups, how individuals identify groups, and whether they see them as having a positive or negative image. Social psychologists also attempt to measure the changes that occur in group self-image over time; they can then infer that social or political movements have affected that image. Studies involving African American children for whom the essential identifying element is a physical one, race, provide an example.

In the landmark 1954 Supreme Court decision *Brown v. Board of Education*, which mandated school desegregation, social scientists presented evidence that educational segregation produced feelings of inferiority in black children. Support was drawn in part from a 1947 study by Kenneth and Mamie Clark, in which they compared the preferences of black and white children between the ages of three and seven for dolls with either dark or fair skin tones. Approximately 60 percent of the black children said that the fair-skinned doll was the "nicer" doll, the "nicer color" doll, or the doll they "preferred to play with." The dark-skinned doll, by contrast, "looked bad." Based on a combination of this negative self-image and the fact that African Americans are objectively bound to their group by their race, social identity theory would predict collective action for social change.

The Civil Rights movement embodied that collective, or voice, activity, and it offered blacks a new context within which to evaluate black identity. Results from studies performed in the 1970's suggest that, indeed, there was a significant rise in black self-esteem during that period. A replication of the Clarks' study by other researchers showed a clear preference for the dark-skinned doll among black children. Later analyses of comparable doll studies showed that such preferences for one's own group were most common among young subjects from areas with large black populations and active black pride movements.

A positive self-image may also emerge when social and cultural themes and historical events are reinterpreted within a group. A group's cultural image may be emphasized; its music, art, and language then become valued. To continue using the African American example, in the twentieth century, black music—work songs and spirituals—which once had been the music of the oppressed evolved into a music that communicated ethnic identity in a new way. Blues and jazz became a focus of group pride; jazz, in particular, become renowned worldwide. The acceptance of jazz as a valuable art form by people of many races and nationalities illustrates another frequent outcome of activity for generating a positive self-concept: It often initiates a response from the larger society that improves the group's relative position in that society.

Jaclyn Rodriguez

Core Resources

Differentiation Between Social Groups: Studies in the Social Psychology of Intergroup Relations (London: Academic Press, 1978), edited by Henri Tajfel, presents the work of the team of European social psychologists that conceptualized and formalized social identity theory. Tajfel's *Human Groups and Social Categories* (Cambridge, England: Cambridge University Press, 1981) is an easy-to-read account of Tajfel's conceptualization of intergroup conflict. Tajfel and John Turner's "The Social Identity Theory of Intergroup Behavior," in *Social Psychology of Intergroup Relations*, edited by Stephen Worchel and William G. Austin (2d ed., Chicago: Nelson-Hall, 1986) is an excellent summary of social identity theory. Turner's *Rediscovering the Social Group: A Self-Categorization Theory* (New York: Basil Blackwell, 1987) provides the reader with a valuable backdrop for understanding many of Tajfel's predictions in a readable blend of theoretical and empirical work.

See also: Black Is Beautiful movement; Black Power movement; Internalized racism; Passing.

Southern Christian Leadership Conference

The SCLC was one of the major organizations instrumental in the Civil Rights movement in the American South in the 1950's and 1960's.

The Southern Christian Leadership Conference originated in a bus boycott organized in 1955 to protest segregation in Montgomery, Alabama. Martin Luther King, Jr., a young minister, led the Montgomery Improvement Association, which spearheaded the boycott. His leadership marked the emergence of African American ministers as organizers in the Civil Rights movement. King and other black ministers became increasingly involved in the Civil Rights movement.

The SCLC was formed in December, 1957, as a result of this church-led protest movement and others that had occurred in southern communities. The SCLC was distinctly different from the National Association for the Advancement of Colored People (NAACP, established in 1909), long the premiere organization involved in the struggle for the rights of African Americans. In contrast to the NAACP, the SCLC was confined to the South. It did not have individual memberships, in part so that it would not be seen as competing with the NAACP. Instead, it was an umbrella organization bringing together local affiliates in a loose alliance. Each affiliate paid the SCLC a fee of twenty-five dollars, in return receiving a certificate of affiliation signed by King. Each affiliate had the right to send five delegates to the group's annual meeting. Most affiliates were composed of African American ministers and their churches. At least two-thirds of the thirty-three members of the governing board were ministers, primarily Baptist. Northern activists, including Bayard Rustin and Stanley Levison, assisted the SCLC in solving problems of organizational cohesion, financial stability, and political direction. The SCLC, however, is identified primarily with King as its leader.

Methods The approach used by the SCLC was a combination of grassroots activism and political strategy. Its major campaigns concentrated on the use of nonviolent direct action techniques such as marches, demonstrations, boycotts, and civil disobedience to protest segregation and discrimination. Politically, the SCLC worked within the system to change laws.

The organization's initial project, in 1958, was a voter registration drive in the South. As the 1960's began, other groups began launching protest movements of various types. In 1960, African American students launched sit-in demonstrations at lunch counters to protest segregation, and in 1961, the Congress of Racial Equality initiated Freedom Rides on interstate buses. These protests served as training in the use of nonviolent protest methods. In 1961, the SCLC became involved in mass nonviolent demonstrations

During its peak years, the SCLC was closely identified with Martin Luther King, Jr., who helped found the organization after leading the Montgomery, Alabama, bus boycott. *(National Archives)*

against segregation in Albany, Georgia, learning how to mobilize the African American community in the process. Although the Albany campaign failed, the SCLC learned the importance of having a strong local base, a clear chain of command, and a coherent strategy. In 1963, the SCLC was successful in desegregating facilities in Birmingham, Alabama. Publicity from that movement, including televised coverage of police officers beating black demonstrators, was a major impetus to passage of the Civil Rights Act of 1964. In 1965, the SCLC was involved in a voting rights campaign in Selma, Alabama. This led directly to passage of the Voting Rights Act of 1965, one of the major achievements of the Civil Rights movement.

After 1965, the SCLC began to look beyond the South. A 1966 attempt to end housing segregation in Chicago failed, in part because the SCLC lacked a base outside the South. King and the SCLC also began to focus on problems of poverty following urban riots in 1964. This effort culminated in the Poor People's Campaign. King was assassinated on April 4, 1968, when he went to Memphis, Tennessee, to support striking sanitation workers as part of his Poor People's Campaign. The campaign continued, and the planned march to Washington, D.C., took place under the leadership of the Reverend Ralph Abernathy. The SCLC held demonstrations in the nation's capital in May and June of 1968.

Following King's death, Abernathy became president of the SCLC. The SCLC subsequently declined in importance. Abernathy lacked King's leadership abilities, and following the major achievements of the 1960's, support for the Civil Rights movement as a whole diminished. In the 1970's, the SCLC faded as an effective force in achieving social and economic progress for African American and poor people. In 1973, Abernathy announced his resignation as president of the SCLC.

Assessment In 1986, King's birthday was made a national holiday in recognition of his civil rights work. King is the leader most clearly identified with the Civil Rights movement. Passage of the Voting Rights Act of 1965 was one of the notable achievements of the SCLC. That act resulted in an increase in African American voter registration from 2 million to approximately 3.8 million in ten years. This in turn led to a large increase in the numbers of African American elected officials and other elected officials responsive to the needs of the African American community. Although that community continued to face problems, the efforts of the SCLC aided black Americans in securing equal rights within the American system of justice. The SCLC later concentrated its efforts on issues involving African American families and voter registration in the South.

William V. Moore

Core Resources

Numerous books document the contributions of King and various civil rights groups. Among them are Taylor Branch's *Parting the Waters: America in the King Years, 1954-63* (New York: Simon & Schuster, 1988); Adam Fairclough's *To Redeem the Soul of America: The Southern Christian Leadership Conference and Martin Luther King, Jr.* (Athens: University of Georgia Press, 1987); David J. Garrow's *Bearing the Cross: Martin Luther King, Jr., and the Southern Christian Leadership Conference* (New York: William Morrow, 1986); Stephen B. Oates's *Let the Trumpet Sound: The Life of Martin Luther King, Jr.* (New York: Harper & Row, 1982); and Robert Weisbrot's *Freedom Bound: A History of America's Civil Rights Movement* (New York: W. W. Norton, 1990).

See also: Children in the Civil Rights movement; Civil Rights Act of 1964; Civil Rights movement; Congress of Racial Equality; Freedom Riders; Greensboro sit-ins; King, Martin Luther, Jr., assassination; Little Rock school desegregation; National Association for the Advancement of Colored People; Segregation: de facto and de jure; Selma-Montgomery march; Student Nonviolent Coordinating Committee; Voting Rights Act of 1965.

Southern Conference for Human Welfare

A small group of southern liberals founded the Southern Conference for Human Welfare (SCHW) in 1938 in response to the *Report on Economic Conditions of the South* (1938), a devastating critique of the region's prospects and leadership. The report was commonly known as the Mellett Report after Lowell Mellett, director of the National Emergency Council, a group of educators, businesspeople, bankers, farmers, and others from the South who prepared the report in response to a request by President Franklin D.

Roosevelt. The president was trying to garner southern support for his second New Deal and needed to demonstrate an understanding of the area's problems. The SCHW remained a small group until the end of World War II, when it spearheaded a widespread reform movement. The SCHW viewed race discrimination as an economic and political problem rather than a social one. Its members advocated strong labor unions, an end to rule by Bourbons (extremely conservative southerners), and the abolition of the poll tax and other disfranchisement laws. By the end of 1946, it had more than ten thousand members. Paid workers lobbied the U.S. Congress and conducted conferences throughout the South. An offshoot, the Southern Conference Education Fund, continued to work for civil rights for black southerners.

The SCHW met its demise in a disastrous attempt to mount a third-party presidential campaign in 1948. Backing Henry Wallace's Progressive Party, the SCHW staged several integrated tours through southern cities. However, as the Cold War heated up, the SCHW became suspect. Although the House Committee on Un-American Activities failed to uncover a single communist in the organization, it tainted the organization with charges of disloyalty. In November, 1948, the SCHW's board of representatives voted to suspend operations.

Robert E. McFarland

See also: Civil rights movement; Labor movement; Roosevelt coalition.

Sports

Although sports are often prized by fans and participants alike as a refuge from mundane concerns, the sporting world has long provided a highly public forum for the debate and resolution of social issues. Matters of race and ethnicity have long been among the most contentious of these.

The rise of organized sports in the mid- to late nineteenth century coincided with the drawing of the "color line" and the institution of formalized, legally sanctioned modes of discrimination in virtually all walks of American life. In sports as in most other contexts, the most virulent discrimination has typically been directed against African Americans. Although relations between whites, Latinos, Native Americans, Jews, and other ethnic minorities would often be strained, both on the playing fields and in the stands, such tensions historically have been relatively minor in comparison to the intense feelings aroused by the participation of black athletes. As one baseball historian has remarked, "With the breaking of the color barrier, other ethnic identities ceased to have much meaning. . . . where the Blacks were, everybody else was just White"—a statement that encapsulates the history of race relations not only in baseball but also in most other American sports. By the latter half of the twentieth century, the integration of most sports was an accomplished fact, but other issues of race and ethnicity continued to swirl around the world of sports.

Baseball and Discrimination in Team Sports Baseball, the most popular and most widely played team sport of nineteenth century America, was also the first major sport to attain a secure organizational footing in North America, and in many respects, it long set the pattern for other American sports. In the early years of organized baseball, a certain degree of racial freedom prevailed on American playing fields; although African Americans, Native Americans, and other ethnic minorities did not commonly compete with white players, neither was their participation formally barred. All-black teams occasionally played all-white squads, and African Americans, Latinos, and Native Americans competed with whites in front of racially mixed audiences in the earliest professional leagues.

By the waning years of the nineteenth century, however, such tolerance was becoming increasingly rare. As white America grappled with the changed legal and social status of blacks in the post-Civil War period, segregated facilities and institutions were established in virtually all walks of American life. In 1896, the U.S. Supreme Court gave its blessing to such arrangements by endorsing the "separate but equal" doctrine in the landmark case *Plessy v. Ferguson.* Segregationists had their way in organized baseball as well, and by the century's close, blacks had been effectively excluded from the sport's highest levels by means of an unwritten but nevertheless effective agreement among team owners and managers. (Sole responsibility for adoption of the ban is often assigned to Adrian "Cap" Anson, a star player and manager and a vocal proponent of segregation. Such an assessment, however, oversimplifies the reality; although Anson was one of the game's leading figures, he was only one among many who worked to exclude blacks from the sport. African Americans were being systematically separated from whites in education, housing, and virtually every other arena, and the segregation of the country's most popular spectator sport was virtually inevitable.)

No such restrictions, however, were placed on the participation of Native Americans and light-skinned Latinos in organized baseball. Louis "Jud" Castro, for example, an infielder from Colombia, played in the inaugural season of the American League in 1902, and such Native Americans as Jim Thorpe and Albert "Chief" Bender had successful major league careers in the first decades of the twentieth century. As a consequence, white managers and owners made occasional attempts to pass off talented African American players as "Indians" or "Cubans"; legendary manager John McGraw, for example, tried unsuccessfully to play infielder Charlie Grant under the allegedly Cherokee name Charlie Tokohamo. Although white teams would sometimes play exhibitions against black teams, and although players of all races competed together in Latin America, the color line had been firmly drawn. For more than half a century, no openly African American players were permitted in the white professional leagues. Moreover, although light-skinned Latinos and Native Americans were not barred from the white leagues, they commonly experienced the same slights and racist treatments accorded ethnic minorities in all facets of American life—a fact perhaps reflected by the patronizing nicknames given even to star players; the nickname "Chief," for example, was routinely applied to Native American players, while Jewish players were often nicknamed "Moe." In addition to Bender and Thorpe, Native American pioneers included John "Chief" Meyers, a star catcher for the New York Giants; the most successful Latino player of the early century was Adolpho "Dolf" Luque, a Cuban American pitcher also nicknamed "the Pride of Havana." (In the early part of the century, when many Americans were first- or second-generation European immigrants, ethnic identification was strong even among white players, and the achievements of athletes of Irish, Italian, German, Polish, or Jewish ancestry were celebrated by their respective communities to an extent unknown to later generations. Nicknames that called attention to a player's ethnicity were common; German American superstar Honus Wagner, for example, was known as "the Flying Dutchman.")

Barred from the white leagues, African American professionals competed against one another in the Negro Leagues, a loose association of teams that flourished in the first half of the twentieth century. Negro League stars such as Oscar Charleston, Josh Gibson, Satchel Paige, and Buck Leonard were widely regarded as the equals of the best white players, but they were allowed to compete against them only in exhibitions, barnstorming tours, and foreign leagues.

In 1946, however, in a move that would have repercussions well beyond baseball or sports in general, baseball's color line was broken by Brooklyn Dodgers executive Branch Rickey, who signed Jackie Robinson, a rising star in the Negro Leagues, to a minor league contract. Robinson reached the majors the following season. Though he endured taunts and harassment both on and off the field, he quickly attained stardom (among Robinson's notable supporters was Hank Greenberg, a Jewish superstar who had long crusaded against anti-Semitism). Robinson's on-field success was matched by the remarkable dignity and restraint with which he bore the torrents of abuse directed at him, and his shining example deprived baseball's powers of any further excuse for continuing to segregate the sport. A flood of talented black players entered the white leagues, and every major league team was integrated by 1958. As a consequence, the Negro Leagues, deprived of their reason for existing, soon shriveled and disappeared.

Football, Basketball, and Integration When the color line was drawn in baseball, football was in its infancy, and professional structures did not exist. In the early years of the sport's evolution, however, a number of black players excelled at the collegiate level, often while playing for such all-black schools as Howard and Tuskegee Universities. Several black players, moreover, attained collegiate stardom at predominantly white schools; William Henry Lewis was named an All-American in 1892 and 1893 while playing for Amherst, and Paul Robeson starred for Rutgers before becoming famous as a singer and actor. When the first professional leagues were formed in the 1920's, moreover, no color line existed, and Robeson, Brown University graduate Frederick Douglass "Fritz" Pollard, and University of Iowa product Fred "Duke" Slater, among others, were among the best of the early professionals. In the early 1930's, however, professional football followed baseball's lead and excluded black players. Notable early players of other ethnic backgrounds included Jewish stars Sid Luckman and Bennie Friedman and the multitalented Native American Thorpe, whose football achievements surpassed his baseball success.

Long after color lines were broken in professional sports, more subtle forms of discrimination persisted— such as the notion that African Americans could not handle leadership positions. Gradually, however, the success on the field of players such as NFL quarterback Warren Moon proved otherwise. *(National Football League)*

At the same time that Robinson was integrating baseball to great publicity, the established National Football League (NFL) had to fend off a challenge from the upstart All-America Football Conference, which signed a number of black players in an effort to compete with the older league. Faced with these twin pressures, the NFL owners rescinded their ban on black players. As in baseball, African Americans soon came to play important roles on every professional team.

Basketball, like football, was slow to develop viable professional structures. As in football, therefore, the collegiate level of play was the highest level widely available; although black teams were generally unable to play white opponents, basketball flourished at black colleges. Before the formation of solid professional leagues, traveling professional teams played all comers; among the most successful of these teams were the all-black Harlem Renaissance (or "Rens") and the Harlem Globetrotters. Both teams enjoyed success against white competition; in order, in part, to deflect hostility from white crowds, the Globetrotters learned to supplement their play with minstrel-like antics, and the team eventually evolved into an entertainment vehicle rather than a competitive unit. Jewish players and teams were also important to the rise of the sport, and such stars as Moe Goldman, Red Holtzman, and Eddie Gottlieb endured anti-Semitic taunts from opposing teams and crowds while helping to establish the basis for the first successful professional leagues.

Prior to 1950, blacks were excluded from the National Basketball Association (NBA) and its predecessor organizations. That year, three African Americans were signed by NBA teams; within two decades, African American players would come to dominate the sport. Segregation at the college level would persist for decades, as a number of southern schools refused to use black players or to play against integrated teams. In 1966, in a game sometimes referred to as "the *Brown v. Board of Education* of college basketball," an all-black Texas Western team defeated all-white, heavily favored Kentucky for the national collegiate championship.

Individual and Olympic Sports Sports based on individual excellence rather than on team play have historically proven somewhat less amenable to overt racism than structured team and league sports; in addition, international competitions such as the Olympic Games have been relatively unaffected by parochial color lines. Nevertheless, issues of race have repeatedly reared their heads in international and individual sports. White boxing champions of the nineteenth and early twentieth centuries often refused to fight black competitors, and the 1908 capture of the world heavyweight championship by Jack Johnson, a flamboyant African American who flouted convention by consorting with white women, led to a prolonged search for a "Great White Hope" who could humble Johnson (who was concurrently persecuted by police).

In contrast, the midcentury heavyweight champion Joe Louis was applauded by many whites for his humility; when successors such as the irrepressible Muhammad Ali refused to defer to white sensibilities, racial alarms again were sounded. Among his many celebrated and controversial actions, Ali in 1964 became the first of many prominent black athletes to change his birth name (Cassius Clay) to a name reflecting his African heritage.

Among other individual sports, the "elitist" games of tennis and golf have proven least amenable to widescale integration. In part, this state of affairs has reflected economic realities, as relatively few minority competitors have been able to afford the club memberships and private instruction that most successful players require. Yet the intractability of racist sentiment has played an undeniable part in limiting minority success in both sports. Tennis stars of the 1950's and 1960's such as the Latino legend Pancho Gonzales and the African Americans Althea Gibson and Arthur Ashe often had to battle for permission to compete at race-restricted tournaments and clubs as did leading black golfers such as Lee Elder and Calvin Peete. Even after the resounding successes of golfing sensation Tiger Woods brought legions of new minority fans and players to the sport in the mid-1990's, country clubs across the United States—including some at which leading tournaments were held—refused to admit minority members.

International competitions such as the Olympic Games have traditionally been more open to minority participation. George Poage in 1904 became the first African American Olympic medalist, and Thorpe, generally acclaimed the world's greatest athlete, won two gold medals at the 1912 Games. In 1936, the African American track star Jesse Owens won four gold medals at the Berlin Olympics to the chagrin of the Nazi hosts who hoped to use the Games to demonstrate Aryan supremacy. In 1968, many of the United States' top black athletes refused to participate in the Games, and two, sprinters John Carlos and Tommie Smith, engendered a worldwide controversy by giving a "black power salute" and refusing to acknowledge the U.S. national anthem while receiving their medals (they were subsequently stripped of their medals and removed from the Olympic team).

Other Controversies As the integration of most sports at the playing level became an accomplished fact, questions of race and ethnicity in the sports world came increasingly to focus on other issues. Perhaps the most persistent of these was the fact that although minorities had made vital contributions as athletes in every major sport, only a handful had risen to fill managerial, administrative, and executive positions. In 1987, a furor erupted when Los Angeles Dodgers executive Al Campanis—who, ironically, had been a teammate and longtime friend of Jackie Robinson—told a television interviewer that blacks were underrepresented in front-office sports jobs because they "lack the necessities" to fill such positions. Although many commentators dismissed Campanis's remarks as the confused, out-of-context ramblings of a tired old man, the incident touched off a round of recriminations and investigations. Yet though baseball and other sports appointed panels to study the situation, more than a decade later, minorities had yet to achieve more than token representation in the power structures of most American sports. A similar reception greeted golfer Fuzzy Zoeller's indiscreet 1997 remarks that Tiger Woods, who is partly of African American heritage, might have a preference for stereotypically "black" foods such as watermelon and fried chicken. These and other such incidents served as ongoing reminders that racial and ethnic divisions persist in the world of sports to the same extent as they do elsewhere in American society.

Glenn Canyon

Core Resources

Arthur Ashe's *A Hard Road to Glory: A History of the African American Athlete Since 1946* (New York: Warner Books, 1988) is a thorough overview of the black legacy to American sport; two companion volumes carry the discussion back to the earliest days of American history. Sociologist Harry Edwards, who was hired by major league baseball as a consultant in the wake of the Campanis incident, has written numerous thought-provoking analyses of race and sports; his groundbreaking *The Sociology of Sport* (1973) remains useful. *The Bill James Historical Baseball Abstract* (rev. ed., New York: Villard Books, 1988) is a fascinating miscellany with many insightful comments of the history of race relations in the "national pastime." Robert Peterson's *Only the Ball Was White* (Englewood Cliffs, N.J.: Prentice-Hall, 1970) was the first and is still among the best of the many histories of the Negro Leagues.

See also: Baseball; Segregation: de facto and de jure.

Stereotype

A stereotype is a generalized belief about the characteristics of a group of people. Stereotypes are a natural outgrowth of people's psychological need

One of the most persistent white stereotypes of African American women is that of the black "mammy"—a woman selflessly devoted to caring for her master's children. *(Library of Congress)*

to simplify and organize the information that they encounter in their lives. In order to meet these needs, people put information into categories; stereotypes are categories of people.

Stereotypes can be beneficial or harmful depending on the truthfulness of the information they contain and the purposes for which they are used. To say that teachers should know more about the subject they are teaching than their students presents stereotypes of students and teachers. These stereotypes are certainly useful, for example, in determining whether to hire a sixth-grade teacher. Furthermore, the promotion of cultural diversity assumes that there are some categorical differences among people of various cultural groups, otherwise people would just talk about individual diversity.

Stereotyping is harmful when negative impressions create and/or reinforce prejudice and discrimination against people. These negative impressions are often based on false information and are frequently exaggerated in order to justify hateful thoughts and hurtful actions. Furthermore, stereotypes tend to be resistant to change ("stereotype" originally referred to a printing plate). People focus more on information that confirms rather than contradicts stereotypical images, perpetuating destructive attitudes.

Paul J. Chara, Jr.

See also: African American women; Psychology of racism; Race as a concept.

Structural racism

Scholars, along with the general public, historically have viewed racism as consisting of individual behaviors or institutional policies that intentionally discriminate against minority groups. Sociologist Fred Pincus, in his article "From Individual to Structural Discrimination," in *Race and Ethnic Conflict: Connecting Views on Prejudice, Discrimination, and Ethnoviolence,* edited by Fred L. Pincus and Howard J. Ehrlich (Boulder, Colo.: Westview, 1994), introduced the concept of structural racism, which was designed to broaden the understanding of racism by focusing on effect rather than intent. Structural racism is defined as institutional policies conceived by the dominant group as race-neutral but that have harmful effects on minority groups. Examples might include college entrance requirements organized primarily around standardized test scores, on which minority groups historically have scored lower than the dominant group; or business layoff systems organized around seniority in a society where minority groups historically have been hired last. If these example policies were instituted, minority groups would be considerably underrepresented in colleges and in the labor force. These policies, intended to be nondiscriminatory, would have negative effects on minority groups. Structural racism is less visible than individual or institutional racism, making it harder to address. The effects, though, perpetuate the subordination of minority groups to the dominant group.

Cheryl D. Childers

See also: College admissions; College entrance examinations; Individual racism; Institutional racism; Racism: history of the concept.

Student Nonviolent Coordinating Committee

The insistence of four African American students from the North Carolina Agricultural and Technical College that they be served at a Woolworth's lunch counter in Greensboro, North Carolina, in February of 1960 sparked the student sit-ins of the 1960's. The students' sit-in at the Woolworth's lunch counter precipitated similar protests in more than sixty-five cities. The need to coordinate what began as spontaneous and haphazard events resulted in the establishment of the Student Nonviolent Coordinating Committee (SNCC).

SNCC was founded in April of 1960 by a group of southern African American students, many of whom participated in the sit-ins. They were assisted by long-time civil rights leader Josephine Baker, who insisted that the new student organization pursue its own path. SNCC concentrated its efforts in the South, as its leadership determined that the more immediate problems of racial discrimination and the denial of constitutional rights were occurring there. SNCC spent most of its early years, especially in 1964 and 1965, attempting to register African Americans to vote. The voter registration campaign that SNCC and the Congress of Racial Equality (CORE) carried out, along with the passage of the 1965 Voting Rights Act, proved to have a tremendous impact on southern politics, especially within the Democratic Party.

Despite its various successes, SNCC appeared to be an organization that was in constant turmoil. It was continually struggling over which direction it should take as an incipient social justice organization. SNCC's uncertainty was reflected in the group's frequent changes in leadership. James Farmer, a former Chicago teacher and the first executive secretary of SNCC, attempted to mold it into a highly structured and formal organization. He was replaced by John Lewis, who was committed to nonviolent integrated struggle. In 1966 Lewis was replaced by Stokely Carmichael (Kwame Toure), who advocated total black membership and would later initiate the move toward

H. Rap Brown at a SNCC press conference. *(Library of Congress)*

"black power." SNCC officially adopted "black power" as its slogan at its 1966 convention. Under Carmichael, SNCC decided to stop using integrated teams of field-workers. He took the position that if whites really wanted to help, then they should organize whites in their communities. By 1969 Carmichael had been replaced by H. Rap Brown, who was perceived to be even more militant and changed the group's name to the Student National Coordinating Committee.

SNCC's new philosophy alienated whites, but more important, it put SNCC (along with CORE) at odds with the more traditional civil rights organizations, especially the National Association for the Advancement of Colored People (NAACP) and the Southern Christian Leadership Conference (SCLC). While its new philosophy was embraced by many young African Americans, it moved SNCC further from what many perceived to be the paradigm of the civil rights struggle. Consequently, much of the group's financial support dried up, and the young people who were committed to nonviolent integrated struggle slowly deserted its ranks. By 1970, SNCC had ceased to exist.

Charles C. Jackson

See also: Black Panther Party; Black Power movement; Civil Rights movement; Congress of Racial Equality; Freedom Riders; Greensboro sit-ins; National Association for the Advancement of Colored People; Southern Christian Leadership Conference.

Summit Meeting of National Negro Leaders

After five years in office and repeated requests from civil rights activists for an audience, U.S. president Dwight D. Eisenhower held a "summit meeting" in June, 1958, with four African American leaders: Dr. Martin Luther King, Jr.; A. Philip Randolph; Roy Wilkins of the National Association for the Advancement of Colored People; and Lester B. Granger of the National Urban League. The purpose of the summit was to address strategies for dealing with the approaching wave of school integration and to express concerns over the reluctance of the Eisenhower administration to support civil rights and enforce court orders mandating desegregated public schools; yet the significance of the summit lay in the fact that it was Eisenhower's first such meeting with black leaders.

The meeting itself was by all accounts brief and uneventful. The leaders presented Eisenhower with a carefully worded statement calling for increased federal visibility and involvement in advancing civil rights causes and tactfully criticized the president for his previous statement urging them to "be patient" about civil rights. Eisenhower promised the leaders that he would take their statement under consideration but responded evasively to their requests for a national conference on civil rights. The 1958 summit would be the only White House conference of black leaders during the Eisenhower administration; subsequent requests for additional meetings were denied.

Michael H. Burchett

See also: Civil Rights movement; King, Martin Luther, Jr.; National Association for the Advancement of Colored People; National Urban League.

Supreme Court and ethnic representation

A broadening of the ethnic base of the United States Supreme Court began with the appointment of Louis D. Brandeis to the Court in 1916 by President Woodrow Wilson. Brandeis was Jewish, a Boston public interest attorney whose defense of the labor movement and reform legislation made him prominent. He had revolutionized legal practice by using economic and sociological facts in his brief in *Muller v. Oregon* (1908), a famous Supreme Court case. The principal architect of President Woodrow Wilson's economic program, he was the first Jew appointed to the Court. Anti-Semitism was prevalent in the United States at that time, and considerable opposition arose to Brandeis's confirmation.

Some members of the bar opposed Brandeis on the pretext that he had engaged in improper practices as a private attorney. President Wilson stood by Brandeis, and after stormy hearings at which the charges against Brandeis were discredited, the Senate approved his appointment. Brandeis began service on June 5, 1916, and served the Court with distinction until old age forced him to retire in 1939. Another Jew, Benjamin Cardozo, was appointed to the Court by President Herbert Hoover in 1932. Cardozo died in 1939 and was replaced by Felix Frankfurter, also Jewish. In this way began the tradition of there being a "Jewish seat" on the Court. Frankfurter, who retired in 1962, was replaced by Arthur Goldberg, also Jewish. In the closing years of the twentieth century, there were two Jewish members of the Court, Ruth Bader Ginsburg and Stephen Breyer.

The first African American to sit on the Supreme Court was Thurgood Marshall. From 1930 to 1933, Marshall attended Howard University's law school, then the only black law school in the country. Howard attracted a great many young black men who wished to participate in the civil rights struggle. After graduation, Marshall affiliated himself with the efforts of the National Association for the Advancement of Colored People Legal Defense and Educational Fund and became an extremely successful civil rights lawyer. His work as an advocate reached its peak with his successful argument in *Brown v. Board of Education* (1954), the case that struck down racial segregation in schools and eventually in all public institutions. Marshall was appointed to the U.S. Court of Appeals for the Second Circuit by President John F. Kennedy in 1961 and, after a brief stint as solicitor-general of the United States, was nominated to the Supreme Court by President Lyndon B. Johnson in 1967. He was the ninety-sixth person to be appointed to the Court and the first African American. Racism was diminishing at the time, and Marshall's nomination met with no significant opposition in the Senate.

Marshall served on the Court until 1991, and after his retirement, President George Bush nominated another African American, Clarence Thomas, to replace him. The nomination became fiercely controversial when Thomas was charged with sexual harassment by Anita Hill, an African American law professor who had been one of Thomas's colleagues. After sensational public hearings, Thomas's nomination was confirmed in a close vote, and he took his seat on the court in 1992.

Robert Jacobs

See also: Criminal justice system; Marshall, Thurgood; Thomas/Hill hearings.

Swann v. Charlotte-Mecklenburg Board of Education

In the 1971 *Swann v. Charlotte-Mecklenburg Board of Education* decision, the U.S. Supreme Court determined that lower courts may properly order local school boards to use extensive school busing to desegregate urban schools.

By the end of the 1960's, a significant percentage of southern school boards had desegregated their schools. The primary exception to this trend was urban schools. Many urban schools by the end of the 1960's were still segregated because of significant residential segregation. In 1968, in *Green v. County School Board of New Kent County*, the Supreme Court ruled that school boards had an "affirmative duty" to take all necessary actions to integrate schools. The question after the *Green* decision was what type of affirmative action must an urban school board faced with considerable residential segregation take in order to integrate its schools.

In the late 1960's, a group of black parents, with the assistance of the National Association for the Advancement of Colored People Legal Defense and Educational Fund, filed a lawsuit seeking to force the school board in Charlotte, North Carolina, to implement an extensive school busing plan to integrate its schools. Prior to the litigation, children in the Charlotte-Mecklenburg school system were assigned to schools on the basis of their residence. As a result, many schools remained all-white or all-black because of the city's residential segregation.

In February of 1970, federal district court judge James McMillan ordered the Charlotte-Mecklenburg Board of Education to adopt an extensive busing plan that would integrate every school in the school system. McMillan's busing plan sparked a firestorm of opposition, with politicians throughout the state and nation, including President Richard M. Nixon, criticizing his action. In June, 1970, the U.S. Supreme Court decided to review the case to decide whether urban school boards were required to engage in extensive school busing to overcome residential segregation. It was understood throughout the country that the *Swann* case would settle the issue of whether school boards would be obliged to engage in school busing to integrate their schools.

In April, 1971, the U.S. Supreme Court unanimously held that school busing was an appropriate method for eliminating segregated schools and that Judge McMillan had acted properly in ordering the Charlotte-Mecklenburg School Board to engage in extensive busing. The Court did say that not every majority black school had to be eliminated in order to satisfy constitutional demands, but it did strongly affirm the legitimacy of busing as a means of integrating urban schools.

In the wake of the *Swann* decision, lower court judges throughout the South ordered urban school boards to adopt school busing plans. In the meantime, members of Congress sought passage of both legislation and constitutional amendments restricting the application of the *Swann* decision. Efforts to amend the Constitution failed, and the legislation that Congress enacted did not significantly inhibit the ability of courts to require school busing. As a result of the *Swann* decision, most urban school systems eventually adopted pupil-assignment plans involving school busing.

Davison M. Douglas

See also: *Brown v. Board of Education*; Busing and integration; *Green v. County School Board of New Kent County*; *Milliken v. Bradley*; Segregation: de facto and de jure.

Sweatt v. Painter

Plessy v. Ferguson (1896) established the "separate but equal" doctrine that provided the legal justification for segregation. Civil rights organizations, including the National Association for the Advancement of Colored People (NAACP), although opposed to "separate but equal," decided to use the courts in an attempt to make sure that the "equal" part of the "separate but equal" doctrine was being enforced. In a series of cases running from 1936 to the *Sweatt* decision in 1950, the NAACP attacked the lack of law schools and graduate programs for blacks throughout the South.

If no professional schools existed, clearly the "separate but equal" doctrine was not being met. When African Americans started seeking admission to professional schools throughout the South, many states established "overnight" law schools and professional schools in order to comply with *Plessy*. These schools were certainly separate, but were they equal? Herman Sweatt, a Houston, Texas, postal worker, applied for admission to the University of Texas Law School in 1946. He was denied admission on the grounds that Texas had just created a law school for blacks. To avoid integration, Texas had rented a few rooms in Houston and hired two black lawyers as its faculty.

Sweatt refused to attend the "black law school," saying that it was inferior and he would be deprived of the "equal protection of the law." A unanimous Supreme Court sided with Sweatt, whose case was argued by Thurgood Marshall of the NAACP. Even if the facilities at the two Texas schools were equal, the Court concluded that inequality might exist with respect to other factors "which make for greatness in a law school." Such factors include the reputation of the faculty and administration and the prestige of the alumni. "It is difficult to believe," said Chief Justice Fred M. Vinson, Jr., "that one who had a free choice between these law schools would consider the question close."

The Court ordered that Sweatt be admitted to the University of Texas Law School. The *Sweatt* case marked the first time the Supreme Court found a black professional school to be unequal in quality. Although the Court refused to reexamine *Plessy v. Ferguson,* the decision in *Sweatt* paved the way for the NAACP to launch a direct assault in overturning *Plessy* in *Brown v. Board of Education* only four years later.

Darryl Paulson

See also: *Brown v. Board of Education*; Civil Rights movement; National Association for the Advancement of Colored People; *Plessy v. Ferguson.*

Symbolic racism

The concept of modern, or symbolic, racism was created by social psychologists in the early 1980's in response to the fact that the form of white Americans' racism toward blacks had changed since the early years of research into prejudice.

When scientists first began studying racism in the 1930's, not only did most white Americans have prejudiced beliefs about blacks but also most of them were quite candid in their expression of those beliefs. Researchers would typically give people a checklist of attributes and stereotypes and ask people to indicate those traits that they felt were characteristics of blacks. The majority of white respondents chose much more negative traits for blacks than they did for whites. Whites would also express rejection of integration in schools, neighborhoods, and the workplace.

By the 1970's, however, researchers found that these old methods of measuring racism no longer worked very well. Overt bigotry was no longer considered socially acceptable, and whites were no longer willing to indicate such obviously biased views. They ascribed fewer negative stereotypes to blacks and supported integration. However, racism clearly had not disappeared. Whites were still reluctant to vote for black political candidates, and they continued to oppose such policies as affirmative action. Researchers such as John McConahay, David Sears, Lawrence Bobo, John Dovidio, and Samuel Gaertner called this new form "symbolic" or "modern" racism.

Symbolic racists assert that racism is bad, and they reject most of the old-fashioned stereotypes. They believe in equal opportunities. However, they believe that discrimination no longer exists and that blacks are demanding and receiving unfair benefits at the expense of whites.

People who are high in symbolic racism will often respond to certain "code words" that have come to *symbolize* blacks in the United States (hence the term "symbolic" racism). Examples of these code words are "affirmative action," "crime," and "welfare." According to the researchers, these individuals still harbor antiblack feelings, although they are often not consciously aware of them. These feelings conflict with their beliefs in equality, resulting in ambivalence and conflict. Furthermore, because prejudice is not generally socially acceptable, these people must cloak their feelings in a manner that can be explained by factors other than prejudice, such as fear of crime.

To measure symbolic racism, McConahay created the Modern Racism Scale. The items in this scale attempt to determine the degree to which respondents believe that African Americans have pushed too hard and received more than they deserve. Some have criticized that the scale really measures some other factor, such as political conservatism, rather than racism. However, scores on the Modern Racism Scale have been found to correlate with attitudes toward busing, feeling toward African Americans, voting decisions, and race-based hiring decisions.

Those who study symbolic racism have acknowledged that the form racism takes in the United States is likely to continue to change, and the methods of measuring racism will have to change accordingly. It is unlikely, however, that bigotry and racism will disappear altogether.

Phyllis B. Gerstenfeld

See also: Bigotry; Racism: changing nature of; "Reverse" racism.

Talented Tenth

"Talented Tenth" is a term coined in 1903 by black scholar and activist W. E. B. Du Bois to denote a black intellectual elite that he hoped would provide the leadership necessary to facilitate the advancement of black Americans. Du Bois, who in 1895 became the first African American to receive a doctoral degree from Harvard, drew upon a tradition of northern-based black intellectualism predating the Civil War to promote the development of a classically trained vanguard of "leaders, thinkers, and artists" to educate and uplift oppressed, lower-class blacks. Du Bois's Talented Tenth proposal was largely a response to accommodationists such as Booker T. Washington, who emphasized vocational education as a means for blacks to establish themselves economically and socially in a manner nonthreatening to whites.

Originally a follower of Washington, Du Bois began to dissent from accommodationist policy when Washington's emphasis on industrial education and his influence with northern philanthropists drew resources away from southern liberal arts colleges such as Atlanta University, where Du Bois was a professor of sociology. Although Du Bois's scathing criticisms of accommodationism echoed those of other "radical" black leaders such as Monroe Trotter (who denounced Washington as a race traitor), Du Bois's call for a

Talented Tenth was essentially an elitist variation of the doctrine of self-help and racial solidarity that was at the core of accommodationism. Like Washington, Du Bois advocated education as a means of strengthening black communities by alleviating social pathologies brought on by generations of oppression and cultural alienation. While recognizing the necessity of vocational training for young blacks, Du Bois insisted that the true aim of education was "not to make men carpenters (but) to make carpenters men" by imbuing them with a sense of culture and an elevated awareness of their place in the world. To accomplish this, Du Bois argued, it would be necessary to maintain a small number of quality black liberal-arts institutions dedicated to developing and motivating liberally educated black teachers and professionals.

The idea of a Talented Tenth of black leadership is significant not only as the essence of Du Bois's racial policy but also as a reflection of the changing spirit of black activism in early twentieth century America. By combining elements of accommodationism with strains of postbellum agitation, Du Bois advanced a new synthesis of black protest thought that exerted considerable influence upon the early Civil Rights movement; at the heart of this synthesis was his advocacy of leadership by the Talented Tenth. The Niagara Movement, organized by Du Bois in 1905, consisted mainly of upper- and middle-class black intellectuals from northern states and emphasized agitation as a means of protest. In 1909, key members of the Niagara Movement, including Du Bois, joined forces with progressive upper-and middle-class whites to establish the National Association for the Advancement of Colored People (NAACP), whose strategy of legalism and direct action relied heavily upon the leadership of attorneys and academics. Despite the success of this strategy of legalism and the prominent leadership of scholars such as Martin Luther King, Jr., enthusiasm for the idea of a Talented Tenth waned through the twentieth century as the focus of the Civil Rights movement shifted from the interests of a biracial elite to those of a predominantly black working class.

Michael H. Burchett

See also: Accommodationism; Black colleges and universities; Civil Rights movement; National Association for the Advancement of Colored People; Niagara Movement.

Thirteenth Amendment

The first of the Civil War Amendments states that "neither slavery nor involuntary servitude . . . shall exist within the United States."

The Thirteenth Amendment (1865) was one of three amendments known as the Civil War Amendments. The combined purpose of these three amend-

The involuntary servitude of plantation slaves, such as the members of this family, was legally ended—once and for all—by ratification of the Thirteenth Amendment. *(Library of Congress)*

ments was to free the slaves and promote their participation in their country. The Thirteenth Amendment states, in full, "1. Neither slavery nor involuntary servitude, except as a punishment for crime whereof the party shall have been duly convicted, shall exist within the United States, or any place subject to its jurisdiction. 2. Congress shall have power to enforce this article by appropriate legislation."

One of the battles surrounding the Thirteenth Amendment in particular, and all the Civil War Amendments in general, concerned the interpretation of the Tenth Amendment. The Tenth Amendment stated that no federal legislation could detract from the power of state government. Those who opposed the Thirteenth Amendment claimed that the right to allow slavery was not specifically denied in the Constitution and therefore fell within the authority of the state.

With the passage of this amendment, the long fight to abolish slavery was over. The amendment was ratified on December 6, 1865, and officially announced on December 18, 1865. For some abolitionists, such as William Lloyd Garrison, the battle had been won: Slavery was ended. Others saw the Thirteenth Amendment as only a beginning.

Frederick Douglass did not have the same high hopes held by Garrison. Douglass believed that slavery would not be abolished until the former slaves acquired the right to vote. The passage of the Civil Rights Act of 1866 did not provide this right. It was not until the passage of the Fourteenth Amendment, in 1868, that citizenship and the rights thereof were guaranteed to "all persons born or naturalized in the United States." Finally, in 1870, with the passage of the Fifteenth Amendment, former slaves were expressly given the right to vote. Within weeks, the first African American in the U.S. Senate, Hiram R. Revels, took his seat.

Sharon L. Larson

Core Resources

John Hope Franklin's *From Slavery to Freedom: A History of Negro Americans* (3d ed., New York: Alfred A. Knopf, 1967) details the changes undergone by African Americans during the movement toward abolition and after they achieved citizenship. J. C. Furnas's *The Road to Harpers Ferry* (London: Faber & Faber, 1961) contains an enlightening discussion of the problems created or observed in the abolitionist movement. Robert Dale Owen's *The Wrong of Slavery, the Right of Emancipation, and the Future of the African Race in the United States* (Philadelphia: J. B. Lippincott, 1864) collects writings on the issue of slavery in the United States from an abolitionist of the slave era. *1791 to 1991: The Bill of Rights and Beyond* (Washington, D.C.: Commission on the Bicentennial of the U.S. Constitution, 1991) discusses the abolitionist movement and passage of the Civil War Amendments in relation to each other.

See also: Abolition; Civil Rights Acts of 1866-1875; Fifteenth Amendment; Fourteenth Amendment; Lincoln-Douglas debates.

Thomas/Hill hearings

U.S. president George Bush's decision to nominate Clarence Thomas, an African American and former head of the Equal Employment Opportunity Commission (EEOC), to fill Thurgood Marshall's seat on the U.S. Supreme Court was immediately controversial because Thomas was a conservative who was opposed to affirmative action and because he was meant to fill the seat left open by the justice who was most closely identified with the Civil Rights movement and who was the first African American on the Supreme Court. Members of the civil rights community and of the broader Left accused Bush of cynically using Thomas as a token black man in order to advance an agenda that was hostile to racial minorities. At the same time, other prominent African Americans, including author and poet Maya Angelou, argued in favor of Thomas's nomination for the associate justice post because of the supposed importance of having an African American on the Court. African Americans and the nation as a whole were already divided in their assessment of Thomas's nomination well before allegations surfaced that Thomas had sexually harassed a black woman named Anita Hill while he was her supervisor at the EEOC.

When word of Hill's allegations reached the media, the congressional confirmation hearings that normally accompany such presidential appointments became a national media spectacle. More than 27 million households tuned in on October 11, 1991, to the first day of the portion of Thomas's confirmation hearings that were meant to examine Hill's allegations and became known as the Thomas/Hill hearings. Some commentators argued that the hearings constituted a watershed in terms of the mass media's representation of African Americans, a rare opportunity to allow the American public to see African American professionals articulately discuss their lives. Others claimed that there was really very little that was new because public interrogations of African American sexuality had been integral to American racial politics from the nation's inception. Thomas himself hit upon this idea forcefully when he claimed that he was the victim of "a high-tech lynching." Thomas's lynching metaphor was perhaps the most rhetorically powerful moment of the hearings, as it served to direct attention away from Hill's allegations and toward the possibility that Thomas was the victim of racism. Although Thomas's charge succeeded in galvanizing support from some sectors of the black community, it alienated other African Americans, who noted that no black man was ever lynched at the behest of a black woman. One of the most important long-term effects of the Thomas/Hill hearings may well be that they rendered the very notion of a monolithic "black community" obsolete, as a mass audience was exposed to struggles within that community.

Thomas was confirmed as an associate justice on October 13, 1991, and in the years since the hearings, he and Hill have become iconic figures on the American cultural landscape. Hill has become an important feminist symbol, and women's outrage at her treatment during the hearings has been widely seen as a contributing factor to a series of women's electoral victories in 1992, which has been dubbed "the year of the woman." The most far-reaching consequence of the hearings, however, may well be the appointment of one of the most conservative Supreme Court justices in recent memory. Thomas's judicial decisions were expected to have an impact for years to come.

Jonathan Markovitz

See also: Lynchings; Race card; Supreme Court and ethnic representation.

Three-fifths compromise

The Constitutional Convention in 1787 adopted the three-fifths compromise, whereby five slaves were counted as three people for purposes of taxation and representation. The idea originated as part of a 1783 congressional plan to base taxation on population. Congress rejected the three-fifths idea, but delegate James Wilson of Pennsylvania resurrected it as an amendment to the Virginia plan at the Constitutional Convention.

The Wilson amendment provoked heated debate over the counting of slaves. Most northern delegates regarded slaves as property and not deserving representation, while southern delegates insisted that blacks be counted equally with whites for purposes of representation. Northern delegates wanted slaves counted for taxation, while southern delegates disagreed.

Delegates also debated whether the Congress or a census every ten years should determine the apportionment of representatives in the national legislature. Several northern delegates wanted Congress to control apportionment because the West was developing rapidly. They considered the three-fifths idea pro-South and opposed its adoption. Southern delegates, meanwhile, threatened to reject the three-fifths idea if Congress controlled representation. Northern delegates eventually agreed to accept a census every ten years and count slaves as people rather than property, demonstrating the numerical strength of the proslavery interests. Until the Civil War, therefore, slaves were counted as three-fifths of nonslaves for purposes of taxation and representation.

David L. Porter

See also: Censuses, U.S.; Constitutional racism; Representation: gerrymandering, malapportionment, and reapportionment.

Tokenism

Tokenism is a form of discrimination whereby minorities (such as members of racial and ethnic groups and women) fill roles usually reserved for dominant group members, especially white men. Tokenism can occur in all sorts of settings, including schools, government agencies, and private industry.

In bureaucratic and/or corporate settings, where pressure toward conformity is strong, the inclusion of a small number of "different" individuals is a common practice. Faced with legal and social pressures, tokenism in these settings gives the illusion that white male employers are addressing the issue of discrimination without really challenging the existing balance of power.

Tokenism can have myriad effects on people who fill these roles, including high visibility, increased pressure to perform, and loneliness resulting from their status as outsiders. Tokens also have difficulty advancing because they are often barred from access to the formal and informal networking that is essential for movement up the hierarchy. Studies involving African Americans in corporations have found that token blacks are often placed in staff positions where they either have little power or are restricted to servicing other minorities. Restricted opportunities often lead to high turnover, and pressures to overachieve may result in burnout.

Eleanor A. LaPointe

See also: Desegregation: public schools; Discrimination: behaviors; Quotas.

Tolerance

Tolerance is defined, from both a psychological and a sociological perspective, as the ability to look at issues from multiple perspectives, show empathy for other persons' points of view, and be open-minded toward and accepting of cultural and other forms of diversity. An individual's level of tolerance is influenced by family, religious, and community values. People with ultraconservative political and religious viewpoints usually show low levels of tolerance toward cultural diversity. Very liberal individuals also tend to be intolerant of opposing ideas. Thus, tolerance tends to be associated with political and religious ideological extremes.

Swiss psychologist Jean Piaget first identified stages of human development, and Lawrence Kohlberg wrote about stages of moral development. After researching human development, James Banks advanced the theory that as individuals develop and socialize, they go through stages of ethnicity. These stages are ethnic and psychological captivity (negative beliefs about one's identity and low self-esteem), ethnic encapsulation (ethnic isolation and voluntary separatism), ethnic identity clarification (acceptance of ethnic self-identity, a prerequisite for beginning to understand other cultures), bi-ethnicity (a healthy sense of self-identity and an ability to function in two cultures), multiethnicity (the ability to function within several ethnic environments), and finally, the highest stage, globalism and global competency. Individuals who have reached the highest stage are tolerant; they become comfortably reflective in relationships with those who are culturally different. They have the knowledge and skills for effective and meaningful crosscultural communication.

Social theories of acculturation also have ramifications for tolerance. Acculturation, or adaptation to a culture, can take the form of assimilation or cultural pluralism. Assimilation theories such as the melting pot theory and Anglo-conformity assume that individuals will gradually become like the dominant group of white Anglo-Saxon Protestants. Under cultural pluralism, which is described using a salad bowl metaphor, individuals still identify with their primary culture and language but function and communicate effectively within the society as a whole. Typically, cultural pluralism promotes biculturalism and bilingualism and functional multiculturalism and interculturalism. Therefore, cultural pluralism tends to promote tolerance whereas assimilation views diversity as something that will gradually be eliminated.

Other concepts related to tolerance include xenophobia, ethnocentrism, and cultural relativism. Xenophobics display ignorance and fear toward those who are culturally different and adopt separatist and segregationist attitudes rather than attitudes of tolerance. Ethnocentrics believe that their own culture is superior and preferred over any other culture. They use their own cultural lenses to judge other groups; extreme ethnocentric views lead to stereotyping, prejudice, and discrimination.

Maria A. Pacino

See also: Afrocentrism; Friendships, interracial/interethnic; Interracial and interethnic marriage.

Triple oppression

Modern societies such as the United States are composed of many subgroups, occupying various racial, ethnic, gender, and social class positions. Members of these groups often have less access to resources such as wealth, power, and prestige than do members of the dominant society. The notion of "triple oppression" applies when a person simultaneously occupies three oppressed groups at once. The term was coined by sociologist Denise A. Segura and promulgated in "Chicanas and Triple Oppression in the Labor Force" (*Chicana Voices: Intersections of Class, Race, and Gender,* edited by Teresa Cordova et al., 1986).

Using the context of work as an example, Segura described how race, class, and gender all play roles in determining occupational attainment and earnings. In general, in countries with capitalist economic systems, poor people do not have the economic and educational resources necessary for business ownership, and their access to well-paying, upwardly mobile jobs is more limited than that of their middle-class and wealth-owning counterparts. In addition, occupational sex segregation limits the job options of women of all races, ethnicities, and classes. Finally, nonwhite men and women routinely encounter race-based discrimination despite the existence of laws designed to ensure equal opportunities.

Taken together, then, those who experience triple oppression are nonwhite (that is, African American, Latina, Asian American, Native American) working-class women, who because of the triple status are inhibited from socioeconomic advancement. In their daily lives the effects of class, race, and gender are both interactive and cumulative in nature.

Eleanor A. LaPointe

See also: Discrimination: racial and ethnic; Economics and race.

Turner's slave insurrection

The 1831 slave revolt led by Nat Turner sent fear through the southern white community and prompted legislation prohibiting the assembly, education, and movement of plantation slaves.

Although neither the first attempted slave rebellion nor the last during the more than two centuries of African American slavery, Nat Turner's assault against the whites in southeastern Virginia marked the only time a group of black slaves banded together to strike successfully against their white masters.

Background Turner, as far as is known, spent his entire life as a slave in his native Southampton County, where he had been born on October 2, 1800, on the plantation of Benjamin Turner. His mother was probably a native African, who taught him at an early age to believe that he possessed supernatural powers. He was both a mystic and oriented toward religion. In addition to possessing those traits, he could read, and historians have surmised that he learned this skill from the Turner family. Nat became a Christian through the instruction of his grandmother, Bridget, and mostly read the Bible. Perhaps because of his knowledge of the Bible, he became a Baptist preacher. Because of his mysticism, his ability to read, and his activities as a minister, Turner gained considerable influence over his fellow slaves.

Samuel Turner, Benjamin's son, inherited Nat during times of economic depression in Virginia. A newly hired overseer drove the slaves to work harder, and as a consequence, Nat ran away. Although Nat eluded capture for thirty days, he turned himself in to his owner. His return went unpunished, but in the days that followed, Nat saw that his own freedom could not be realized without his people's freedom.

Nat married a slave named Cherry in the early 1820's, and they had three children. Cherry would later conceal coded maps and lists that Turner used in his revolt, which experts have never been able to decode. When Samuel Turner died in 1922, Nat's family was broken up and sold to different families. Nat went to a neighboring farm owner, Thomas Moore. He was sold again to Joseph Travis in 1831.

Nat Turner thought of himself as an instrument of God. Between 1825 and 1830, Turner gained respect as a traveling neighborhood preacher. He became deeply religious, fasting and praying in solitude. In his own mind he had been ordained—like the prophets of old—to perform a special mission. He professed that God communicated with him through voices and signs in the heavens. On May 12, 1828, Turner heard a "great noise" and saw "white spirits" and "black spirits" battling.

The Revolt In February, 1831, a certain blueness in the atmosphere—a solar eclipse—persuaded him that God was announcing that the time had come for the slaves to attack their white masters. Turner communicated this message to his band of followers; the rebellion ensued on August 21, when Turner and seven fellow slaves murdered the Travis family. Within twenty-four hours after the rebellion began, the band of rebels numbered seventy-five slaves. In the next two days, an additional fifty-one whites were killed. No evidence exists to indicate that Turner's movement was a part of any larger scheme. One slave, Nat Turner, used the power at his command to attempt to break his shackles and those of his followers.

Turner directed his attack toward the county seat, Jerusalem, and the weapons in its armory; he never made it. The white community responded promptly, and with an overpowering force of armed owners and militia, it routed the poorly armed slaves during the second day of the rebellion. Although he eluded capture for six weeks, Turner and all the rebels were either killed or captured and executed. Hundreds of other nonparticipating and innocent slaves were slain as a result of fright in the white community. Turner's court-appointed attorney, Thomas Gray, recorded Turner's "confessions" on November 1, and on November 11, 1831, Turner was hanged. Gray later remarked on Turner's intelligence and knowledge of military tactics.

Effects Although Turner's revolt took place in a relatively isolated section of Virginia, the uprising caused the entire South to tremble. Many white

Contemporary drawing of Nat Turner's capture. *(Library of Congress)*

southerners called for more stringent laws regulating slaves' behavior, such as making it a crime to teach a slave to read or write. Turner's revolt coincided with the blossoming of the abolition movement in the North, for the rebellion occurred in the same year that William Lloyd Garrison began his unremitting assault on the South's "peculiar institution." Although no one has been able to demonstrate that abolitionist activity had any influence at all on Turner, white southerners were horrified at the seeming coincidence. They described abolitionists as persons who wanted not only to end slavery but also to sponsor a massacre of southern whites. The white South stood as one against any outside interference with its system.

Although white people throughout the South looked anew at slavery, in no place did they look more closely than in Virginia. During the legislative session of 1831-1832, there occurred the most thorough public discussion of slavery in southern history prior to 1861. Only four months after Turner's revolt, the legislature appointed a committee to recommend to the state a course of action in dealing with slavery.

Those Virginians opposed to slavery made their case. They argued that slavery was a prime cause of Virginia's economic backwardness; that it injured white manners and morals; and that, as witnessed by Turner's revolt, it was basically dangerous. While they did talk about abolition as benefiting the slaves, they primarily maintained that white Virginians would reap the greatest rewards, for the African Americans, after a gradual and possibly compensated emancipation, would be removed from the state. These abolitionists, most of whom were from western Virginia (modern West Virginia), an area of few slaves, could not agree on a specific plan to accomplish their purpose. Slavery's defenders countered by boasting of Virginia's economic well-being and the good treatment and contentment of the slaves. Referring to the well-established belief in the sanctity of private property, they denied that the legislature had any right to meddle with slave property.

The Virginia legislature decided not to tamper with slavery. It rebuffed those who wanted to put Virginia on the road to emancipation. After these debates, white southerners no longer seriously considered any alternative to slavery. In the aftermath of Turner's revolt and Virginia's debate, the South erected a massive defense of its peculiar institution. That defense permeated southern politics, religion, literature, and science. Nat Turner's revolt—the only successful slave uprising in the South—heralded and confirmed the total southern commitment to black slavery. However, Turner left a profound legacy: Slaves would fight for their freedom. Turner's rebellion has inspired black activists since, including Marcus Garvey and Malcolm X.

William J. Cooper, Jr., updated by Marilyn Elizabeth Perry

Core Resources

Terry Bisson's *Nat Turner* (Los Angeles: Melrose Square, 1988) is an easy-to-read account of Nat Turner's life and motivations. Thomas R. Gray's *The Confessions of Nat Turner: The Leader of the Late Insurrection in Southampton,*

Va. (1831; reprint, Miami: Mnemosyne, 1969) contains Turner's own account of his revolt, as given to an official of the court that tried him. William Styron's *Confessions of Nat Turner* (New York: Random House, 1967) is a controversial novel that aimed to show an understanding of Turner's revolt and the institution of slavery but was sharply attacked by African American intellectuals. Henry Irving Tragle's *The Southampton Slave Revolt of 1831: A Compilation of Source Material* (Amherst: University of Massachusetts Press, 1971) reprints primary source material: newspaper accounts, trial records, and other documents written at the time of the revolt.

See also: Abolition; *Amistad* slave revolt; John Brown's raid; *Liberator, The*; Slave rebellions.

Tuskegee Airmen

African Americans made noteworthy gains during World War II, particularly in the Air Force. Despite opposition from southern legislators, African American recruits began training at Tuskegee, Alabama. Challenged by substandard training conditions, discrimination, and segregation, the Tuskegee Airmen responded with resolve and discipline. Between 1942 and 1946, 996 African Americans received their silver wings at Tuskegee Army Air Field. Some 450 of these pilots flew with the 99th Fighter Squadron and later, the 332d Fighter Group. They became known as the "red tails" for the scarlet coloring on the tail and nose of their P-51B Mustang aircraft. After their baptism of fire in North Africa, the Tuskegee Airmen moved into Italy.

Their commanding officer was Colonel Benjamin O. Davis, Jr. Particularly notable is a daring strafing mission that Davis led in Austria. Despite intense group fire, Davis and his squadron destroyed or damaged thirty-five locomotives, six of which are credited to Davis. At about this time, another pilot in the 332d destroyed a German destroyer single-handedly with machine guns. The Tuskegee Airmen were the first U.S. pilots to down a German jet. The 332d achieved lasting fame when it assumed escort duties for U.S. bombers striking deep into Germany. The 332d established a record for never losing a single bomber in approximately two hundred missions, a truly extraordinary accomplishment. The group's heroics in the air and dignity on the ground won them many medals and broke the color barriers of the U.S. military. By the end of World War II, one out of sixteen aviators in the U.S. Army Air Force was an African American.

Douglas W. Richmond

See also: Military and racial/ethnic relations; Military desegregation.

Underclass theories

In his 1968 book *The Unheavenly City,* Edward Banfield bluntly stated that much of what appears to African Americans to be race prejudice is actually class prejudice and that much of what whites interpret as black behavior is actually lower-class behavior. According to Banfield, "lower-class" behavior might involve a large number of specific activities, but their common element was a strong fixation on the immediate present and a very low awareness of and concern for the more distant future. This particular time awareness was manifested in negative attitudes toward schooling and career development, indulgence in alcohol and drug abuse, sexual promiscuity with little concern for pregnancy or disease, eagerness to find "action" in violence, vandalism, and crime, and rejection of "respectable" standards of dress, personal grooming, and speech.

Because personality and behavior patterns are linked to social class, young people tend to adopt these patterns from their family members and from others who appear to be part of their reference group. Clearly lower-class lifestyles, defined in this manner, produce people who have a high probability of living in poverty—indeed, "culture of poverty" is usually identified with the same types of lifestyle and personality.

In his 1994 book *Prescription for Failure,* Byron M. Roth developed these themes still further. Strongly influenced by black economist Thomas Sowell, Roth argued that "most of the problems blacks face in America today are directly attributable to patterns of behavior that have become common in black underclass communities . . . : welfare dependency, crime, illegitimacy, and educational failure, all of which seriously undercut black economic and social advancement, and in addition serve to undermine efforts to facilitate racial integration." Such examples of lower-class behavior are found in all racial and ethnic groups, with the same predictable consequences. To attribute the economic difficulties of African Americans, Native Americans, or Latinos to white racism is, in Roth's view, inaccurate and unfair. Roth contended that even if racism suddenly disappeared, the life of most African Americans would not improve measurably until the "debilitating conditions of life in the underclass" were remedied. On the other hand, if lower-class behaviors—crime, illegitimacy, educational failure—could be halted, Roth believed that African Americans would experience real social and economic growth despite white racism.

Roth notes that much of the disparity between the incomes of blacks and whites arises from factors other than prejudice. Median family income for blacks failed to rise relative to whites over the period 1967 to 1990. However, vastly more of the black families were headed by women and had only one wage earner. For black families headed by married couples, the average income increased from 68 percent of white income in 1967 to 84 percent in

1990. The ratio was even higher for black married-couple families under age forty-four.

Like political scientist Charles Murray, Roth argues that blaming the economic problems of the black underclass on "white racism" has led to public policies regarding education, crime, and welfare that have actually aggravated the problems. He also states that the members of the black underclass themselves have been encouraged to develop defeatist and self-destructive attitudes toward their own situation.

Paul B. Trescott

See also: Class theories of racial/ethnic relations; Culture of poverty; Poverty and race.

Underground Railroad

The Underground Railroad was a loose network of secret routes by which fugitive slaves made their way from the southern slave states north to freedom, often as far as Canada. Parts of the Underground Railroad may have been in place as early as 1786.

By 1850, southern slave owners were claiming enormous loss of slave property to the Underground Railroad, although many believe these claims were exaggerated. It is impossible to know how many slaves made their way to freedom—estimates range from sixty thousand to a hundred thousand between 1800 and 1865.

Many slaves reached freedom without the aid of the Underground Railroad, and many, especially those in the Deep South, did not flee north but went instead to Mexico or found refuge with the Seminole, Cherokee, or other Native American tribes. However, the majority of fugitive slaves escaped from the border states and fled north. Usually, the most dangerous leg of their journey was reaching a station on the underground line; once there, conductors would pass them from site to site toward safety.

It was almost impossible for a runaway slave to reach freedom successfully without assistance. Most slaves had little or no knowledge of geography and fled with only vague notions of where they were headed; most left with no money and few provisions and had to risk asking strangers along the way for food, shelter, and protection from pursuers. For the most part, persons helping runaways performed impulsive acts of compassion and did not consider themselves to be part of a resistance group. In parts of the country, however, the numbers of fugitives coming through were so great that predetermined escape routes, safe houses, and plans of action were organized. In time, some Underground Railroad lines were highly organized, and at least some routes existed in most of the states between the South and Canada.

A novel method that a few African Americans used to escape from southern slavery was to have themselves shipped to the North in boxes. *(Library of Congress)*

The two most frequent escape corridors were from Kentucky and Virginia into Ohio and from there north, and up the Eastern Seaboard through New England. Ohio especially was crisscrossed with routes of escape, as were western Pennsylvania and New York, eastern Indiana, and northwestern Illinois. The Middle Atlantic states and New England also had many well-established routes; lines existed west of Ohio and even, to some degree, in the South. After passage of the Fugitive Slave Law of 1850, organized aid to runaways grew, as the threats to free African Americans as well as fugitive slaves increased and more antislavery sympathizers felt the moral obligation to risk civil disobedience.

Organization No one knows when or how the name Underground Railroad began, although legend has it that it was coined after a frustrated slavecatcher swore that the fugitives he was pursuing had disappeared as thoroughly and suddenly as if they had found an underground road. As knowledge of the existence of escape routes spread, so did the railroad terminology, with words such as "conductors," "stations," "stationkeepers," and "lines."

Conductors often used inventive means to transport fugitives safely from station to station. Many were hidden under goods or in secret compartments in wagons. A few, such as Henry "Box" Brown, were actually boxed and shipped by train or boat. At least once, slaves were hidden in carriages forming a fake funeral procession. There were so many routing options along some lines that tracing was difficult. Barns, thickets, attics, spare rooms, woodsheds, smokehouses, and cellars were used as stations. Fugitives often were disguised: A hoe could make a runaway look like a hired-out day laborer; fine clothes could disguise a runaway field hand as a servant of gentlefolk; cross-dressing could keep fugitives from matching descriptions on handbills. Mulattoes could sometimes pass as whites. Perhaps the most famous escape effected through disguise was that of husband and wife William and Ellen Craft, who, with Ellen disguised as a white Southern gentleman and William as her valet, made it from Georgia to Philadelphia, where the Underground Railroad then transported them to safety. Once at a station, fugitives were given shelter, food, clothing, and sometimes money, as well as help in reaching the next stop.

Quakers—mostly of the Hicksite sect—played a large and early role in maintaining the Underground Railroad; in 1797, George Washington complained of Quakers helping one of his slaves escape. Other sects, such as Covenanters and Wesleyan Methodists, also contributed a number of agents. Particular locations, such as Oberlin College in Ohio, became important centers of activity. Women as well as men played active roles, especially in providing food and clothing to fugitives, and women often organized auxiliaries to support the more visible vigilance and abolitionist committees.

The role played by white antislavery sympathizers, although important, has tended to be overemphasized. In southern states, fellow slaves usually were the source of food and a hiding place for escapees. In border states, free blacks provided the most important help to fugitives, both in all-black settlements and in cities where black abolitionists worked alongside their white counterparts. Many African American churches and vigilance committees extended protection, support, and help in relocation to fugitives who reached the free states.

Whites rarely took the initiative to go south and effect escapes, but a number of former slaves returned to help friends and family flee. The most famous conductor to recruit escapees was the remarkable Harriet Tubman. Having herself escaped from slavery, she made some nineteen daring and successful trips into southern states to bring out groups of slaves, despite the forty-thousand-dollar bounty on her head. She is credited with personally leading more than three hundred slaves to safety, never losing anyone in her charge, and earned the title "the Moses of her people."

The period of greatest activity for the Underground Railroad was from 1850 to 1860. Among the most active white stationkeepers was Levi Coffin: In thirty-five years of activism in Indiana and Ohio, Coffin helped three thousand fugitive slaves on their way north. Quaker Thomas Garrett of Wilmington, Delaware, aided several thousand fugitives over a forty-year period; he lost all of his property to court fines as a result but refused to cease his work.

Important black members of the Underground Railroad included the Reverend William H. Mitchell of Ohio, who in twelve years provided temporary shelter for thirteen hundred fleeing slaves; Robert Purvis of Philadelphia, Pennsylvania; William Whipper of Columbia, Pennsylvania; Henry Highland Garnet of New York; Lewis Hayden of Boston, Massachusetts; Frederick Douglass of Rochester, New York; and William Wells Brown of Buffalo, New York.

However, most of those who hid, fed, transported, and otherwise aided fugitive slaves have remained anonymous. Likewise, records about the fugitives themselves are scarce. Following the Civil War, several prominent activists published memoirs about their Underground Railroad activities that included accounts of some of the slaves they aided. Black stationkeeper William Still of Philadelphia kept notes on almost seven hundred fugitives he helped, providing valuable statistics. His records indicate that 80 percent of runaways were male and that significant numbers of house servants as well as field hands fled. However, the names and profiles of the vast majority of the thousands of men, women, and children who braved the hazards of flight in desperate bids for freedom remain unknown.

Grace McEntee

Core Resources

Henrietta Buckmaster's *Let My People Go: The Story of the Underground Railroad and the Growth of the Abolition Movement* (Boston: Beacon Press, 1941) discusses the Underground Railroad within the broader context of the growth of antislavery sentiment. Levi Coffin's *Reminiscences of Levi Coffin* (New York: Arno Press, 1968) is an important primary source; this work reprints his third edition of 1898. Larry Gara's *The Liberty Line: The Legend of the Underground Railroad* (Lexington: University of Kentucky Press, 1961) counters popular notions that exaggerate the role of white abolitionists and underplay blacks' contributions in helping fugitive slaves. Wilbur H. Siebert's *The Underground Railroad from Slavery to Freedom* (1898; reprint, New York: Arno Press, 1968) is a landmark history of much value. William Still's *The Underground Railroad* (1872; reprint, Chicago: Johnson, 1972) is a vast collection of narratives and sketches, focusing on the fugitives' stories.

See also: Abolition; Antislavery laws of 1777 and 1807; Fugitive slave laws; Slavery: history.

United Negro College Fund

Under the direction of Frederick D. Patterson, president of Tuskegee Institute, the United Negro College Fund (UNCF) was established on April 25, 1944, with twenty-seven member colleges and a combined enrollment of fourteen thousand students. The goal was to become one of the world's leading education assistance organizations. With a few exceptions, most

UNCF member institutions had been founded by religious societies from the North after the Civil War and before the turn of the century. Located principally in the Southeast and in eastern Texas, these institutions operate with a variety of organizational structures and program offerings.

Since its inception, UNCF has grown to become the United States' oldest and most successful African American higher-education assistance organization. In 1998, UNCF provided support for a consortium of forty-one private, accredited four-year black colleges and universities. UNCF raises operating money for its member schools so that they can maintain the highest academic standards and prepare their students for demanding professions and careers. Although these institutions constitute only about 3 percent of all colleges and universities in the United States, they graduate more than one-quarter of all African Americans who earn the baccalaureate degree and nearly 40 percent of African Americans who later earn a doctoral degree. These graduates help build a stronger nation as community leaders and educators and in numerous other vocations.

Alvin K. Benson

See also: Black colleges and universities; Education and African Americans.

United States v. Cruikshank

In 1875, William Cruikshank and two others were convicted in a federal court of participating in the lynching of two African Americans. The 1870 Reconstruction statute under which they were convicted was broadly written to make it unlawful to interfere with most rights of citizens. The constitutional authority claimed for this federal statute was the Fourteenth Amendment. Cruikshank and his codefendants, who were charged with interfering with the right and privilege "peaceably to assemble," argued that the Fourteenth Amendment does not authorize the federal government to establish so broad a criminal statute because the amendment was written to limit state governments, not private persons.

In 1876, the U.S. Supreme Court, in an opinion written by Chief Justice Morrison R. Waite, unanimously agreed with Cruikshank. The Fourteenth Amendment, which establishes citizenship and then says, "No State shall make or enforce any law which shall abridge the privileges or immunities of citizens of the United States," applies in the first instance to state, not private, action. Private action such as the lynching in which Cruikshank participated may be punished by the federal government only if it can be shown that the intent was to deprive a specific constitutional right—and even then the indictment must specify the intent very narrowly. The decision effectively sanctioned the lynchings of African Americans for the next few decades.

Robert Jacobs

See also: Dyer antilynching bill; Lynchings; Sexual fears and racism.

United States v. Reese

United States v. Reese (1876) marked the first major test of voting rights under the Fifteenth Amendment, which had been passed in 1870 and stated that the right to vote "shall not be denied or abridged by the United States or by any State on account of race, color, or previous condition of servitude." A Kentucky voting official was indicted for refusing to let an African American, who had offered to pay his poll tax, vote in a municipal election. The U.S. Supreme Court, by an 8-1 margin, declared unconstitutional the Enforcement Act of 1870, the law on which the indictment was based. The Enforcement Act provided penalties for obstructing or hindering persons from voting in an election. In the majority decision delivered by Chief Justice Morison R. Waite, the Supreme Court ruled that the U.S. Congress had overreached its powers by seeking to punish the denial of voting rights on any grounds and could only legislate against discrimination based on race.

According to the U.S. Supreme Court, the Fifteenth Amendment did not confer the right of suffrage on anyone but merely prohibited the United States from excluding a person from voting because of race, color, or previous condition of servitude. The ruling made it constitutionally possible for southern states to deny the right to vote on any grounds except race, thus allowing the use of poll taxes, literacy tests, good character tests, understanding clauses, and other devices to disfranchise African Americans.

David L. Porter

See also: Disfranchisement laws in Mississippi; Fifteenth Amendment; Literacy tests; Poll tax.

United Steelworkers of America v. Weber

In the 1979 *United Steelworkers of America v. Weber* decision, the U.S. Supreme Court ruled that an employer could establish voluntary programs of racial preference, including quotas, in order to eliminate manifest racial imbalance, even without evidence that the employer was guilty of discrimination.

Title VII of the Civil Rights Act of 1964 made it illegal "to discriminate against any individual because of his race, color, religion, sex, or national origin." Within a few years, federal agencies began to use "racial imbalance" as *prima facie* evidence of invidious discrimination, and they encouraged employers to use numerical goals, timetables, and sometimes quotas to promote minority participation in areas of employment where they had been traditionally underrepresented. The Kaiser Corporation's plant in Gramercy, Louisiana, found that while African Americans made up 39 percent of the local workforce, they occupied less than 2 percent of the craft positions in the plant. Fearing that this imbalance might jeopardize government contracts, the corporation and the labor union agreed to a "voluntary" affirmative action plan that included a special training program for craft positions. Admission to the training program was based on seniority, except that half the positions were reserved for African Americans even if they had less seniority.

Brian Weber, a white employee with five years of experience, was disappointed when he was not admitted into the program while two black employees with less seniority did gain admission. He sued both the company and the union with the argument that he was a victim of discrimination in violation of the 1964 Civil Rights Act. After Weber prevailed in both the district court and the court of appeals, the union petitioned the U.S. Supreme Court to review the judgments.

The Court's Decision The Court voted 5 to 2 to reverse the lower courts' decision and to uphold the affirmative action program at the Gramercy plant. Writing for the majority, Justice William J. Brennan looked to the spirit rather than the literal wording of Title VII. Since the purpose of the law was to advance employment opportunities for members of racial minorities, he reasoned that the law did not prohibit preferences as a means of integrating minorities into the mainstream of American society. The program, moreover, did not "unnecessarily trammel" the interests of Weber; it was only a "temporary measure," to end when a target was reached. Further, it had the limited goal of ending "a manifest racial imbalance." Finally, Brennan noted that if the Court had "misperceived" the intent of Congress, the decision could be corrected easily by legislative action.

In a strongly worded dissent, Justice William H. Rehnquist proclaimed that "no racial discrimination in employment is permissible under Title VII." Noting the explicit wording of the law, he also quoted extensively from the congressional debates to show that the framers of Title VII envisioned a law allowing no preference based on race or gender.

The *Weber* decision was one of the Court's most controversial cases to deal with the question of "reverse discrimination." Supporters of race-conscious remedies for past societal discrimination were delighted that the Court did not apply the strict scrutiny test to an affirmative action program that involved racial preference and quotas. In later cases the justices would continue to be divided over the issue of *Weber*; they would tend to alternate between approving and disapproving affirmative action programs.

Thomas T. Lewis

See also: Affirmative action; *Bakke* case; Civil Rights Act of 1964; *Fullilove v. Klutznick*; Quotas; "Reverse" racism; *Richmond v. J. A. Croson Company*; Set-asides.

Universal Negro Improvement Association

The Universal Negro Improvement Association, an organization dedicated to supporting African American racial pride, did much to advance the growth of black nationalism.

In March, 1916, a young black Jamaican, Marcus Mosiah Garvey, arrived in New York City. He had come to the United States in the hope of securing financial help for the Universal Negro Improvement Association (UNIA), which he had founded in Jamaica two years earlier. After delivering his first public speech in Harlem in May, Garvey began a long speaking tour that took him through thirty-eight states. In May, 1917, he returned to Harlem and—with the help of his secretary and future wife, Amy Ashwood—organized the first American chapter of the UNIA. Though hardly noticed at the time, the establishment of this organization was a significant first step in the growth of black nationalism in the United States. Within a few years, the UNIA would claim millions of members and hundreds of branches throughout the United States, the Caribbean region, and Africa, and Garvey would be one of the most famous black people in the world.

The Beginnings of the UNIA Born in St. Ann's Bay, Jamaica, in 1887, Garvey claimed to be of pure African descent. His father was a descendant of the maroons, or Jamaican slaves, who successfully revolted against their British masters in 1739. During his early years, Garvey gradually became aware that his color was considered by some in his society to be a badge of inferiority. Jamaica, unlike the United States, placed the mulatto in a higher caste as a buffer against the unlettered black masses. This reality caused a sense of racial isolation and yet pride to grow in the young black man. By his twentieth birthday, Garvey had started a program to change the lives of black Jamaicans. While working as a foreman in a printing shop in 1907, he joined a labor strike as a leader. The strike, quickly broken by the shop owners, caused Garvey to lose faith in reform through labor unions. In 1910, he started publishing a newspaper, *Garvey's Watchman*, and helped form a political organization, the National Club. These efforts, which were not particularly fruitful, gave impetus to Garvey's visit to Central America where he was able to observe the wretched conditions of black people in Costa Rica and Panama.

Garvey's travels led him to London, the center of the British Empire. There the young man met Dusé Mohamed Ali, an Egyptian scholar, who increased the young Jamaican's knowledge and awareness of Africa. During his stay in England, Garvey also became acquainted with the plight of African Americans through reading Booker T. Washington's *Up from Slavery*. Washington's autobiography raised questions in Garvey's mind: "I asked, where is the black man's Government? Where is his King and his Kingdom? Where is his President, his country and his ambassador, his army, his navy, his men of big affairs? I could not find them, and then I declared, I will help to make them."

Returning to Jamaica in 1914, Garvey created a self-help organization for black people to which he gave the imposing title, the Universal Negro Improvement and Conservation Association and African Communities League. This new organization, renamed the Universal Negro Improvement

Students at Tuskegee Institute, established in 1881 by Booker T. Washington; its reputation drew Marcus Garvey to the United States, where he wished to study Washington's schemes for racial uplift. *(Library of Congress)*

Association, based its philosophy on the need to unite "all people of Negro or African parentage." The goals of the UNIA were to increase racial pride, to aid black people throughout the world, and "to establish a central nation for the race." Garvey, elected the first president of UNIA, realized that black people would have to achieve these goals without assistance from white people. This self-help concept, similar to the philosophy (but not the practice) of Booker T. Washington, led Garvey to propose a black trade school in Kingston, Jamaica, similar to Washington's Tuskegee Institute. The idea did not attract wide support and Garvey was temporarily frustrated.

In 1915, Garvey decided to come to the United States in order to seek aid for his Jamaica-based organization. Although he had corresponded with Washington, the black leader had died before Garvey arrived in the United States in 1916. Garvey went directly to Harlem, which in the early twentieth century was becoming a center of black culture

The lives of African Americans were rapidly changing in the first two decades of the twentieth century. Metropolitan areas in the North were experiencing mass migrations of African Americans from the South. In New York City, for example, the black population increased from 91,709 in 1910 to 152,467 in 1920. African Americans were attracted by the promise of jobs and by the possibility of escaping the rigid system of segregation in the South.

African Americans found, however, that they could not escape racism simply by moving. Northern whites also believed in the racial inferiority of African Americans and opposed black competitors for their jobs. The new immigrants, like their foreign-born counterparts, were crowded into the northern ghettos without proper housing or the possibility of escape. Racial violence broke out in several northern cities. The North proved not to be a utopia for African Americans.

These harsh realities aided Garvey in establishing the UNIA in New York. The population of Harlem was not attracted to the accommodationist philosophy of Washington or the middle-class goals of the National Association for the Advancement of Colored People. Indeed, urban African Americans were wary of all prophets, even Garvey; but the young Jamaican was able to obtain support from the Jamaican immigrants in Harlem, who felt isolated, and he established a branch of UNIA there in 1917. At first, the organization encountered difficulties. Local politicians tried to gain control of it, and Garvey had to fight to save its autonomy. The original branch of the UNIA was dissolved, and a charter was obtained from the state of New York which prevented other groups from using the organization's name. By 1918, under Garvey's exciting leadership, the New York chapter of the UNIA boasted 3,500 members. By 1919, Garvey optimistically claimed 2 million members for his organization throughout the world and 200,000 subscribers for his weekly newspaper, *The Negro World.*

The Black Star Line and the Collapse of the UNIA In an effort to promote the economic welfare of blacks under the auspices of the UNIA,

Garvey established in 1919 two joint stock companies—the Black Star Line, an international commercial shipping company, and the Negro Factories Corporation, which was to "build and operate factories . . . to manufacture every marketable commodity." Stock in these companies was sold only to black investors. The Black Star Line was to establish commerce with Africa and transport willing emigrants "back to Africa." Although both companies were financial failures, they gave many black people a feeling of dignity. As a result of his promotional efforts in behalf of the Black Star Line, the federal government, prodded by rival black leaders, had Garvey indicted for fraudulent use of the mails in 1922. He was tried, found guilty, and sent to prison in 1923. Although his second wife, Amy Jacques-Garvey, worked to hold the UNIA together, it declined rapidly. In 1927, Garvey was released from prison and deported as an undesirable alien. He returned to Jamaica and then went to London and Paris and tried to resurrect the UNIA, but with little success. He died in poverty in London in 1940. Although a bad businessman, Garvey was a master propagandist and popular leader who made a major contribution to race consciousness among African Americans.

John C. Gardner, updated by R. Kent Rasmussen

Core Resources

E. David Cronon's *Black Moses: The Story of Marcus Garvey and the Universal Negro Improvement Association* (Madison: University of Wisconsin Press, 1955) remains the best introduction to Garvey's life. Marcus Garvey's *Philosophy and Opinions of Marcus Garvey*, edited by Amy Jacques-Garvey, with new introduction by Robert A. Hill (New York: Atheneum, 1992), is a classic collection of Garvey's speeches and writings assembled by his wife. *The Marcus Garvey and Universal Negro Improvement Association Papers* (9 vols., Berkeley: University of California Press, 1983-1996), edited by Robert A. Hill et al., is the most extensive collection of original documents by and about Garvey and his movement.

See also: Black nationalism; National Association for the Advancement of Colored People; Niagara Movement.

Urban underclass and the rural poor

"Urban underclass" has come to refer to a segment of the population that resides in urban or central-city areas and experiences high and persistent poverty, social isolation, anomie, and a sense of hopelessness. The "rural poor" consist of poverty-stricken persons living in small or sparsely populated communities.

The use of the terms "urban underclass" and "rural poor" is controversial, and there seems to be no consensus regarding how best to define them. It is estimated that 33 million poor people lived in the United States in 1990. Journalist Ken Auletta, in *The Underclass* (1983), estimated the number of American underclass to be anywhere from 2 to 18 million, while Joel A. Devine and James D. Wright, in *The Greatest of Evils: Urban Poverty and the American Underclass* (1993), cited figures of 3 million to 3.5 million. The number of rural poor in the United States was more than 9 million. These dramatically different figures and discrepancies in the totals reflect continued debate surrounding the definitions of both rural and urban poverty.

Urban Underclass A number of subgroups are more likely to be among the urban underclass than others, including children, the elderly, women, nonwhites, and members of female-headed households. Of these, racial affiliation is perhaps the most noted in research. Sociologist William J. Wilson points out that underclass neighborhoods "are populated almost exclusively by the most disadvantaged segments of the black urban community." This has not changed significantly since anthropologist Gunnar Myrdal wrote in 1962: "The largest and still most handicapped minority group in America is that of the Negroes."

Increased crime and deviant behavior are two of the most disturbing characteristics of the urban underclass. The entrenched hopelessness found on inner-city streets provides little motivation for members of the underclass to adhere to the norms and values of mainstream society. Consequently, drug dealing, use of drugs and alcohol, prostitution, theft, and other forms of crime are prevalent among members of the urban underclass.

Rural Underclass As defined by the U.S. Bureau of the Census, "rural" generally applies to settlements with concentrated populations of less than 2,500. Demographic studies show that the rural poor are concentrated heavily in the southern region of the United States. For example, the 1987 rural poverty rate in the South was 21.2 percent, 7.6 percent higher than that of the rest of the country. Moreover, in excess of half the rural poor in the United States lived in the South in 1987.

The majority of the rural poor are white. This is not to say that rural blacks, Hispanics, and American Indians do not experience high poverty rates. Statistics show that these subgroups have poverty rates of 44 percent, 35 percent, and at least 35 percent, respectively. These figures represent poverty rates several times higher than those of their white counterparts. Those suffering from persistent rural poverty are more likely to be elderly, black, female, or members of a female-headed household.

There are a number of reasons that many members of the rural population are unable to work. Most noteworthy is the fact that many are children too young to work. Illness and disability are additional reasons that many of the rural poor are not among the workforce. Overriding all this, a large percentage of the rural poor are simply unable to find work because of factory closings or manufacturing cutbacks.

Urban-Rural Comparisons On the surface it might appear that the only difference between the urban underclass and the rural poor is their geographic location and concentration of population. A closer look at the population subgroups (such as elderly, female-headed households, and nonwhites) reveals that this is not the case. In 1987, for example, the rural elderly had a higher poverty rate than the urban elderly. Also, a significantly smaller number of impoverished rural families live in female-headed households than in urban areas.

It appears that behavior is the key to distinguishing the urban underclass from the rural poor. In his provocative book *The Truly Disadvantaged: The Inner City, the Underclass, and Public Policy* (1987), Wilson maintains that "there is a heterogeneous grouping of inner-city families and individuals whose behavior contrasts sharply with that of mainstream America." The anomie or normlessness displayed among the urban underclass manifests itself through high rates of out-of-wedlock births, welfare, unemployment or underemployment, low educational attainment, drug and alcohol abuse, and crime.

According to numerous studies, the rural poor exhibit attitudes toward work that are different from the attitudes of the urban underclass. For example, U.S. census data from 1973 and 1987 indicate that the percentage of rural poor who worked was a full 10 percent higher than the working urban poor.

Economics and the Poor From the end of World War II until the late 1960's, the United States experienced an economic boom. There was little urban poverty, and rural poverty declined as a result of migration to cities. During this period of general prosperity, the eyes of the country turned to the less fortunate. When President Lyndon B. Johnson declared unconditional War on Poverty in 1964, the federal government established an official poverty line and assistance programs. Not all elements of the poor population were helped by federal programs; the focus was mainly on the Appalachia area and poor children and mothers. Sociological research on poverty increased in the 1960's and flourished until the mid-1970's.

Following national economic restructuring beginning in 1979, rural areas experienced economic growth; manufacturers built factories and brought new jobs to small towns. Prices for farm products increased, domestic energy industries expanded, and retirees began moving to rural areas. As Duncan notes, however, this "rural turnaround" was short-lived. Rural poverty began to rise again, mainly because the national economy was hit hard by high inflation, recessions, low wages, unemployment, and slow job growth—the results of international competition, factory closings, and layoffs.

The formation of the urban underclass from the 1960's to the 1990's is generally attributed to the mass exodus of the middle-and working-class residents from cities to the suburbs, and to the simultaneous decline in semiskilled and unskilled employment opportunities in the inner cities. In the early 1980's, many middle-class African Americans left the urban areas to take advantage of educational and employment opportunities in the suburbs.

With the absence of middle-class families and their incomes came a substantial decrease in the tax base available to support public schools and other government-run programs. The quality of education declined and urban youths found opportunities slipping even further out of reach and thus became caught in the poverty trap. The departure of the middle class eventually destroyed other stabilizing social institutions, including black churches and local businesses.

During President Ronald Reagan's administration in the 1980's, the situation worsened. Republican constituents were not, in general, poor or black, but rather middle- and working-class people who were tired of their tax dollars supporting the welfare state. This attitude led to the further neglect of the inner-city poor, which brought with it an increase in underclass violence. Incidents such as the Los Angeles riots in 1992 are evidence of the dysfunctional behavior and anomie characteristic of the underclass.

Liesel A. Miller

Core Resources

Joel A. Devine and James D. Wright's *The Greatest of Evils: Urban Poverty and the American Underclass* (New York: Aldine de Gruyter, 1993) is a thorough study, at the same time nontechnical and interesting. *Rural Poverty in America,* edited by Cynthia M. Duncan (New York: Auburn House, 1992), contends that rural poverty is different from urban poverty and that social, economic, and political barriers keep the rural poor economically disadvantaged. David T. Ellwood's *Poor Support: Poverty in the American Family* (New York: Basic Books, 1988) suggests specific steps to eradicate poverty in logical yet general terms. Michael Harrington's *The New American Poverty* (New York: Penguin Books, 1985) provides readers with a provocative and insightful look at the social and political roots of poverty. Christopher Jencks's *Rethinking Social Policy: Race, Poverty, and the Underclass* (Cambridge, Mass.: Harvard University Press, 1992) deals with affirmative action, intergenerational poverty, urban ghettos, and the size and extent of the urban underclass, making recommendations for welfare reform. *The Urban Underclass,* edited by Christopher Jencks and Paul E. Peterson (Washington, D.C.: Brookings Institution, 1991), provides case studies with solid data, tables, and charts.

See also: Economics and race; Poverty and race; Underclass theories.

Vote, right to

The ability to influence the choice of public officials and policy by participation in free elections permits citizens to participate in the making of law through the choice of lawmakers and provides a means of holding government accountable to the people.

The right to vote is one of the most fundamental rights of American citizenship, and its widespread distribution is one of the essential features of American democracy. The expansion of voting rights has been an important theme in the evolution of American democracy, as has been the increasing role of the federal government in defining such rights.

Early Voting Rights In colonial America, voting rights were limited to adult white males who could meet a property qualification. It was generally felt that ownership of property was necessary to prove a stake in society. During and after the American Revolution, property qualifications were reduced or replaced with a requirement that a voter be a taxpayer. Voting continued to be seen as a privilege rather than a basic right of citizenship.

The U.S. Constitution of 1787 said little about voting rights. The definition of who could vote was left to the states, with the proviso that the requirements for voting for members of the House of Representatives be the same as those for voting for members of the largest house of the state legislature. The franchise remained almost exclusively limited to white males.

Expansion of Voting Rights By the 1830's, there was a noticeable trend in the direction of manhood suffrage—that is, toward allowing adult white male citizens to vote whether they owned property or not. Though all women and most black men continued to be excluded from voting, manhood suffrage was an important step in establishing a connection between citizenship and voting rights.

The Civil War set the stage for a significant broadening of voting rights as well as for a growing federal role in their definition. During Reconstruction, Congress required that the former Confederate states allow adult male African Americans to vote. The Fourteenth Amendment (1868) reinforced this by including a provision (never actually used) that allowed reduction of a state's representation in Congress if it denied the vote to its adult male citizens. The Fifteenth Amendment (1870) went even further, saying that the right to vote could not be denied on the basis of race, color, or previous condition of servitude. Since blacks were already voting in the South under congressionally mandated changes in state constitutions, the most immediate effect of the Fifteenth Amendment was to enfranchise blacks in the North, where most states still limited suffrage to whites.

The Fifteenth Amendment illustrates the point that the right to vote and its actual use are two different things. By the 1890's, southern states were finding ways to limit black voting without formally restricting the right to vote on a racial basis. Techniques such as unevenly applied literacy tests, poll taxes, and the all-white primary (sometimes backed up by the threat of violence) effectively reduced African American voting to insignificance.

Promotion of universal suffrage has been a principle of the National Association for the Advancement of Colored People since its inception in the early twentieth century. *(Library of Congress)*

During the same period, the woman suffrage movement exerted increasing pressure in an effort to gain access to the ballot. Beginning with Wyoming in 1890, a number of states recognized the right of women to vote; however, women could not vote on a nationwide basis until ratification of the Nineteenth Amendment in 1920.

The Civil Rights Movement Reviving the Fifteenth Amendment and ending restrictions on black voting rights in the southern and border states became a major goal of the Civil Rights movement that developed after World War II. Early civil rights laws made limited attempts to protect voting rights, and in 1964, the Twenty-fourth Amendment banned the poll tax in federal elections. It was not, however, until the Selma-to-Montgomery civil rights march dramatized the issue that Congress acted effectively. The result was the Voting Rights Act of 1965. The act provided for federal supervision of elections in southern counties where African Americans did not vote in numbers consistent with their presence in the population. Originally limited to five years, the act was subsequently renewed and extended to cover Native Americans and Hispanics.

The trend toward greater federal definition of voting rights continued in other ways. The Twenty-sixth Amendment (1971) enfranchised millions of new voters by lowering the voting age to eighteen. The federal courts also struck down many state laws limiting the vote to longtime residents. By the 1970's, residency requirements of longer than thirty days were no longer permitted.

Late Twentieth Century Controversies Despite the extension of voting rights to virtually all adult American citizens, the right to vote continued to excite controversy. The Supreme Court expanded its definition of the right to vote beyond access to the ballot itself. Beginning with *Baker v. Carr* (1962), the Court adopted a "one person, one vote" rule that forced changes in the apportionment of state legislatures and local governments. During the 1970's, claims by racial and ethnic groups that apportionment should take into account not only population but also the presence and interests of previously underrepresented groups received a sympathetic hearing. By the 1990's, this approach had created a complicated and controversial area of the law. Less controversial, but troubling, was the irony that as the right to vote expanded, the proportion of Americans actually voting declined.

William C. Lowe

Core Resources

Five works that offer informative historical perspectives on voting in the United States are Lorn S. Foster, ed., *The Voting Rights Act: Consequences and Implications* (New York: Praeger, 1985); Steven Lawson, *Black Ballots: Voting Rights in the South, 1944-1969* (New York: Columbia University Press, 1976); Frances Fox Piven and Richard A. Cloward, *Why Americans Don't Vote* (New York: Pantheon Books, 1988); Donald W. Rogers, ed., *Voting and the Spirit of*

American Democracy (Urbana: University of Illinois Press, 1992); Chilton Williamson, *American Suffrage: From Property to Democracy, 1760-1860* (Princeton, N.J.: Princeton University Press, 1960).

See also: Disfranchisement laws in Mississippi; Fifteenth Amendment; Minority voting districts; Selma-to-Montgomery march; Voting Rights Act of 1965.

Voting Rights Act of 1965

This legislation essentially abolished a number of practices that had been used at various times to disqualify African American voters, primarily in the South, including literacy, education, and character tests. It authorized the U.S. attorney general to send federal examiners into areas where voter discrimination was suspected; in effect, it allowed federal voting registrars to supersede state ones. Affected jurisdictions could be free from federal scrutiny once they showed that they had not employed discriminatory practices for five years from the time of initial federal intervention. Yet perhaps the most sweeping part of the act was its "preclearance requirements," which applied to areas with low voter registration or participation: They required that any reapportionment plans or proposed changes in electoral requirements be approved by the Justice Department before they could take effect. The act also included a finding that poll taxes were preventing blacks from voting in state elections, spurring the Supreme Court to hold that poll taxes were illegal in 1966 (poll taxes in federal elections had been abolished in 1964).

The act was amended in 1970, 1975, and 1982. The 1970 amendment prohibited literacy tests throughout the country until 1975. The 1975 amendment maintained the provisions of the 1970 amendment, suspending literacy tests indefinitely, after failing to enlist enough supporters to apply the Voting Rights Act to language minorities as well as racial minorities. The 1982 amendment, effective for twenty-five years, directed the federal courts to examine the effect, in addition to the intent, of practices that discriminated against black voting opportunities. This amendment was passed as a result of a 1980 Supreme Court decision (*City of Mobile v. Bolden*) stating that civil rights litigants had to prove that municipalities intended to discriminate against blacks by adopting particular voting procedures.

Passage of the act resulted in a dramatic increase in African American voter registration. By the end of the 1960's, more than 60 percent of blacks in the Deep South were registered. This increase in black voter registration also meant that significant numbers of African Americans were elected to office, although primarily at the local, county, and state levels. The act has proved to be a landmark piece of legislation in ensuring that all American citizens can exercise their constitutionally guaranteed right to vote, a fundamental precept of American citizenship and justice.

Craig M. Eckert

See also: Civil Rights Act of 1964; Grandfather clauses; Literacy tests; Poll tax; Representation: gerrymandering, malapportionment, and reapportionment.

Washington v. Davis

African American members of the Washington, D.C., Metropolitan Police Department, as well as unsuccessful applicants to the department, sued the department, claiming that its hiring and promotion policies were racially discriminatory. In particular, they cited a written test that a disproportionately high number of blacks failed. The district court found for the police department, but the appellate court, relying on the Supreme Court precedent of *Griggs v. Duke Power Company* (1971), reversed that decision, finding the disparate impact of the test to be evidence of employment discrimination. When *Washington v. Davis* came before the Supreme Court, however, Justice Byron White's opinion for the Court stated unequivocally that evidence of discriminatory purpose must be present for such tests to be found unconstitutional. The lower appellate court was reversed.

Griggs had been a landmark employment discrimination case which made disparate impact the test for employment discrimination under Title VII of the 1964 Civil Rights Act. In *Washington,* however, the plaintiffs were claiming that the police department's employment practices violated their right to equal protection under the due process clause of the Fifth Amendment. The standards for determining discrimination proscribed under Title VII were not, said the Court, the same as those applied to a claim of unconstitutional racial discrimination, which requires some evidence of intent to discriminate. Here, the Court found, the personnel test at issue was neutral on its face; in addition, it was rationally related to a legitimate purpose: improving employees' communications skills.

The Court indicated that intent to discriminate could be inferred from a totality of circumstances, including disparate impact, but it declined to spell out a more precise test for unconstitutional employment discrimination. In fact, the majority opinion confused the issue. As Justice John Paul Stevens indicates in his concurring opinion, disparate impact and discriminatory purpose are often indistinguishable. When disparate impact becomes proof of discriminatory purpose, the two standards are conflated. Furthermore, by augmenting the consequences of past discrimination, employment policies not intended to be discriminatory can produce results identical to those resulting from conspicuously discriminatory ones.

The test for what constitutes evidence of discriminatory intent was left indeterminate until the Supreme Court strengthened it in *Personnel Administrator of Massachusetts v. Feeney* (1979) to the advantage of employers. In *Feeney*, the Court held that even if discriminatory results of a prospective statute are foreseeable at the time it is passed by the legislature, it is only unconstitutional if these results constitute the reason for passage. The consequences for subsequent civil rights litigants pressing discrimination suits against state employers were profound.

Lisa Paddock

See also: Civil Rights Act of 1964; *Griggs v. Duke Power Company*.

Watts riot

The outbreak of racial violence on August 11, 1965, shattered the summer calm of Los Angeles, California, and eroded the elation felt by many people when President Lyndon B. Johnson had signed the 1965 Voting Rights Act into law only five days earlier. Official investigations confirmed that the causes of the upheaval were deeply rooted in the conditions of ghetto life in the sprawling metropolis. In less immediate terms, however, the upsurge of anarchistic energy stemmed from the existence of intolerable tensions in relations between whites and blacks within U.S. society.

The Watts area of Los Angeles in 1965 provided a perfect setting for racial conflict. The neighborhood had long been the center of African American life in the city. As a result, Watts offered its inhabitants full exposure to the hazards of ghetto existence. More than 30 percent of the workforce was unemployed. Approximately 14 percent of the population was functionally illiterate. The black residents of Watts faced serious barriers in their pursuit of better housing, more remunerative jobs, and improved education. Separated from white society, Watts was a storehouse of combustible material on the southeast side of Los Angeles.

Beginnings A minor clash between police and African American residents caused the explosion that ripped through Watts. Along the edge of the ghetto, on the night of August 11, a California Highway Patrol officer arrested two young African Americans for reckless driving. While the officer administered a sobriety test, a hostile crowd gathered. The confrontation led to more arrests. Finally, the police departed amid a hail of rocks thrown by irate blacks. Rumors of police brutality spread through Watts. In the hours before midnight, a full-scale riot developed. Automobiles traveling through the ghetto were pelted with rocks and bottles. Police moved back into the area at 11:00 P.M., but flurries of violence continued throughout the night.

After a day filled with tension, the rioters returned to the streets on the night of August 12. Commercial buildings were set ablaze, and firemen who responded to the alarms were greeted with rocks and gunfire. California state officials received reports that estimated the number of rioters at eight thousand. The police were unable to prevent widespread burning and looting.

The upheaval reached its climax on the night of August 13. Crowds of angry African Americans surged through Watts. Arsonists began the systematic destruction of whole city blocks in the ghetto. Police and firemen faced added peril from snipers who took up positions in the ruins. At its height, the riot encompassed an area of more than fifty blocks.

Reaction In the early hours of August 14, law enforcement officers began to regain control of the streets. At the request of city officials, National Guard troops joined the Los Angeles Police Department in battling the rioters. Ultimately, nearly fourteen thousand members of the National Guard entered the fray. Burning and looting continued sporadically, but the presence of fully armed soldiers in large numbers gradually restored quiet to the riot-torn area. A dusk-to-dawn curfew went into effect on Saturday night, August 14. Three days later the curfew was lifted, and most of the National Guard troops left the city. Amid the rubble, the people of Watts returned to their everyday concerns. The six days of rioting had wreaked widespread destruction on the African American neighborhood. Thirty-four deaths were reported, and police made more than three thousand arrests. Property damage reached the forty-million-dollar mark, as 288 businesses and private buildings and 14 public buildings were damaged and/or looted, and 1 public and 207 private buildings were destroyed.

Yet the most significant harm caused by the riot was beyond specific assessment. In the realm of race relations, the outbreak of violence exacerbated tensions between blacks and whites throughout the United States. Watts became the first chapter in a history of race riots that included upheavals in Detroit, Michigan, and Newark, New Jersey, in 1967, and Washington, D.C., in 1968. Faced with repeated outbreaks of violence, the Civil Rights movement, with its emphasis on civil disobedience and interracial cooperation, suffered a significant setback in the short run. Beginning with the explosion at Watts, U.S. race relations entered a new, more ominous phase.

The riot did not, however, mean the end of nonviolent direct action or the total reversal of the multiracial cooperation that had brought important legal victories for desegregation in the United States. The history of civil rights reform after 1965 was marked by a growing realization that the socioeconomic conditions in which African Americans, Mexican Americans, and other minorities lived could not be ignored in the quest for social justice and personal fulfillment for all U.S. citizens. The last major effort by civil rights leader Dr. Martin Luther King, Jr.—who visited Watts at the time of the rioting and asked the insurgents to change their motto from "Burn, baby, burn" to "Build, baby, build"—was a Poor People's Campaign that was implemented two months after his assassination on April 4, 1968.

John G. Clark, updated by Thomas R. Peake

Core Resources

The Governor's Commission on the Los Angeles Riots' *Violence in the City: An End or a Beginning?* (Los Angeles: Author, 1965) focuses on the details and location of damage, with useful maps. Thomas R. Peake's *Keeping the Dream Alive: A History of the Southern Christian Leadership Conference from King to the Nineteen-Eighties* (New York: Peter Lang, 1987) includes extensive material on the urban riots and post-1965 efforts to deal with social problems in big-city ghettos. David O. Sears and John B. McConahay's *The Politics of Violence: The New Urban Blacks and the Watts Riot* (Boston: Houghton Mifflin, 1973) reviews the history of the crisis, the views and actions of urban blacks, and official reactions. The Watts Writers' Workshop's *From the Ashes: Voices of Watts,* edited and with an introduction by Budd Schulberg (New York: New American Library, 1967), contains writings by residents of Watts during the time of the 1965 riots and their aftermath, showing their frustrations as well as their hopes for better answers to social, personal, and economic problems.

See also: Detroit riot; Los Angeles riots of 1992; Miami riots of 1980; Newark race riots; Race riots of the twentieth century.

Weber v. Kaiser Aluminum and Chemical Corporation

Brian Weber, a white worker, challenged a voluntary affirmative action plan created by the United Steelworkers of America Union and the Kaiser Corporation. A quota of 50 percent of new skilled craft trainees were to be African American until the percentage of African Americans in a Louisiana plant equaled the percentage of blacks in the local labor force. Lower federal courts judged that this affirmative action plan violated Title VII of the Civil Rights Act of 1964, which prohibits racial discrimination in employment of people such as Weber.

On June 27, 1979, the U.S. Supreme Court reversed the lower court decisions and ruled that Congress did not intend to prohibit all voluntary, race-conscious affirmative action plans designed to break down patterns of racial segregation. This decision opened employment opportunities historically closed to African Americans.

Steve J. Mazurana

See also: Affirmative action; Civil Rights Act of 1964; Employment among African Americans.

Welfare reform: impact on racial/ethnic relations

Certain racial groups—notably African Americans—receive a disproportionate level of welfare benefits. Attempts to modify the welfare system therefore trigger the issue of race.

Any attempt to alter the distribution of government assistance inevitably encounters intense lobbying by groups who stand to gain and lose benefits. Welfare reform is a case in point. Both recipients of welfare benefits and the taxpayers who fund welfare programs have strong economic interests in how the program is run. In addition, the matter of welfare reform is connected to deeper racial issues. Because a disproportionate number of certain racial groups receive welfare benefits, efforts to reduce welfare spending are sometimes viewed as racially motivated.

Calls for Welfare Reform The U.S. welfare system was created in the 1930's during the Great Depression. It was greatly expanded in the 1960's under President Lyndon B. Johnson's Great Society program. Although elements of the system have been altered almost continuously, calls for thorough reform reached a crescendo in the 1980's. These calls were spurred by two factors: First, mounting government debt and increasing hostility to taxes created a political environment that encouraged a reduction in social spending. Second, a consensus began to form that after two decades, the War on Poverty initiated by Johnson had largely failed. In fact, by some measures, poverty had increased even with expanded welfare spending.

The issue of welfare reform had for years been largely associated with the Republican Party. President Ronald Reagan, a Republican, promoted some efforts to reduce welfare spending and tighten eligibility criteria, but the Democrat-controlled Congress was hostile to any serious reduction in welfare benefits. Liberals called the Republican proposals mean-spirited and selfish. More to the point, many minority leaders charged that welfare reform proposals were racist. Although by far whites constituted the largest racial group receiving welfare benefits, a much larger proportion, or percentage, of African Americans (up to 30 percent) received welfare benefits, compared with about 10 percent of Americans overall.

Welfare reform thus became a racially charged topic, with minority groups and African American leaders charging that "welfare" had become a code word for "black," and thus welfare reform was an insidious form of attack against African Americans. In such an environment, only the most incremental welfare reform proposals could make it through the legislative process. Meanwhile, pressure continued to mount from white and other nonblack groups who were becoming frustrated with the inability of the government to address the ineffectiveness of the welfare system. This frustration was dubbed "donor fatigue," whereby many taxpayers despaired that the Great Society programs of the 1960's could ever significantly reduce the problems they were designed to eradicate.

The Republican "Revolution" It was in this environment that the Republican Party won a majority in both houses of Congress in 1994. After decades as the minority party, the Republicans sought to tap in to the rising conservative mood of the electorate and reverse long-standing programs they derided as too liberal. Welfare was one of these. President Bill Clinton, a Democrat, quickly agreed to work with the Republicans to "end welfare as we know it"—itself an indicator of how potent the public mood was gauged to be. Clinton was criticized by members of his own party for allegedly capitulating to the conservative mood, but the prevailing political environment made defense of the status quo a fatal stance in most districts.

In the next few years, a monumental welfare reform bill was created in Congress. The bill, formally titled the Personal Responsibility and Work Opportunity Reconciliation Act, passed in Congress and was signed by President Clinton in 1996. The act had a number of provisions that were racially controversial. One of these denied welfare benefits to immigrants who entered the country after August 22, 1996 (although these immigrants could later receive benefits upon securing U.S. citizenship). Noncitizens living in the country before this deadline would also be ineligible for benefits, unless they had worked in the United States for at least ten years.

Supporters of the National Welfare Rights Organization picketing a retail store in Washington, D.C., in 1969 to protest its refusal to advance credit to poor customers. *(Library of Congress)*

Latino and Hispanic leaders were especially opposed to this provision, since by far the largest number of noncitizen immigrants were from Mexico and Central American countries. Although he signed the bill, Clinton promised to fight to "fix" the welfare reform law at a later time. The immigrant provision was removed as part of the following year's budget bill.

The much more important provision of the 1996 welfare reform law terminated the government's Aid to Families with Dependent Children (AFDC) program and converted its funding into grants for state programs. The states would have considerable flexibility in implementing their programs, but several nationwide standards would be imposed. Among these were the limitation of two consecutive years for receiving assistance, a lifetime maximum of five years, and the requirement that persons receiving this aid be actively looking for work, going to school, or performing public work.

Evaluation Although it would be years before the success of the individual state programs could be evaluated, many immediately weighed in with their assessments of the landmark reform. As regards racial and ethnic relations, groups promoting the interests of African Americans and Latinos tended to be critical of the reforms, although the United States population in general tended to support the reforms. Disagreements focused on two major issues: First, since the reforms required welfare recipients to make a quick transition to the workforce, did the nation's economic system provide opportunities for all, regardless of race and ethnicity, to earn a living wage? Second, was some form of welfare system necessary to help more people of color join the economic mainstream of society?

In general, the welfare reform of 1996 is premised on the belief that welfare should be a form of temporary assistance rather than a long-term way of life. Opponents argue that although that sentiment may be laudable, the existing economic system makes the goal of self-sufficiency unrealistic for some people. Some argue that the legacy of past racial discrimination, and perhaps even continuing discrimination, make economic self-sufficiency impossible for certain groups, at least within the parameters of the reforms.

Proponents of welfare reform counter that poverty is due to economic rather than racial factors. They further argue that the welfare system of the 1960's and 1970's created disincentives in the areas of work, education, and personal responsibility. The 1996 welfare reform attempts to create a new incentive structure that encourages work and facilitates training and education.

At the end of the twentieth century, it was unlikely that racial issues connected with welfare reform would disappear until there were no significant differences in wealth and work between different racial and ethnic groups, and it remained unclear whether the 1996 welfare reform bill or the programs being implemented at the state level would achieve that goal.

Steve D. Boilard

Core Resources

A detailed analysis of racial factors in white people's attitudes about welfare is available in Martin Gilens's "'Race Coding' and White Opposition to Welfare," in *American Political Science Review* (September, 1996). More extensive, though more dated, analysis is available in Fay Lomax Cook and Edith J. Barrett's *Support for the American Welfare State: The Views of Congress and the Public* (1992). The Public Broadcasting Service (PBS) has produced a ninety-minute documentary entitled *Ending Welfare as We Know It,* which examines how six women on welfare strive to cope with the new welfare system. The documentary was first aired in June, 1998. The Urban Institute also has examined the effects of the 1996 welfare reform program and has published its findings in "One Year After Federal Welfare Reform: A Description of State Temporary Assistance for Needy Families (TANF) Decisions as of October, 1997" (May, 1998). The report is available through the institute's internet site (http://newfederalism.urban.org/html/1year.html). A more positive evaluation is offered by Daniel Casse in "Why Welfare Reform Is Working," in *Commentary* (104, no. 3, September, 1997).

See also: Economics and race; Employment among African Americans; Welfare's impact on racial/ethnic relations.

Wilson-Willie debate

The debate between William J. Wilson and Charles V. Willie concerns a central issue in race relations: Is racial inequality primarily a product of historical forces or is it maintained by continuing racism and discrimination?

In the summer of 1977, Wilson, then a professor of sociology at the University of Chicago, reported to a meeting of the Sociological Research Association that social class had become more important than race in determining the access of African Americans to economic resources and political power. The following year, this claim became the basis of Wilson's book, *The Declining Significance of Race* (1978). Wilson maintained that racial discrimination had, historically, limited the life chances of African Americans. Under slavery and the Jim Crow system, African Americans had been legally excluded from many areas of American life. The discrimination continued as the United States became increasingly industrialized. By the 1970's, though, official discrimination had been outlawed by civil rights legislation, and unofficial discrimination had decreased greatly. However, according to Wilson, African Americans continued to experience much greater rates of poverty than whites because historical discrimination had left African Americans with fewer job skills and lower levels of education than whites.

An excerpt from Wilson's book was published in the July/August, 1978, issue of the periodical *Society*. The periodical also published a response from Harvard sociologist Charles Vert Willie, who maintained that the significance of race in American society was not declining but "inclining." Willie argued, on the basis of statistics, that African Americans suffered systematic disadvantages in income and employment, in access to education, and in housing. These disadvantages, according to Willie, could be maintained only by continuing discrimination. Further, Willie suggested that as school desegregation and affirmative action programs brought African Americans into closer contact with whites, race became more—rather than less—important in determining black identities. Middle-class African Americans, who were under pressure to constantly prove themselves, had become obsessed with race, in Willie's view.

Responding to Willie's criticism, Wilson cited evidence that African Americans were achieving higher levels of education than ever before. He argued that the black-white gap in income was steadily decreasing among the well-educated and well-trained. He granted that some of those in the black middle class might feel psychological pressure but suggested that this was an entirely different matter from having their life chances limited by racial discrimination.

The Wilson-Willie debate continued in publications throughout the 1980's. It is a central issue in race relations, one that has been compared to the famous debate between Booker T. Washington and W. E. B. Du Bois in the early twentieth century regarding how to overcome the heritage of slavery. To the extent that social class is the basis of racial inequality, the problem requires class-based solutions such as job training for all poor, black or white. To the extent that discrimination is the basis, tough laws protecting minorities and affirmative action programs may be the best types of solutions.

Carl L. Bankston III

See also: Accommodationism; Affirmative action; Black middle class/black underclass relations; Discrimination: racial and ethnic; Underclass theories.

Wisconsin v. Mitchell

Following a showing of the 1988 film *Mississippi Burning*, several African American men and boys congregated at an apartment complex to talk about the film. After a discussion of a scene in the film in which a young African American boy is beaten by a white man, the accused, Todd Mitchell, asked those who joined him outside if they were ready to go after a white man.

Walking on the opposite side of the street and saying nothing, fourteen-year-old Gregory Riddick approached the complex. Mitchell selected three individuals from the group to go after Riddick. The victim was beaten, and his tennis shoes were stolen.

In a Kenosha, Wisconsin, trial court, Mitchell was convicted as a party to the crime of aggravated battery. By Wisconsin law, this crime carried a maximum prison sentence of two years. Mitchell's sentence was extended to four years, however, under a state statute commonly known as the "hate crimes" statute. This statute provided for sentence extensions if it could be determined that the victim was selected because of his or her race, religion, color, disability, sexual orientation, national origin, or ancestry.

Mitchell appealed his conviction and the extended sentence. His conviction was upheld by the court of appeals, but the Supreme Court of Wisconsin reversed the decision of the appellate court. Wisconsin's Supreme Court held that the "hate crimes" statute violated the defendant's First Amendment protection for freedom of speech because it was unconstitutionally overbroad and punished only what the state legislature found to be offensive. Moreover, the state Supreme Court believed that this statute would have a "chilling effect" on a citizen's freedom of speech; that is, a citizen would fear reprisal for actions that might follow the utterance of prejudiced or biased speech.

The U.S. Supreme Court reversed the state court's decision. Chief Justice William H. Rehnquist wrote the opinion in this unanimous decision. The Court held that Mitchell's First Amendment rights to free speech had not been violated.

The Court pointed out that the statute was not aimed at speech but at conduct, which is not protected by the First Amendment. The Court also addressed the concern about the "chilling effect" of the statute, finding that such would not be the case and that the state Supreme Court's hypothesis was far too speculative to be entertained. This decision indicates that the Supreme Court appears ready to uphold legislation designed to enhance punishment for criminal acts based on bigotry and bias without making bigoted or biased speech itself a crime.

Donna Addkison Simmons

See also: *R.A.V. v. City of St. Paul.*

Zoning

Zoning affords local governments the power to address a range of justice issues, including the affordability of housing, the integration of neighborhoods, and the preservation of quality of life; however, zoning also raises legal questions about just compensation for the "taking" of a property's use. Almost all land in the incorporated cities and towns of the United States, and much land in the surrounding counties, is subject to land-use controls established by local ordinances. Zoning is the designating of the various parcels of land for specific purposes, such as residential, commercial, industrial, and open space. In addition to specifying permissible use, zoning ordinances typically regulate the acceptable types of construction and other improvements on the property. The benefits of zoning are obvious in terms of community planning, as they facilitate the logical and orderly development of neighborhoods, commercial districts, park lands, and sanitation districts. Zoning permits long-range planning and allows purchasers of property to know the nature of the surrounding areas once it is built out—possibly some decades in the future.

Beyond its practical benefits, zoning involves several justice issues. Particularly in terms of residential zoning, housing affordability and discrimination are relevant. By specifying maximum density (units per acre) of residential construction, zoning affects the affordability of housing through land costs. Low-density housing requirements can make housing prohibitively expensive for lower-income households. Off-street parking requirements, floor area ratios, and other zoning standards may add to housing costs. Highly restrictive zoning may effectively turn neighborhoods and even entire towns into elite enclaves. Some have gone so far as to charge that such situations amount to *de facto* racial discrimination. Conversely, a broad range of residential zoning standards in a single area (for example, including apartments, condominiums, mobile homes, and single-family homes) can encourage the creation of financially and racially integrated neighborhoods. Federal and various state fair housing laws prohibit intentional discrimination through zoning, but it is difficult to distinguish between regulations which stem from legitimate purposes, such as public health and safety, and those which unfairly place excessive "quality of life" standards above the need for affordable housing within a region.

Zoning also raises justice issues for the owners of land. By definition, land use controls such as zoning place some limits on the rights of ownership. This fact raises questions about just compensation: Do governmental restrictions upon one's land constitute a "taking" of all or part of the land's value, thus requiring compensation? Moreover, how should compensation, if necessary, be calculated? Over time, the courts have broadened the tolerable level of abridgment of property rights in the public interest. Nevertheless, standards vary from court to court and from place to place, leaving much room for controversy.

Steve D. Boilard

See also: Housing; Redlining; Restrictive covenants.

Notable African American Figures in Civil Rights History

Abernathy, Ralph David (1926-1990): Christian minister and civil rights activist; became close friends with Martin Luther King, Jr., when both took Baptist pastorates in Montgomery, Alabama, around 1951; helped coordinate the Montgomery bus boycott in 1955 and organize the Southern Christian Leadership Conference (SCLC) in 1957; succeeded King as president of the SCLC, 1968-1977; stood unsuccessfully for Congress in 1977; published a controversial autobiography, *And the Walls Came Tumbling Down* (1989), which included details of King's extramarital affairs.

Ali, Muhammad (1942-): Boxer; born Cassius Marcellus Clay, Jr., started boxing at an early age in Louisville, Kentucky; won Olympic gold medal as a light-heavyweight in 1960; converted to the Black Muslim religion and changed his name in 1964; won heavyweight championship four times (1964, 1967, 1974, 1978); stripped of title when he refused induction into the U.S. Army in 1967, though the U.S. Supreme Court reversed the draft evasion conviction in 1971; became a symbol of black pride during the 1960's.

Angelou, Maya (1928-): Novelist, poet; born Marguerite Johnson, she worked as a nightclub singer in New York and San Francisco, as an editor for the English-language *Arab Observer* (Cairo), and as a teacher of music and drama in Ghana; became a national figure with publication of the first volume of her autobiography, *I Know Why the Caged Bird Sings* (1970), detailing her experience of southern racism and sexual abuse; nominated for an Emmy Award for her performance as Nyo Boto in the television series *Roots* (1977); invited to read her poem "On the Pulse of Morning" at the inauguration of President Bill Clinton in 1993.

Asante, Molefi Kete (1942-): Scholar; born Arthur Lee Smith, Jr., but legally changed his name in 1975; after receiving a doctoral degree in communications from the University of California, Los Angeles (UCLA) in 1968, taught at Purdue, UCLA, State University of New York, Howard University, and Temple University; named director of the Center for Afro-American Studies at UCLA; wrote more than two dozen books, including *Afrocentricity: The Theory of Social Change* (1980), *African Culture: The Rhythms of Unity* (1985), and *The Historical and Cultural Atlas of African-Americans* (1991); was founding editor of the *Journal of Black Studies.*

Baker, Josephine (1903-1986): Civil rights activist; after graduating as valedictorian with a bachelor's degree from Shaw Boarding School in 1927, moved to New York City where she became deeply involved with progressive politics; became director of the Young Negroes Cooperative League in 1931, helping to provide reasonably priced food to members during the Depression (1930's); worked with the literacy program of the Works Progress Administration; set up and directed branch offices of the National Association for the Advancement of Colored People during the 1940's; moved to Atlanta to work with the Southern Christian Leadership Conference in 1958; was unofficial adviser to the Student Nonviolent Coordinating Committee in the 1960's; helped organize the Mississippi Freedom Democratic Party; raised money for freedom fighters in Rhodesia and South Africa.

Baldwin, James Arthur (1924-1987): Author and playwright; often praised for his ability to make readers feel the destructive power of racial prejudice on both blacks and whites; his books include two autobiographical works, *Notes of a Native Son* (1955) and *Nobody Knows My Name* (1961); several powerful novels, including *Go Tell It on the Mountain* (1953), *Another Country* (1962), and *Just Above My Head* (1979); and a number of plays, including *Blues for Mister Charlie* (1964) and *The Amen Corner* (1964); spent the final years of his life in France, where he was made commander of the Legion of Honor, France's highest civilian award.

Baraka, Imamu Amiri (1934-): Poet, playwright; born LeRoi Jones, founded *Yugen* magazine and Totem Press in 1958 and the Black Arts Repertory Theater in 1964; achieved fame with honest treatment of racism in plays such as *Dutchman* (1964), *The Slave* (1966), and *Four Revolutionary Plays* (1968); was leading spokesperson for the Black Power movement in Newark, New Jersey, heading the activist Temple of Kawaida; chair of the National Black Political Convention in 1972.

Bethune, Mary McLeod (1875-1955): Educator; after teaching at various schools in Georgia and Florida, founded the Daytona Educational and Industrial School for Negro Girls in 1904 and McLeod Hospital in 1911; the Daytona school merged with the Cookman Institute to become Bethune-Cookman College in 1922, with Bethune serving as president until 1942; served on conferences under Herbert Hoover in the 1920's; served as director of the Division of Negro Affairs of the National Youth Administration, 1936-1944; was special assistant to the secretary of war during World War II; served as special adviser on minority affairs to President Franklin D. Roosevelt, 1935-1944; played important roles in the National Urban League, National Association for the Advancement of Colored People, and National Council of Negro Women.

Bond, Julian (1940-): Politician, civil rights activist; student founder of the Committee on Appeal for Human Rights; attracted attention of Martin Luther King, Jr., and helped found the Student Nonviolent Coordinating Committee, serving as its first director of communications, 1961-1966; was Democratic member of the Georgia house of representatives, 1965-1975, and the Georgia senate, 1975-1987; helped found the Southern Poverty Law Center in 1971; served as president of the Atlanta branch of the National Association for the Advancement of Colored People (NAACP), 1974-1989; appointed chair of the NAACP in 1998; hosted the television program *America's Black Forum* and narrated the Public Broadcasting Service civil rights series *Eyes on the Prize.*

Bradley, Thomas (1917-1998): Politician; held various positions with the Los Angeles Police Department, 1940-1961; after earning a law degree in the 1950's, became the first African American elected to the Los Angeles city council, 1963-1973; served as mayor of Los Angeles, 1973-1989; was a founding member of the Black Achievers Committee of the National Association for the Advancement of Colored People.

Braun, Carol Moseley (1947-): Politician; assistant U.S. attorney for the northern district of Illinois, 1973-1977; served as Illinois state representative, 1979-1987, establishing a reputation as an ardent supporter of civil rights legislation; was Cook County recorder of deeds, 1987-1993; became first African American woman to be elected to the U.S. Senate (Democrat, Illinois) in 1992. She served from 1993-1999.

Brown, H. Rap (1943-): Civil rights activist; became leader of the Student Nonviolent Coordinating Committee in 1967; charged with inciting riot in Cambridge, Maryland, in 1968 and convicted of carrying a gun across state lines; published *Die Nigger Die* (1969); while in prison for a robbery conviction, converted to Islam, taking the name Jamil Abdullah Al-Amin; leader of Community Mosque in Atlanta, Georgia.

Bruce, Blanche Kelso (1841-1898): Politician; born a slave, after the Civil War built a fortune as a plantation owner; served in various local and state positions in Mississippi; was a U.S. senator from Mississippi (Republican), 1875-1881, and became the first African American to serve a full term; was a staunch defender of black, Chinese, and American Indian rights; worked with U.S. register of treasury, 1881-1889, 1895-1898; worked as recorder of deeds, District of Columbia, 1889-1895.

Bunche, Ralph (1904-1971): Diplomat; head of the department of political science, Howard University, 1928-1932; during World War II served as senior social analyst for the Office of the Coordinator of Information in African and Far Eastern Affairs and with the African section of the Office of Strategic Services; recognized as a colonial expert when he joined the State Department in 1944; served as delegate or adviser to nine international conferences in four years; was chief assistant on the United Nations Palestine Commission; became first African American to receive the Nobel Peace Prize in 1950, for his role in the Arab-Israeli cease-fire of 1948-1949; served as U.N. undersecretary of Special Political Affairs, 1957-1967, and undersecretary general of the United Nations, 1968-1971.

Carmichael, Stokely (1941-1998): Political activist; born in Trinidad; after attending Howard University, he became an accomplished organizer for the Student Nonviolent Coordinating Committee (SNCC) of which he was elected chair in 1966; popularized the controversial phrase "black power" as well as radical policies, which led to his expulsion from SNCC in 1968; joined the Black Panther Party in 1968, but resigned the following year and moved to Guinea, Africa; since the 1970's consistently supported Pan-Africanism; changed his name in 1978 to Kwame Toure, in honor of African leaders Sékou Touré and Kwame Nkrumah.

Chavis, Benjamin (1948-): Civil rights activist; after training as a theologian, became a civil rights organizer for the Southern Christian Leadership Conference and the United Church of Christ; indicted in 1971 as one of the Wilmington Ten for the firebombing of a store in Wilmington, Delaware; convicted but granted parole, his conviction was reversed in 1980; appointed executive director of the Commission for Racial Justice in 1985; served as executive director of the National Association for the Advancement of Colored People, 1993-1994, a position from which he was forced to resign because of a financial scandal; served as national director of the 1995 Million Man March.

Chisholm, Shirley (1924-): Politician; after an early career in child care and education, elected New York State assemblywoman in 1964; served as U.S. representative (Democrat), 1969-1983, becoming the first African American woman in Congress; published her autobiography, *Unbossed and Unbought* (1970); cofounded the National Political Congress of Black Women.

Cleaver, Eldridge (1935-1998): Civil rights activist; after serving a prison sentence from 1958 to 1966, joined the Black Panther Party and became one of the most vocal proponents of the doctrine of black power; his book *Soul on Ice* (1968) became one of the most powerful statements of the movement; after involvement in a 1968 shooting, fled to Algeria; returned to the United States in 1975.

Cone, James (1938-): Theologian; faculty member at Union Theological Seminary from 1969; provided systematic case for divine support of the black liberation struggle in the United States and elsewhere; wrote many books, including *Black Theology and Black Power* (1969), *For My People: Black Theology and the Black Church* (1984), and *Martin and Malcolm and America: A Dream or a Nightmare?* (1991).

Cosby, Bill (1937-): Actor, comedian; by the mid-1960's, was playing top nightclubs with his comedy routine and regularly appearing on television; became first African American star of prime time television with three-time Emmy-winning role in *I Spy* (1965-1968); throughout the 1970's appeared in films and television series and in Las Vegas, Reno, and Tahoe nightclubs; *The Cosby Show* (1985-1992) presented upper-middle-class black family life to mainstream American audiences; earned five Grammy Awards; wrote *Fatherhood* (1986) and *TimeFlies* (1987), and starred in other television series.

Crummell, Alexander (1819-1898): Christian minister, author; born in New York City; after earning a degree at Queens College, Cambridge, in England, served as professor of mental and moral science at the College of Liberia, 1853-1873; was minister of St. Luke's Protestant Episcopal Church in Washington, D.C., 1876-1898; helped found the American Negro Academy in 1897; published many books, including *Future of Africa* (1862) and *Africa and America* (1892).

Davis, Angela (1944-): Political activist, scholar; after an extensive education at Brandeis University, the Sorbonne, and the University of Frankfurt, took a teaching job at the University of California, Los Angeles; joined the Communist Party in 1969; became involved with the Black Panther Party and was implicated in a courtroom shooting in 1970; went underground but eventually was arrested; acquitted of all charges in 1972; cochair of the National Alliance against Racism and Political Repression; wrote *If They Come in the Morning* (1971), *Women, Race, and Class* (1983), and *Women, Culture, and Politics* (1989).

Delany, Martin Robison (1812-1885): Doctor, author, abolitionist; born in West Virginia but fled north when it was learned that he could read; edited *The Mystery* and *The North Star* in support of the antislavery movement; disappointed with treatment of blacks in the United States, he recommended founding an African American colony in Africa or South America; first African American commissioned a major in the U.S. Army in 1863; published *Principal of Ethnology: The Origin of Races and Color* (1879).

Douglass, Frederick (c. 1817-1895): Abolitionist; fled slavery in 1838; brilliant orator who became famous as an agent of the Massachusetts Anti-Slavery Society in the 1840's; published *Narrative of the Life of Frederick Douglass* (1845); lectured in England and Ireland, 1845-1847, earning enough money to purchase his freedom; founded and served as coeditor of *The North Star*, 1847-1860 (*Frederick Douglass's Paper* from 1851); opposed radical abolitionism of William Lloyd Garrison and John Brown; was U.S. marshal for District of Columbia, 1877-1881; was recorder of deeds, District of Columbia, 1881-1886; served as U.S. minister to Haiti, 1889-1891.

Du Bois, W. E. B. (1868-1963): Civil rights activist, scholar, author; leader of the Niagara Movement, 1905-1909; helped found the National Association for the Advancement of Colored People (NAACP), 1909; acted as director of publications for the NAACP and editor of *The Crisis*, 1909-1934; was a professor of sociology at Atlanta University, 1932-1944; served as head of special research department of the NAACP, 1944-1948; dissatisfied with the pace of racial change, joined the Communist Party and emigrated to Africa in 1961 to become editor in chief of the Pan-Africanist *Encyclopedia Africana*, sponsored by Ghanaian president Kwame Nkrumah; wrote numerous books, including *The Souls of Black Folk* (1903), *The Negro* (1915), *The Gift of Black Folk* (1924), *Color and Democracy* (1945), *The World and Africa* (1947), and the *Black Flame* trilogy (1957-1961).

Evers, Medgar (1925-1963): Civil rights activist; appointed Mississippi field secretary of the National Association for the Advancement of Colored People, 1954; actively fought for enforcement of school integration and advocated the right of blacks to vote and the boycotting of merchants who discriminated against African Americans; when murdered in 1963 became one of the first martyrs of the Civil Rights movement.

Farmer, James (1920-   ): Civil rights leader; organizer of the Congress of Racial Equality (CORE), 1942, the first nonviolent protest organization;

staged the first successful sit-in, at a Chicago restaurant in 1943; program director of the National Association for the Advancement of Colored People, 1959-1961; introduced the tactic of the Freedom Ride in 1961 to test principles of desegregation; left CORE in 1966; appointed assistant secretary of health, education, and welfare in 1969; became associate director of the Coalition of American Public Employees in 1976.

Farrakhan, Louis (1933-): Minister; born Louis Eugene Walcott; joined the Nation of Islam in the 1950's; denounced Malcolm X (following his split with Elijah Muhammad) and succeeded him as leader of the Harlem mosque; left Nation of Islam when it began to accept whites in the mid-1970's, founding a rival organization, later known by the same name; supported Jesse Jackson in the 1984 presidential campaign, marking a turning point in Black Muslim political involvement; organized 1995 Million Man March.

Father Divine (1879-1965): Religious leader; probably born George Baker; early life mysterious; joined various Christian sects before returning to native Georgia around 1910 to proclaim himself a "divine messenger"; driven from Georgia, settled in New York City in 1915, where he fed the poor and homeless and established a communitarian religious group based on racial equality; his Peace Mission movement spread in the 1930's and 1940's, becoming a cult in which Father Divine was worshiped as God incarnate on earth.

Forten, James (1766-1842): Abolitionist, entrepreneur; born of free parents in Philadelphia, served aboard a privateer during the American Revolution; captured and held prisoner for seven months; while in England became acquainted with abolitionist philosophy; by 1798 owned a prosperous maritime company; became active in the abolitionist movement in the 1830's, including membership in the American Anti-Slavery Society; helped raise funds for William Lloyd Garrison's newspaper *The Liberator*; founded the American Moral Reform Society.

Fortune, T. Thomas (1856-1928): Journalist, editor; worked in various positions for the *New York Sun* from 1878; founded the *New York Age* (1883), the leading black journal of opinion in the United States; crusaded against school segregation; joined Booker T. Washington in organizing the National Negro Business League in 1900; coined the term "Afro-American" as a substitute for "Negro" in the New York press.

Garvey, Marcus (1887-1940): Black nationalist leader; Jamaican-born founder of the Universal Negro Improvement Association (UNIA) in 1914; came to United States in 1916, founding branches of the UNIA in northern ghettos; at the UNIA's first convention in New York City in 1920, outlined plan for the establishment of an African nation-state for black Americans; preached racial pride through civil rights and economic self-sufficiency; convicted of fraud in 1925; sentence commuted by President Calvin Coolidge and deported to Jamaica in 1927, where he continued to be active in progressive politics.

Gordy, Berry, Jr. (1929-): Songwriter, producer; served with U.S. Army in Korea; after a number of failed or unsatisfying jobs in Detroit, Michigan, began writing hit songs with his sister Gwen and Billy Davis; formed Motown Record Corporation and a number of related businesses in 1959; by the mid-1960's had brought black soul music to mainstream American audiences with highly polished performances by artists such as the Supremes, Smokey Robinson, the Four Tops, the Marvelettes, Marvin Gaye, the Jackson Five, Lionel Richie, and Stevie Wonder; inducted into the Rock and Roll Hall of Fame in 1988.

Grace, Charles Emmanuel "Sweet Daddy" (1881-1960): Religious leader; born Marcelino Manoel de Graca in the Cape Verde Islands; established the United House of Prayer for All People (c. 1921), with ministry style rooted in faith healing and speaking in tongues; products such as "Daddy Grace" coffee, tea, and creams were believed to heal; by 1960, his church had some 25,000 adherents in 375 congregations.

Graves, Earl (1935-): Publisher, editor; officer, U.S. Army Green Berets, 1957-1960; administrative assistant to Robert F. Kennedy, 1964-1968; launched *Black Enterprise* (1970) to provide African Americans with practical help for succeeding in business; by the late 1990's, *Black Enterprise* had a subscription base of more than 300,000; wrote *How to Succeed in Business Without Being White* (1997).

Haley, Alex (1921-1992): Journalist, author; chief journalist for the U.S. Coast Guard, 1952-1959; interviewed Malcolm X for *Playboy*, which led to his first book, *The Autobiography of Malcolm X* (1965); spent a dozen years researching family history, leading to publication of the novel *Roots* (1976), based on the life of a West African youth named Kunta Kinte who was brought to America as a slave; the novel led to a twelve-hour television series, hundreds of interviews and articles, instructional packets and tapes, and sparked intense interest in African American genealogy and history.

Hamer, Fannie Lou (1917-1977): Civil rights activist; after forty years of work on the same plantation, lost her job when she tried to vote; began working with the Student Nonviolent Coordinating Committee to register black voters in 1962; helped form the Mississippi Freedom Democratic Party and spoke eloquently in favor of seating black delegates to the Democratic National Convention in 1964; became one of the first delegates to the Democratic convention in 1968; founded Freedom Farms Corporation, 1969; toured and spoke widely on behalf of civil rights legislation.

Hill, Anita (1956-): Professor of law; a relatively unknown law professor at the University of Oklahoma when she gained national attention during Senate confirmation hearings for U.S. Supreme Court justice nominee Clarence Thomas in 1991; charged that she had been sexually harassed when working for Thomas at the Equal Employment Opportunities Commission in the early 1980's; withstood attempts by some lawmakers to have the University of Oklahoma Law School fire her; spoke widely around the country throughout the 1990's in favor of civil rights and women's rights.

Hooks, Benjamin (1925-): Lawyer, preacher, civil rights leader; first African American to serve as judge in criminal court in Shelby County, Tennessee; served as executive director of the National Association for the Advancement of Colored People, 1977-1992, where he vigorously promoted integration, pro-African foreign policy, and employment legislation.

Hughes, Langston (1902-1967): Writer; after dropping out of Columbia University, wrote poetry and worked as a cabin boy on a freighter; major figure in the 1920's Harlem Renaissance; "The Negro Writer and the Racial Mountain" (1926) established an early ethic of black pride; wrote in many fields, including poetry (*The Weary Blues*, 1926; *Fine Clothes to the Jew*, 1927; *Shakespeare in Harlem*, 1942; *Montage of a Dream Deferred*, 1951); librettos (*Street Scene*, 1947); plays (*Mulatto*, 1935); and autobiography (*The Big Sea*, 1940; *I Wonder as I Wander*, 1956).

Innis, Roy (1934-): Civil rights leader; joined Congress of Racial Equality (CORE) in 1963, becoming national director in 1968; founded Harlem Commonwealth Council designed to promote black businesses; controversy over recruitment of black Vietnam veterans for the civil war in Angola and misappropriation of funds led to important defections from CORE, which became largely inactive in the 1980's.

Jackson, Jesse (1941-): Civil rights activist, Baptist minister; joined the Southern Christian Leadership Conference (SCLC) in 1965; served as executive director of SCLC's Operation Breadbasket, 1967-1971; founded Operation PUSH (People United to Save Humanity) in 1971; his PUSH-EXCEL program for encouraging young students to improve academically received funding from the administration of U.S. president Jimmy Carter, 1977-1981; ran for the Democratic nomination for president in 1984 and 1988; finished a strong second to Michael Dukakis in 1988, demonstrating the viability of an African American candidate; continued to press for child care, health care reform, housing reform, and statehood for the District of Columbia.

Johnson, Jack (1878-1946): Boxer; first black heavyweight champion, 1908-1915; became the center of racial controversy as the public called for Jim Jeffries, the white former champion, to come out of retirement; Johnson defeated Jeffries in 1910.

Johnson, James Weldon (1871-1938): Poet, diplomat, civil rights leader; as a young man known principally as a lyricist for popular songs, including "Lift Every Voice and Sing" (1899); served as U.S. consul in Puerto Cabello, Venezuela, 1906-1909, and Corinto, Nicaragua, 1909-1912; was executive secretary of the National Association for the Advancement of Colored People, 1920-1930; wrote many books, including *The Autobiography of an Ex-Colored Man* (1912), *The Book of American Negro Poetry* (1922), *God's Trombones* (1927), and *Negro Americans, What Now* (1934).

Johnson, John H. (1918-): Publisher; addressed the need for mainstream black publications with the establishment of the *Negro Digest* (1942) and *Ebony* (1945); member of advisory council of Harvard Graduate School of Business; director for the Chamber of Commerce of the United States.

Jordan, Vernon (1935-): Lawyer, civil rights leader; field secretary for the Georgia Branch of the National Association for the Advancement of Colored People, 1962-1964; director of the Voter Education Project of the Southern Regional Council, 1964-1968; appointed executive director of the United Negro College Fund, 1970-1972; served as executive director of the National Urban League, 1972-1981; became political confidante of President Bill Clinton in 1992.

King, Martin Luther, Jr. (1929-1968): Civil rights activist, Baptist minister; received doctorate from Crozer Theological Seminary, 1955; accepted pastorate of the Dexter Avenue Baptist Church in Montgomery, Alabama, in 1956; organized the Montgomery bus boycott in 1956; founded the Southern Christian Leadership Conference, serving as first president in 1957; was copastor of Ebenezer Baptist Church, Atlanta, 1960-1968; arrested for protesting segregation and unfair hiring practices in Birmingham, Alabama, in 1963, leading to his classic "Letter from a Birmingham Jail"; delivered his "I Have a Dream" speech at the historic March on Washington in 1963; *Time* Man of the Year in 1963; awarded Nobel Peace Prize in 1964; began to speak out forcefully against the Vietnam War and urban poverty, leading many black leaders to question his tactics in achieving full civil rights; assassinated in Memphis, Tennessee, in 1968; consistently promoted a policy of nonviolent protest. (See also article in the main text.)

Lee, Spike (1957-): Filmmaker; while attending New York University's Institute of Film and Television, won the Student Award presented by the Academy of Motion Picture Arts and Sciences for *Joe's Bed-Sty Barbershop: We Cut Heads* (1982); his controversial films, highlighting past and present struggles of African Americans in a land of alien values, include *She's Gotta Have It* (1986), *Do the Right Thing* (1989), *Mo' Better Blues* (1990), *Malcolm X* (1992), and *He Got Game* (1998).

Locke, Alain (1886-1954): Philosopher, writer; after study at Harvard University, Oxford University, and the University of Berlin, served on faculty at Howard University, 1912-1953; celebrated black cultural contributions in works such as *The New Negro: An Interpretation* (1925) and a special issue of the journal *Survey Graphic*, which announced the arrival of a "Harlem Renaissance" and published work by Langston Hughes, Zora Neale Hurston, and W. E. B. Du Bois; also wrote or edited *Race Contacts and Inter-Racial Relations* (1916), *Opportunity* (an annual review of the state of black writing), *Negro Art: Past and Present* (1936), and *The Negro and His Music* (1940).

Lowery, Joseph E. (1924-): Pastor, civil rights leader; pastor of the

Warren Street Church in Birmingham, Alabama, 1952-1961; cofounder of the Southern Negro Leaders Conference (later the Southern Christian Leadership Conference, SCLC) in 1957, serving as its first vice president under Martin Luther King, Jr.; became president of the SCLC in 1977; pastor of Cascade United Methodist Church in Atlanta from 1986.

McKissick, Floyd (1922-1991): Lawyer, civil rights leader; sued the University of North Carolina at Chapel Hill for admission to their law school and became the first African American to earn a degree there; head of Congress fn Racial Equality, 1966-1968; between 1968 and 1980 worked unsuccessfully to establish a new and self-sufficient community in Warren County, North Carolina, known as Soul City.

Malcolm X (1925-1965): Black nationalist; born Malcolm Little, to a family committed to Marcus Garvey's United Negro Improvement Association; after his father's murder, left school for New York, where he was convicted of burglary; converted to Nation of Islam while in prison; a brilliant speaker, he began making provocative, anti-white statements, for which he was expelled from the Nation of Islam by Elijah Muhammad; formed Organization of Afro-American Unity and Muslim Mosque Inc. in 1964; after pilgrimage to Mecca, converted to orthodox Islam, took the name El-Hajj Malik El-Shabazz, and moderated his views; shot to death by Black Muslims; author (with Alex Haley) of *The Autobiography of Malcolm X* (1965).

Marshall, Thurgood (1908-1993): Lawyer, judge, civil rights activist; served as chief legal counsel for the National Association for the Advancement of Colored People, 1938-1961; played key role in *Brown v. Board of Education* case (1954), in which the U.S. Supreme Court overturned the "separate but equal" doctrine in public education; won twenty-nine of the thirty-two cases he argued before the Supreme Court; became federal circuit judge, 1961-1967; appointed first African American associate justice of the U.S. Supreme Court, 1967-1991. (See also article in the main text.)

Meredith, James (1933-): Civil rights activist; became first African American to attend the University of Mississippi in 1962, generating riots and the stationing of federal troops on the campus; led march to encourage black voter registration in 1966, shot by sniper, but recovered; wrote *Three Years in Mississippi* (1966).

Morrison, Toni (1931-): Writer; born Chloe Anthony Wofford; incorporated African and African American folklore, legend, and mythology into her novels; works contain many autobiographical references; *Beloved* (1987), which examines the brutality of American slavery, won the Pulitzer Prize in fiction in 1988 and was adapted to film in 1998; won Nobel Prize in Literature in 1993; also wrote *The Bluest Eye* (1970), *Sula* (1974), *Song of Solomon* (1977), *Tar Baby* (1981), *Jazz* (1992), and *Paradise* (1998).

Muhammad, Elijah (1897-1975): Religious leader and black nationalist; born Elijah Poole to a former slave; became chief assistant to W. D. Fard, founder of the Lost-Found Nation of Islam, in 1930; upon Fard's disappearance in 1934, succeeded to leadership of the Nation of Islam; preached racial segregation, black integrity, and the need for economic independence from whites; support for Japan in World War II and the conviction of three members of the Nation of Islam for the assassination of Malcolm X led to unfavorable press coverage, but the movement continued to grow, especially among the underemployed of the major cities.

Newton, Huey P. (1942-1989): Black activist; cofounder, with Bobby Seale, of the Black Panther Party for Self-Defense in 1966, which became a force in California politics; convicted of manslaughter in the 1967 killing of an Oakland police officer, but the conviction was later overturned; helped elect Lionel Wilson as first black mayor of Oakland in 1977; frequently in legal trouble throughout the 1970's and 1980's; killed by a drug dealer.

Owens, Jesse (1913-1980): Track and field athlete; one of the first great all-around track and field athletes, earned four gold medals in the 1936 Berlin Olympics (100- and 200-meter races, 400-meter relay, broad jump); became internationally famous when German Nazi leader Adolf Hitler refused to honor him personally as he did other medal winners; traveled and spoke widely on the value of sport in breaking down racial barriers.

Parks, Rosa Louise McCauley (1913-): Civil rights activist; secretary of the Montgomery, Alabama, chapter of the National Association for the Advancement of Colored People in the 1950's; arrested and fined for refusing to give up her seat to a white person, sparking a 382-day citywide bus boycott aimed at desegregating public transportation; harassment led Parks and her family to move to Detroit, Michigan, where she worked in the office of Congressman John Conyers and continued to campaign for civil rights.

Patterson, Frederick D. (1901-1988): Educator; faculty member, and later president of, Tuskegee Institute from 1928; chair of the R. R. Moton Memorial Institute; organized United Negro College Fund in 1944 to aid historically black colleges and universities.

Payne, Daniel Alexander (1811-1893): Educator, bishop; born to free parents, opened a school for blacks in Charleston, South Carolina, in 1829; after his school was closed by an act of the South Carolina legislature, traveled north to study, delivering powerful abolitionist speeches throughout the 1840's and 1850's; elected bishop of the African Methodist Episcopal Church in 1852; bought Wilberforce University from the Methodist Episcopal Church in 1863 and devoted the rest of his life to developing the university and overseeing missionary endeavors; wrote *Recollections of Seventy Years* (1888) and *History of the African Methodist Episcopal Church* (1891).

Powell, Adam Clayton, Jr. (1908-1972): Politician; instrumental in securing better treatment for African Americans in Harlem during the Depression

(1930's); succeeded his father as pastor of the Abyssinian Baptist Church in 1936; served in various New York posts until 1944 when he was elected to the U.S. House of Representatives, 1945-1967, 1969-1971; sponsored more than fifty pieces of social legislation, many aimed at ending discrimination against minorities; became chairman of House Committee on Education and Labor in 1960; censured in the House and unseated in 1967 for misuse of public funds but readmitted the following year.

Powell, Colin (1937-): Military leader; served two tours of duty in Vietnam during the 1960's; military assistant to the secretary of defense in 1983; national security adviser to President Ronald Reagan, 1987-1989; served as chairman of the joint chiefs of staff, 1989-1993, from which position he gained international recognition for his role in conducting the Persian Gulf War (1991); popularity and vocal support for personal responsibility made him an attractive political candidate; addressed the 1996 Republican National Convention in San Diego, heightening rumors that he might one day run for high office.

Robeson, Paul (1898-1976): Singer, actor; son of a runaway slave; after earning a law degree from Columbia University, was discovered by playwright Eugene O'Neill and became a successful stage actor in the 1920's; performance in *Emperor Jones* (1923) led to a successful singing career, including 1925 concert debut of all-African-American music; active in national and international civil and human rights campaigns, he spoke out vigorously for independence for African colonies; trips to the Soviet Union and other association with communists led to the government's revocation of his passport in 1950 and a decline in his career; regained passport after an eight-year legal battle in 1958 and moved to London, where he lived until 1963; wrote *Here I Stand* (1958).

Robinson, Jackie (1919-1972): Baseball player; after a stellar career at the University of California, Los Angeles, left in his junior year to play professional football for the Los Angeles Bulldogs, and then to serve as a lieutenant in the U.S. Army during World War II; played baseball with the Kansas City Monarchs of the Negro American League in 1945; became the first black player in modern major league baseball in 1947, beginning a ten-year career with the Brooklyn Dodgers; responded to much public hostility with grace and outstanding play, paving the way for expansion of opportunities for black athletes; inducted into Baseball Hall of Fame in 1962.

Rustin, Bayard (1910-1987): Civil rights leader; organizer of the Young Communist League, 1936-1941; worked with James Farmer in the Chicago Committee of Racial Equality, which developed into the Congress of Racial Equality; was a founding member of the Southern Christian Leadership Conference, 1963; served as organizational coordinator of the 1963 March on Washington; was executive director of the A. Philip Randolph Institute, 1964-1979; founded Organization for Black Americans to Support Israel in 1975; consistent supporter of nonviolent change.

Scott, Dred (1795-1858): Slave, abolitionist; attempted to escape and buy freedom; with help from attorneys, sued for his freedom on the grounds that he had accompanied his master into the free state of Illinois; U.S. Supreme Court ruled in 1857 that Scott, as a slave, was not a legal citizen and therefore had no standing before the courts; freed by owner shortly before his death.

Seale, Bobby (1936-): Black activist; cofounder, with Huey P. Newton, of the Black Panther Party for Self-Defense in 1966; mistrial declared in his 1971 trial for the kidnapping and killing of a suspected police informant; disenchanted with revolutionary politics, left the Panthers in 1974; wrote *Seize the Time: The Story of the Black Panther Party* (1970) and *A Lonely Rage: The Autobiography of Bobby Seale* (1978).

Sharpton, Al (1954-): Pentecostal minister, social activist; after gaining prominence for his preaching in Brooklyn, became active in the Civil Rights movement; appointed youth director of Jesse Jackson's Operation Breadbasket; briefly served as a bodyguard for singer James Brown and became involved with fight promoter Don King; founded the National Youth Movement (later the United African Movement) in 1971; involved with many high-profile racial incidents in New York City, including the Bernhard Goetz murder trial in 1984, the Howard Beach killing in 1986, the Tawana Brawley affair in 1987, and the Bensonhurst killing in 1989; controversial figure whose motives have been questioned by many.

Truth, Sojourner (c. 1797-1883): Abolitionist; born Isabella Baumfree, she was freed by the New York State Emancipation Act in 1827; preached and lectured widely to abolitionist audiences, taking the name Sojourner Truth in 1843; raised money to aid runaway slaves and soldiers during the Civil War; served as councilor with the National Freedmen's Relief Association, 1864; dictated *The Narrative of Sojourner Truth* (1850).

Tubman, Harriet (c. 1820-1913): Civil rights activist; born Araminta Ross, escaped slavery in 1848; rescued more than three hundred slaves before the Civil War in nineteen forays along the Underground Railroad; aided John Brown in recruiting soldiers for his raid on Harper's Ferry, 1858; spoke widely on emancipation and women's rights after 1860; served as nurse and spy for the Union army during the Civil War; buried with military honors.

Turner, Henry McNeal (1834-1915): Religious leader; born to free parents; tutored by lawyers for whom he worked as a janitor; became a preacher in the Methodist Episcopal Church South, 1853; switched affiliation and preached for African Methodist Episcopal (AME) churches in Baltimore, Maryland, and Washington, D.C., 1858-1863; was chaplain of First U.S. Colored Troops, 1863; served as Georgia state representative, 1868-1869, 1870; elected AME bishop in 1880; supported voting rights for blacks and advocated a return to Africa when the Civil Rights Act was overturned by the Supreme Court in 1883; proclaimed that "God is a Negro"; forerunner of modern black theology.

Walker, Alice (1944-): Writer; poet; her works deal principally with the experience of black women living in a racist and sexist society; early books were critically acclaimed, though she did not become widely popular until she published her third novel, *The Color Purple* (1982), which won a Pulitzer Prize in fiction and was adapted to film in 1985; champion of the works of Zora Neale Hurston; published in several genres, including poetry: *Once* (1968) and *Revolutionary Petunias and Other Poems* (1973); novels: *The Third Life of Grange Copeland* (1970), *Meridian* (1976), and *Possessing the Secret of Joy* (1992); short stories: "In Love and Trouble" (1973) and "You Can't Keep a Good Woman Down" (1976); and criticism: *A Zora Neale Hurston Reader* (1980).

Washington, Booker T. (1856-1915): Educator, political activist; born a slave, became committed to the idea that education would raise African Americans to equality; taught American Indians at Hampton Institute, 1879-1881; founded Tuskegee Normal and Industrial Institute, 1881, and served as its president; founded National Negro Business League, 1900; advised Presidents William Howard Taft and Theodore Roosevelt on racial issues; promoted what is sometimes called the "Atlanta Compromise," accepting segregation of African Americans in return for economic opportunities; his conservative racial views appealed to many white Americans who feared more radical change; wrote *Up from Slavery* (1901); opposed by W. E. B. Du Bois.

Wells-Barnett, Ida B. (1862-1931): Editor; editor and part owner of the black newspaper *Memphis Free Speech* from 1889; campaigned vigorously against lynching, leading to a mob attack on the newspaper's offices; with Frederick Douglass and Ferdinand L. Barnett, wrote "The Reason Why the Colored American Is Not in the World's Columbian Exposition" (1893); published the antilynching pamphlet, "Red Record" (1895); defended W. E. B. Du Bois's criticism of Booker T. Washington in *The Souls of Black Folk*; helped found the National Association for the Advancement of Colored People, 1909.

Wilkins, Roy (1901-1981): Journalist, civil rights leader; on the staff of the Kansas City *Call*, 1923-1931; served as assistant executive secretary of the National Association for the Advancement of Colored People (NAACP), 1931-1955; succeeded W. E. B. Du Bois as editor of *The Crisis*, 1934-1949; was executive secretary of the NAACP, 1955-1964; served as executive director of the NAACP, 1965-1977; chairman of the Leadership Conference on Civil Rights.

Woodson, Carter (1875-1950): Scholar; known as the "Father of Modern Black History"; formed the Association for the Study of Negro Life and History (later the Association for the Study of Afro-American Life and History), 1915, which established the *Journal of Negro History* (1916); founded Associated Publishers, 1920, and Negro History Bulletin, 1921; created Negro History Week (later Black History Month); wrote many books, including *The Education of the Negro Prior to 1861* (1915); *The Negro* *in Our History* (1922), *The Miseducation of the Negro* (1933), and *African Heroes and Heroines* (1939).

Wright, Richard (1908-1960): Novelist; member of the Communist Party, 1933-1944; used personal experience from his Mississippi youth to dramatize the brutal effects of racism in books such as *Uncle Tom's Children* (Best Work of Fiction by a Works Progress Administration writer, 1938), *Native Son* (1940), and the largely autobiographical *Black Boy* (1945); moved to Paris in 1946; there continued writing, including *The Outsider* (1953), *Black Power* (1954), *White Man Listen* (1957), and *Eight Men* (1961); *American Hunger* (1977) was a continuation of his autobiography.

Young, Andrew (1932-): Civil rights activist, politician, diplomat; aide and confidant of Martin Luther King, Jr., in the early 1960's; was executive vice president of the Southern Christian Leadership Conference, 1967; served as Georgia state representative, 1973-1977; was U.S. ambassador to the United Nations, 1977-1979; served as mayor of Atlanta, 1981-1989; chair of the Atlanta Committee for the Olympic Games.

Young, Whitney (1921-1971): Educator, civil rights leader; executive director of the St. Paul chapter of the Minnesota Urban League, 1950-1954; was dean of Atlanta University School of Social Work, 1954-1961; served as executive director of National Urban League, 1961-1971; called for a "domestic Marshall Plan" to end black poverty, and helped President Lyndon B. Johnson craft his War on Poverty; received Medal of Freedom in 1969; wrote *To Be Equal* (1964) and *Beyond Racism* (1969).

John Powell

Time Line

1619 First Africans are brought to the Colony of Virginia as indentured servants.

1641 Massachusetts Colony recognizes the legality of slavery.

1662 British government grants a monopoly to the Royal African Slave Company, marking the shift away from indentured servitude toward slavery.

1662 Virginia legislature rules that children of unions of slave and free parents are slave or free according to their mothers' status.

1664 Maryland enacts the first law outlawing marriage between white women and black men.

1688 Pennsylvania Mennonites protest slavery.

1691 Virginia law restricts manumissions to prevent the growth of a free black class.

1705 Virginia bars African Americans and Indians from holding ecclesiastic, civil, or military offices.

1712 Slave revolt in New York results in the execution of twenty-one slaves and the suicides of six others.

1723 Virginia denies African Americans the right to vote.

1775 First abolitionist organization in the United States, the Pennsylvania Society for the Abolition of Slavery, is formed.

1793 Virginia outlaws entry of free African Americans into the state.

1793 Fugitive Slave Act requires the return of escaped slaves to their owners.

1793 Invention of the cotton gin encourages the spread of slavery in the South.

1808 Federal government bans importation of slaves into the United States, but illegal importation continues.

1820 Congress enacts the Missouri Compromise, under which Missouri is admitted to the Union as a slave state, Maine is admitted as a free state, and slavery is prohibited in the remaining territories north of Missouri's southern boundary.

1822 Denmark Vesey is executed for conspiring to lead a slave insurrection in South Carolina.

1827 First African American newspaper, *Freedman's Journal*, is published.

1831 Nat Turner leads a slave insurrection in Virginia.

1832 New England Anti-Slavery Society is organized.

1843 Sojourner Truth begins giving abolitionist lectures.

1852 Harriet Beecher Stowe publishes *Uncle Tom's Cabin*, which attacks slavery.

1854 Republican Party is founded by antislavery members of the Whig, Democratic, and Free Soil parties.

1857 Supreme Court's *Dred Scott* decision declares that African Americans are not citizens of the United States and that the Missouri Compromise is unconstitutional.

1859 Abolitionist John Brown is hanged after his raid on the federal arsenal at Harpers Ferry, Virginia.

1861 Civil War begins (April).

1863 President Abraham Lincoln issues the Emancipation Proclamation, declaring slaves in states still in rebellion against the Union to be free (January 1).

1865 Civil War ends (April 9).

1865 Ratification of the Thirteenth Amendment to the U.S. Constitution prohibits slavery or other involuntary servitude (December).

1865 Southern states begin to enforce black laws, which severely limit liberties of newly freed African Americans.

1865 Ku Klux Klan is founded in Tennessee.

1866 Congress enacts the Civil Rights Act of 1866, declaring that persons born in the United States are, without regard to race, citizens of the United States entitled to equal protection of the law.

1867 Congress passes the first Reconstruction Act, which divides the former Confederate states into five military districts (March).

1868 Ratification of the Fourteenth Amendment grants citizenship to all persons born in the United States, without regard to race, and requires states to accord individuals equal protection of the law and due process of the law (July).

1870 Ratification of the Fifteenth Amendment guarantees the right to vote without regard to race, color, or previous condition of servitude (February).

1871 Congress enacts the Ku Klux Klan Act in an attempt to restrain the violence perpetrated by the organization.

1875 Congress enacts the Civil Rights Act of 1875, prohibiting racial discrimination in transportation, hotels, inns, theaters, and places of public amusement.

1877 Reconstruction ends as President Rutherford B. Hayes withdraws the last Union troops from the South.

1879 Supreme Court's *Strauder v. West Virginia* decision holds that exclusion of African Americans from jury service violates the equal protection clause.

1881 Booker T. Washington founds the Tuskegee Institute.

1883 Supreme Court's *Civil Rights* cases decision declares the Civil Rights Act of 1875 unconstitutional.

1896 Supreme Court's *Plessy v. Ferguson* decision establishes the separate-but-equal principle by holding that a legally mandated provision for separate railway cars for whites and blacks does not violate the equal protection clause.

1899 Supreme Court's *Cumming v. Richmond County Board of Education* decision holds that a school district can provide high school education for white students but not for blacks.

1905 Niagara Movement, predecessor of the National Association for the Advancement of Colored People, is organized with the help of W. E. B. Du Bois.

1909 National Association for the Advancement of Colored People (NAACP) is founded.

1911 National Urban League is organized to protect the rights of African Americans who migrate to northern cities from the South.

1915 Supreme Court's *Guinn v. United States* decision invalidates state voter literacy requirements intended to prevent African Americans from voting.

1915 *The Birth of a Nation*, pathbreaking feature film about the Civil War and Reconstruction, demonstrates the pervasiveness of anti-black racism in the United States.

1916 Marcus Garvey arrives in the United States from Jamaica and becomes a leading advocate of black nationalism.

1920 American Civil Liberties Union (ACLU) is founded.

1927 Supreme Court's *Nixon v. Herndon* decision finds unconstitutional the exclusion of blacks from voting in state Democratic primaries.

1930 Wallace Fard founds the Nation of Islam.

1931 Trial of the Scottsboro Nine begins in Alabama.

1935 Supreme Court's *Grovey v. Townsend* decision upholds a state Democratic Party's limitation of membership to whites.

1935 Mary McLeod Bethune founds the National Council of Negro Women.

1938 Supreme Court's *Missouri ex rel. Gaines v. Canada* decision holds that refusal of a state to allow African Americans to attend a state's only public law school violates the equal protection clause.

1939 NAACP creates the Legal Defense and Educational Fund to oppose racially discriminatory laws, and Thurgood Marshall takes charge of these efforts.

1941 In response to A. Philip Randolph's call for African Americans to march on Washington to protest racial discrimination in the armed forces, defense industries, and federal employment generally, President Franklin D. Roosevelt issues an executive order temporarily establishing the Fair Employment Practices Committee.

1942 James Farmer and students at the University of Chicago establish the Congress of Racial Equality (CORE).

1944 Supreme Court's *Smith v. Allwright* decision finds that exclusion of African Americans from participation in party primaries violates the Constitution.

1946 President Harry S Truman issues an executive order establishing the President's Committee on Civil Rights.

1947 Jackie Robinson becomes the first African American to play major league baseball.

1947 President's Committee on Civil Rights produces a report entitled *To Secure These Rights*, which condemns racial discrimination in the United States.

1948 When the Democratic Party National Convention adopts a strong civil rights plank, southern Democrats withdraw to form the Dixiecrat Party, with Strom Thurmond as their presidential candidate.

1948 Supreme Court's *Shelley v. Kraemer* decision holds that the Constitution prevents state courts from enforcing racially restrictive real estate covenants.

1948 President Harry S Truman signs Executive Order 9981 prohibiting racial discrimination in the armed forces and other federal employment.

1950 Supreme Court's *Sweatt v. Painter* decision holds that Texas' attempt to establish a separate law school for blacks rather than admit black applicants to the University of Texas Law School violates the equal protection clause.

1952 McCarran-Walter Act eliminates race as a bar to immigration but continues the national origins quota system.

1954 Supreme Court's *Brown v. Board of Education of Topeka, Kansas* decision finds that racial segregation in public schools violates the equal protection clause (May 17).

1955 Interstate Commerce Commission bans racial segregation on interstate buses and trains.

1955 Fifteen-year-old African American Emmett Till is murdered in Mississippi after allegedly flirting with a white woman; a jury ultimately acquits two white men charged with his murder.

1955 Supreme Court issues a second opinion in the *Brown v. Board of Education* case (*Brown II*), requiring desegregation of public schools "with all deliberate speed."

1955 Rosa Parks's defiance of segregated seating rules on a Montgomery, Alabama, bus touches off a year-long bus boycott.

1956 Most southern members of Congress sign the "Southern Manifesto" denouncing the Supreme Court's *Brown v. Board of Education* decision.

1957 Martin Luther King, Jr., and other African American leaders found the Southern Christian Leadership Conference (SCLC).

1957 Congress passes the first civil rights act since Reconstruction, banning discrimination in public places based on race, color, religion, or national origin.

1957 After Arkansas' governor uses National Guard troops to block African American children from entering Little Rock's Central High School, President Dwight D. Eisenhower federalizes the guard and mobilizes additional federal armed forces to ensure that the school is peacefully integrated.

1958 Supreme Court's *Cooper v. Aaron* decision rejects state attempt to delay desegregation of public schools on the grounds of potential racial turmoil.

1960 Student sit-ins begin at lunch counters in Greensboro, North Carolina.

1960 Passage of the Civil Rights Act of 1960 expands protections of voting rights.

1960 Student Non-Violent Coordinating Committee (SNCC) is founded.

1961 President John F. Kennedy issues executive order that establishes the Equal Employment Opportunity Commission and requires businesses with government contracts to take "affirmative action" in the equal treatment of employees.

1961 Freedom rides sponsored by CORE test the ban on segregation in interstate buses; riders are beaten, and a bus is burned in Birmingham, Alabama.

1962 President John F. Kennedy signs an executive order banning racial discrimination in federally financed housing.

1962 Voter registration drives begin in southern states under the direction of the Council of Federated Organizations (COFO).

1962 James Meredith enrolls in the University of Mississippi over the defiant protest of Governor Ross R. Barnett and in the face of mob violence.

1963 During demonstrations in Birmingham, Alabama, Police Commissioner Eugene (Bull) Connor orders the use of dogs and fire hoses against demonstrators.

1963 Medgar W. Evers, field secretary for the Mississippi NAACP, is assassinated (June 12).

1963 March on Washington is sponsored by civil rights, labor, and religious organizations; featured speaker Martin Luther King, Jr., delivers his "I Have a Dream" speech (August 28).

1963 In his inaugural address, newly elected Alabama governor George C. Wallace declares "Segregation now, segregation tomorrow, segregation forever."

1963 Four African American girls are killed when a bomb explodes at the Sixteenth Street Baptist Church in Birmingham, Alabama (September 15).

1964 Council of Federated Organizations, a group of associated civil rights groups, organizes the Freedom Summer project to register African Americans to vote in Mississippi.

1964 Ratification of the Twenty-fourth Amendment prohibits poll taxes in federal elections.

1964 Civil rights workers James Chaney, Michael Schwerner, and Andrew Goodman are killed near Philadelphia, Mississippi (June).

1964 Supreme Court's *Griffin v. Prince Edward County School Board* decision finds that school districts cannot simply close public schools in an attempt to avoid desegregating them.

1964 Congress passes the Civil Rights Act of 1964, which prohibits racial, religious, sexual, and other forms of discrimination in a variety of contexts.

1964 Martin Luther King, Jr., is awarded the Nobel Peace Prize.

1964 Supreme Court's *Heart of Atlanta Motel v. United States* decision upholds the power of Congress to prohibit racial discrimination in privately owned hotels and inns.

1965 Malcolm X is assassinated (February 21).

1965 Martin Luther King, Jr., leads a march from Selma to Montgomery, Alabama, to protest voting discrimination (March).

1965 Congress passes the Voting Rights Act.

1965 President Lyndon B. Johnson signs an executive order requiring businesses with federal contracts to undertake affirmative action measures.

1965 Watts riot flares in Los Angeles.

1965 Thurgood Marshall becomes solicitor general of the United States.

1965 Congress amends the McCarran-Walter Act to abolish the national origins quota system.

1966 Supreme Court overrules the attempt by Georgia's legislature to deny Julian Bond a seat in the legislature because of his association with SNCC.

1966 Massachussetts makes Edward W. Brooke the first black U.S. senator elected since Reconstruction.

1966 Black Panther Party is organized in Oakland, California, by Bobby Seale and Huey P. Newton.

1966 Constance Bake Motley becomes the first African American woman appointed to serve as a federal judge.

1966 Stokely Carmichael takes over leadership of SNCC and coins the phrase "Black Power" to advocate more militant responses to continued racial discrimination.

1967 Thurgood Marshall is appointed by President Lyndon Johnson as the U.S. Supreme Court's first black justice.

1967 Summer race riots disrupt many northern cities.

1967 Supreme Court's *Loving v. Virginia* decision holds that a state law barring interracial marriages is unconstitutional.

1968 Supreme Court's *Green v. County School Board* decision finds that a "freedom of choice" plan adopted by a school district does not satisfy the district's constitutional obligation to desegregate public schools.

1968 National Advisory Committee on Civil Disorders (the Kerner Commission) releases its report concerning urban riots, claiming as key reasons white racism and increasing racial and economic stratification.

1968 Supreme Court's *Jones v. Alfred H. Mayer Co.* decision finds that Congress has the power to prohibit racial discrimination in housing sales.

1968 Martin Luther King, Jr., is assassinated in Memphis, Tennessee, a few days after leading a protest march for striking sanitation workers (April 4).

1968 Congress passes the Civil Rights Act of 1968, which prohibits discrimination in the sale and rental of housing and in home financing.

1968 Shirley Chisholm of New York becomes the first African American woman elected to Congress.

1969-1971 Richard M. Nixon administration requires federal contractors to set specific goals and timetables for minority hiring.

1971 Supreme Court's *Griffin v. Breckenridge* decision upholds a federal law punishing racially motivated assaults on public highways.

1971 Jesse Jackson organizes Operation PUSH.

1971 In *Griggs v. Duke Power Company*, the Supreme Court bans non-job-related tests that might unfairly screen minorities.

1971 Attica Prison riot leaves more than forty people dead.

1971 Ratification of the Twenty-sixth Amendment to the U.S. Constitution lowers the minimum voting age to eighteen.

1971 Supreme Court's *Swann v. Charlotte-Mecklenburg Board of Education* decision authorizes busing to desegregate school district.

1976 Supreme Court's *Washington v. Davis* decision holds that laws having a disproportionately burdensome effect on racial minorities are not subject to the same rigorous review as laws purposefully discriminating on grounds of race.

1978 In *Regents of the University of California v. Bakke,* the Supreme Court rules against the use of quotas to achieve racial balance in colleges and universities but allows an applicant's race to be considered in the admissions process.

1979 Supreme Court's *United Steel Workers of America v. Weber* decision upholds the ability of private employers to adopt affirmative action plans.

1980 In *Fullilove v. Klutznick,* the Supreme Court upholds minority set-aside contracts established by Congress for federal programs.

1980 Race riots leave eighteen people dead in Miami after four Miami police officers are acquitted of charges of beating a black insurance executive to death.

1982 Congress extends the effect of the Voting Rights Act of 1965.

1984 Civil Rights Commission ends the use of quotas in employment promotions for African Americans.

1986 Supreme Court's *Batson v. Kentucky* decision holds that a prosecutor's attempt to disqualify possible jurors because of their race violates the equal protection clause of the Fourteenth Amendment.

1986 In *Wygant v. Jackson Board of Education,* the Supreme Court rules that the jobs of newly hired black teachers cannot be protected by laying off senior white teachers.

1986 Holiday honoring Martin Luther King, Jr., is celebrated officially for the first time.

1987 Twenty thousand people participate in a racial brotherhood march in Cummings, Georgia, following disruption of an earlier march by the Ku Klux Klan.

1987 Shooting of an unarmed black teenager by a white police officer leads to widespread protest from Montreal's black community.

1987 Three white teenagers are convicted of manslaughter following a racially motivated attack on three black men in the Howard Beach section of New York City a year earlier.

1987 Supreme Court's *McCleskey v. Kemp* decision holds that mere proof of a racially disproportionate impact of death penalty sentences on African Americans does not violate the Constitution.

1988 Federal jury orders the Ku Klux Klan, the Southern White Knights, and eleven individuals to pay $1 million in damages to protesters attacked during a 1987 civil rights march.

1988 Fair Housing Amendments Act establishes a procedure for imposing fines for those found guilty of housing discrimination based on race, color, sex, religion, or national origin.

1988 Civil Rights Restoration Act restricts federal funding to institutions that discriminate on the basis of race, gender, disability, and age, reversing a 1984 Supreme Court decision that narrowed the scope of federal antidiscrimination laws.

1988 House of Representatives extends antidiscrimination job protection to its own employees, overriding its previous exemption.

1988 City of Yonkers, New York, accepts a court-ordered plan to integrate both housing and schools, ending a legal battle begun in 1980.

1989 Supreme Court's *Richmond v. J. A. Croson, Co.* decision holds that state and local affirmative action programs must be subject to "strict scrutiny," a constitutional standard requiring the most compelling government justifications.

1989 Douglas Wilder is elected governor of Virginia, becoming the first elected black state governor in the United States.

1989 In *Martin v. Wilks,* the Supreme Court allows white firefighters in Birmingham, Alabama, to challenge a 1981 court-approved affirmative action program designed to increase minority representation and promotion.

1989 Racial unrest on the campus of the University of Massachusetts in Amherst leads to the introduction of mounted police patrols on campus.

1989 In protest of the Supreme Court's decision in *Patterson v. McLean Credit* to limit the application of an 1866 civil rights law to job-discrimination cases, more than 35,000 protesters silently file past the Supreme Court Building and the Capitol.

1989 William Barclay Allen resigns as chairman of the U.S. Commission on Civil Rights following a number of controversial actions, culminating in a California speech entitled "Blacks, Animals, and Homosexuals: Who Is a Minority?"

1989 Following a 1988 federal court ruling that Mississippi judicial districts must be redrawn, voters elect five black trial court judges.

1989 Memorial inscribed with the names of forty people who died in the 1960's Civil Rights movement is dedicated in Montgomery, Alabama.

1990 The march of 150 people from Selma to Montgomery marks the twenty-fifth anniversary of the historic march to gain equal voting rights for African Americans.

1990 Milwaukee, Wisconsin, school board votes to open two schools for blacks utilizing a special curriculum focusing on black culture and featuring programs designed to develop self-esteem and personal responsibility.

1990 President George Bush vetoes the Civil Rights Act, which would have overturned five recent Supreme Court rulings making it more difficult to win discrimination lawsuits against employers.

1990 In *The Content of Our Character,* Shelby Steele presents an African American case against affirmative action, arguing that it contributes to a "victim-focused identity."

1990 Using themes of racial resentment, former Ku Klux Klansman David Duke makes a strong showing in the U.S. Senate primary in Louisiana.

1991 Supreme Court's *Board of Education of Oklahoma City Public Schools v. Dowell* decision holds that a school district is entitled to have a desegregation order lifted when it has complied in good faith with a desegregation decree since it was entered and when vestiges of past discrimination have been eliminated to the extent practicable.

1991 U.S. district court strikes down a University of Wisconsin, Madison, policy banning speech demeaning to a person's race, sex, religion, color, creed, disability, sexual orientation, or ancestry.

1991 Dinesh D'Souza argues against political correctness and ideological education in *Illiberal Education: The Politics of Race and Sex on Campus.*

1991 Advisory panel to the New York state commissioner of education publishes "One Nation, Many Peoples: A Declaration of Cultural Interdependence," calling for the inclusion of more nonwhite and non-European views in the public school curriculum.

1991 President George Bush signs the Civil Rights Bill, making it easier for employees to sue employers for discrimination, but only after changes are made to a vetoed 1990 bill that might have created racial quotas.

1991 Clarence Thomas succeeds Thurgood Marshall as the second black Supreme Court justice, despite protests from civil rights groups decrying his opposition to affirmative action programs and busing for school desegregation.

1991 National Civil Rights Museum, dedicated to the 1950's and 1960's struggle for racial equality in the United States, is opened in Memphis, Tennessee.

1991 Eight FBI agents are disciplined and an internal review is initiated following a $1 million racial settlement with Donald Rochon, a black former agent.

1991 U.S. Education Department proposes regulations banning most race-based college scholarships.

1991 Studies by the Urban Institute find that hiring and housing discrimination against blacks is "widespread and entrenched."

1992 Four Los Angeles police officers are acquitted of charges stemming from the 1991 beating of black motorist Rodney King, touching off five days of rioting in Los Angeles that result in more than fifty deaths and $1 billion in property damage.

1992 Supreme Court prohibits criminal defendants from excluding potential jurors on the basis of race.

1992 FBI agrees to promote, reassign, or grant back pay to more than fifty black agents.

1992 U.S. Department of Education determines that the admissions policy of the University of California at Berkeley's law school violates the Civil Rights Act of 1964 by comparing prospective candidates only against others in their own racial group.

1992 Following the killing of a black man, Raymond Lawrence, by a white police officer, rioters in Toronto go on a two-hour rampage in the city's first ever race riot.

1992 In settlement of the first case of mortgage discrimination, the Justice Department forces Decatur Federal Savings and Loan of Atlanta to pay $1 million to forty-eight black families who had been unfairly denied mortgages between 1988 and 1992.

1992 In *United States v. Fordice,* the Supreme Court rules that remnants of segregation remain in the Mississippi system of higher education and that positive steps must be taken to remedy such segregation.

1992 In *R.A.V. v. City of St. Paul*, the Supreme Court unanimously rules that a St. Paul, Minnesota, law making the use of racist language a criminal offense is a violation of First Amendment guarantees of free speech.

1993 President Bill Clinton angers civil rights groups when he withdraws Lani Guinier's nomination for head of the Civil Rights Division of the Justice Department following opposition by critics who cite her radical proposals for helping minorities gain political power.

1993 Shoney's restaurant company agrees to a $105 million settlement with 40,000 current or former employees who claim racial bias in hiring, firing, and promoting practices.

1993 Los Angeles police officers Stacey Koon and Laurence Powell are sentenced to prison for violating the civil rights of Rodney King in a 1991 beating incident.

1993 In *Wisconsin v. Mitchell*, the Supreme Court rules that states can punish racially motivated crimes more harshly than similar crimes not motivated by bias.

1993 Some 75,000 civil rights activists march on Washington, D.C., to celebrate the thirtieth anniversary of the first march on Washington and call for a renewed commitment to civil rights.

1993 Supreme Court votes to return to a lower court a challenge to the creation of two strangely shaped congressional districts that favor minority candidates, arguing that such gerrymandering might violate the rights of white voters.

1994 Seventy-three-year-old white supremacist Byron De La Beckwith is convicted of the 1963 murder of civil rights leader Medgar Evers and is sentenced to life in prison.

1994 Parent Flagstar Company agrees to pay $45.7 million in a class-action settlement stemming from 4,300 racial bias complaints against Denny's restaurant chain.

1994 Federal jury orders the city of Los Angeles to pay Rodney King $3.8 million in damages stemming from a 1991 beating by white police officers.

1995 Supreme Court's *Miller v. Johnson* decision finds that state congressional districts deliberately drawn to include a majority of African American residents violates equal protection.

1995 Supreme Court upholds a lower-court ruling abolishing a University of Maryland scholarship program specifically designed for African American students.

1995 Delegates to the annual convention of Southern Baptists, the nation's largest Protestant denomination, pass a resolution denouncing racism and apologizing for "historic acts of evil such as slavery."

1995 In *Adarand Constructors, Inc. v. Pena*, the Supreme Court requires that federal contracts based on affirmative action set-asides are valid only in cases where those benefiting have suffered actual discrimination in the past.

1995 Governor Pete Wilson abolishes some 150 boards that advised California state agencies on minority hiring.

1995 Governing board of the University of California votes to end preferential treatment for minorities in their hiring process.

1995 O. J. Simpson's acquittal of the 1994 murder of his wife and a companion divides the country along racial lines.

1995 Approximately 700,000 people, mostiy African American men, attend Louis Farrakhan's Million Man March, a Washington, D.C., rally highlighting male family responsibilities and addressing problems plaguing the black community in America.

1995 Maryland Democratic Representative Kweisi Mfume becomes chief executive of the NAACP following longstanding controversies over improper financial practices of former directors William F. Gibson, Benjamin Chavis, and Benjamin L. Hooks.

1996 At a Theater Communications Group conference, African American playwright August Wilson decries the lack of funding for minority theaters and suggests that many critics are incapable of appreciating works with minority themes.

1996 California voters approve Proposition 209, designed to end all forms of affirmative action in "the operation of public employment, public education, or public contracting."

1996 U.S. Fifth Circuit Court of Appeals decision in *Hopwood v. Texas* bars the University of Texas Law School from considering race as a factor in the admissions process.

1996 President Bill Clinton signs the Church Arson Prevention Act, making destruction of religious property "on the basis of race, color, or ethnicity" a federal crime.

1996 Texaco Incorporated agrees to pay $176.1 million to settle a discrimation suit filed on behalf of 1,500 current and former black employees.

1996 Oakland, California, school board determines that the English dialect spoken by many African Americans is a separate language (Ebonics) based upon West African roots, thus qualifying for federal funds approved for bilingual education.

1997 National Church Arson Task Force, appointed by President Clinton in 1996, reports that racism was only one of many factors contributing to more than four hundred church fires that had been set during the 1990's.

1997 President Bill Clinton launches a year-long debate on race relations in America by appointing black historian John Hope Franklin to lead a panel consisting of three whites, two blacks, one Hispanic, and one Korean American.

1998 Sam Bowers, a former Imperial Wizard of the Ku Klux Klan in Mississippi, is sentenced to life in prison for ordering the 1966 murder of civil rights activist Vernon Dahmer.

John Powell

U.S. Constitution

We the People of the United States, in Order to form a more perfect Union, establish Justice, insure domestic Tranquility, provide for the common defence, promote the general Welfare, and secure the Blessings of Liberty to ourselves and our Posterity, do ordain and establish this Constitution for the United States of America.

Article I.

SECTION 1. All legislative Powers herein granted shall be vested in a Congress of the United States, which shall consist of a Senate and House of Representatives.

SECTION 2. The House of Representatives shall be composed of Members chosen every second Year by the People of the several States, and the Electors in each State shall have the Qualifications requisite for Electors of the most numerous Branch of the State Legislature.

No Person shall be a Representative who shall not have attained to the Age of twenty five Years, and been seven Years a Citizen of the United States, and who shall not, when elected, be an Inhabitant of that State in which he shall be chosen.

Representatives and direct Taxes shall be apportioned among the several States which may be included within this Union, according to their respective Numbers, which shall be determined by adding to the whole Number of free Persons, including those bound to Service for a Term of Years, and excluding Indians not taxed, three fifths of all other Persons. The actual Enumeration shall be made within three Years after the first Meeting of the Congress of the United States, and within every subsequent Term of ten Years, in such Manner as they shall by Law direct. The number of Representatives shall not exceed one for every thirty Thousand, but each State shall have at Least one Representative; and until such enumeration shall be made, the State of New Hampshire shall be entitled to chuse three, Massachusetts eight, Rhode-Island and Providence Plantations one, Connecticut five, New York six, New Jersey four, Pennsylvania eight, Delaware one, Maryland six, Virginia ten, North Carolina five, South Carolina five, and Georgia three.

When vacancies happen in the Representation from any State, the Executive Authority thereof shall issue Writs of Election to fill such Vacancies.

The House of Representatives shall chuse their Speaker and other Officers; and shall have the sole Power of Impeachment.

SECTION 3. The Senate of the United States shall be composed of two Senators from each State, chosen by the Legislature thereof, for six Years; and each Senator shall have one Vote.

Immediately after they shall be assembled in Consequence of the first Election, they shall be divided as equally as may be into three Classes. The Seats of the Senators of the first Class shall be vacated at the Expiration of the second Year, of the second Class at the Expiration of the fourth Year, and of the third Class at the Expiration of the sixth Year, so that one third may be chosen every second Year; and if Vacancies happen by Resignation, or otherwise, during the Recess of the Legislature of any State, the Executive thereof may make temporary Appointments until the next Meeting of the Legislature, which shall then fill such Vacancies.

No Person shall be a Senator who shall not have attained to the Age of thirty Years, and been nine Years a Citizen of the United States, and who shall not, when elected, be an Inhabitant of that State for which he shall be chosen.

The Vice President of the United States shall be President of the Senate, but shall have no Vote, unless they be equally divided.

The Senate shall chuse their other Officers, and also a President pro tempore, in the Absence of the Vice President, or when he shall exercise the Office of President of the United States.

The Senate shall have the sole Power to try all Impeachments. When sitting for that Purpose, they shall be on Oath or Affirmation. When the President of the United States is tried, the Chief Justice shall preside: And no Person shall be convicted without the Concurrence of two thirds of the Members present.

Judgment in Cases of Impeachment shall not extend further than to removal from Office, and disqualification to hold and enjoy any Office of honor, Trust or Profit under the United States: but the Party convicted shall nevertheless be liable and subject to Indictment, Trial, Judgment and Punishment, according to Law.

SECTION 4. The Times, Places and Manner of holding Elections for Senators and Representatives, shall be prescribed in each State by the Legislature thereof; but the Congress may at any time by Law make or alter such Regulations, except as to the Places of chusing Senators.

The Congress shall assemble at least once in every Year, and such Meeting shall be on the first Monday in December, unless they shall by Law appoint a different Day.

SECTION 5. Each House shall be the Judge of the Elections, Returns and Qualifications of its own Members, and a Majority of each shall constitute a Quorum to do Business; but a smaller Number may adjourn from day to day, and may be authorized to compel the Attendance of absent Members, in such Manner, and under such Penalties as each House may provide.

Each House may determine the Rules of its Proceedings, punish its Members for disorderly Behaviour, and, with the Concurrence of two thirds, expel a Member.

Each House shall keep a Journal of its Proceedings, and from time to time publish the same, excepting such Parts as may in their Judgment require Secrecy; and the Yeas and Nays of the Members of either House on any question shall, at the Desire of one fifth of those Present, be entered on the Journal.

Neither House, during the Session of Congress, shall, without the Consent of the other, adjourn for more than three days, nor to any other Place than that in which the two Houses shall be sitting.

SECTION 6. The Senators and Representatives shall receive a Compensation for their Services, to be ascertained by Law, and paid out of the Treasury of the United States. They shall in all Cases, except Treason, Felony and Breach of the Peace, be privileged from Arrest during their Attendance at the Session of their respective Houses, and in going to and returning from the same; and for any Speech or Debate in either House, they shall not be questioned in any other Place.

No Senator or Representative shall, during the Time for which he was elected, be appointed to any civil Office under the Authority of the United States, which shall have been created, or the Emoluments whereof shall have been increased during such time; and no Person holding any Office under the United States, shall be a Member of either House during his Continuance in Office.

SECTION 7. All Bills for raising Revenue shall originate in the House of Representatives; but the Senate may propose or concur with Amendments as on other Bills.

Every Bill which shall have passed the House of Representatives and the Senate, shall, before it becomes a Law, be presented to the President of the United States; If he approve he shall sign it, but if not he shall return it, with his Objections to that House in which it shall have originated, who shall enter the Objections at large on their Journal, and proceed to reconsider it. If after such Reconsideration two thirds of that House shall agree to pass the Bill, it shall be sent, together with the Objections, to the other House, by which it shall likewise be reconsidered, and if approved by two thirds of that House, it shall become a Law. But in all such Cases the Votes of both Houses shall be determined by Yeas and Nays, and the Names of the Persons voting for and against the Bill shall be entered on the Journal of each House respectively. If any Bill shall not be returned by the President within ten Days (Sundays excepted) after it shall have been presented to him, the Same shall be a Law, in like Manner as if he had signed it, unless the Congress by their Adjournment prevent its Return, in which Case it shall not be a Law.

Every Order, Resolution, or Vote to which the Concurrence of the Senate and House of Representatives may be necessary (except on a question of Adjournment) shall be presented to the President of the United States; and before the Same shall take Effect, shall be approved by him, or being disapproved by him, shall be repassed by two thirds of the Senate and House of Representatives, according to the Rules and Limitations prescribed in the Case of a Bill.

SECTION 8. The Congress shall have Power To lay and collect Taxes, Duties, Imposts and Excises, to pay the Debts and provide for the common Defence and general Welfare of the United States; but all Duties, Imposts and Excises shall be uniform throughout the United States;

To borrow Money on the credit of the United States;

To regulate Commerce with foreign Nations, and among the several States, and with the Indian Tribes;

To establish an uniform Rule of Naturalization, and uniform Laws on the subject of Bankruptcies throughout the United States;

To coin Money, regulate the Value thereof, and of foreign Coin, and fix the Standard of Weights and Measures;

To provide for the Punishment of counterfeiting the Securities and current Coin of the United States;

To establish Post Offices and post Roads;

To promote the Progress of Science and useful Arts, by securing for limited Times to Authors and Inventors the exclusive Right to their respective Writings and Discoveries;

To constitute Tribunals inferior to the supreme Court;

To define and punish Piracies and Felonies committed on the high Seas, and Offenses against the Law of Nations;

To declare War, grant Letters of Marque and Reprisal, and make Rules concerning Captures on Land and Water;

To raise and support Armies, but no Appropriation of Money to that Use shall be for a longer Term than two Years;

To provide and maintain a Navy;

To make Rules for the Government and Regulation of the land and naval Forces;

To provide for calling forth the Militia to execute the Laws of the Union, suppress Insurrections and repel Invasions;

To provide for organizing, arming, and disciplining the Militia, and for governing such Part of them as may be employed in the Service of the United States, reserving to the States respectively, the Appointment of the Officers, and the Authority of training the Militia according to the discipline prescribed by Congress;

To exercise exclusive Legislation in all Cases whatsoever, over such District (not exceeding ten Miles square) as may, by Cession of particular States, and the Acceptance of Congress, become the Seat of the Government of the United States, and to exercise like Authority over all Places purchased by the Consent of the Legislature of the State in which the Same shall be, for the Erection of Forts, Magazines, Arsenals, dock-Yards and other needful Buildings;—And

To make all Laws which shall be necessary and proper for carrying into Execution the foregoing Powers, and all other Powers vested by this Constitution in the Government of the United States, or in any Department or Officer thereof.

SECTION 9. The Migration or Importation of such Persons as any of the States now existing shall think proper to admit, shall not be prohibited by the Congress prior to the Year one thousand eight hundred and eight, but a Tax or duty may be imposed on such Importation, not exceeding ten dollars for each Person.

The Privilege of the Writ of Habeas Corpus shall not be suspended, unless when in Cases of Rebellion or Invasion the public Safety may require it.

No Bill of Attainder or ex post facto Law shall be passed.

No Capitation, or other direct, Tax shall be laid, unless in Proportion to the Census or Enumeration herein before directed to be taken.

No Tax or Duty shall be laid on Articles exported from any State.

No Preference shall be given by any Regulation of Commerce or Revenue to the Ports of one State over those of another: nor shall Vessels bound to, or from, one State, be obliged to enter, clear, or pay Duties in another.

No Money shall be drawn from the Treasury, but in Consequence of Appropriations made by Law; and a regular Statement and Account of the Receipts and Expenditures of all public Money shall be published from time to time.

No Title of Nobility shall be granted by the United States: And no Person holding any Office of Profit or Trust under them, shall, without the Consent of the Congress, accept of any present, Emolument, Office, or Title, of any kind whatever, from any King, Prince, or foreign State.

SECTION 10. No State shall enter into any Treaty, Alliance, or Confederation; grant Letters of Marque and Reprisal; coin Money; emit Bills of Credit; make any Thing but gold and silver Coin a Tender in Payment of Debts; pass any Bill of Attainder, ex post facto Law, or Law impairing the Obligation of Contracts, or grant any Title of Nobility.

No State shall, without the Consent of the Congress, lay any Imposts or Duties on Imports or Exports, except what may be absolutely necessary for executing it's inspection Laws: and the net Produce of all Duties and Imposts, laid by any State on Imports or Exports, shall be for the Use of the Treasury of the United States; and all such Laws shall be subject to the Revision and Control of the Congress.

No State shall, without the Consent of Congress, lay any Duty of Tonnage, keep Troops, or Ships of War in time of Peace, enter into any Agreement or Compact with another State, or with a foreign Power, or engage in War, unless actually invaded, or in such imminent Danger as will not admit of delay.

Article II.

SECTION 1. The executive Power shall be vested in a President of the United States of America. He shall hold his Office during the Term of four Years, and, together with the Vice President, chosen for the same Term, be elected, as follows:

Each State shall appoint, in such Manner as the Legislature thereof may direct, a Number of Electors, equal to the whole Number of Senators and Representatives to which the State may be entitled in the Congress: but no Senator or Representative, or Person holding an Office of Trust or Profit under the United States, shall be appointed an Elector.

The Electors shall meet in their respective States, and vote by Ballot for two Persons, of whom one at least shall not be an Inhabitant of the same State with themselves. And they shall make a List of all the Persons voted for, and of the Number of Votes for each; which List they shall sign and certify, and transmit sealed to the Seat of the Government of the United States, directed to the President of the Senate. The President of the Senate shall, in the Presence of the Senate and House of Representatives, open all the Certificates, and the Votes shall then be counted. The Person having the greatest Number of Votes shall be the President, if such Number be a Majority of the whole Number of Electors appointed; and if there be more than one who have such Majority, and have an equal Number of Votes, then the House of Representatives shall immediately chuse by Ballot one of them for President; and if no Person have a Majority, then from the five highest on the List the said House shall in like manner chuse the President. But in chusing the President, the Votes shall be taken by States, the Representation from each State having one Vote; A quorum for this Purpose shall consist of a Member or Members from two thirds of the States, and a Majority of all the States shall be necessary to a Choice. In every Case, after the Choice of the President, the Person having the greatest Number of Votes of the Electors shall be the Vice President. But if there should remain two or more who have equal Votes, the Senate shall chuse from them by Ballot the Vice President.

The Congress may determine the Time of chusing the Electors, and the Day on which they shall give their Votes; which Day shall be the same throughout the United States.

No Person except a natural born Citizen, or a Citizen of the United States, at the time of the Adoption of this Constitution, shall be eligible to the Office of the President; neither shall any person be eligible to that Office who shall not have attained to the Age of thirty five Years, and been fourteen Years a Resident within the United States.

In Case of the Removal of the President from Office, or of his Death, Resignation, or Inability to discharge the Powers and Duties of the said Office, the Same shall devolve on the Vice President, and the Congress may by Law provide for the Case of Removal, Death, Resignation or Inability, both of the President and Vice President, declaring what Officer shall then act as President, and such Officer shall act accordingly, until the Disability be removed, or a President shall be elected.

The President shall, at stated Times, receive for his Services, a Compensation, which shall neither be increased nor diminished during the Period for which he shall have been elected, and he shall not receive within that Period any other Emolument from the United States, or any of them.

Before he enter the Execution of his Office, he shall take the following Oath or Affirmation:—"I do solemnly swear (or affirm) that I will faithfully execute the Office of President of the United States, and will to the best of my Ability, preserve, protect and defend the Constitution of the United States."

SECTION 2. The President shall be Commander in Chief of the Army and Navy of the United States, and of the Militia of the several States, when called into the actual Service of the United States; he may require the Opinion, in writing, of the principal Officer in each of the executive Departments, upon any Subject relating to the Duties of their respective Offices, and he shall have Power to grant Reprieves and Pardons for Offenses against the United States, except in Cases of Impeachment.

He shall have Power, by and with the Advice and Consent of the Senate, to make Treaties, provided two thirds of the Senators present concur; and he shall nominate, and by and with the Advice and Consent of the Senate, shall appoint Ambassadors, other public Ministers and Consuls, Judges of the supreme Court, and all other Officers of the United States, whose Appointments are not herein otherwise provided for, and which shall be established by Law: but the Congress may by Law vest the Appointment of such inferior Officers, as they think proper, in the President alone, in the Courts of Law, or in the Heads of Departments.

The President shall have Power to fill up all Vacancies that may happen during the Recess of the Senate, by granting Commissions which shall expire at the End of their next Session.

SECTION 3. He shall from time to time give to the Congress Information of the State of the Union, and recommend to their Consideration such Measures as he shall judge necessary and expedient; he may, on extraordinary Occasions, convene both Houses, or either of them, and in Case of Disagreement between them, with Respect to the Time of Adjournment, he may adjourn them to such Time as he shall think proper; he shall receive Ambassadors and other public Ministers; he shall take Care that the Laws be faithfully executed, and shall Commission all the Officers of the United States.

SECTION 4. The President, Vice President and all civil Officers of the United States, shall be removed from Office on Impeachment for, and Conviction of, Treason, Bribery, or other high Crimes and Misdemeanors.

Article III.

SECTION 1. The judicial Power of the United States, shall be vested in one supreme Court, and in such inferior Courts as the Congress may from time to time ordain and establish. The Judges, both of the supreme and inferior Courts, shall hold their Offices during good Behavior, and shall, at stated Times, receive for their Services, a Compensation, which shall not be diminished during their Continuance in Office.

SECTION 2. The judicial Power shall extend to all Cases, in Law and Equity, arising under this Constitution, the Laws of the United States, and Treaties made, or which shall be made, under their Authority;—to all Cases affecting Ambassadors, other public Ministers and Consuls;—to all Cases of admiralty and maritime Jurisdiction;—to Controversies to which the United States shall be a Party;—to Controversies between two or more States; between a

State and Citizens of another State; between Citizens of different States;—between Citizens of the same State claiming Lands under Grants of different States;—and between a State, or the Citizens thereof, and foreign States, Citizens or Subjects.

In all Cases affecting Ambassadors, other public Ministers and Consuls, and those in which a State shall be Party, the supreme Court shall have original Jurisdiction. In all the other Cases before mentioned, the supreme Court shall have appellate Jurisdiction, both as to Law and Fact, with such Exceptions, and under such Regulations as the Congress shall make.

The Trial of all Crimes, except in Cases of Impeachment, shall be by Jury; and such Trial shall be held in the State where the said Crimes shall have been committed; but when not committed within any State, the Trial shall be at such Place or Places as the Congress may by Law have directed.

SECTION 3. Treason against the United States, shall consist only in levying War against them, or in adhering to their Enemies, giving them Aid and Comfort. No Person shall be convicted of Treason unless on the Testimony of two Witnesses to the same overt Act, or on Confession in open Court.

The Congress shall have Power to declare the Punishment of Treason, but no Attainder of Treason shall work Corruption of Blood, or Forfeiture except during the Life of the Person attainted.

Article IV.

SECTION 1. Full Faith and Credit shall be given in each State to the public Acts, Records, and judicial Proceedings of every other State; And the Congress may by general Laws prescribe the Manner in which such Acts, Records and Proceedings shall be proved, and the Effect thereof.

SECTION 2. The Citizens of each State shall be entitled to all Privileges and Immunities of Citizens in the several States.

A Person charged in any State with Treason, Felony, or other Crime, who shall flee from Justice, and be found in another State, shall on Demand of the executive Authority of the State from which he fled, be delivered up, to be removed to the State having Jurisdiction of the Crime.

No person held to Service or Labour in one State, under the Laws thereof, escaping into another, shall, in Consequence of any Law or Regulation therein, be discharged from such Service or Labour, but shall be delivered up on Claim of the Party to whom such Service or Labour may be due.

SECTION 3. New States may be admitted by the Congress into this Union; but no new State shall be formed or erected within the Jurisdiction of any other State; nor any State be formed by the Junction of two or more States, or parts of States, without the Consent of the Legislatures of the States concerned as well as of the Congress.

The Congress shall have Power to dispose of and make all needful Rules and Regulations respecting the Territory or other Property belonging to the United States; and nothing in this Constitution shall be so construed as to Prejudice any Claims of the United States, or of any particular State.

SECTION 4. The United States shall guarantee to every State in this Union a Republican Form of Government, and shall protect each of them against Invasion; and on Application of the Legislature, or of the Executive (when the Legislature cannot be convened) against domestic Violence.

Article V.

The Congress, whenever two thirds of both Houses shall deem it necessary, shall propose Amendments to this Constitution, or, on the Application of the Legislatures of two thirds of the several States, shall call a Convention for proposing Amendments, which, in either Case, shall be valid to all Intents and Purposes, as Part of this Constitution, when ratified by the Legislatures of three fourths of the several States, or by Conventions in three fourths thereof, as the one or the other Mode of Ratification may be proposed by the Congress; Provided that no Amendment which may be made prior to the Year One thousand eight hundred and eight shall in any Manner affect the first and fourth Clauses in the Ninth Section of the first Article; and that no State, without its Consent, shall be deprived of it's equal Suffrage in the Senate.

Article VI.

All Debts contracted and Engagements entered into, before the Adoption of this Constitution, shall be as valid against the United States under this Constitution, as under the Confederation.

This Constitution, and the Laws of the United States which shall be made in Pursuance thereof; and all Treaties made, or which shall be made, under the Authority of the United States, shall be the supreme Law of the Land; and the Judges in every State shall be bound thereby, any Thing in the Constitution or Laws of any State to the Contrary notwithstanding.

The Senators and Representatives before mentioned, and the Members of the several State Legislatures, and all executive and judicial Officers, both of the United States and of the several States, shall be bound by Oath or Affirmation, to support this Constitution; but no religious Test shall ever be required as a Qualification to any Office or public Trust under the United States.

Article VII.

The Ratification of the Conventions of nine States, shall be sufficient for the Establishment of this Constitution between the States so ratifying the Same.

Done in Convention by the Unanimous Consent of the States present the Seventeenth Day of September in the Year of our Lord one thousand seven hundred and Eighty seven and of the Independence of the United States of America the Twelfth. In Witness whereof We have hereunto subscribed our Names,

Go. Washington—Presidt and deputy from Virginia

Amendments to the U.S. Constitution

Amendment I.

Congress shall make no law respecting an establishment of religion, or prohibiting the free exercise thereof; or abridging the freedom of speech, or of the press, or the right of the people peaceably to assemble, and to petition the Government for a redress of grievances.

[ratified December, 1791]

Amendment II.

A well regulated Militia, being necessary to the security of a free State, the right of the people to keep and bear Arms, shall not be infringed.

[ratified December, 1791]

Amendment III.

No Soldier shall, in time of peace be quartered in any house, without the consent of the Owner, nor in time of war, but in a manner to be prescribed by law.

[ratified December, 1791]

Amendment IV.

The right of the people to be secure in their persons, houses, papers, and effects, against unreasonable searches and seizures, shall not be violated, and no Warrants shall issue, but upon probable cause, supported by Oath or affirmation, and particularly describing the place to be searched, and the persons or things to be seized.

[ratified December, 1791]

Amendment V.

No person shall be held to answer for a capital, or otherwise infamous crime, unless on a presentment or indictment of a Grand Jury, except in cases arising in the land or naval forces, or in the Militia, when in actual service in time of War or public danger; nor shall any person be subject for the same offence to be twice put in jeopardy of life or limb, nor shall be compelled in any criminal case to be a witness against himself, nor be deprived of life, liberty, or property, without due process of law; nor shall private property be taken for public use without just compensation.

[ratified December, 1791]

Amendment VI.

In all criminal prosecutions, the accused shall enjoy the right to a speedy and public trial, by an impartial jury of the State and district wherein the crime shall have been committed; which district shall have been previously ascertained by law, and to be informed of the nature and cause of the accusation; to be confronted with the witnesses against him; to have compulsory process for obtaining witnesses in his favor, and to have the assistance of counsel for his defence.

[ratified December, 1791]

Amendment VII.

In Suits at common law, where the value in controversy shall exceed twenty dollars, the right of trial by jury shall be preserved, and no fact tried by a jury shall be otherwise re-4examined in any Court of the United States, than according to the rules of the common law.

[ratified December, 1791]

Amendment VIII.

Excessive bail shall not be required, nor excessive fines imposed, nor cruel and unusual punishments inflicted.

[ratified December, 1791]

Amendment IX.

The enumeration in the Constitution, of certain rights, shall not be construed to deny or disparage others retained by the people.

[ratified December, 1791]

Amendment X.

The powers not delegated to the United States by the Constitution, nor prohibited by it to the States, are reserved to the States respectively, or to the people.

[ratified December, 1791]

Amendment XI.

The Judicial power of the United States shall not be construed to extend to any suit in law or equity, commenced or prosecuted against one of the United States by Citizens of another State, or by Citizens or Subjects of any Foreign State.

[ratified February, 1795]

Amendment XII.

The Electors shall meet in their respective states, and vote by ballot for President and Vice President, one of whom, at least, shall not be an inhabitant of the same state with themselves; they shall name in their ballots the person voted for as President, and in distinct ballots the person voted for as Vice-President, and they shall make distinct lists of all persons voted for as President, and of all persons voted for as Vice-President, and of the number of votes for each, which lists they shall sign and certify, and transmit sealed to the seat of the government of the United States, directed to the President of the Senate;—The President of the Senate shall, in the presence of the Senate and House of Representatives, open all the certificates and the votes shall then be counted;— The person having the greatest number of votes for President, shall be the President, if such number be a majority of the whole number of Electors appointed; and if no person have such majority, then from the persons having the highest numbers not exceeding three on the list of those voted for as President, the House of Representatives shall choose immediately, by ballot, the President. But in choosing the President, the votes shall be taken by states, the representation from each state having one vote; a quorum for this purpose shall consist of a member or members from two-thirds of the states, and a majority of all the states shall be necessary to a choice. And if the House of Representatives shall not choose a President whenever the right of choice shall devolve upon them, before the fourth day of March next following, then the Vice-President shall act as President, as in the case of the death or other constitutional disability of the President.—The person having the greatest number of votes as Vice-President, shall be the Vice-President, if such number be a majority of the whole number of Electors appointed, and if no person have a majority, then from the two highest numbers on the list, the Senate shall choose the Vice-President; a quorum for the purpose shall consist of two-thirds of the whole number of Senators, and a majority of the whole number shall be necessary to a choice. But no person constitutionally ineligible to the office of President shall be eligible to that of Vice-President of the United States.

[ratified June, 1804]

Amendment XIII.

SECTION 1. Neither slavery nor involuntary servitude, except as a punishment for crime whereof the party shall have been duly convicted, shall exist within the United States, or any place subject to their jurisdiction.

SECTION 2. Congress shall have power to enforce this article by appropriate legislation.

[ratified December, 1865]

Amendment XIV.

SECTION 1. All persons born or naturalized in the United States and subject to the jurisdiction thereof, are citizens of the United States and of the State wherein they reside. No State shall make or enforce any law which shall abridge the privileges or immunities of citizens of the United States; nor shall any State deprive any person of life, liberty, or property, without due process of law; nor deny to any person within its jurisdiction the equal protection of the laws.

SECTION 2. Representatives shall be apportioned among the several States according to their respective numbers, counting the whole number of persons in each State, excluding Indians not taxed. But when the right to vote at any election for the choice of electors for President and Vice President of the United States, Representatives in Congress, the Executive and Judicial officers of a State, or the members of the Legislature thereof, is denied to any of the male inhabitants of such State, being twenty-one years of age, and citizens of the United States, or in any way abridged, except for participation in rebellion, or other crime, the basis of representation therein shall be reduced in the proportion which the number of such male citizens shall bear to the whole number of male citizens twenty-one years of age in such State.

SECTION 3. No person shall be a Senator or Representative in Congress, or elector of President and Vice President, or hold any office, civil or military, under the United States, or under any State, who, having previously taken an oath, as a member of Congress, or as an officer of the United States, or as a member of any State legislature, or as an executive or judicial officer of any State, to support the Constitution of the United States, shall have engaged in insurrection or rebellion against the same, or given aid or comfort to the enemies thereof. But Congress may by a vote of two-thirds of each House, remove such disability.

SECTION 4. The validity of the public debt of the United States, authorized by law, including debts incurred for payment of pensions and bounties for services in suppressing insurrection or rebellion, shall not be questioned. But neither the United States nor any State shall assume or pay any debt or obligation incurred in aid of insurrection or rebellion against the United States, or any claim for the loss or emancipation of any slave; but all such debts, obligations and claims shall be held illegal and void.

SECTION 5. The Congress shall have power to enforce, by appropriate legislation, the provisions of this article.

[ratified July, 1868]

Amendment XV.

SECTION 1. The right of citizens of the United States to vote shall not be denied or abridged by the United States or by any State on account of race, color, or previous condition of servitude.

SECTION 2. The Congress shall have power to enforce this article by appropriate legislation.

[ratified February, 1870]

Amendment XVI.

The Congress shall have power to lay and collect taxes on incomes, from whatever source derived, without apportionment among the several States, and without regard to any census or enumeration.

[ratified February, 1913]

Amendment XVII.

The Senate of the United States shall be composed of two Senators from each State, elected by the people thereof, for six years; and each Senator shall have one vote. The electors in each State shall have the qualifications requisite for electors of the most numerous branch of the State legislatures.

When vacancies happen in the representation of any State in the Senate, the executive authority of such State shall issue writs of election to fill such vacancies: *Provided,* That the legislature of any State may empower the executive thereof to make temporary appointments until the people fill the vacancies by election as the legislature may direct.

This amendment shall not be so construed as to affect the election or term of any Senator chosen before it becomes valid as part of the Constitution.

[ratified April, 1913]

Amendment XVIII.

SECTION 1. After one year from the ratification of this article the manufacture, sale, or transportation of intoxicating liquors within, the importation thereof into, or the exportation thereof from the United States and all territory subject to the jurisdiction thereof for beverage purposes is hereby prohibited.

SECTION 2. The Congress and the several States shall have concurrent power to enforce this article by appropriate legislation.

SECTION 3. This article shall be inoperative unless it shall have been ratified as an amendment to the Constitution by the legislatures of the several States, as provided in the Constitution, within seven years from the date of the submission hereof to the States by the Congress.

[ratified January, 1919, repealed December, 1933]

Amendment XIX.

The right of citizens of the United States to vote shall not be denied or abridged by the United States or by any State on account of sex.

Congress shall have power to enforce this article by appropriate legislation.

[ratified August, 1920]

Amendment XX.

SECTION 1. The terms of the President and Vice President shall end at noon on the 20th day of January, and the terms of Senators and Representatives at noon on the 3d day of January, of the years in which such terms would have ended if this article had not been ratified; and the terms of their successors shall then begin.

SECTION 2. The Congress shall assemble at least once in every year, and such meeting shall begin at noon on the 3d day of January, unless they shall by law appoint a different day.

SECTION 3. If, at the time fixed for the beginning of the term of the President, the President elect shall have died, the Vice President elect shall become President. If a President shall not have been chosen before the time fixed for the beginning of his term, or if the President elect shall have failed to qualify, then the Vice President elect shall act as President until a President shall have qualified; and the Congress may by law provide for the case wherein neither a President elect nor a Vice President elect shall have qualified, declaring who shall then act as President, or the manner in which one who is to act shall be selected, and such person shall act accordingly until a President or Vice President shall have qualified.

SECTION 4. The Congress may by law provide for the case of the death of any of the persons from whom the House of Representatives may choose a President whenever the right of choice shall have devolved upon them, and for the case of the death of any of the persons from whom the Senate may choose a Vice President whenever the right of choice shall have devolved upon them.

SECTION 5. Sections 1 and 2 shall take effect on the 15th day of October following the ratification of this article.

SECTION 6. This article shall be inoperative unless it shall have been ratified as an amendment to the Constitution by the legislatures of three-fourths of the several States within seven years from the date of its submission.

[ratified January, 1933]

Amendment XXI.

SECTION 1. The eighteenth article of amendment to the Constitution of the United States is hereby repealed.

SECTION 2. The transportation or importation into any State, Territory, or possession of the United States for delivery or use therein of intoxicating liquors, in violation of the laws thereof, is hereby prohibited.

SECTION 3. This article shall be inoperative unless it shall have been ratified as an amendment to the Constitution by conventions in the several States, as provided in the Constitution, within seven years from the date of the submission hereof to the States by the Congress.

[ratified December, 1933]

Amendment XXII.

SECTION 1. No person shall be elected to the office of the President more than twice, and no person who has held the office of President, or acted as President, for more than two years of a term to which some other person was elected President shall be elected to the office of the President more than once. But this Article shall not apply to any person holding the office of President when this Article was proposed by the Congress, and shall not prevent any person who may be holding the office of President, or acting as President, during the term within which this Article becomes operative from holding the office of President or acting as President during the remainder of such term.

SECTION 2. This article shall be inoperative unless it shall have been ratified as an amendment to the Constitution by the legislatures of three-fourths of the several States within seven years from the date of its submission to the States by the Congress.

[ratified February, 1951]

Amendment XXIII.

SECTION 1. The District constituting the seat of Government of the United States shall appoint in such manner as the Congress may direct:

A number of electors of President and Vice President equal to the whole number of Senators and Representatives in Congress to which the District would be entitled if it were a State, but in no event more than the least populous State; they shall be in addition to those appointed by the States, but they shall be considered, for the purposes of the election of President and Vice President, to be electors appointed by a State; and they shall meet in the District and perform such duties as provided by the twelfth article of amendment.

SECTION 2. The Congress shall have power to enforce this article by appropriate legislation.

[ratified March, 1961]

Amendment XXIV.

SECTION 1. The right of citizens of the United States to vote in any primary or other election for President or Vice President, for electors for President or Vice President, or for Senator or Representative in Congress, shall not be denied or abridged by the United States or any State by reason of failure to pay any poll tax or other tax.

SECTION 2. The Congress shall have power to enforce this article by appropriate legislation.

[ratified January, 1964]

Amendment XXV.

SECTION 1. In case of the removal of the President from office or of his death or resignation, the Vice President shall become President.

SECTION 2. Whenever there is a vacancy in the office of the Vice President, the President shall nominate a Vice President who shall take office upon confirmation by a majority vote of both Houses of Congress.

SECTION 3. Whenever the President transmits to the President pro tempore of the Senate and the Speaker of the House of Representatives his written declaration that he is unable to discharge the powers and duties of his office, and until he transmits to them a written declaration to the contrary, such powers and duties shall be discharged by the Vice President as Acting President.

SECTION 4. Whenever the Vice President and a majority of either the principal officers of the executive departments or of such other body as Congress may by law provide, transmit to the President pro tempore of the Senate and the Speaker of the House of Representatives their written declaration that the President is unable to discharge the powers and duties of his office, the Vice President shall immediately assume the powers and duties of the office as Acting President.

Thereafter, when the President transmits to the President pro tempore of the Senate and the Speaker of the House of Representatives his written declaration that no inability exists, he shall resume the powers and duties of his office unless the Vice President and a majority of either the principal officers of the executive department or of such other body as Congress may by law provide, transmit within four days to the President pro tempore of the Senate and the Speaker of the House of Representatives their written declaration that the President is unable to discharge the powers and duties of his office. Thereupon Congress shall decide the issue, assembling within forty-eight hours for that purpose if not in session. If the Congress, within twenty-one days after receipt of the latter written declaration, or, if Congress is not in session, within twenty-one days after Congress is required to assemble, determines by two-thirds vote of both Houses that the President is unable to discharge the powers and duties of his office, the Vice President shall continue to discharge the same as Acting President; otherwise, the President shall resume the powers and duties of his office.

[ratified February, 1967]

Amendment XXVI.

SECTION 1. The right of citizens of the United States, who are eighteen years of age or older, to vote shall not be denied or abridged by the United States or by any State on account of age.

SECTION 2. The Congress shall have power to enforce this article by appropriate legislation.

[ratified July, 1971]

Amendment XXVII.

No law, varying the compensation for the services of the Senators and Representatives, shall take effect, until an election of Representatives shall have intervened.

[ratified May 7, 1992]

Bibliography

1. Background

Allen, Bonnie. *We Are Overcome: Thoughts on Being Black in America.* New York: Crown, 1995.

Allen, Robert L. *Black Awakening in Capitalist America.* Garden City, N.Y.: Doubleday/Anchor, 1970.

America, Richard F. *Paying the Social Debt: What White America Owes Black America.* Westport, Conn.: Praeger, 1993.

Appiah, Kwame Anthony. *In My Father's House: Africa in the Philosophy of Culture.* New York: Oxford University Press, 1992.

Armour, Jody David. *Negrophobia and Reasonable Racism: The Hidden Costs of Being Black in America.* New York: New York University Press, 1997.

Asante, Molefi Kete. *The Afrocentric Idea.* Philadelphia: Temple University Press, 1987.

__________. *Afrocentricity.* Trenton, N.J.: Africa World Press, 1988.

Baldwin, James. *The Fire Next Time.* New York: Dell, 1963.

Berry, Mary Frances, and John Blassingame. *Long Memory: The Black Experience in America.* New York: Oxford University Press, 1982.

Blauner, Bob. *Black Lives, White Lives: Three Decades of Race Relations in America.* Berkeley: University of California Press, 1989.

Boxill, Bernard R. *Blacks and Social Justice.* Totowa, N.J.: Rowman & Allanheld, 1984.

Brock, Lisa, and Digna Castañeda Fuertes, eds. *Between Race and Empire: African-Americans and Cubans Before the Cuban Revolution.* Philadelphia: Temple University Press, 1998.

Brooks, Roy L. *Rethinking the American Race Problem.* Berkeley: University of California Press, 1990.

Broussard, Albert S. *Black San Francisco: The Struggle for Racial Equality in the West, 1900-1954.* Lawrence: University Press of Kansas, 1993.

Brown, Tony. *Black Lies, White Lies: The Truth According to Tony Brown.* New York: Wm. C. Morrow, 1995.

Carlson, Lewis H., and George A. Colburn, eds. *In Their Place: White America Defines Her Minorities, 1850-1950.* New York: Wiley, 1972.

Clark, Kenneth B. *Dark Ghetto: Dilemmas of Social Power.* New York: Harper & Row, 1965.

Cleaver, Eldridge. *Soul on Ice.* New York: McGraw-Hill, 1968.

Coleman, Jonathan. *Long Way to Go: Black and White in America.* New York: Atlantic Monthly Press, 1997.

Collier, Peter, and David Horowitz. *The Race Card: White Guilt, Black Resentment, and the Assault on Truth and Justice.* Rocklin, Calif.: Prima Publishing, 1997.

Croucher, Sheila. *Imagining Miami.* Charlottesville: University Press of Virginia, 1997.

Cruse, Harold. *Plural but Equal: A Critical Study of Blacks and Minorities in America's Plural Society.* New York: William Morrow, 1987.

Davis-Adeshoté, Jeanette, et al. *Black Survival in White America: From Past History to the Next Century.* Orange, N.J.: Bryant and Dillon, 1995.

Dorman, James H., and Robert R. Jones. *The Afro-American Experience.* New York: Wiley, 1974.

Du Bois, W. E. B. *The Souls of Black Folk.* 1903. Reprint. New York: Vintage Books, 1990.

Dunn, Marvin. *Black Miami in the Twentieth Century.* Tallahassee: University of Florida Press, 1997.

Dvorak, Katharine L. *An African American Exodus.* Brooklyn, N.Y.: Carlson, 1991.

Gaillard, Frye. *The Dream Long Deferred.* Chapel Hill: University of North Carolina Press, 1988.

Goldschmid, Marcel L., ed. *Black Americans and White Racism: Theory and Research.* New York: Holt, Rinehart and Winston, 1970.

Gubar, Susan. *Racechanges: White Skin, Black Face in American Culture.* New York: Oxford University Press, 1997.

Guerrero, Ed. *Framing Blackness.* Philadelphia: Temple University Press, 1993.

Hacker, Andrew. *Two Nations: Black and White, Separate, Hostile, Unequal.* New York: Charles Scribner's Sons, 1992.

Holden, Matthew. *The White Man's Burden.* New York: Chandler, 1973.

Johnson, Charles S. *The Negro in American Civilization: A Study of Negro Life and Race Relations in the Light of Social Research.* New York: Henry Holt, 1930.

Jordan, Winthrop D. *White over Black: American Attitudes Toward the Negro, 1550-1812.* New York: W. W. Norton, 1968, 1995.

Keyes, Alan L. *Masters of the Dream: The Strength and Betrayal of Black America.* New York: William Morrow, 1995.

Kochman, Thomas. *Black and White Styles in Conflict.* Chicago: University of Chicago Press, 1981.

Lefkowitz, Mary. *Not out of Africa: How Afrocentrism Became an Excuse to Teach Myth.* New York: Basic Books, 1996.

Long, Richard A. *African Americans: A Portrait.* New York: Crescent Books, 1993.

Lyman, Stanford M. *The Black American in Sociological Thought.* New York: Putnam, 1972.

McWilliams, Carey. *Brothers Under the Skin.* Rev. ed. Boston: Little, Brown, 1964.

Mills, Charles W. *Blackness Visible: Essays on Philosophy and Race.* Ithaca, N.Y.: Cornell University Press, 1998.

Munford, Clarence J. *Race and Reparations: A Black Perspective for the Twenty-first Century.* Trenton, N.J.: Africa World Press, 1996.

Myrdal, Gunnar. *An American Dilemma: The Negro Problem and American Democracy.* New York: Harper & Row, 1944; McGraw-Hill, 1964.

Parsons, Talcott, and Kenneth B. Clark, eds. *The Negro American.* Boston: Houghton Mifflin, 1966.

Pettigrew, Thomas F. *A Profile of the Negro American.* Princeton, N.J.: D. Van Nostrand, 1964.

Pieterse, Jan Nederveen. *White on Black.* New Haven, Conn.: Yale University Press, 1992.

Ploski, Harry A., and James Williams, eds. *The Negro Almanac: A Reference Work on the African American.* Detroit, Mich.: Gale Research, 1989.

Shipler, David K. *A Country of Strangers: Blacks and Whites in America.* New York: Knopf, 1997.

Sigelman, Lee, and Susan Welch. *Black Americans' Views of Racial Inequality.* Cambridge, England: Cambridge University Press, 1991.

Silberman, Charles E. *Crisis in Black and White.* New York: Vintage Books, 1964.

Smith, Lillian. *Killers of the Dream.* New York: W. W. Norton, 1949.

Steele, Shelby. *A Dream Deferred: The Second Betrayal of Black Freedom in America.* New York: HarperCollins, 1998.

Thernstrom, Stephan, and Abigail Thernstrom. *America in Black and White: One Nation Indivisible.* New York: Random House, 1997.

West, Cornell. *Race Matters.* New York: Random House, 1993.

__________. *Restoring Hope: Conversations on the Future of Black America.* Boston: Beacon Press, 1997.

Wonkeryor, Edward Lama. *On Afrocentricity, Intercultural Communication, and Racism.* Lewiston, N.Y.: Edwin Mellin Press, 1998.

2. History

Anderson, Eric, and Alfred A. Moss, Jr., eds. *The Facts of Reconstruction: Essays in Honor of John Hope Franklin.* Baton Rouge: Louisiana State University Press, 1991.

Aptheker, Herbert. *Anti-Racism in U.S. History: The First Two Hundred Years.* New York: Greenwood Press, 1992.

Bell, Howard Holman. *A Survey of the Negro Convention Movement, 1830-1861.* New York: Arno Press, 1969.

Benedict, Michael Les. *A Compromise of Principle: Congressional Republicans and Reconstruction, 1863-1869.* New York: W. W. Norton, 1974.

Bonnett, Aubrey W., and G. Llewellyn Watson, eds. *Emerging Perspectives on the Black Diaspora.* Lanham, Md.: University Press of America, 1990.

Brown, Richard H. *The Missouri Compromise: Political Statesmanship or Unwise Evasion?* Boston: D. C. Heath, 1964.

Carter, Dan T. *Scottsboro: A Tragedy of the American South.* Rev. ed. Baton Rouge: Louisiana State University Press, 1979.

__________. *When the War Was Over: The Failure of Self-Reconstruction in the South, 1865-1867.* Baton Rouge: Louisiana State University Press, 1985.

Chalmers, Allan Knight. *They Shall Be Free.* Garden City, N.Y.: Doubleday, 1951.

Collins, Bruce. *The Origins of America's Civil War.* New York: Holmes & Meier, 1981.

Conniff, Michael L., and Thomas J. Davis. *Africans in the Americas: A History of the Black Diaspora.* New York: St. Martin's Press, 1994.

Cox, LaWanda. *Lincoln and Black Freedom: A Study in Presidential Leadership.* Columbia: University of South Carolina Press, 1981.

Cox, LaWanda, and John H. Cox. *Politics, Principle, and Prejudice: Dilemma of Reconstruction America, 1865-1866.* New York: Free Press, 1963.

Cronon, E. David. *Black Moses: The Story of Marcus Garvey and the Universal Negro Improvement Association.* Madison: University of Wisconsin Press, 1955.

Crouch, Barry A. *The Freedmen's Bureau and Black Texans.* Austin: University of Texas Press, 1992.

Dykstra, Robert R. *Bright Radical Star: Black Freedom and White Supremacy on the Hawkeye Frontier.* Cambridge, Mass.: Harvard University Press, 1993.

Finkelman, Paul, ed. *Race, Law, and American History, 1700-1900.* 11 vols. New York: Garland, 1992.

Foner, Eric. *Nothing but Freedom: Emancipation and Its Legacy.* Baton Rouge: Louisiana State University Press, 1983.

__________. *Reconstruction: America's Unfinished Revolution.* New York: Harper & Row, 1988.

Franklin, John Hope. *The Emancipation Proclamation.* Garden City, N.Y.: Doubleday, 1963.

__________. *Reconstruction: After the Civil War.* Chicago: University of Chicago Press, 1961.

Franklin, John Hope, and Alfred A. Moss, Jr. *From Slavery to Freedom: A History of African Americans.* 7th ed. New York: McGraw-Hill, 1994.

Frazier, Thomas R., ed. *Afro-American History: Primary Sources.* New York: Harcourt, Brace & World, 1970.

Frederickson, George M. *The Arrogance of Race: Historical Perspectives.* Middletown, Conn.: Wesleyan University Press, 1988.

Garvey, Amy Jacques. *Garvey and Garveyism.* 1963. Reprint. New York: Collier, 1976.

Garvey, Marcus. *Philosophy and Opinions of Marcus Garvey.* Edited by Amy Jacques-Garvey, with new introduction by Robert A. Hill. New York: Atheneum, 1992.

Goodfriend, Joyce D. *Before the Melting Pot: Society and Culture in Colonial New York City, 1664-1730.* Princeton, N.J.: Princeton University Press, 1992.

Hamilton, Holman. *Prologue to Conflict: The Crisis and Compromise of 1850.* New York: W. W. Norton, 1964.

Harlan, Louis R. *Booker T. Washington in Perspective: Essays of Louis R. Harlan.* Edited by Raymond W. Smock. Jackson: University Press of Mississippi, 1988.

__________. *Booker T. Washington: The Making of a Black Leader, 1856-1901.* New York: Oxford University Press, 1972.

__________. *Booker T. Washington: The Wizard of Tuskegee, 1901-1915.* New York: Oxford University Press, 1983.

Hill, Robert A., and Barbara Bair, eds. *Marcus Garvey: Life and Lessons.* Berkeley: University of California Press, 1987.

Holman, Hamilton. *Prologue to Conflict: The Crisis and Compromise of 1850.* New York: W. W. Norton, 1966.

Holt, Michael. *The Political Crisis of the 1850's.* New York: W. W. Norton, 1978.

Hornsby, Alton, Jr. *Chronology of African-American History.* Detroit, Mich.: Gale Research, 1991.

Keegan, Frank L. *Blacktown, U.S.A.* Boston: Little, Brown, 1971.

Kellogg, Charles Flint. *NAACP: A History of the National Association for the Advancement of Colored People.* Baltimore: The Johns Hopkins University Press, 1964.

Kusmer, Kenneth L., ed. *Black Communities and Urban Development in America, 1720-1990.* New York: Garland, 1991.

Lasch-Quinn, Elisabeth. *Black Neighbors: Race and the Limits of Reform in the American Settlement House Movement, 1890-1945.* Chapel Hill: University of North Carolina Press, 1993.

Leckie, William H. *The Buffalo Soldiers: A Narrative of the Negro Cavalry in the West.* Norman: University of Oklahoma Press, 1967.

Lemann, Nicholas. *The Promised Land: The Great Black Migration and How It Changed America.* New York: Alfred A. Knopf, 1991.

Lewis, David Levering. *W. E. B. Du Bois: Biography of a Race, 1868-1919.* New York: Henry Holt, 1993.

Lewis, Rupert, and Maureen Warner-Lewis, eds. *Garvey: Africa, Europe, the Americas.* Kingston, Jamaica: Institute of Social and Economic Research, University of the West Indies, 1986.

Lofgren, Charles A. *The Plessy Case: A Legal-Historical Interpretation.* New York: Oxford University Press, 1987.

Lubiano, Wahneema, ed. *The House That Race Built: Black Americans, U.S. Terrain.* New York: Pantheon, 1997.

McPherson, James M. *The Battle Cry of Freedom: The Civil War Era.* Oxford, England: Oxford University Press, 1988.

__________. *The Negro in the Civil War.* New York: Vintage Books, 1965.

__________. *Ordeal by Fire: The Civil War and Reconstruction.* 2d ed. New York: McGraw-Hill, 1992.

__________. *The Struggle for Equality: Abolitionists and the Negro in the Civil War and Reconstruction.* Princeton, N.J.: Princeton University Press, 1964.

Magdol, Edward. *A Right to the Land: Essays on the Freedmen's Community.* Westport, Conn.: Greenwood Press, 1977.

Mathurin, Owen Charles. *Henry Sylvester Williams and the Origins of the Pan-African Movement, 1869-1911.* Westport, Conn.: Greenwood Press, 1976.

Meier, August. *Negro Thought in America, 1880-1915: Racial Ideologies in the Age of Booker T. Washington.* Ann Arbor: University of Michigan Press, 1988.

Miller, Loren. *The Petitioners: The Story of the Supreme Court of the United States and the Negro.* New York: Pantheon Books, 1966.

Moses, Wilson Jeremiah. *The Golden Age of Black Nationalism, 1850-1925.* New York: Oxford University Press, 1978.

Nevins, Allen. *A House Dividing, 1852-1857.* Vol. 2 in *Ordeal of the Union.* New York: Charles Scribner's Sons, 1947.

Nieman, Donald G. *Promises to Keep: African-Americans and the Constitutional Order, 1776 to the Present.* New York: Oxford University Press, 1991.

Norris, Clarence, and Sybil D. Washington. *The Last of the Scottsboro Boys.* New York: Putnam, 1979.

Oates, Stephen B. *Our Fiery Trial: Abraham Lincoln, John Brown, and the Civil War Era.* Amherst: University of Massachusetts Press, 1979.

Ovington, Mary White, et al. *Black and White Sat Down Together: The Reminiscences of an NAACP Founder.* New York: Feminist Press of City University of New York, 1996.

Patterson, Haywood, and Earl Conrad. *Scottsboro Boy.* Garden City, N.Y.: Doubleday, 1950.

Potter, David M. *The Impending Crisis, 1848-1861.* Completed and edited by Don. E. Fehrenbacher. New York: Harper & Row, 1976.

Quarles, Benjamin. *Lincoln and the Negro.* New York: Oxford University Press, 1962.

__________. *The Negro in the Civil War.* Boston: Little, Brown, 1953.

Rabinowitz, Howard N., and George W. Frederickson. *Race Relations in the Urban South, 1865-1890.* New York: Oxford University Press, 1996.

Rasmussen, R. Kent. *Farewell to Jim Crow: The Rise and Fall of Segregation in America.* New York: Facts On File, 1998.

Rymer, Russ. *American Beach: A Saga of Race, Wealth, and Memory.* New York: HarperCollins, 1998.

Shropshire, Kenneth L., and Kellen Winslow. *In Black and White: Race and Sports in America.* New York: New York University Press, 1996.

Stampp, Kenneth, ed. *The Causes of the Civil War.* Rev. ed. Englewood Cliffs, N.J.: Prentice-Hall, 1974.

__________. *The Era of Reconstruction, 1865-1877.* New York: Alfred A. Knopf, 1965.

Tygiel, Jules. *Baseball's Great Experiment: Jackie Robinson and His Legacy*. New York: Vintage, 1984.

Van Denburg, William L., ed. *Modern Black Nationalism: From Marcus Garvey to Louis Farrakhan*. New York: New York University Press, 1997.

Van Sertima, Ivan, ed. *African Presence in Early America*. New Brunswick, N.J.: Transaction, 1992.

Walvin, James. *Black and White: The Negro and English Society, 1555-1945*. London: Penguin Press, 1973.

Williams, Vernon J. *From a Caste to a Minority: Changing Attitudes of American Sociologists Toward Afro-Americans, 1896-1945*. New York: Greenwood Press, 1989.

Wood, Peter H. *Black Majority: Negroes in Colonial South Carolina from 1670 Through the Stono Rebellion*. New York: W. W. Norton, 1974.

3. Slavery

Abbott, Richard H. *Cotton and Capital: Boston Businessmen and Antislavery Reform, 1854-1868*. Amherst: University of Massachusetts Press, 1991.

Angle, Paul M., ed. *Created Equal? The Complete Lincoln-Douglas Debates of 1858*. Chicago: University of Chicago Press, 1958.

Aptheker, Herbert. *American Negro Slave Revolts*. 1943. Rev. ed. New York: Columbia University Press, 1969.

Ball, Edward. *Slaves in the Family*. New York: Farrar, Straus & Giroux, 1998.

Barber, John Warner. *A History of the Amistad Captives*. New York: Arno Press, 1969.

Barnes, Gilbert Hobbs. *The Antislavery Impulse: 1830-1844*. New York: Harcourt, Brace & World, 1964.

Bender, Thomas, ed. *The Antislavery Debate: Capitalism and Abolitionism as a Problem in Historical Interpretation*. Berkeley: University of California Press, 1992.

Berlin, Ira. *Many Thousands Gone: The First Two Centuries of Slavery in North America*. Cambridge, Mass.: Belknap Press, 1998.

Berlin, Ira, et al. *Slaves No More: Three Essays on Emancipation and the Civil War*. Cambridge, England: Cambridge University Press, 1992.

Blackburn, Robin. *The Overthrow of Colonial Slavery, 1776-1848*. New York: Verso, 1988.

Blassingame, John W. *The Slave Community: Plantation Life in the Antebellum South*. New York: Oxford University Press, 1972.

Blassingame, John W., and John R. McKivigan, eds. *The Frederick Douglass Papers*. Series 1, *Speeches, Debates, and Interviews*. Vol. 3, *1855-1863*. New Haven, Conn.: Yale University Press, 1991.

Bontemps, Arna, ed. *Great Slave Narratives*. Boston: Beacon Press, n.d.

Boskin, Joseph. *Into Slavery: Racial Decisions in the Virginia Colony*. Philadelphia: J. B. Lippincott, 1976.

Boyer, Richard O. *The Legend of John Brown: A Biography and a History*. New York: Alfred A. Knopf, 1972.

Buckmaster, Henrietta. *Let My People Go: The Story of the Underground Railroad and the Growth of the Abolition Movement.* Boston: Beacon Press, 1941.

Campbell, Stanley. *The Slave Catchers: Enforcement of the Fugitive Slave Law, 1850-1860.* Chapel Hill: University of North Carolina Press, 1970.

Catterall, Helen T., ed. *Judicial Cases Concerning American Slavery and the Negro.* 5 vols. New York: Octagon Books, 1968.

Curtin, Philip D. *The Atlantic Slave Trade.* Madison: University of Wisconsin Press, 1969.

Daniel, Pete. *The Shadow of Slavery: Peonage in the South, 1901-1969.* Urbana: University of Illinois Press, 1972.

Davis, David Brion. *The Problem of Slavery in the Age of Revolution, 1770-1823.* Ithaca, N.Y.: Cornell University Press, 1975.

__________. *The Problem of Slavery in Western Culture.* Ithaca, N.Y.: Cornell University Press, 1966.

__________. *Slavery and Human Progress.* New York: Oxford University Press, 1984.

Degler, Carl N. *Neither Black nor White: Slavery and Race Relations in Brazil and the United States.* 1971. Madison: University of Wisconsin Press, 1986.

Duberman, Martin, ed. *The Antislavery Vanguard: New Essays on the Abolitionists.* Princeton, N.J.: Princeton University Press, 1965.

Elkins, Stanley M. *Slavery: A Problem in American Institutional and Intellectual Life.* Chicago: University of Chicago Press, 1959.

Eltis, David, and James Walvin, eds. *The Abolition of the Atlantic Slave Trade: Origins and Effects in Europe, Africa, and the Americas.* Madison: University of Wisconsin Press, 1981.

Faust, Drew Glipin. *The Ideology of Slavery: Proslavery Thought in the Antebellum South, 1830-1860.* Baton Rouge: Louisiana State University Press, 1981.

Filler, Louis. *The Crusade Against Slavery, 1830-1860.* New York: Harper & Row, 1960.

Finkelman, Paul, ed. *Slavery and the Founders: Race and Liberty in the Age of Jefferson.* Armonk, N.Y.: M. E. Sharpe, 1996.

Finley, Moses I. *Ancient Slavery and Modern Ideology.* New York: Viking Press, 1980.

Fogel, Robert. *Without Consent or Contract: The Rise and Fall of American Slavery.* New York: W. W. Norton, 1989.

Franklin, Raymond S. *Shadows of Race and Class.* Minneapolis: University of Minnesota Press, 1991.

Friedman, Lawrence J. *Gregarious Saints: Self and Community in American Abolitionism, 1830-1870.* New York: Cambridge University Press, 1982.

Frost, J. William, ed. *The Quaker Origins of Antislavery.* Norwood, Pa.: Norwood Editions, 1980.

Gara, Larry. *The Liberty Line: The Legend of the Underground Railroad.* Lexington: University of Kentucky Press, 1961.

Genovese, Eugene D. *Roll, Jordan, Roll: The World the Slaves Made.* New York: Pantheon Books, 1974.

__________. *The Slaverholders' Dilemma: Freedom and Progress in Southern Conservative Thought, 1820-1860.* Columbia: University of South Carolina Press, 1992.

Goldwin, Robert A., and Art Kaufman. *Slavery and Its Consequences: The Constitution, Equality, and Race.* Washington, D.C.: American Enterprise Institute Press, 1988.

Goodheart, Lawrence, Richard D. Brown, and Stephen Rabe, eds. *Slavery in American Society.* 3d ed. Lexington, Mass.: Heath, 1993.

Goodman, Paul. *Of One Blood: Abolitionism and the Origins of Racial Equality.* Berkeley: University of California Press, 1998.

Gutman, Herbert. *The Black Family in Slavery and Freedom, 1750-1925.* New York: Pantheon, 1976.

Harris, Marvin. *Patterns of Race Relations in America.* New York: Walker, 1964.

Hoetink, H. *Slavery and Race Relations in the Americas: Notes on Their Nature and Nexus.* New York: Harper & Row, 1973.

Holzer, Harold, ed. *The Lincoln-Douglas Debates: The First Complete, Unexpurgated Text.* New York: HarperCollins, 1993.

Howard, Warren S. *American Slavers and the Federal Law: 1837-1862.* Berkeley: University of California Press, 1963.

Huggins, Nathan Irvin. *Slave and Citizen: The Life of Frederick Douglass.* Boston: Little, Brown, 1980.

James, Sydney V. *A People Among Peoples: Quaker Benevolence in Eighteenth Century America.* Cambridge, Mass.: Harvard University Press, 1963.

Jenkins, William S. *Pro-Slavery Thought in the Old South.* Chapel Hill: University of North Carolina Press, 1935.

Kolchin, Peter. *American Slavery: 1619-1877.* New York: Hill & Wang, 1993.

Kraditor, Aileen S. *Means and Ends in American Abolitionism: Garrison and His Critics on Strategy and Tactics, 1834-1850.* New York: Vintage Books, 1970.

Kraut, Alan M., ed. *Crusaders and Compromisers: Essays on the Relationship of the Antislavery Struggle to the Antebellum Party System.* Westport, Conn.: Greenwood Press, 1983.

Levine, Alan J. *Race Relations Within Western Expansion.* Westport, Conn.: Praeger, 1996.

Litwack, Leon F. *Been in the Storm So Long: The Aftermath of Slavery.* New York: Alfred A. Knopf, 1979.

__________. *North of Slavery: The Negro in the Free States: 1790-1860.* Chicago: University of Chicago Press, 1961.

McGary, Howard, and Bill E. Lawson. *Between Slavery and Freedom: Philosophy and American Slavery.* Bloomington: Indiana University Press, 1992.

McKivigan, John R. *The War Against Proslavery Religion: Abolitionism and the Northern Churches, 1830-1865.* Ithaca, N.Y.: Cornell University Press, 1984.

MacLeod, Duncan J. *Slavery, Race, and the American Revolution.* London: Cambridge University Press, 1974.

McManus, Edgar J. *A History of Negro Slavery in New York.* Syracuse, N.Y.: Syracuse University Press, 1966.

Martin, Christopher. *The "Amistad" Affair.* New York: Abelard-Schuman, 1970.

Martin, Waldo E. *The Mind of Frederick Douglass.* Chapel Hill: University of North Carolina Press, 1984.

Melish, Joanne Pope. *Disowning Slavery: Gradual Emancipation and "Race" in New England, 1780-1860.* Ithaca: Cornell University Press, 1998.

Meltzer, Milton, ed. *Frederick Douglass, in His Own Words.* San Diego, Calif.: Harcourt, Brace, 1995.

Merrill, Walter M. *Against Wind and Tide: A Biography of William Lloyd Garrison.* Cambridge, Mass.: Harvard University Press, 1963.

Morgan, Edmund S. *American Slavery, American Freedom: The Ordeal of Colonial Virginia.* New York: W. W. Norton, 1975.

Morris, Thomas D. *Free Men All: The Personal Liberty Laws of the North, 1780-1861.* Baltimore: The Johns Hopkins University Press, 1974.

Mullin, Michael. *Africa in America: Slave Acculturation and Resistance in the American South and the British Caribbean, 1736-1831.* Urbana: University of Illinois Press, 1992.

Nye, Russel B. *William Lloyd Garrison and the Humanitarian Reformers.* Boston: Little, Brown, 1955.

Oakes, James. *The Ruling Race: A History of American Slaveholders.* New York: Alfred A. Knopf, 1982.

__________. *Slavery and Freedom: An Interpretation of the Old South.* New York: Alfred A. Knopf, 1990.

Owen, Robert Dale. *The Wrong of Slavery, the Right of Emancipation, and the Future of the African Race in the United States.* Philadelphia: J. B. Lippincott, 1864.

Owens, William A. *Black Mutiny: The Revolt on the Schooner "Amistad."* Philadelphia: Pilgrim Press, 1968.

Patterson, Orlando. *Slavery and Social Death: A Comparative Study.* Cambridge, Mass.: Harvard University Press, 1982.

__________. *The Sociology of Slavery.* Rutherford, N.J.: Fairleigh Dickinson University Press, 1975.

Perry, Lewis, and Michael Fellman, eds. *Antislavery Reconsidered: New Perspectives on the Abolitionists.* Baton Rouge: Louisiana State University Press, 1979.

Phillips, Ulrich B. *American Negro Slavery.* Baton Rouge: Louisiana State University Press, 1966.

Phillips, William D. *Slavery from Roman Times to the Early Transatlantic Trade.* Minneapolis: University of Minnesota Press, 1985.

Quarles, Benjamin. *Black Abolitionists.* New York: Oxford University Press, 1969.

Rawley, James A. *The Transatlantic Slave Trade: A History.* New York: W. W. Norton, 1981.

Rogers, William B. *"We Are All Together Now": Frederick Douglass, William Lloyd Garrison, and the Prophetic Tradition.* New York: Garland, 1995.

Schwartz, Philip J. *Twice Condemned: Slaves and the Criminal Laws of Virginia, 1705-1865.* Baton Rouge: Louisiana State University Press, 1988.

Shaw, Robert B. *A Legal History of Slavery in the United States.* Potsdam, N.Y.: Northern Press, 1991.

Siebert, Wilbur H. *The Underground Railroad from Slavery to Freedom.* 1898. Reprint. New York: Arno Press, 1968.

Smith, John D. *Black Slavery in the Americas: An Interdisciplinary Bibliography, 1865-1980.* 2 vols. Westport, Conn.: Greenwood Press, 1982.

Sorin, Gerald. *Abolitionism: A New Perspective.* New York: Praeger, 1972.

Stampp, Kenneth M. *The Peculiar Institution: Slavery in the Ante-Bellum South.* New York: Alfred A. Knopf, 1956.

Stewart, James Brewer. *Holy Warriors: The Abolitionists and American Slavery.* New York: Hill & Wang, 1976.

__________. *William Lloyd Garrison and the Challenge of Emancipation.* Arlington Heights, Ill.: Harlan Davidson, 1992.

Still, William. *The Underground Railroad.* 1872. Reprint. Chicago: Johnson, 1972.

Stuckey, Sterling. *Slave Culture.* New York: Oxford University Press, 1987.

Styron, William. *Confessions of Nat Turner.* New York: Random House, 1967.

Thomas, John L. *The Liberator: William Lloyd Garrison, A Biography.* Boston: Little, Brown, 1963.

Tise, Larry E. *Proslavery: A History of the Defense of Slavery in America, 1701-1840.* Athens: University of Georgia Press, 1987.

Tushnet, Mark V. *The American Law of Slavery, 1810-1860: Considerations of Humanity and Interest.* Princeton, N.J.: Princeton University Press, 1981.

Washington, Booker T. *Up from Slavery.* 1901. Reprint. New York: Gramercy Books, 1993.

Watson, Alan. *Slave Law in the Americas.* Athens: University of Georgia Press, 1989.

White, Shane. *Somewhat More Independent: The End of Slavery in New York City, 1770-1810.* Athens: University of Georgia Press, 1991.

Wilson, Carol. *Freedom at Risk: The Kidnapping of Free Blacks in America,* 1780-1865. Lexington: University Press of Kentucky, 1994.

Woodward, C. Vann. *American Counterpoint: Slavery and Racism in the North-South Dialogue.* Boston: Little, Brown, 1971.

Zilversmit, Arthur. *The First Emancipation: The Abolition of Slavery in the North.* Chicago: University of Chicago Press, 1967.

4. The South and Segregation

Baer, Hans A., and Yvonne Jones, eds. *African Americans in the South: Issues of Race, Class, and Gender.* Athens: University of Georgia Press, 1992.

Bartley, Numan V. *The New South: 1945-1980.* Baton Rouge: Louisiana State University Press, 1995.

Bayor, Ronald H. *Race and the Shaping of Twentieth-Century Atlanta.* Chapel Hill: University of North Carolina Press, 1996.

Davis, Allison, Burleigh B. Gardner, and Mary R. Gardner. *Deep South: A Social Anthropological Study of Caste and Class.* Chicago: University of Chicago Press, 1941.

Dollard, John. *Caste and Class in a Southern Town.* New Haven, Conn: Yale University Press, 1947.

Fossett, Mark A., and Therese Siebert. *Long Time Coming: Racial Inequality in the Nonmetropolitan South, 1940-1990.* Boulder, Colo.: Westview Press, 1997.

Goldfield, David R. *Black, White, and Southern: Race Relations in Southern Culture, 1940 to the Present.* Baton Rouge: Louisiana State University Press, 1990.

__________. *Region, Race and Cities: Interpreting the Urban South.* Baton Rouge: Louisiana State University Press, 1997.

Hale, Grace Elizabeth. *Making Whiteness: The Culture of Segregation in the South, 1890-1940.* New York: Pantheon, 1998.

Larson, Edward J. *Sex, Race, and Science: Eugenics in the Deep South.* Baltimore: The Johns Hopkins University Press, 1995.

McLaurin, Melton A. *Separate Pasts: Growing Up White in the Segregated South.* Athens: University of Georgia Press, 1987.

McMillen, Neil R. *Dark Journey: Black Mississippians in the Age of Jim Crow.* Urbana: University of Illinois Press, 1990.

Newby, I. A. *Jim Crow's Defense.* Baton Rouge: Louisiana State University Press, 1965.

Odum, Howard W. *Race and Rumors of Race: The American South in the Early Forties.* Baltimore: The Johns Hopkins University Press, 1997.

Stokes, Melvyn, and Rick Halpern, eds. *Race and Class in the American South Since 1890.* Providence, R.I.: Berg, 1994.

Williamson, Joel. *A Rage for Order: Black-White Relations in the American South Since Emancipation.* New York: Oxford University Press, 1986.

Wilson, Theodore B. *The Black Codes of the South.* Tuscaloosa: University of Alabama Press, 1965.

Woodward, C. Vann. *The Strange Career of Jim Crow.* 3d rev. ed. New York: Oxford University Press, 1974.

5. Modern Civil Rights Movement Era

Abernathy, Ralph. *And the Walls Came Tumbling Down.* New York: Harper & Row, 1989.

Ashmore, Harry S. *"Civil Rights and Wrongs": A Memoir of Race and Politics, 1944-1996.* Rev. and expanded ed. Columbia: University of South Carolina Press, 1997.

Bartley, Numan V. *The Rise of Massive Resistance: Race and Politics in the South During the 1950's.* Baton Rouge: Louisiana State University Press, 1969.

Bates, Daisy. *The Long Shadow of Little Rock: A Memoir.* New York: David McKay, 1962.

Blaustein, Albert P., and Robert L. Zangrando, eds. *Civil Rights and the American Negro: A Documentary History.* New York: Trident Press, 1968.

Bloom, Jack D. *Class, Race, and the Civil Rights Movement.* Bloomington: Indiana University Press, 1987.

Blossom, Virgil T. *It Has Happened Here.* New York: Harper and Brothers, 1959.

Blumberg, Rhoda L. *Civil Rights: The 1960's Freedom Struggle.* Boston: Twayne, 1984.

Burk, Robert Frederick. *The Eisenhower Administration and Black Civil Rights.* Knoxville: University of Tennessee Press, 1984.

Burns, W. Haywood. *The Voices of Negro Protest in America.* New York: Oxford University Press, 1963.

Carmichael, Stokely, and Charles V. Hamilton. *Black Power: The Politics of Liberation in America.* New York: Random House, 1967.

Carson, Clayborne. *In Struggle: SNCC and the Black Awakening of the 1960's.* Cambridge: Mass.: Harvard University Press, 1981.

Carson, Clayborne, et al., eds. *Eyes on the Prize Civil Rights Reader: Documents, Speeches, and Firsthand Accounts from the Black Freedom Struggle, 1954-1990.* New York: Penguin, 1991.

Chappell, David L. *Inside Agitators: White Southerners in the Civil Rights Movement.* Baltimore: The Johns Hopkins University Press, 1994.

Chong, Dennis. *Collective Action and the Civil Rights Movement.* Chicago: University of Chicago Press, 1991.

Churchill, Ward, and Jim Vander Wall. *Agents of Repression: The FBI's Secret Wars Against the Black Panther Party and the American Indian Movement.* Boston: South End Press, 1988.

Couto, Richard A. *Ain't Gonna Let Nobody Turn Me Round: The Pursuit of Racial Justice in the Rural South.* Philadelphia: Temple University Press, 1991.

D'Emilio, John. *The Civil Rights Struggle: Leaders in Profile.* New York: Facts On File, 1979.

Dees, Morris. *The Gathering Storm.* New York: HarperCollins, 1996.

Dees, Morris, with Steve Fiffer. *A Season for Justice: The Life and Times of Civil Rights Lawyer Morris Dees.* New York: Maxwell Macmillan International, 1991.

Dittmer, John. *Local People: The Struggle for Civil Rights in Mississippi.* Urbana: University of Illinois Press, 1994.

Draper, Alan. *Conflict of Interests: Organized Labor and the Civil Rights Movement in the South, 1954-1968.* Ithaca, N.Y.: ILR Press, 1994.

Dunbar, Leslie W. *Minority Report: What Has Happened to Blacks, American Indians, and Other Minorities in the Eighties.* New York: Pantheon, 1984.

Farmer, James. *Freedom—When?* New York: Random House, 1965.

__________. *Lay Bare the Heart: The Autobiography of the Civil Rights Movement.* New York: New American Library, 1985.

Finch, Minnie. *The NAACP: Its Fight for Justice.* Metuchen, N.J.: Scarecrow Press, 1981.

Forman, James. *The Making of Black Revolutionaries.* 1972. 2d ed. Washington, D.C.: Open Hand, 1985.

Freyer, Tony. *The Little Rock Crisis: A Constitutional Interpretation.* Westport, Conn.: Greenwood Press, 1984.

Garrow, David J., ed. *We Shall Overcome: The Civil Rights Movement in the United States in the 1950's and 1960's.* 3 vols. Brooklyn, N.Y.: Carlson, 1989.

Graham, Hugh Davis. *The Civil Rights Era: Origins and Development of National Policy.* New York: Oxford University Press, 1990.

Hamilton, Charles, and Stokely Carmichael. *Black Power.* New York: Random House, 1967.

Harvey, James C. *Black Civil Rights During the Johnson Administration.* Jackson: University and College Press of Mississippi, 1973.

Higham, John, ed. *Civil Rights and Social Wrongs: Black-White Relations Since World War II.* University Park: Pennsylvania State University Press, 1997.

Hill, Herbert, and James E. Jones, Jr., eds. *Race in America: The Struggle for Equality.* Madison: University of Wisconsin Press, 1993.

Kosof, Anna. *The Civil Rights Movement and Its Legacy.* New York: Watts, 1989.

Levy, Peter B. *The Civil Rights Movement.* Westport, Conn.: Greenwood Press, 1998.

McKissack, Pat, and Fredrick McKissack. *The Civil Rights Movement in America from 1865 to the Present.* 2d ed. Chicago: Children's Press, 1991.

McMillen, Neil R. *The Citizens' Council: Organized Resistance to the Second Reconstruction, 1954-1964.* Urbana: University of Illinois Press, 1971.

Marsh, Charles. *God's Long Summer: Stories of Faith and Civil Rights.* Princeton, N.J.: Princeton University Press, 1997.

Meier, August, and Elliot Rudwick. *CORE: A Study in the Civil Rights Movement, 1942-1968.* Urbana: University of Illinois Press, 1975.

Meredith, James H. *Three Years in Mississippi.* Bloomington: Indiana University Press, 1966.

Meriwether, Louise. *Don't Ride the Bus on Mondays: The Rosa Parks Story.* Englewood Cliffs, N. J.: Prentice Hall, 1973.

Miller, Marilyn. *The Bridge at Selma.* Morristown, N.J.: Silver Burdett, 1985.

Morris, Aldon B. *The Origins of the Civil Rights Movement: Black Communities Organizing for Change.* New York: Free Press, 1984.

Newton, Huey P. *To Die for the People.* New York: Random House, 1972.

__________. *War Against the Panthers: A Study of Repression in America.* New York: Harlem River Press, 1996.

O'Neill, William L. *Coming Apart: An Informal History of America in the 1960's.* Chicago: Quadrangle Books, 1971.

Oppenheimer, Martin. *The Sit-in Movement of 1960.* Brooklyn, N.Y.: Carlson, 1989.

O'Reilly, Kenneth. *Racial Matters: The FBI's Secret File on Black America, 1960-1972.* New York: Free Press, 1989.

Powledge, Fred. *Free at Last? The Civil Rights Movement and the People Who Made It.* Boston: Little, Brown, 1991.

Price, Steven D., comp. *Civil Rights, 1967-68.* Vol. 2. New York: Facts On File, 1973.

Record, Wilson, and Jane Cassels Record, eds. *Little Rock, U.S.A.* San Francisco: Chandler, 1960.

Robinson, Jo Ann Gibson. *The Montgomery Bus Boycott and the Women Who Started It: The Memoir of Jo Ann Gibson Robinson.* Knoxville: University of Tennessee Press, 1987.

Rothschild, Mary Aickin. *A Case of Black and White: Northern Volunteers and the Southern Freedom Summers, 1964-1965.* Westport, Conn.: Greenwood Press, 1982.

Seale, Bobby. *Seize the Time: The Story of the Black Panther Party and Huey P. Newton.* New York: Random House, 1968.

Sitkoff, Harvard. *The New Deal for Blacks: The Emergence of Civil Rights as a National Issue.* New York: Oxford University Press, 1978.

__________. *The Struggle for Black Equality, 1954-1980.* New York: Hill and Wang, 1993.

Van Dyke, Vernon. *The Human Rights, Ethnicity, and Discrimination.* Westport, Conn.: Greenwood Press, 1985.

Weisbrot, Robert. *Freedom Bound: A History of America's Civil Rights Movement.* New York: W. W. Norton, 1990.

Wexler, Sanford. *The Civil Rights Movement: An Eyewitness History.* New York: Facts On File, 1993.

Williams, Juan. *Eyes on the Prize: America's Civil Rights Years, 1954-1965.* New York: Viking, 1987.

Young, Andrew. *An Easy Burden: The Civil Rights Movement and the Transformation of America.* New York: HarperCollins, 1996.

6. Affirmative Action

Annals of the American Academy of Political and Social Science 523 (September, 1992). Special issue, Affirmative Action Revisited.

Badgett, M. V. Lee, Andrew F. Brimmer, Cecilia A. Conrad, and Heidi Hartmann. *Economic Perspectives on Affirmative Action.* Washington, D.C.: Joint Center for Political and Economic Studies, 1995.

Beckwith, Francis J., and Todd E. Jones, eds. *Affirmative Action: Social Justice or Reverse Discrimination?* Amherst, N.Y.: Prometheus, 1997.

Benokraitis, Nijole, and Joe R. Feagin. *Affirmative Action and Equal Opportunity: Action, Inaction, Reaction.* Boulder, Colo.: Westview Press, 1978.

Bolick, Clint. *The Affirmative Action Fraud: Can We Restore the American Civil Rights Vision?* Washington, D.C.: Cato Institute, 1996.

Bowen, William G., and Derek Bok. *The Shape of the River: Long-Term Consequences of Considering Race in College and University Admissions.* Princeton, N.J.: Princeton University Press, 1998.

Bowie, Norman E., ed. *Equal Opportunity.* Boulder, Colo.: Westview Press, 1988.

Burstein, Paul. "Affirmative Action, Jobs, and American Democracy: What Has Happened to the Quest for Equal Opportunity?" *Law and Society Review* 26, no. 4 (1992): 901-922.

Carter, Stephen L. *Reflections of an Affirmative Action Baby.* New York: Basic Books, 1992.

Clayton, Susan D., and Faye J. Crosby. *Justice, Gender and Affirmative Action.* Ann Arbor: University of Michigan Press, 1992.

Cohen, Carl. *Naked Racial Preferences: The Case Against Affirmative Action.* Lanham, Md.: Madison Books, 1995.

Delgado, Richard. *The Coming Race War? And Other Apocalyptic Tales of America After Affirmative Action and Welfare.* New York: New York University Press, 1996.

Dworkin, Ronald. "What Did *Bakke* Really Decide?" In *A Matter of Principle.* Cambridge, Mass.: Harvard University Press, 1985.

Eastland, Terry. *Ending Affirmative Action: The Case for Colorblind Justice.* New York: Basic Books, 1996.

Edley, Christopher F., Jr. *Not All Black and White: Affirmative Action, Race, and American Values.* New York: Hill & Wang, 1996.

Ezorsky, Gertrude. *Racism and Justice: The Case for Affirmative Action.* Ithaca, N.Y.: Cornell University Press, 1991.

Fiscus, Ronald J. *The Constitutional Logic of Affirmative Action.* Durham, N.C.: Duke University Press, 1992.

Fullinwider, Robert. *The Reverse Discrimination Controversy.* Totowa, N.J.: Rowman and Littlefield, 1980.

Glazer, Nathan. *Affirmative Discrimination: Ethnic Inequality and Public Policy.* New York: Basic Books, 1975.

Greene, Kathanne W. *Affirmative Action and Principles of Justice.* New York: Greenwood Press, 1989.

Greenwalt, Kent. *Discrimination and Reverse Discrimination.* New York: Alfred A. Knopf, 1983.

Horne, Gerald. *Reversing Discrimination: The Case for Affirmative Action.* New York: International, 1992.

Jackson, Charles C. "Affirmative Action: Controversy and Retrenchment." *The Western Journal of Black Studies* 16, no. 4 (Winter, 1992).

Jones, Augustus J. *Affirmative Talk, Affirmative Action: A Comparative Study of the Politics of Affirmative Action.* New York: Praeger, 1991.

Kahlenberg, Richard D. *The Remedy: Class, Race, and Affirmative Action.* New York: BasicBooks, 1996.

Leonard, Jonathan. "The Federal Anti-Bias Effort." In *Essays on the Economics of Discrimination,* edited by Emily P. Hoffman. Kalamazoo, Mich.: W. E. Upjohn Institute, 1991.

Lerner, Robert, and Althea K. Nigai. *Racial Preferences in Undergraduate Enrollment at the University of California, Berkeley, 1993-1995: A Preliminary Report.* Washington, D.C.: Center for Equal Opportunity, 1996.

McCormack, Wayne. *The Bakke Decision: Implications for Higher Education Admissions.* Washington, D.C.: American Council on Education and the Association of American Law Schools, 1978.

McWhirter, Darien A. *The End of Affirmative Action: Where Do We Go from Here?* New York: Carol Publishing Group, 1996.

Maguire, Daniel. *A Case for Affirmative Action.* Dubuque, Iowa: Shepherd, 1992.

Post, Robert, and Michael Paul Rogin, eds. *Race and Representation: Affirmative Action.* New York: Zone Books, 1998.

Roberts, Paul Craig, and Lawrence M. Stratton, Jr. *The New Color Line: How Quotas and Privilege Destroy Democracy.* Washington, D.C.: Regnery, 1995.

Rosenfeld, Michel. *Affirmative Action and Justice: A Philosophical and Constitutional Inquiry.* New Haven, Conn.: Yale University Press, 1991.

Sindler, Allan P. *Bakke, Defunis, and Minority Admissions: The Quest for Equal Opportunity.* New York: Longman, 1978.

Sowell, Thomas. *Preferential Policies: An International Perspective.* New York: William Morrow, 1990.

Steinberg, Stephen. *Turning Back: The Retreat from Racial Justice in American Thought and Policy.* Boston: Beacon Press, 1995.

Swain, Carol M., ed. *Race Versus Class: The New Affirmative Action Debate.* Lanham, Md.: University Press of America, 1996.

Thernstrom, Abigail. *Whose Votes Count? Affirmative Action and Minority Voting Rights.* Cambridge, Mass.: Harvard University Press, 1987.

U.S. Commission on Civil Rights. *Affirmative Action in 1980's: Dismantling the Process of Discrimination: A Statement of the United States Commission on Civil Rights.* Washington, D.C.: Author, 1981.

Urofsky, Melvin I. *A Conflict of Rights: The Supreme Court and Affirmative Action.* New York: Charles Scribner's Sons, 1991.

Zelnick, Bob. *Backfire: A Reporter's Look at Affirmative Action.* Chicago: Henry Regnery, 1996.

7. Desegregation

Armor, David J. *Forced Justice: School Desegregation and the Law.* New York: Oxford University Press, 1995.

Barnes, Catherine A. *Journey from Jim Crow: The Desegregation of Southern Transit.* New York: Columbia University Press, 1981.

Barrett, Russell H. *Integration at Ole Miss.* Chicago: Quadrangle Press, 1965.

Brooks, Roy L. *Integration or Separation? A Strategy for Racial Equality.* Cambridge, Mass.: Harvard University Press, 1996.

Clark, E. Culpepper. *The Schoolhouse Door: Segregation's Last Stand at the University of Alabama.* New York: Oxford University Press, 1993.

Cohodas, Nadine. *The Band Played Dixie: Race and the Liberal Conscience at Ole Miss.* New York: Free Press, 1997.

Hochschild, Jennifer L. *The New American Dilemma: Liberal Democracy and School Desegregation.* New Haven, Conn.: Yale University Press, 1984.

Hughes, Larry W., William M. Gordon, and Larry W. Hillman. *Desegregating American Schools.* New York: Longman, 1980.

Jacoby, Tamar. *Someone Else's House: America's Unfinished Struggle for Integration.* New York: Free Press, 1998.

Jones, Leon. *From Brown to Boston: Desegregation in Education, 1954-1974.*

Metuchen, N.J.: Scarecrow Press, 1979.

Kluger, Richard. *Simple Justice: The History of Brown v. Board of Education and Black America's Struggle for Equality*. New York: Alfred A. Knopf, 1976.

Kohn, Howard. *We Had a Dream: A Tale of the Struggles for Integration in America.* New York: Simon & Schuster, 1998.

Loevy, Robert D. *To End All Segregation: The Politics of the Passage of the Civil Rights Act of 1964.* Lanham, Md.: University Press of America, 1990.

Metcalf, George R. *From Little Rock to Boston: The History of School Desegregation.* Westport, Conn.: Greenwood Press, 1983.

Molotch, Harvey. *Managed Integration: Dilemmas of Doing Good in the City.* Berkeley: University of California Press, 1972.

Patterson, Orlando. *The Ordeal of Integration: Progress and Resentment in America's Racial Crisis.* Counterpoint, dist. by Publishers Group West, 1997.

Schwartz, Bernard. *Swann's Way: The School Busing Case and the Supreme Court.* New York: Oxford University Press, 1986.

Small, Stephen. *Racialized Barriers: The Black Experience in the United States and England in the 1980's.* London: Routledge, 1994.

Wicker, Tom. *Tragic Failure: Racial Integration in America.* New York: William Morrow, 1996.

Wilkinson, J. Harvie, III. *From "Brown" to "Bakke": The Supreme Court and School Integration: 1954-1978.* New York: Oxford University Press, 1979.

Wolters, Raymond. *The Burden of Brown: Thirty Years of School Desegregation.* Knoxville: University of Tennessee Press, 1984.

Ziegler, Benjamin, ed. *Desegregation and the Supreme Court.* Boston: D. C. Heath, 1958.

8. Civil Rights Law

Abernathy, Charles F. *Civil Rights and Constitutional Litigation: Cases and Materials.* 2d ed. St. Paul, Minn.: West, 1992.

Abernathy, M. Glenn. *Civil Liberties Under the Constitution.* 5th ed. Columbia: University of South Carolina Press, 1989.

Bardolph, Richard, ed. *The Civil Rights Record: Black Americans and the Law, 1849-1870.* New York: Thomas Crowell, 1970.

Bell, Derrick A., Jr. *Race, Racism, and American Law.* 2d ed. Boston: Little, Brown, 1980.

Berman, Daniel M. *A Bill Becomes a Law: Congress Enacts Civil Rights Legislation.* New York: Macmillan, 1966.

Berry, Mary Frances. *Black Resistance/White Law: A History of Constitutional Racism in America.* Rev. ed. New York: Penguin, 1994.

Curtis, Michael Kent. *No State Shall Abridge.* Durham, N.C.: Duke University Press, 1986.

Davidson, Chandler, and Bernard Grofman, eds. *Quiet Revolution in the South: The Impact of the Voting Rights Act, 1965-1990.* Princeton, N.J.: Princeton University Press, 1994.

Flagg, Barbara J. *Was Blind, but Now I See: White Race Consciousness and the Law.*

New York: New York University Press, 1998.

Grofman, Bernard, and Chandler Davidson, eds. *Controversies in Minority Voting: The Voting Rights Act in Perspective.* Washington, D.C.: Brookings Institution, 1992.

Halpern, Steven C. *On the Limits of the Law: The Ironic Legacy of Title VI of the 1964 Civil Rights Act.* Baltimore: The Johns Hopkins University Press, 1995.

Hoemann, George H. *What God Hath Wrought: The Embodiment of Freedom in the Thirteenth Amendment.* New York: Garland Press, 1987.

Hyman, Harold M., and William M. Wiecek. *Equal Justice Under Law: Constitutional Development, 1835-1875.* New York: Harper & Row, 1982.

Kull, Andrew. *The Color-Blind Constitution.* Cambridge, Mass.: Harvard University Press, 1992.

Lively, Donald E. *The Constitution and Race.* New York: Praeger, 1992.

McDonald, Laughlin. *Rights of Racial Minorities: The Basic ACLU Guide to Racial Minority Rights.* 2d ed. Carbondale: Southern Illinois University Press, 1993.

Nelson, William. *The Fourteenth Amendment.* Cambridge, Mass.: Harvard University Press, 1988.

Reams, Bernard D., Jr., and Paul E. Wilson, eds. *Segregation and the Fourteenth Amendment in the States: A Survey of State Segregation Laws, 1865-1953, Prepared for United States Supreme Court in re Brown vs. Board of Education of Topeka.* Buffalo, N.Y.: W. S. Hein, 1975. Includes indexes and bibliography.

Roberts, Ronald S. *Clarence Thomas and the Tough Love Crowd: Counterfeit Heroes and Unhappy Truths.* New York: New York University Press, 1995.

Tushnet, Mark V. *Making Civil Rights Law: Thurgood Marshall and the Supreme Court, 1936-1961.* New York: Oxford University Press, 1994.

U.S. Commission on Civil Rights. *The Voting Rights Act: Unfulfilled Goals.* Washington, D.C.: Government Printing Office, 1981.

Whalen, Charles, and Barbara Whalen. *The Longest Debate: A Legislative History of the 1964 Civil Rights Act.* Washington, D.C.: Seven Locks Press, 1985.

9. Martin Luther King, Jr.

Ansbro, John J. *Martin Luther King, Jr.: The Making of a Mind.* Maryknoll, N.Y.: Orbis Books, 1982.

Branch, Taylor. *Parting the Waters: America in the King Years, 1954-1963.* New York: Simon & Schuster, 1988.

Clark, Kenneth B., ed. *The Negro Protest: James Baldwin, Malcolm X, Martin Luther King Talk with Kenneth B. Clark.* Boston: Beacon Press, 1963.

Colaiaco, James A. *Martin Luther King, Jr.: Apostle of Militant Nonviolence.* New York: St. Martin's Press, 1988.

Fairclough, Adam. *Martin Luther King, Jr.* Athens: University of Georgia Press, 1990.

__________. *To Redeem the Soul of America: The Southern Christian Leadership Conference and Martin Luther King, Jr.* Athens: University of Georgia Press, 1987.

Frank, Gerold. *An American Death: The True Story of the Assassination of Dr. Martin Luther King, Jr.* Garden City, N.Y.: Doubleday, 1972.

Garrow, David J. *Bearing the Cross: Martin Luther King, Jr., and the Southern Christian Leadership Conference.* New York: William Morrow, 1986.

__________. *Protest at Selma: Martin Luther King, Jr., and the Voting Rights Act of 1965.* New Haven: Yale University Press, 1978.

Hanigan, James P. *Martin Luther King, Jr., and the Foundations of Nonviolence.* Lanham, Md.: University Press of America, 1984.

King, Martin Luther, Jr. *Stride Toward Freedom: The Montgomery Story.* New York: Harper & Row, 1958.

Lewis, David L. *King: A Critical Biography.* New York: Praeger, 1970.

McPhee, Penelope, and Flip Schulke. *King Remembered.* New York: Pocket Books, 1986.

Oates, Stephen B. *Let the Trumpet Sound: The Life of Martin Luther King, Jr.* New York: Harper & Row, 1982.

Oppenheimer, Martin. *Martin Luther King, Jr., and the Civil Rights Movement.* University of Pennsylvania, 1963.

Peake, Thomas R. *Keeping the Dream Alive: A History of the Southern Christian Leadership Conference from King to the Nineteen-Eighties.* New York: Peter Lang, 1987.

Ward, Brian, and Tony Badger. *The Making of Martin Luther King and the Civil Rights Movement.* Washington Square, N.Y.: New York University Press, 1996.

10. Other Minorities and African Americans

Berman, Paul, ed. *Blacks and Jews: Alliance and Arguments.* New York: Delacorte Press, 1994.

Collum, Danny Duncan. *Black and White Together: The Search for Common Ground.* Maryknoll, N.Y.: Orbis Books, 1996.

Daughtry, Herbert D., Sr. *No Monopoly on Suffering: Blacks and Jews in Crown Heights.* Trenton, N.J.: Africa World Press, 1997.

Diner, Hasia R. *In the Almost Promised Land: American Jews and Blacks, 1919-1935.* Westport, Conn.: Westview, 1977.

Forbes, Jack D. *Black Africans and Native Americans: Color, Race, and Caste in the Evolution of Red-Black Peoples.* Urbana: University of Illinois Press, 1993.

Kaufman, Jonathan. *Broken Alliance: The Turbulent Times Between Blacks and Jews in America.* New York: Scribner's, 1988.

Lerner, Michael, and Cornel West. *Jews and Blacks: Let the Healing Begin.* New York: G. P. Putnam's Sons, 1995.

Lieberson, Stanley. *A Piece of the Pie: Blacks and White Immigrants Since 1880.* Berkeley: University of California Press, 1980.

Ownby, Ted, ed. *Black and White Cultural Interaction in the Antebellum South.* Jackson: University Press of Mississippi, 1993.

Phillips, William M., Jr. *An Unillustrious Alliance: The African American and Jewish American Communities.* Westport, Conn.: Greenwood Press, 1991.

Piatt, Bill, et al. *Black and Brown in America: The Case for Cooperation.* New York: New York University Press, 1997.

Salzman, Jack, and Cornel West, eds. *Struggles in the Promised Land: Towards a History of Black-Jewish Relations in the United States.* New York: Oxford University Press, 1997.

Waldinger, Roger. *Still the Promised City? African-Americans and the New Immigrants in Post-Industrial New York.* Cambridge, Mass.: Harvard University Press, 1996.

Williams, Richard E. *Hierarchical Structures and Social Value: The Creation of Black and Irish Identities in the United States.* Cambridge, England: Cambridge University Press, 1990.

11. The Military

Bogart, Leo. *Social Research and Desegregation of the United States Army.* Chicago: Markham, 1969.

Brandt, Nat. *Harlem at War: The Black Experience in WWII.* Syracuse: Syracuse University Press, 1996.

Dalifiume, Richard. *Desegregation of the U.S. Armed Forces: Fighting on Two Fronts, 1939-1953.* Columbia: University of Missouri Press, 1969.

Mershon, Sherie, and Steven L. Schlossman. *Foxholes and Color Lines: Desegregating the U.S. Armed Forces.* Baltimore: The Johns Hopkins University Press, 1998.

Moskos, Charles C. *All That We Can Be: Black Leadership and Racial Integration the Army Way.* New York: Basic Books, 1996.

Nalty, Bernard C. *Strength for the Fight: A History of Black Americans in the Military.* New York: Free Press, 1986.

Stillman, Richard. *Integration of the Negro in the U.S. Armed Forces.* New York: Frederick A. Praeger, 1968.

U.S. Department of Defense. Office of the Deputy Assistant Secretary of Defense for Civilian Personnel Policy/Equal Opportunity. *Black Americans in Defense of Our Nation.* Washington, D.C.: Government Printing Office, 1991.

12. Education

Anderson, Talmadge. *Introduction to African American Studies.* Dubuque, Iowa: Kendall/Hunt, 1994.

Atkinson, Pansye S. *Brown vs. Topeka: An African American's View: Desegregation and Miseducation.* Chicago: African American Images, 1993.

Bell, Derrick, ed. *Shades of Brown: New Perspectives on School Desegregation.* New York: Teachers College Press, 1980.

Berry, Gordon LaVern, and Joy Keiko Asamen, eds. *Black Students: Psychosocial Issues and Academic Achievement.* Newbury Park, Calif.: Sage Publications, 1989.

Feagin, Joe R., et al. *The Agony of Education: Black Students at White Colleges and Universities.* New York: Routledge, 1996.

Ford, Donna V. *Reversing Underachievement Among Gifted Black Students: Promising Practices and Programs.* New York: Teachers College Press, 1996.

Formisano, Ronald P. *Boston Against Busing: Race, Class, and Ethnicity in the 1960's and 1970's.* Chapel Hill: University of North Carolina Press, 1991.

Gill, Walter. *Issues in African American Education.* Nashville, Tenn.: One Horn Press, 1991.

Graglia, Lino A. *Disaster by Decree: The Supreme Court Decisions on Race and the Schools.* Ithaca, N.Y.: Cornell University Press, 1976.

Hill, Leven, ed. *Black American Colleges and Universities.* Detroit, Mich.: Gale Research, 1994.

Jacoby, Russell, and Naomi Glauberman, eds. *The Bell Curve Debate: History, Documents, Opinions.* New York: Times Books (Random House), 1995.

Jones-Wilson, Faustine C. *The Encyclopedia of African American Education.* Westport, Conn.: Greenwood Press, 1996.

Levin, Michael. *Why Race Matters: Race Differences and What They Mean.* Westport, Conn.: Praeger, 1997.

Margo, Robert A. *Race and Schooling in the South, 1880-1950: An Economic History.* Chicago: University of Chicago Press, 1990.

Razack, Sherene H. *Looking White People in the Eye: Gender, Race, and Culture in Courtrooms and Classrooms.* Toronto: University of Toronto Press, 1998.

Roebuck, Julian, and Komanduri Murty. *Historically Black Colleges and Universities: Their Place in American Higher Education.* Westport, Conn.: Praeger, 1993.

Rossell, Christine H., and Willis D. Hawley, eds. *The Consequences of School Desegregation.* Philadelphia: Temple University Press, 1983.

Seller, Maxine, and Lois Weis, eds. *Beyond Black and White: New Faces and Voices in U.S. Schools.* Albany: State University of New York Press, 1997.

Tesconi, Charles A., Jr., and Emanuel Hurwitz, Jr. *Education for Whom? The Question of Equal Educational Opportunity.* New York: Dodd, Mead, 1974.

Troyna, Barry. *Racism and Education: Research Perspectives.* Philadelphia: Open University Press, 1993.

Walsh, Catherine. *Pedagogy and the Struggle for Voice.* New York: Bergin and Garvey, 1991.

Weis, Lois, ed. *Class, Race, and Gender in American Education.* Albany: State University of New York Press, 1988.

Wollenberg, Charles. *All Deliberate Speed: Segregation and Exclusion in California Schools, 1855-1975.* Berkeley: University of California Press, 1976.

Zweigenhaft, Richard L., and G. William Domhoff. *Blacks in the White Establishment? A Study of Race and Class in America.* New Haven, Conn.: Yale University Press, 1991.

Index

A page number or range in **boldface** type indicates a full article devoted to that topic.